Gay, Lesbian, and Transgender Clients
A Lawyer's Guide

JOAN M. BURDA

GP|Solo
ABA General Practice, Solo & Small Firm Division

Cover design by ABA Publishing

The materials contained herein represent the opinions and views of the authors and/or the editors, and should not be construed to be the views or opinions of the law firms or companies with whom such persons are in partnership with, associated with, or employed by, nor of the American Bar Association unless adopted pursuant to the bylaws of the Association.

Nothing contained in this book is to be considered as the rendering of legal advice for specific cases, and readers are responsible for obtaining such advice from their own legal counsel. This book and any forms and agreements herein are intended for educational and informational purposes only.

© 2008 American Bar Association. All rights reserved. No part of this publication may be reproduced, stored in a retrieval system, or transmitted in any form or by any means, electronic, mechanical, photocopying, recording, or otherwise, without the prior written permission of the publisher. For permission contact the ABA Copyrights & Contracts Department, copyright@abanet.org or via fax at (312) 988-6030.

11 10 09 08 07   5 4 3 2 1

Cataloging-in-Publication data is on file with the Library of Congress

Family law and lesbian and gay clients / Burda, Joan M.

Discounts are available for books ordered in bulk. Special consideration is given to state bars, CLE programs, and other bar-related organizations. Inquire at Book Publishing, ABA Publishing, American Bar Association, 321 North Clark Street, Chicago, Illinois 60610.

www.ababooks.org

Contents

Dedication xi

About the Author xiii

Acknowledgments xv

Introduction xvii

Chapter One
Representing Lesbian, Gay, and Transgender Clients 1
    A. Significant Case Law 2
    B. Language 3
    C. What Should We Call This? 4
    D. Attitude 4
    E. Potential Conflicts 6
    F. Ethical Considerations 7
    G. Representing Transgender Clients 8
    H. Conclusion 9

Chapter Two
LGT Relationships 11
    A. Massachusetts 12
    B. Current Situation 13
    C. Some History 14
    D. Terminology 16
    E. Defense of Marriage Act 16
    F. Marriage 17
    G. Federal Marriage Rights 20
    H. Other Rights/Benefits/Tax Consequences 21
    I. Traditional Marriage 22
    J. Foreign Recognition of Same-Sex Marriage 24
    K. Domestic Partnerships/Civil Unions 25
    L. State Employees and Domestic Partnership Benefits 26
    M. Unmarried Cohabitants 29
    N. Reciprocal Beneficiaries Law 30
    O. Religion and Marriage 31
    P. Alternatives to Traditional Marriages and "Family" 32
    Q. Starting a Relationship 34

    R. The Party's Over 40
    S. Termination Protocol 43
    T. Update 46
    U. Conclusion 47

Chapter Three
LGT Families 51
    A. Issues Facing Lesbian and Gay Families 53
    B. Family Law 55
    C. LGT Legal Documents 57
    D. Families Moving to Another State 58
    E. Conclusion 59

Chapter Four
Children 61
    A. No Difference Between Straight and Gay Parents 63
    B. Let's Start a Family 64
        1. Artificial Reproductive Technology 65
        2. Surrogacy 66
        3. Surrogacy Considerations 69
    C. Contracts 70
        1. Egg/Sperm Donor Contracts 72
        2. Egg Donation from One Lesbian Partner to the Other 73
    D. Best Friends 73
    E. Parental Rights 75
        1. Illegitimacy 76
        2. Adopted Children 76
    F. Benefits of Families 77
    G. Canada Started 2007 Right: Three Legal Parents 81
    H. Conclusion 82

Chapter Five
Adoption 85
    A. Private Adoptions 89
    B. International Adoptions 89
    C. Second-Parent Adoptions 90
    D. Adoption Costs 92
    E. Adoptions by Lesbian and Gay Individuals and Couples 92
    F. Developing Law 94
    G. Conclusion 96

Chapter Six
Parenting Rights **99**
    A. Applicable Laws Establishing Parenting Rights 100
        1. Parental Kidnapping Prevention Act (PKPA) 100
        2. Uniform Child-Custody Jurisdiction and Enforcement Act (UCCJEA) 102
        3. Uniform Parentage Act (2002) 105
    B. Miller-Jenkins v. Miller-Jenkins 107
    C. Changing Ways to Become a Parent 109
    D. Who Is a Parent? 110
    E. Co-parenting Agreements 119
    F. Same-Sex Parenting Case Law 123
    G. Conclusion 131

Chapter Seven
LGBT Students and Schools **137**
    A. Definitions 138
    B. Harris Interactive and GLSEN Study 139
    C. GSA/Transgender Law Center/NCLR Report 140
    D. Handling Discrimination and Harassment 142
    E. What Does the Law Say? 145
        1. Title IX 145
        2. Equal Protection Clause 146
        3. The First Amendment and the Due Process Clause 147
        4. State Laws 147
    F. Gay-Straight Alliances (GSAs) 147
    G. Harassed Students and What They Did About It 150
    H. Conclusion 153

Chapter Eight
Representing Transgender/Transsexual Clients **155**
    A. Representing Transgender Clients 157
    B. Statutory Protections 158
    C. Family Law Issues 160
        1. Terminating Parental Rights 166
        2. Marriage 167
        3. Estate Planning 168
    D. Employment 169
        1. Disability Laws 172
        2. Federal Laws 173
    E. Sex Reassignment Surgery 174
    F. Transsexuals in Prison 176

    G. Identification 180
        1. Determining a Person's Legal Sex 180
        2. Birth Certificates 181
        3. Name Changes 182
    H. Conclusion 183

Chapter Nine
Lesbian, Gay, and Transgender Elders 189
    A. "Out & Aging: The Metlife Study of Lesbian and Gay Baby Boomers" 191
    B. Older Americans Act (OAA) 192
    C. Social Security 193
    D. Medicaid 196
        1. Estate Recovery Programs 196
        2. Look-Back Period 198
        3. Penalty Period 198
        4. Hardship Waiver 199
        5. Annuities 199
        6. Principal Residence 199
        7. Continuing Care Retirement Communities 199
        8. Life Estates 199
        9. Long-Term Care Partnerships 199
        10. Life Insurance 200
    E. Effect on Lesbian, Gay, Transgender, and Transsexual Elders 200
    F. Counseling of Elders 203
    G. LGT Elders Who Are Military Veterans 203
    H. Retirement Accounts 204
    I. Public Accommodations 205
    J. Nursing Homes and Hospice Care 206
    K. Healthcare Issues Affecting Lesbian, Gay, Transgender, and Transsexual Seniors 210
    L. LGT Elders and Aids 211
    M. Insurance Concerns of Lesbian, Gay, Transgender, and Transsexual Seniors 212
    N. Transgender and Transsexual Elders 213
    O. Conclusion 214

Chapter Ten
Estate Planning 217
    A. Last Will and Testament 218
        1. Guardian of Minor Children 220
        2. Recognizing the Relationship 220

Contents vii

   3. Funeral Expenses 221
   4. "In Terrorum" Clauses 222
   5. Beneficiary Designations 223
   6. Pet Clauses 223
 B. Trusts 225
   1. Testamentary Trusts 227
   2. Inter Vivos Trusts 228
   3. Grantor Retained Income Trusts (GRITs) 230
   4. Total Return Trust 231
   5. Grantor Retained Annuity Trust (GRAT) 232
 C. Charitable Remainder Trusts and Annuities 232
   1. Charitable Lead Trust (CLT) 232
   2. Charitable Remainder Unitrust (CRUT) 233
   3. Charitable Remainder Annuity Trust (CRAT) 234
   4. Charitable Gift Annuity (CGA) 234
   5. Remainder Interests in Real Estate/Retained Life Estate ... 234
   6. Qualified Retirement and IRA Assets 234
   7. Life Insurance Gifts 235
 D. Advance Directives 235
   1. Living Will 236
   2. Health Care Power of Attorney 236
   3. Health Insurance Portability and Accountability Act (HIPAA) 237
 E. Designation of Agent 238
 F. Durable Power of Attorney for Finances 239
   1. Nomination of Guardian 239
 G. Payable on Death (POD) Bank Accounts 241
 H. Funeral Arrangements 241
 I. Unified Estate and Gift Tax Credit 242
 J. Other Ideas for Estate Distribution 243
 K. Inherited Individual Retirement Plans 244
 L. Conclusion 245

Chapter Eleven
Immigration 247
 A. Immigration Law Background 247
 B. Basic Immigration Law 250
 C. Visas 251
 D. Asylum 251
 E. Immigration for Employment Purposes 254
 F. Green Card Lottery 254
 G. Transgender and Transsexual Persons 255

- H. Sham Marriages ... 255
- I. Persons Living with HIV/AIDS ... 256
- J. Pending Congressional Action ... 256
- K. Who Can Help ... 257
- L. Conclusion ... 258

APPENDIX A
Case Law ... 261
- A. United States Supreme Court Cases ... 261
- B. Federal Cases ... 261
- C. Equal Access Act ... 262
- D. Dress Code ... 262
- E. Curriculum ... 262
- F. School Board/Districts Liability Harassment Discrimination ... 262
- G. School Activities/Restrictions on Speech/Viewpoints ... 263
- H. Bankruptcy ... 263
- I. State Cases ... 263
- J. Second Parent Adoptions ... 264
- K. Custody Cases ... 264
- L. Awarding Property Rights to Unmarried Cohabitants ... 265
- M. Statutes ... 265
- N. State Law Decisions re: Same-Sex Marriage & Related Issues ... 265

APPENDIX B
Legal Resources ... 271
- Part I: Law Review/Articles/Books ... 271
  - Law Review & Journal Articles ... 271
  - Books ... 276
- Part II: Information on Benefits for Same-Sex Couples ... 276
- Part III: Pension Protection Act of 2006 ... 278
- Part IV: Sec. 402. Taxability of Beneficiary of Employees' Trust ... 279

APPENDIX C
Forms ... 295
- Confidential Will Questionnaire ... 296
- Last Will and Testament ... 305
- Client Estate-Planning Checklist ... 311
- Designation of Agent with Authority Re: Health Care Visitation, Receipt of Personal Property, Disposition of Remains, and Making Funeral Arrangements. ... 314
- General Durable Power of Attorney ... 317
- Springing General Durable Power of Attorney ... 323

Notice of Revocation of Power of Attorney 330
Authorization to Release Health Insurance and/or Medical Records
 Protected Under the Health Information Portability and
 Accountability Act (HIPAA) 331
Nomination of Guardian for Estate and Person of a Minor Child 334
Parental Consent to Authorize Medical Treatment of Minor 338
Authorization to Consent to Medical, Surgical or Dental Examination
 or Treatment of a Minor and Authorization to Deal With
 Minor's School 339
Domestic Partnership Agreement (Complex) 342
Simple Domestic Partner Agreement Maintaining Separate Property 356
Simple Domestic Partner Agreement Sharing Most Property 360
Termination of Domestic Partnership 364
Sample Shared Parenting Agreement 367
Memorandum of Understanding 375
Confirmation of Ownership and Beneficiary Designations 378
Definition 379
Donor Insemination Agreement 380
For Transgender Individuals Entering into Heterosexual Marriage/
 Relationship 385
HIPAA Authorization 388
Sample Living Together Agreement 390
Possible Definitions for Legal Documents 396
Dissolution Agreement 398
Client Intake Checklist 404

APPENDIX D
State Laws **407**
 Birth Certificate Statutes 407
 States with Pro-LGBT Non-discrimination Laws 409
 State Adoption Laws 410
 Anti-LGBT Adoption Laws 413
 States with Civil Unions, Marriage, and Domestic Partnerships 414

APPENDIX E
LGBT Community Resources **415**

APPENDIX F
Uniform Child Custody Jurisdiction Enforcement Act Adoptions **425**

Index **427**

Dedication

To my parents, Jack and Mildred Burda, who have been married for 60 years, raised four kids, and provide an example to emulate.

To Marty Webb and Debra Dunkle, together in a committed relationship for 26 years and who are, indubitably, a perfect match.

To my good friends Glenn and Bill and Bob and George, each couple enjoying a long-standing committed relationship.

To all lesbian, gay, and transgender/transsexual individuals and couples, and their children, who live in committed relationships and who daily defy a conservative backlash intent on denying their rights to their love, their lives, and their families.

To the children of lesbian, gay, transgender, and transsexual parents who are reminded daily that their families are not legitimate and their parents are not important. They face these trials and grow up to be wonderful, productive members of society.

To Emily (and her moms), for taking the time to tell everyone about her family.

And to my partner and beloved companion, Betsy, whose love, patience, and support over 17 years keeps me grounded. I can count on her to always be there, for better, for worse, for richer and poorer, in sickness and in health, until—well, you know the rest.

About the Author

Joan M. Burda is a native of Ohio and attended Holy Name High School (must get a plug in for the Green Wave). She practices law in Lakewood, Ohio. Joan received her Bachelor's degree from Bowling Green State University in Bowling Green, Ohio, and her Juris Doctor from Pepperdine University School of Law in Malibu, California.

She is admitted to the Ohio bar and is licensed to practice before the United States District Court of Ohio, Northern Division. She is also admitted to practice before the U.S. Court of Appeals for the Armed Forces.

Joan is a member of the Cleveland Bar Association, the Ohio State Bar Association, the National Lesbian and Gay Law Association, and the American Bar Association. She serves on the General Practice Section Council of the Ohio Bar Association. She is also a member of the General Practice, Solo and Small Firm Division of the American Bar Association, where she serves on the Division Council, the Long-Range Planning Committee, and the Editorial Board of the Division magazine, *GPSOLO*, and serves as the editor-in-chief.

She is the author of *Estate Planning for Same-Sex Couples* (American Bar Association, 2004) and *An Overview of Federal Consumer Law* (American Bar Association, 1998). The estate-planning book received a Benjamin Franklin Award in 2005, the first ABA book so honored. She is also the author of numerous articles on various legal topics. She has been a featured presenter in several American Bar Association forums as well as at the Lavender Law Conference sponsored by the National Lesbian and Gay Law Association.

Joan has a solo estate-planning practice. She is also the program director of the Cleveland Homeless Legal Assistance Program. In her spare time, she teaches in the Legal Studies Program at Ursuline College in Pepper Pike, Ohio, and serves as an arbitrator with the Cleveland Better Business Bureau.

She lives in Lakewood, Ohio, with her partner of 17 years, Betsy Ashley.

Acknowledgments

This book is a long time in the making. As a practicing attorney representing lesbian and gay clients, I often face questions for which there are no answers. I needed a resource to help me address my clients' goals. The General Practice, Solo and Small Firm (GPSSF) Division gave me the opportunity to write this book, and I am deeply grateful to them.

Any shortcomings or oversights in this book are mine. I welcome questions, suggestions, and criticisms from my colleagues. The time you take to let me know what you think helps me make the next edition better. I am grateful if you find the book helpful in representing your lesbian, gay, and transgender clients.

Dwight Smith, Lee Kolczun, and John Macy are among the Division leaders who encouraged me in writing this book as they had with my previous book, *Estate Planning for Same-Sex Couples*. I will always be grateful for their continued support.

My editor is Rick Paszkiet. He has been a man of great patience and encouragement throughout this endeavor. Rick is quick with suggestions, guidance, and ideas, all of which I appreciate, because he is oh so right.

Melanie Bragg is my liaison with the GPSSF Publications Board. She is the perfect person for the job because she sees things I miss and helps point the way to clarifying my ideas. She is a remarkable person and I value her input.

Martha Church, a former member of the GPSSF Publications Board and now a valued member of the *GPSOLO* magazine Editorial Board, also read the draft manuscript. She went out of her way to dissect and comment on the draft. Her comments, critique and criticisms were valid, well-considered, and welcome. Martha helped me make this book even better.

Michael Hurley, chair of the GPSSF Division's Publications Board, is a long-time supporter. I value his friendship and appreciate his encouragement and cheerleading.

As a member of the *GPSOLO* magazine Editorial Board, I have had the great privilege of working with many extraordinary people. They are unique individuals, and my experiences with them have made me a better writer and person. They are unequaled in their dedication to writing and the legal profession. I am especially grateful to Jennifer Rose, editor-in-chief of *GPSOLO* and soon-to-be Division chair. Aside from rooming together during ABA meetings, we share ideas and opinions. She is a friend whose friendship is valued, whose opinion is important, and whose support is always present.

Kelly Fox, a law student in Chicago, gave me well-considered and reasoned feedback on the first draft. I am grateful for the time she took and the thoroughness of her comments.

I want to acknowledge the people who contributed their thoughts and feelings about their lives. I've included their stories in the body of the book as well as sidebars. It is through individual stories that we realize what is at stake. I am grateful to all of them for letting all of you know them just a little.

I especially want to thank Cole Thaler, staff attorney with Lambda Legal Defense and Education Fund's Transgender Rights Project. Cole reviewed the chapter on transgender/transsexual clients and made an enormous difference in the final product. I do not claim to be an authority in this area of the law, and I recognized its importance and wanted the best information available. To achieve that goal, I went to Cole. I have learned a great deal from him and encourage anyone with more questions to contact him for counsel and advice. His email address is: cthaler@lambdalegal.org.

I also thank the Very Rev. Tracey Lind, dean of Trinity Cathedral in Cleveland, for permitting me to quote from her book, *Interrupted by God: Glimpses from the Edge*. She gives me much to ponder.

Dr. Martha Webb had the indubitable knack of pushing me when I felt overwhelmed by the task before me. She gave me the benefit of her insights with patience and humor. She and her partner of 26 years, Dr. Debra Dunkle, are a perfect example of the wonder of a long-term relationship. I am grateful for Marty's ongoing support and encouragement.

If I missed anyone, please forgive me. I'm over 30 and the memory is the first thing to go!

Nothing would be possible without my partner, Betsy Ashley. We've been together for over 17 years, and every day she gives me love and support. She has been continually supportive of my writing even when it meant she became responsible for work around the yard and house. I owe her so much, and I am very lucky to have her in my life.

Joan M. Burda
Lakewood, Ohio
jmburda@mac.com

Introduction

According to the 2000 United States census, the number of married couples in the United States increased 7% since the 1990 census. The census also found that the number of unmarried couples increased 71% during the same period. The 2000 census marked the first time "partner" was added as a household member category.

A major gay rights organization, the Human Rights Campaign, estimates there are more than 3.1 million same-sex households in this country. This is a significantly larger number than is reflected in data released by the 2000 census. That data counted more than 600,000 same-sex households in the United States. However, even that number reflects a dramatic increase of more than 145,000 households over those counted in the 1990 census.

A 2001 study estimates the lesbian and gay population to be 5% of the total U.S. population of 209,128,094.[1]

Many family law issues affecting same-sex and transgender couples are similar to those faced by opposite-sex couples. There are major differences, however, because the law may not recognize or protect the families of same-sex and transgender couples.

Some lawyers may wonder why this book is necessary. Guaranteeing the rights of a minority group against the prejudices of the majority is one role that lawyers play. As officers of the court, lawyers are uniquely positioned to assist clients and teach judges and the public about why equality under the law is vital and not subject to negotiation. When restrictions are placed on the rights of one group of citizens, everyone is, in some way, also restricted. Our system of justice relies on the foundation that all are equal before the law. It is the lawyer's job to ensure that the system applies to his or her clients.

The purpose of this book is to introduce lawyers and their clients to the legal landscape as it relates to lesbian, gay, and transgender persons today. This is an amorphous situation. State courts, legislatures, and society are changing the laws, definitions, and understandings of LGT (lesbian, gay, and transgender) issues almost daily. The conflicts arising because of competing laws on the local, state, and national levels create confusion and consternation for those affected.

The techniques and tactics used in representing clients are also changing. Lawyers can use this book as a beginning reference. It provides the opportunity to look at issues from different perspectives. Lawyers can start with this book and move forward in applying the law to the facts of their individual cases.

This is a different kind of law book. In addition to case law, statutes, and a discussion of legal issues, this book also introduces the reader to the people who make up the LGT community. For lawyers who currently represent members of this client base, the discussion may be unnecessary. But for those who want to market to the LGT community, it will be helpful to understand who is in the community and their common issues.

While this book addresses the issues faced by lesbian, gay, and transgender clients and their families, it will not deal separately with individuals who identify themselves as bisexual. A bisexual person in an opposite-sex relationship is governed by existing laws dealing with heterosexuals. Bisexuals in a same-sex relationship are covered by the discussions set forth in this book.

This book can be used as a starting point to develop theories of law to protect your clients, to trigger new ideas of what is possible in your jurisdiction, and to identify legal issues that can be successfully challenged.

Why is this book important? The Very Rev. Tracey Lind, dean of Trinity Cathedral in Cleveland, Ohio, wrote with great eloquence: "To exist in a homophobic society in silence, conformity, fear, acquiescence, and collaboration; to hide in our closets for fear of being caught, rejected, fired, abused, disowned, disinherited, ridiculed and despised; to covet 'safety' or 'security' on the conditions prescribed by the state or the church causes moral insanity and the death of one's soul. To come out, to state honestly and clearly who one is and who one loves is *not* flaunting one's sexuality, but rather, to be faithful to one's integrity, to choose freedom over oppression, and to claim life in the midst of death."[2]

Notes

1. David M. Smith & Dr. Gary J. Gates, Gay and Lesbian Families in the United States: Same-Sex Unmarried Partner Households, A Preliminary Analysis of 2000 United States Census Data, 8/22/2001.

2. INTERRUPTED BY GOD: GLIMPSES FROM THE EDGE, Photographs and Essays by Tracey Lind, The Pilgrim Press (2004).

CHAPTER ONE

Representing Lesbian, Gay, and Transgender Clients

There are few ground rules and little precedent in the area of family law that affect lesbian, gay, and transgender clients and their families. This is an emerging area of law, and decisions are being issued with increasing frequency. These decisions are preserving the status quo or carving out new interpretations of existing law to apply to nontraditional families.

Attorneys must be cognizant of the challenges inherent in any new area of law. But in this area, there is also the satisfaction of representing clients who face enormous obstacles in their lives. Unlike traditional family law cases, those involving families headed by lesbian, gay, or transgender (LGT) parents present an opportunity to create new law or expand existing law.

The legal issues affecting the LGT client base are both unclear and rapidly changing. Attorneys are asked to advise clients on the laws of other states because what is legal in State A may be illegal in State B. Legal documents that are valid in the client's home state may be unenforceable in another. Heterosexual clients and their families may face some of these issues, but there is no organized attempt to limit the rights of heterosexuals in state laws.

For example, there is no question that heterosexual parents traveling with their children are protected in every state. Lesbian and gay parents, however, face situations like the recently overturned Oklahoma Adoption Invalidation Act, which provided that adoptions involving same-sex parents would not be recognized in Oklahoma. If a lesbian family traveling through Oklahoma was in a collision and the biological parent was killed, under the Oklahoma law, the children could be taken as wards of the state. The 10th Circuit Court of Appeals issued its decision on August 3, 2007, affirming the federal district court decision in *Finstuen v. Edmondson*.[1]

It is essential that lawyers representing lesbian and gay clients and their families be familiar with what is happening throughout the country. Lawyers must maintain current knowledge and understanding of not only the law but also social trends in this area.

Attorneys who wish to expand their practice in this area should become familiar with the legal history of lesbian and gay families in the United States. There are precedent-setting cases affecting LGT clients that attorneys need to be familiar with if they want to be considered players in this field. (Note: Legal issues specifically addressing transgender clients and their families are addressed in a later chapter.)

A. Significant Case Law

- *Romer v. Evans*[2] is a 1996 United States Supreme Court case out of Colorado. Colorado voters approved a constitutional amendment (Amendment Two) that barred all local protection for gays and lesbians. The Court found that the amendment violated the federal Constitution's Equal Protection Clause.
- In 2000, the United States Supreme Court, in *Dale v. Boy Scouts*,[3] dealt with the decision by the Boy Scouts of America to prohibit gay Scoutmasters. The Court held that the Scouts' First Amendment freedom of association rights trumped the New Jersey antidiscrimination law on public accommodation. So, the Scouts have free rein to discriminate based on sexual orientation. This includes discriminating against potential Scouts who are gay and those who do not share the organization's religious values. The downside, from the Scouts' position, is that other entities may refuse to allow the Scouts the use of public facilities that were provided in the past. The Scouts' protests about these restrictions have, thus far, been unsuccessful.
- *Lawrence v. Texas*[4] reversed the Supreme Court's 1986 decision in *Bowers v. Hardwick*.[5] The *Lawrence* Court determined that the Texas sodomy law violated the federal Constitution's Due Process Clause. The Court held that private sexual conduct between consenting adults is protected behavior.
- *Loving v. Virginia*[6] involved an interracial couple whose marriage violated the Virginia miscegenation statute. The Lovings were convicted and received a suspended sentence, provided they did not return to the commonwealth of Virginia. The Supreme Court held the miscegenation statute was unconstitutional on myriad levels. This decision is often seen as the basis for overturning the federal Defense of Marriage Act (DOMA)

as well as state statutes and constitutional provisions against same-sex marriage. To date, the argument has been unsuccessful.
- *Griswold v. Connecticut*[7] involved the right to privacy. Specifically, the case dealt with a state law prohibiting the use of contraceptives by married couples. The United States Supreme Court declared that law unconstitutional.

B. Language

For attorneys practicing in this area, word choice is a topic you must pay particular attention to. Lawyers representing lesbian and gay clients must understand how words can interfere with the attorney-client relationship.

Terms that may appear neutral or non-controversial to a lawyer may be offensive to a lesbian or gay client. At the very least, some terms may make prospective clients uncomfortable and question whether the lawyer and his staff are able to properly represent their interests. "Homosexuals," "sexual preference," and "gay lifestyle" are some terms that can be problematic. Use the language preferred by your clients. If in doubt, ask for the client's preference.

Straight lawyers may wonder why these terms might present a problem.

"Homosexual" is a term usually used in a clinical or confrontational setting. Gay and lesbian individuals do not use the word to describe themselves. Some members of the lesbian/gay/bisexual/transgender community use the term "queer" to describe themselves in an effort to reclaim a word that is used as an insult. Some lesbians describe themselves as "dykes," but it is safe to assume that it is not a term a lawyer will use with a client. Likewise, gay men may use the word "faggot" or "fag" among themselves, but it is usually seen in the heterosexual world as an insult.

"Sexual preference" is a term that is often heard to describe someone's sexuality. The term reflects the belief of some that gay men and lesbians made a choice to be homosexual. Because there is no legitimate scientific data supporting that position, "sexual orientation" is the more realistic term.

"Gay lifestyle" also causes problems, primarily because it defies definition. Ask most lesbians and gay men and they will find it difficult to define the term. It is difficult to see the difference between a gay male couple with a house, mortgage, car payments, dogs, children, jobs, and taxes from their heterosexual married neighbors.

Using the terms "gay," "lesbian," "partners," and "transgender" is a safe way to proceed with LGT clients. Again, the clients are in the best position to relay the language with which they are most comfortable.

It is also important for lawyers to understand how same-sex relationships are defined in the states where they are licensed. There are resources available to assist lawyers in getting this information. The Human Rights Campaign[8] and Lambda Legal[9] are two organizations that maintain information on developments on the state and national levels. Understanding this will help a lawyer develop the appropriate language to use with LGT clients.

C. What Should We Call This?

Civil same-sex marriages are synonymous with heterosexual marriage. Massachusetts is still the only state that permits same-sex marriage. Litigation is pending in some states, such as Iowa and California, on the issue of same-sex marriage.

Civil unions are comparable to marriage, but not synonymous. Vermont was the first state to permit civil unions. Civil unions grant many of the same rights as a state's marriage laws, but there are no federal rights conferred. Connecticut's law, passed by a state legislature without court intervention, recognizes civil unions from other states; but does not recognize same-sex marriages entered into in Massachusetts.

Hawaii has reciprocal beneficiary relationships that may apply to heterosexual and gay or lesbian couples. The law also applies to relatives (e.g., mother and daughter).

Finally, domestic partnerships, like reciprocal beneficiary relationships, are not the same as marriage. In California, domestic partnerships provide many of the same rights as marriage in some states. In other states, few rights are granted to couples entering into these relationships.

D. Attitude

Clients may be reluctant to contact a lawyer unless they are assured they will be received with respect and professionalism. Attorneys who are uncomfortable representing lesbian or gay clients, for whatever reason, should not do so. That seems obvious; however, some lawyers do not have the luxury of declining a client. And there is a misconception that all LGT clients are wealthy.

Such a lawyer will be well served by discussing the matter with a more senior attorney and seeking a reassignment. If the lawyer's attitude becomes obvious, the client will leave anyway. The firm loses a client and may develop the reputation of being intolerant.

A lawyer who cannot set aside his or her personal views concerning objections to lesbian or gay relationships may want to decline representation. It is not unrealistic to expect dissatisfied clients to believe their lawyer sabotaged their case because of personal animosity. Remember, though, that a client's sexual orientation may have nothing to do with the type of case he or she needs assistance on. Not all LGT clients retain lawyers because of issues arising from their sexual orientation.

Clients want to know how the law affects their case. It is important for a lawyer to be honest and forthcoming, the same way he or she would be with other clients. When sexual orientation is the basis for a possible claim, explain the current status of the law, the types of legal arguments available, and whether any of those arguments are applicable to that client's case. The law involving LGT individuals and couples is evolving. The process is slow and cumbersome. There are no quick resolutions, and clients need to be aware of this.

Clients want the lawyer's opinion and the best legal services possible. This is particularly true if the legal issues create a case of first impression for a court. Clients must also be aware that a trial court's ruling can be appealed.

Practice Tips

1. Put yourself in the client's shoes. Try to understand what it is like to live in a world that treats you differently simply because of who you love or who you are attracted to; consider the varying and subtle forms of discrimination the client may experience.
2. Ask questions. Lawyers ask questions for a living. Direct questions are fine; they clear the air and provide information not otherwise readily available or apparent.
3. If you are uncomfortable, turn the case over to someone else. Keeping the case is not good for you or the client.
4. Consider holding a training session with your staff to orient them to issues facing LGT clients. This will also help you understand any concerns your staff may have and give you a chance to address them.
5. In many places, the LGT community is small. Not every town and city is like New York, Chicago, San Francisco, or Los Angeles. People know each other, and clients may be concerned about others in the community learning about their business with you. Some clients may assume you know their friends and associates and wonder if you will discuss their situation. Do not assume that clients know that you will not discuss their legal issues with others. Reassure them that the attorney-client relationship is sacrosanct.

E. Potential Conflicts

When a lesbian or gay couple sees a lawyer, there is an inherent conflict. Individually, they are legal strangers to each other. Even with scads of legal documents memorializing their relationship, the couple generally has no legal standing in their respective states. In fact, there may be state laws that specifically prohibit the recognition of any relationship that looks like a marriage.

Lawyers represent husbands and wives on a regular basis. While the possibility of a conflict exists, it usually is not considered a problem. Joint representation of a couple, and the potential ethical considerations involved, is always a concern. Many same-sex couples seek legal assistance to develop a variety of documents to protect and establish their relationship. For this reason, a lawyer representing this couple must establish the parameters of his or her representation.

When drafting legal documents such as a domestic partnership agreement, or an agreement similar to a prenuptial agreement, lawyers must ensure that clients understand the limits of the representation. A lawyer may want to consult his or her malpractice carrier before accepting such a case.

A separate acknowledgment, signed by the clients, will notify them that in the event of disagreements, the lawyer will withdraw from the case and both clients must seek new counsel. The lawyer must also explain that he cannot keep the secrets of one partner from the other. The standard attorney-client relationship is different in this situation. If one partner asks the lawyer to do something that will adversely affect the rights of the other partner, the lawyer is obligated to disclose that information to the other person.

For example, the lawyer is preparing an estate plan for the clients. After the initial meeting, one partner contacts the attorney to change his will and leave out the other partner. The client must be told that the attorney has an ethical duty to inform the other partner of the change. This may create a problem between the couple. If that happens, the attorney should withdraw and have the clients find new representation.

Clients must also be advised of the transitory nature of the law involving lesbian and gay families. Use the retainer agreement as the vehicle to acknowledge that the law is subject to change, and that documents drafted by the lawyer may be unenforceable or may not survive a court challenge. These documents can include a Last Will and Testament, Domestic Partnership Agreements, Co-Parenting Agreements, custody, and visitation and support agreements. A retainer agreement allows the clients to give informed consent before representation begins. Lawyers need to take the time to ensure that clients fully understand any limits that may exist.

It is imperative that lawyers work closely with their clients. There are few areas of law where clients' direct participation in the process is so important. It is as important to discover what a client wants as it is to decide how to achieve the client's goals.

F. Ethical Considerations

Joint representation of clients is often troublesome. Unlike a heterosexual married couple, in most states there is no legally recognized relationship between a lesbian or gay male couple. Any lawyer engaged in representing these clients must take extra steps to ensure that clients understand they are entitled to separate counsel, the advantages of individual counsel, and the disadvantages of both using the same lawyer. Take estate planning as an example.

Most estate planners assist clients with post-mortem planning and arranging their affairs during their lifetime. The Last Will and Testament allows a client to determine how her individual estate will be distributed after she dies. Advance Directives, Durable Powers of Attorney for Finances, Designation of Agent, and similar documents provide clients with the opportunity to achieve peace of mind during their lifetimes. Both aspects of estate planning are important.

Any estate plan may include the transfer of assets, which may result in conflict between the partners. And the attorney may find herself in the middle.

The American Bar Association's 2004 Model Rule of Professional Conduct (RPC) 1.7(b) addresses conflicts of interest with current clients.

> "Notwithstanding the existence of a concurrent conflict of interest under paragraph (a), a lawyer may represent a client if:
> (1) the lawyer reasonably believes that the lawyer will be able to provide competent and diligent representation of each affected client;
> (2) the representation is not prohibited by law;
> (3) the representation does not involve the assertion of a claim by one client against another client represented by the lawyer in the same litigation or other proceeding before a tribunal; and
> (4) each affected client gives informed consent, confirmed in writing."

Questions about joint representation crop up regularly. The ABA RPC gives guidance to lawyers representing a lesbian or gay couple. The basic advice: have both clients sign an acknowledgment that provides informed consent. Be sure to include a statement that if problems arise, you will withdraw and be unable to represent either party. It is also incumbent on any lawyer to determine if there is a probability of problems. Better to nip a potential problem at the start than find yourself in a quagmire down the road.

G. Representing Transgender Clients

A longtime client calls for an appointment. But the person expected is not the one entering the office. Since you last saw the client, Greg has become Barb. This situation can pose unique problems for the lawyer, her staff, and the client. All transgender persons know what they will face when they begin the process of living as a member of the other gender. This is a difficult time emotionally, physically, and psychologically for such clients, and the way they are treated in your office can have an enormous impact.

> **Practice Tips**
>
> - Use the client's post-transition name whenever possible; acknowledge the pre- and post-transition name in legal documents; the situation is comparable to a name change, even if a formal name change has not been granted.
> - Do not assume the client is coming in about transgender issues; transgender people have non-gender legal issues too. Long-time clients still have the same legal issues they consulted you about in the past.
> - Watch for assumptions about gender, including stereotypes based on sex or sexual orientation.
> - Be open to the client's sense of self-identity.
> - When in doubt, ask.

The initial meeting may be uncomfortable for the lawyer, her staff, and the client. But with time, everyone will move past the initial reaction and continue to work together. Issues involving transgender clients are covered in detail in Chapter 8.

H. Conclusion

Lawyers who represent lesbian, gay, and transgender clients in family law cases are pioneers in a rapidly growing field of law. Also, these lawyers face myriad obstacles to achieving legal objectives for their clients.

Some lawyers represent a lesbian or gay biological parent and use the existing laws to thwart the efforts of a former partner/de facto parent from maintaining a parent-child relationship. This places the child in a terrible position. There is no justification for making a child choose between parents. This scenario plays out often in heterosexual divorces, and it is inexcusable for a similar situation to exist in lesbian and gay "divorces.

Representing lesbian, gay, and transgender families is to engage in a law practice that is on the cutting edge of jurisprudence. It can be frustrating, disheartening, and thrilling. Creative lawyering involving intuition, vigorous advocacy, and passion is essential in this practice area.

Notes

1. Finstuen v. Edmondson, No. 06-6213 (10th Cir. Ct. App., Aug. 3, 2007).
2. 517 U.S. 620 (1996).
3. 530 U.S. 640 (2000).
4. 539 U.S. 558 (2003).
5. 478 U.S. 186 (1986), *rev'd*, Lawrence v. Texas, 539 U.S. 558 (2003).
6. 388 U.S. 1 (1967).
7. 381 U.S. 479 (1965).
8. www.hrc.org
9. www.lambdalegal.org

CHAPTER TWO

LGT Relationships

When the relationship issues of lesbians and gay men are involved, they can include the intricacies of marriage, civil unions, domestic partnerships, and relationships that do not fit any particular model.

Marriage, domestic partner laws, and civil unions are three ways lesbian and gay couples can add legal status to their relationships, but those opportunities are limited to a few states. Most states provide no legal recognition for the committed relationships of same-sex couples. Only one state, Massachusetts, permits gay marriage, but no other state recognizes those marriages.

Lawyers representing same-sex couples are asked to prepare written documents that reflect the parties' intentions about their relationship. The Appendices contain forms lawyers can use to assist their clients in realizing their goals.

In 1996, the United States Congress, fearing an onslaught of gay men and lesbians demanding to be married, enacted the Defense of Marriage Act (DOMA).[1] The law has two effects:

1. No state (or other political subdivision within the United States) need recognize a marriage between persons of the same sex, even if the marriage was concluded or recognized in another state.
2. The federal government may not recognize same-sex or polygamous marriages for any purpose, even if concluded or recognized by one of the states.

This statute permits an exception to recognition of marriages by other states. It happened before when states were not required to recognize marriages entered into by persons of different races.

Many states followed suit and passed "mini-DOMAs" to codify the prohibition against same-sex marriage.

A. Massachusetts

In 2003, the Supreme Judicial Court of Massachusetts, in *Goodridge v. Dept. of Public Health, et al.*,[2] held that the commonwealth's constitution prohibited restricting marriage to opposite-sex couples.

The court stated:

> Marriage is a vital social institution. The exclusive commitment of two individuals to each other nurtures love and mutual support; it brings stability to our society. For those who choose to marry, and for their children, marriage provides an abundance of legal, financial, and social benefits. In return, it imposes weighty legal, financial, and social obligations. . . . We are mindful that our decision marks a change in the history of our marriage law. Many people hold deep-seated religious, moral, and ethical convictions that marriage should be limited to the union of one man and one woman, and that homosexual conduct is immoral. Many hold equally strong religious, moral, and ethical convictions that same-sex couples are entitled to be married, and that homosexual persons should be treated no differently than their heterosexual neighbors.

The *Goodridge* decision prompted other states to amend their state constitutions to prevent a similar judicial outcome. The decision also resulted in increased pressure to pass an amendment to the United States Constitution restricting marriage, and all ensuing rights, to opposite-sex couples.

A 1913 Massachusetts statute[3] prohibits the recognition of a marriage between nonresidents if the marriage will not be recognized in the parties' home state. For 27 years the Department of Public Health instructed city and town clerks that they were not to enforce eligibility requirements, including the residency requirements. On April 26, 2004, former Massachusetts Governor Romney instructed the commonwealth's justices of the peace that they were required to ask for proof of residency. He instituted this policy shortly before Massachusetts began issuing marriage licenses to same-sex couples. Massachusetts' current governor rescinded that order. Romney's order was challenged in court.

The Massachusetts Supreme Judicial Court upheld the constitutionality of this statute on March 30, 2006, in *Cote-Whitacre v. Department of Public Health*.[4] The Massachusetts court agreed that the law could be used to prevent same-sex couples from other New England states from marrying in the commonwealth.

The court refrained from ruling on whether couples from New York and Rhode Island were prevented from marrying. The court took this action because the laws in those two states are unclear. Since that decision, New York's highest court has ruled that same-sex couples cannot marry in the state.

In his dissent in *Cote-Whitacre*, Associate Justice Roderick L. Ireland wrote, "Finally, the Commonwealth's resurrection and selective enforcement of a moribund statute, dormant for almost one hundred years, not only violates the 'spirit' of *Goodridge*, as stated by the judge below, but also offends notions of equal protection. It is, at its core, fundamentally unfair."[5]

B. Current Situation

The situation in the United States today is fluid. In 2004, 13 states adopted amendments to their state constitutions banning same-sex marriages. Some states—Ohio, for example—restrict recognition of any relationship or granting of benefits to people in relationships that "approximate" marriage. Yet, there is no definition of relationships that "approximate" marriage. Deciphering the meaning of those words will be a job for the courts.

Proponents argue that these state constitutional amendments are needed to protect the "sanctity" of marriage. These laws follow on the heels of the federal and state Defense of Marriage Acts passed by Congress and many states.

When Long-Time Partners Are Denied Equal Protection Under the Law

We have been together in Ohio as a couple since 1984 and were legally married in Canada in July of 2004. Of course, the marriage is not legally recognized in Ohio, but it has meant a great deal to our families, our friends, and us.

We have done and continue to do all the work to maintain our relationship and household like heterosexual couples. However, we are hindered by the denial of legal protections for our property and savings, and access to health insurance and a myriad of financial "discounts" afforded to opposite-sex married couples.

The state truly treats us as "less than" others. Although we love much of the culture and beauty of Ohio, if it weren't for the close ties and support of family and friends, we would move to another state that recognizes and protects all of its citizens.

Judy Maruszan and Susan Ballard, Rocky River, Ohio

In 2004, Virginia enacted the Affirmation of Marriage Act,[6] adding a new section to the Code of Virginia. The section is titled, "Civil unions between persons of same sex." The Code's language is:

A civil union, partnership contract or other arrangement between persons of the same sex purporting to bestow the privileges or obligations of marriage is prohibited. Any such civil union, partnership contract or other arrangement entered into by persons of the same sex in another state or jurisdiction shall be void in all respects in Virginia and any contractual rights created thereby shall be void and unenforceable.

Henry F. Fradella, law professor at College of New Jersey, responded to this enactment by saying, "Nothing so homophobic has ever been enacted into law in this nation's history."

No one knows how far this statute will reach or whether it will withstand a court challenge. However, if upheld, it could negate powers of attorney, wills, leases, custody arrangements, joint bank accounts, business contracts, and health insurance offered by private companies in Virginia.

Until that happens, however, the law exists, and lawyers both in and outside of Virginia must be aware of its possible effect on their clients.

C. Some History

The Massachusetts Supreme Judicial Court was not the first court to deal with the issue of same-sex marriages. In 1993, the Hawaii Supreme Court issued a ruling that laws denying same-sex couples the right to marry violated the Hawaii State Constitution. The Hawaii justices held that the state must show a "compelling reason" for discriminating against same-sex couples and remanded the case. In 1996, the trial court declared the state had no compelling reason to deny marriage to same-sex couples.

Before the courts resolved the matter in 1998, Hawaii's voters amended the state constitution to restrict marriage to opposite-sex couples. Following this vote, the legislature enacted legislation establishing a "reciprocal beneficiaries" status for Hawaii residents. Sexual orientation is not an issue with this status. It is available to heterosexuals, gay men, and lesbians. Further, family members may declare a relationship to qualify for benefits under this law. However, the 1998 action by Hawaii's electorate scared the daylights out of people on the mainland and started the DOMA ball rolling.

Vermont's Supreme Court issued a similar decision to the one in Hawaii in *Baker v. Vermont.*[7] The court held that denying marriage rights to same-sex couples violated the Vermont constitution. The court delayed enforcement until the legislature took action.

In 2000, Vermont became the first state to recognize civil unions. Same-sex couples were granted substantially the same benefits, rights, responsibilities, and obligations as married couples. This includes the right to intestate succession, preference in naming a legal guardian, hospital visitation rights, transfer of property between partners without paying a transfer tax, and standing to sue for wrongful death and other types of injury cases if one partner is injured or killed.

Vermont civil unions are also subject to dissolution in the state's family law courts. At least one member of the couple must be a Vermont resident for one year before filing for the court to exercise jurisdiction. Same-sex couples who entered a civil union outside of Vermont may qualify for a dissolution if one of them meets the Vermont residency requirements.

While marriage in Vermont is restricted to heterosexual couples, the legislature created a parallel system of civil unions for lesbian and gay couples. Vermont views civil unions as being a step beyond domestic partnerships. In 2007, the Vermont legislature started discussions about the possibility of enacting legislation providing for same-sex marriages.

In April 2005, Connecticut became the first state to implement legislation permitting civil unions. This happened without a court order. Further, Connecticut law recognizes civil unions from other states, although it will not recognize Massachusetts' same-sex marriages.

Since January 2004, lesbians and gay men living in New Jersey have enjoyed many of the rights claimed by heterosexual married couples. Following a 2006 New Jersey Supreme Court ruling, the New Jersey legislature enacted a law permitting civil unions in the state. Under the law, same-sex couples are to be treated the same as heterosexual married couples.

Although New Jersey businesses are required to provide health coverage to employee spouses, some New Jersey employers are refusing to do so, stating they are bound by the federal Employee Retirement Income and Security Act (ERISA). Since DOMA, federal law does not recognize same-sex couples. This is a continuing problem throughout the country. Legal action will be needed to resolve the differences between state and federal laws.

A certain irony comes from California. In 2006, the state legislature passed a bill permitting same-sex marriage. Governor Schwarzenegger then vetoed it, stating that the courts should resolve the issue. Governor Schwarzenegger thus became the first government official to take the position that a duly elected state legislature cannot change the definition of marriage. In other states, government officials, arguing against "activist judges," have taken the opposite position and stated that only the legislature could make the decision. The California Supreme Court will be hearing appeals on the subject, and the outcome will be most interesting.

D. Terminology[8]

- Civil Marriage: a legal status established through a license issued by a state government granting legal rights to and imposing legal obligations on the two married persons; U.S. citizens may marry in a civil ceremony, a religious ceremony or both; state governments grant priests, rabbis, ministers, and other clergy presiding over a religious marriage the authority of the state to endorse the marriage license and establish a civil marriage.[9] These marriages are recognized by the federal government.
- Religious Marriage: a liturgical rite, a sacrament, or a solemnization of the uniting of two persons that is recognized by the hierarchy and adherents of that religious group.
- Civil Union: a legal mechanism, sanctioned by the civil authorities, intended to grant same-gender couples legal status somewhat similar to civil marriage; not recognized by the federal government.
- Domestic Partnership: a relationship between two individuals, often but not necessarily of the same gender, who live together and mutually support each other as spouses but who are not legally joined in a civil marriage or a civil union; does not reach the legal threshold of civil unions or civil marriages and does not afford to the couples the rights, benefits, obligations, and protections of civil marriage or, in some cases, civil unions.

E. Defense of Marriage Act

The United States Congress enacted the federal Defense of Marriage Act (DOMA) in 1996[10] and President Bill Clinton signed it into law. The federal DOMA bars any recognition of same-sex marriages for the purpose of federal benefits. The statute also permits the states to refuse to recognize same-sex marriages from other jurisdictions.

Until DOMA, the states recognized marriages from other states—even those that would not be allowed in the particular state where recognition is sought. The Full Faith and Credit Clause of the United States Constitution generally requires states to recognize and honor the laws of other states. The exception is when those laws violate a state's strong public policy.

Forty-two states declared that same-sex marriage violates their strong public policy by passing their own mini-DOMAs. Language limiting marriage to "one man and one woman" has been included in the state constitutions of 17 states. Oregon amended its constitution but did not pass a mini-DOMA. Seven states do not have DOMAs: Connecticut, Massachusetts, New Jersey, New Mexico, New York, Rhode Island, and Wisconsin, although some of them are considering such legislation.

To date, neither the federal nor any state DOMA has been successfully challenged on equal protection grounds.

F. Marriage

I've heard the reasons for opposing civil marriage for same-sex couples. Cut through the distractions and they stink of the same fear, hatred and intolerance I have known in racism and in bigotry.[11]

Beyond the religious arguments about the "sanctity" of marriage, marriage is a legal contract between two individuals who possess the capacity to enter into contracts. This legal dimension of marriage is what must be debated, not the religious aspect.

The institution of marriage has changed dramatically over the centuries. The Bible supports plural marriage: Abraham, Sarah, and Hagar, *Genesis* 11-23; Jacob, Leah, and Rachel, *Genesis* 25-35. Solomon had three wives; *Kings* 1 and *Genesis* 38 both demand that a brother marry his surviving sister-in-law. The *Quran* allows four wives. Hinduism does not condone same-sex marriage, but Buddhism is neutral on the subject.

In early American history, many colonies had official religions. Some did not permit civil marriage ceremonies. Only religious marriages, performed under the aegis of the state-approved religion, were allowed.

As late as the 1990s, cohabitation was illegal in six states: Florida, North Carolina, North Dakota, Mississippi, Virginia, and West Virginia.

Many states carried laws that prohibited marriages between the races. Virginia prosecuted a mixed-race couple, the Lovings, for marrying each other. Both husband and wife were convicted and banned from the commonwealth. They appealed their conviction, and the United States Supreme Court declared these miscegenation statutes unconstitutional.[12]

In the decision, the Supreme Court declared that marriage is a fundamental right and struck down the laws prohibiting interracial marriage. In its decision, the Justices found that "[T]he freedom to marry has long been recognized as one of the vital personal rights essential to the orderly pursuit of happiness by free men." The Court further held:

> Marriage is one of the "basic civil rights of man," fundamental to our very existence and survival. To deny freedom on so unsupportable a basis [as racial classification] . . . a classification so directly subversive of the principle of equality at the heart of the Fourteenth Amendment, is surely to deprive all the State's citizens of liberty without due process of law. . . . Under our Constitution, the freedom to marry, or not to marry . . . resides with the individual and cannot be infringed by the State.

The miscegenation statutes were arbitrary exercises of state power that the Supreme Court found unacceptable. To date, however, the *Loving* decision has not been extended to laws discriminating against same-sex couples.

Eleven years later, in *Zablocki v. Redhall*,[13] the United States Supreme Court again addressed the rights of marriage. The Court held, "[t]he right to marry is of fundamental importance for all individuals." This case dealt with a Wisconsin statute that prohibited a resident who had unpaid child support obligations from marrying. The Court held that the statute was a violation of the Equal Protection Clause of the United States Constitution.

The issue of marriage and same-sex couples rose again in a New York case. On July 6, 2006, the New York State Court of Appeals, its highest court, stated, "We hold that the New York Constitution does not compel recognition of marriages between members of the same sex."[14]

The court held that New York's domestic relations law is understood to include only heterosexual couples. The court found two grounds that support the limitation: "First, the Legislature could rationally decide that, for the welfare of children, it is more important to promote stability, and to avoid instability, in opposite-sex than same-sex relationships. Heterosexual intercourse has a natural tendency to lead to the birth of children; homosexual intercourse does not. . . . [T]here is a second reason: The Legislature could rationally believe that it is better . . . for children to grow up with both a mother and a father."[15]

On July 26, 2006, the Washington Supreme Court issued its same-sex marriage decision in *Anderson v. King County*.[16] This was a 5-4 plurality decision. Three justices concurred in Justice Madsen's opinion. There were two opinions concurring in Madsen's decision and a dissent written by Justice Fairhurst, in which Justice Chambers concurred.

The plurality decided that marriage in Washington is limited to opposite-sex couples, reversing decisions by two lower courts. The justices comprising the plurality held that the plaintiffs failed to establish they are members of a suspect class or that they had a fundamental right to marry a person of the same sex. The court used a rational review standard to determine if the plaintiffs' claims trumped the state's position. The court found no violation of the state constitution's privileges and immunities clause or the due process clause.

In response to the court's decision, the Washington State Legislature passed a domestic partnership law. One year later, on July 22, 2007, that law took effect. Washington's law requires that the couple be of the same sex, share a common residence, be at least 18 years old, and not be married to or in a registered domestic partnership with another person. This law also allows heterosexual persons age 62 or older to register.

The benefits under the law include hospital visitation, the right to make medical decisions, intestate inheritance rights, the right to make funeral arrangements, and the right to bring a wrongful death suit for their deceased partner.

Most courts issuing same-sex marriage decisions rely on the procreation argument to support restricting marriage to opposite-sex couples. But selecting one's life partner is not based on sexual intercourse. In the dissent in *Bowers v. Hardwick*,[17] Justice Blackmun wrote, "Clearly, the right to choose one's life partner is quintessentially the kind of decision which our culture recognizes as personal and important. . . . The relevant question is not whether same-sex marriage is so rooted in our traditions that it is a fundamental right, but whether the freedom to choose one's own life partner is so rooted in our traditions."[18]

One question frequently raised addresses whether the application of the Full Faith and Credit Clause of the federal Constitution requires the recognition of same-sex marriages, civil unions, and domestic partnerships. The standard answer is that any state may refuse to recognize a marriage from one state if it violates the strong public policy of another state. The United States Supreme Court has applied the Full Faith and Credit Clause to judgments. But marriages, civil unions, and domestic partnerships are not judgments; they are acts reflecting a status within the state in which they were entered. As they are not judgments, it seems that full faith and credit does not apply.

Of course, adoption decrees, dissolutions, property divisions—where there is a court order—are judgments, and as such, full faith and credit must and does apply.

On October 25, 2006, the New Jersey Supreme Court issued its long-awaited decision on the same-sex marriage case, *Mark Lewis and Dennis Winslow, et al. v. Gwendolyn L. Harris, etc., et al.*[19] The court held:

> [D]enying committed same-sex couples the financial and social benefits and privileges given to their married heterosexual counterparts bears no

substantial relationship to a legitimate governmental interest. The Court holds that under the equal protection guarantee of Article I, Paragraph 1 of the New Jersey Constitution, committed same-sex couples must be afforded on equal terms the same rights and benefits enjoyed by opposite-sex couples under the civil marriage statutes. The name to be given to the statutory scheme that provides full rights and benefits to same-sex couples, whether marriage or some other term, is a matter left to the democratic process.

The court gave the New Jersey Legislature 180 days to comply with the decision. The court's decision came down in October 2006; the legislature passed legislation creating civil unions in New Jersey in December 2006. And New Jersey's lesbian and gay residents became eligible to enter a civil union as of February 2007. Civil unions grant the same rights and responsibilities awarded to heterosexual married couples. But this does not include any federal benefits, nor does it guarantee recognition in other states or by the federal government.

New Jersey joins Vermont and Connecticut in recognizing civil unions as legally sanctioned same-sex relationships. New Jersey civil unions now carry the weight of marriage without the name. However, as with the other states' civil unions and same-sex marriage in Massachusetts, New Jersey civil unions are only recognized by state law, not federal. Further, there is no guarantee the relationship will be recognized by other states. As it stands today, it is likely that most states will not recognize these civil unions.

G. Federal Marriage Rights

In 1997, the Government Accounting Office (GAO) prepared a study on marriage rights. That study[20] found 1,049 federal statutes that included marriage as a factor. In 2004, the GAO updated the study and identified 1,138 federal statutes involving rights, privileges, and responsibilities that revolved around marriage.[21]

Five states conducted similar studies of their state laws: California, Colorado, Hawaii, Massachusetts, and Vermont. (See Appendix for citations.) Each found a variety of rights, privileges, responsibilities, and obligations that were governed by the marital status of the individual. These state laws grant specific rights and privileges only to married couples.

The federal DOMA renders same-sex couples ineligible for tax preferences and other rights enjoyed by married couples under the Internal Revenue Code, Employee Retirement Income Security Act (ERISA), Family Medical Leave Act, and other federal laws.

Same-sex couples cannot draft legal documents that provide coverage denied under federal law. Estranged family members who question the very existence of the couple's relationship may challenge any documents the couple does draft.

H. Other Rights/Benefits/Tax Consequences

In addition to state and federal rights that are explicitly granted by statute or regulation, other benefits are denied to same-sex couples. For example, many employers provide health insurance to their employees, and most provide coverage for the employee's spouse and family. These employment benefits, which are not required by law or regulation, are not usually available to gay or lesbian employees.

These gay and lesbian employees, who are in committed relationships, are treated differently from their fellow employees. Employers argue that the benefits are provided to all married employees and their families. But the law in most states prohibits gay and lesbian employees from marrying. Therefore, they can never meet the basic requirement established by their employer to obtain healthcare coverage for their families.

An increasing number of employers are providing domestic partner benefits for their gay and lesbian employees and their respective families. These employers see this as a business decision necessary to remain competitive. However, there is a major difference when benefits are provided to same-sex couples and their families. The cost of the benefit is added to the employee's income. So, unlike their heterosexual married fellow employees, the gay or lesbian employee is taxed on the cost of those health benefits. Gay and lesbian state employees in Rhode Island recently found this out the hard way. In 2001, the legislature provided domestic partner health and insurance benefits but did not provide for tax deductions on those benefits. The state notified more than 200 employees that the benefits are considered taxable income by the I.R.S. and that back taxes are owed. Some employees may be responsible for up to five years of unpaid taxes. The only positive part is that no penalties or interest will be assessed.

> **Practice Tip**
>
> Lawyers representing lesbian and gay employees opting into employer-sponsored domestic partnership benefits need to advise their clients of the tax liability.

In Rhode Island, many employees had no idea the benefits were taxable because their heterosexual married counterparts are not taxed. The benefits are taxed because the DOMA prohibits recognition of the employee's domestic partnership.

Under Internal Revenue Code (I.R.C.) section 105(b), amounts paid to an employee's dependent domestic partner through a healthcare plan that are attributable to an employee after tax considerations and employer contributions are excluded from the employee's income (sections 104 and 105). However, if the domestic partner is not a dependent under I.R.C. section 152, the fair market value of the health coverage is included in the employee's income. That amount is subject to FICA, FUTA, and withholding taxes. Further, the employee's portion of the premium for coverage of the non-dependent domestic partner must be paid on an after-tax basis.

In a private letter, the I.R.S. states that the fair market value of the domestic partnership healthcare coverage is equal to the fair market value of the group coverage provided to domestic partners.[22]

Even with companies offering health insurance to the partners of their lesbian and gay employees, there is no COBRA[23] coverage for domestic partners if their partners leave that employment.

I. Traditional Marriage

There is an argument that marriage fosters social stability. Accepting that position, the states should encourage more people to enter the stabilizing institution of marriage.

Historically, marriage had nothing to do with love; it was a mandatory political and economic institution. Marriages were arranged. Wives and children were the property of the husband. In the moneyed classes, husbands divorced wives who could not bear children, preferably a male heir. This view of "traditional marriage" is unacceptable in today's society.

Birth control came into vogue in the 19th century, and it was illegal. Under 19th-century law, "husband and wife were one and that one is the husband."

There were state laws of "coverture" prohibiting a married woman from entering contracts or owning property in her name. Until Congress enacted federal laws in the 1960s and 1970s, married women could be denied credit in their name; credit was only issued in the husband's name. Single women also endured discrimination because they were not married.

An 1863 New York judge decided that giving wives independent property rights would "sow the seeds of perpetual discord," thereby dooming marriage.

In 1958, again in New York, only husbands could sue for loss of consortium because wives were expected to provide these services.

Even in the late 1970s, many states had "head and master" laws that gave the husband the authority to determine where the family lived. Under the legal definition of marriage, the man was required to support the family and the woman to keep house, raise the children, and provide sex. This once was "traditional marriage."

Marital rape became recognized as a crime in the 1980s. Before that, society recognized the "rule of thumb." Under that tradition, a husband could beat his wife but was limited to an instrument that was no larger than his thumb, giving us "the rule of thumb."

As society changed, so did marriage. Women gained independent legal existence and did not destroy marriage. Women entered the workforce; men became stay-at-home dads, and that did not destroy marriage. Marriage, as an institution, is constantly changing. It is now more flexible, although some look upon the old days with fondness. The marriages of those who created the baby-boom generation are not the same as those entered into by their grandchildren.

The marriage of history and tradition no longer exists in reality. It exists only in history books.

Common-law marriage is a form of marriage that originally served the needs of people living on the frontier. Ministers and justices of the peace were rare. The state encouraged marriage, and restricting it to those sanctioned by a minister or justice of the peace was impractical. Establishing common-law marriage was a response to the westward movement. It allowed people to marry by holding themselves out as a married couple.

Most states have abandoned common-law marriage as unnecessary in the modern world. However, common-law marriage is another version of "traditional marriage."

Common-Law Marriage
Common-law marriage is still recognized by 11 states: Alabama, Colorado, Iowa, Kansas, Montana, Oklahoma, Pennsylvania, Rhode Island, South Carolina, Texas, and Utah.

Elements of Common-Law Marriage
1. Individuals legally able to enter into a marriage contract;
2. There was a present mutual intention and agreement to be married;
3. The parties lived together as husband and wife; and
4. The couple held themselves out to the world as husband and wife.

Historically, state law governed marriage—its creation and its demise. Recent case law reflects the current state of marriage challenges. In *Hernandez v. Robles*,[24] New York's highest court reversed a lower court decision and declared that the trial court exceeded its mandate and usurped the legislature's responsibility to rewrite statutes. The plaintiffs were same-sex couples challenging the New York law restricting marriage to opposite-sex couples.

The appellate court rejected the plaintiff's argument based on the finding in *Loving v. Virginia*[25] that marriage is a fundamental right. The court stated that the elements that determine the existence of a "fundamental right" are a careful description of the liberty interest and that the interest must be firmly rooted "in the nation's history, legal traditions and practices." Based on the court's decision, the judges did not find that a fundamental interest existed. The court also held:

> Marriage laws are not primarily about adult needs for official recognition and support, but about the well-being of children and society, and such preference constitutes a rational policy decision.

J. Foreign Recognition of Same-Sex Marriage

A growing number of foreign countries are recognizing same-sex marriages. No marriage entered into in any of those countries is recognized in the United States. Same-sex marriage is allowed in the Netherlands, Belgium, Canada, and Spain.

Other countries recognize same-sex relationships as either domestic partnerships or registered partnerships. These countries are Denmark, Norway, Sweden, Iceland, and Finland. Most provide all marriage rights except for adoption and international recognition. In 1995, Hungary extended rights of cohabitation to same-sex couples.

France and Germany allow solidarity pacts (PACs) and recognize same-sex couples. A PAC allows unmarried couples to register and grants them access to certain benefits and responsibilities.

The United Kingdom allowed formal recognition of civil unions between same-sex couples in December 2005.

Laws in Brazil, Colombia, Costa Rica, the Czech Republic, Israel, and New Zealand offer same-sex couples the rights and responsibilities of marriage.

The Republic of Ireland is considering domestic partnership legislation and, possibly, same-sex marriage.

Since Canada recognizes same-sex marriages, many U.S. citizens have crossed the border to tie the knot. Canada does not require residency or medical tests. The only requirements are a license, two witnesses, and someone authorized to officiate. However, there is a one-year residency requirement to dissolve a Canadian marriage. No state in the United States recognizes same-sex marriages performed in Canada.

K. Domestic Partnerships/Civil Unions

Domestic partnerships are recognized in a growing number of states. These, along with civil unions, are often called "marriage light" because they provide some marital rights, but not all. Some activists in the LGBT community see domestic partnerships and civil unions as stepping-stones to full marriage rights for same-sex couples.

Civil unions were first created in Vermont in 2000. This followed the Vermont Supreme Court's decision in *Baker v. Vermont* (supra). Non-residents of Vermont are permitted to take out a license for a civil union. A majority of civil unions entered into in Vermont are between non-residents. Most states do not recognize these civil unions. New Jersey and Connecticut are exceptions.

However, ending those relationships may prove problematical for the parties. There are limited venues available for couples wishing to terminate their civil unions. States with mini-DOMAs will not recognize the civil union and will not permit a "divorce" in their states. Vermont requires at least one partner to be a resident before its courts have jurisdiction to dissolve a civil union entered into in that state.

California has led the way in providing protection to lesbian and gay couples through domestic partnerships. California does restrict marriage to a man and woman; however, the domestic partnership law provides myriad rights to same-sex couples that mirror marital rights. Initially, the rights included:

- The right to sue for the wrongful death of a partner
- Adoptions under the state's stepparent adoption procedures
- The right to make healthcare decisions for an incapacitated partner
- The right to claim state income tax deductions
- The right to claim an exclusion for a partner's medical care and benefits
- The right to be appointed administrator of the deceased partner's estate

The state initiated a statewide domestic partnership registry in 1999.

In 2003, the California Domestic Partner Rights and Responsibilities law required equal treatment of domestic partners and spouses. Couples that register with the state are entitled to hundreds of new rights and responsibilities, including community property (property that a couple acquires after registration is owned equally). Under this expanded law, registered domestic partners have mutual obligations for debts to third parties, inheritance rights, intestacy rights, entitlement to bereavement leave, and the right to make funeral arrangements.

In California, children of same-sex couples have the same rights as children of a married couple. A child born to a registered couple through assisted reproduction is automatically considered the legal child of both parties. The law also requires formal court proceedings to dissolve the relationship.

However, even with the expanded set of rights, responsibilities, and obligations, registered domestic partners in California cannot file joint state tax returns, and the process for entering and dissolving the relationship is different from marriage.

Since many states do not recognize domestic partnerships, parents are encouraged to get a court order acknowledging their legal relationship with the children. The court order assists the parents when they travel or move from California because states are required, under various federal laws, to recognize the judicial decisions of other states. Even individual state mini-DOMAs and state constitutional amendments cannot bar enforcement of another state's court order. This is particularly true where children are concerned.

Some question the cost of state domestic partnership laws. In 2003, the University of Massachusetts at Amherst and the University of California at Los Angeles conducted a study of that question. According to this study, California would save $8.1 million to $10.6 million each year by enacting a domestic partnership law.[26]

New Jersey passed its domestic partnership law in 2004 after showing a projected annual savings of more than $61 million.[27] Following the New Jersey Supreme Court's ruling in October 2006 declaring that same-sex couples must be given the same rights, privileges, obligations, and responsibilities under the state constitution, the state legislature enacted a civil union law. The legislature passed the law in December 2006 and it became effective in February 2007.

L. State Employees and Domestic Partnership Benefits

State-proffered benefits usually include healthcare benefits. But they are very different from benefits offered to heterosexual married couples. The cost of the health insurance is charged as income to lesbian or gay employees, who must pay tax on those benefits.

There have been attempts to use state laws prohibiting recognition of same-sex relationships to prevent government employers from offering benefits to gay and lesbian couples. The argument in favor of these benefits refers to them as incentives to recruit highly qualified employees. They are seen as employment benefits and not as an attempt to recognize same-sex relationships.

Thirteen states offer domestic partnership benefits to state employees.

1. California
2. Connecticut
3. District of Columbia
4. Hawaii
5. Iowa
6. Maine
7. New Mexico
8. New Jersey
9. New York
10. Oregon
11. Vermont
12. Rhode Island
13. Washington

In Ohio, a conservative state legislator filed a taxpayer suit against Miami University of Ohio because it provides benefits to employees in same-sex relationships. The university argued it was not violating the Ohio Constitution by recognizing the relationship. It was only providing an employment package to recruit highly qualified employees. Ultimately, the legislator gave up his suit because of questions about his standing.

In Alaska, the battle to preserve benefits for state employees continues. On October 28, 2005, the Alaska Supreme Court issued a decision that spousal limitations were unconstitutional as applied to public employees with same-sex partners.[28] The justices held that these limitations violated the Alaska State Constitution's Equal Protection Clause. The court remanded the case to the Superior Court for further proceedings.

On June 1, 2006, the court ordered the Superior Court to do what was necessary to ensure compliance by January 7, 2007.[29] This included ordering the state and the city of Anchorage to provide benefits that complied with the October 28, 2005 decision.

The Alaska Commissioner of Administration adopted regulations that conferred employee medical benefits and retirement system benefits on the same-sex partners of state employees. This occurred on October 13, 2006. While the Superior Court found the regulations lacking, the Supreme Court vacated the court's decision and approved the regulations. The Supreme Court, in an order dated December 19, 2006, ordered the state to implement the regulations by the January 7, 2007 deadline.[30]

The benefit most often provided to the same-sex partners of public employees is health insurance. But it must be remembered that the value of these benefits is considered taxable income to the employee. This is not the case with the spouse of a married public employee.

Hundreds of local governments throughout the country also offer benefits to the same-sex partners of their employees. Again, these benefits are considered part of the employee's package and are often part of the union contract negotiated with the local government entity.

In 2005, Michigan's Attorney General opined that government-provided benefits violated the state's constitutional amendment prohibiting recognition of same-sex relationships, enacted in 2004.

Wisconsin, one of the states that passed a constitutional amendment banning same-sex marriage and recognition of same-sex relationships in 2006, is also feeling the effects. Several highly regarded academicians are looking to move to other universities because they fear the loss of benefits for their partners.

The argument about whether these benefits constitute recognition of same-sex relationships or are recruiting tools for qualified employees will continue to fester until rational minds triumph in their efforts to impress on others the inherent injustice of the situation.

New Jersey law allows local governments to determine if they will provide survivor benefits to employees. The need for this became apparent in the case of Laurel Hester, a 23-year employee of the Ocean City Prosecutor's Office. Lt. Hester, suffering from terminal lung cancer, asked the Ocean City freeholders (local government officials) to give her $13,000 death benefit to her partner, Stacey Andree. Lt. Hester made the request because she feared her partner would lose their home after her death.

For months the Ocean City freeholders refused Lt. Hester's request. They reasoned it would set an expensive precedent. However, they did not anticipate the international outrage once word of their parsimony became known. A Republican legislator decided to introduce legislation to provide what the freeholders were refusing.

Facing an onslaught of criticism, the freeholders reversed their decision and voted to authorize payment of the death benefit to Stacey Andree. She was able to keep the home she shared with Laurel, who died in 2006.

A married couple would never face the same situation. This should never happen again with the new civil union law in New Jersey. Public employees in civil unions will be guaranteed the same rights as heterosexual married couples.

The only possible glitch is benefit plans that are controlled by the Employee Retirement Income Security Act of 1974 (ERISA). That is a federal law, and DOMA will trump any state law.

M. Unmarried Cohabitants

In 2003, the New Mexico Supreme Court decided, in *Lozoya v. Sanchez*,[31] that an unmarried cohabitant could make a claim for "loss of consortium." The court will consider the length of the relationship and the degree to which the partners' lives are intertwined as factors in making a decision.

In 2005, the California Supreme Court issued the *Koebke v. Bernardo Hts. Country Club*[32] decision. The plaintiffs were registered domestic partners, one of whom was a member of the defendant country club. They sued because the club treated them differently from married club members in setting golf tee times and permitting the non-member partner to only play as a guest. The plaintiffs argued that the club's policies constituted discrimination under California's Unruh Civil Rights Act.[33]

The trial court granted summary judgment to the defendants, and the plaintiffs appealed. The Supreme Court found that marital status claims are available under the Unruh Act. The court also found there is a distinction between registered domestic partners and other unmarried couples and individuals. According to the court, registered domestic partners are the equivalent of spouses for purposes of the Unruh Act. Businesses that extend benefits to spouses that are not offered to registered domestic partners engage in impermissible marital status discrimination. But businesses may, for legitimate business reasons, draw distinctions between married and unmarried couples. This seems contradictory, but courts often use legitimate business reasons as a standard in discrimination cases.

The court found there was no discrimination by the country club's spousal benefit policy for actions taken *before* the Domestic Partner Act took effect. Legitimate business interests supported the club's policy. The court did find, however, that the plaintiffs might have a viable Unruh Act claim for discriminatory application of the club's policy. The plaintiffs presented evidence that the club did not strictly adhere to its married couple's policy. The club allowed exceptions and non-adherence to the policy on a regular basis. The plaintiffs should have been permitted to argue these facts to the jury.

Since domestic partnerships and civil unions are statutory creations, lawyers can expect courts to strictly construe the statutes that created them. A New York case bears this out. In *Langan v. St. Vincent's Hospital of New York*,[34] a surviving partner sued the hospital for wrongful death.

Mr. Langan and his partner, Neil Conrad Spicehandler, entered into a civil union in Vermont in 2000. In 2002, a car struck Mr. Spicehandler, causing multiple injuries. He died following two surgeries at St. Vincent's Hospital in New York.

The lower court denied a defense motion to dismiss and the defendant appealed. The Supreme Court of New York, Appellate Division, Second Judicial Department reversed that decision. The court decided that only the legislature has the authority to change the statute to provide for same-sex couples. The court, citing *Lawrence v. Texas*,[35] agreed with the dissent, holding that ". . . disapprobation of homosexual conduct is a sufficient basis for virtually any law based on classification of such conduct." The court decided that any decision recognizing same-sex relationships would usurp the legislature's authority.

N. Reciprocal Beneficiaries Law

After the Hawaii Supreme Court held that same-sex couples could not be barred from marrying, the state legislature amended the state constitution to counter that decision. In response to the call for some protection for same-sex couples, the Hawaii Legislature enacted the Reciprocal Beneficiaries Act.[36] The law allows any two single adults, including same-sex partners, blood relatives, or friends, to access some state spousal rights. The number and kind of rights are not readily apparent. Initially, the statute provided workplace medical insurance. However, the Hawaii Attorney General eliminated that benefit by opining that no private business was required to offer domestic partner benefits. This was followed by a court decision limiting health insurance provisions to state employees. Over the years, fewer benefits are available to persons using this law. The number of persons registering is low compared to the population of the islands (1.1 million).

Under the Reciprocal Beneficiary Act, individuals:

- Must be at least 18 years old;
- Must not be married or part of another reciprocal beneficiary relationship;
- Are legally prohibited from marrying under Hawaii's marriage law;
- Are consenting without force, duress or fraud;
- Must sign and file a notarized declaration; and
- Must pay $8 registration fee ($8 to terminate status).

O. Religion and Marriage

According to many religious faiths, marriage shall always be between one man and one woman. But this is not a universal religious belief. Many faiths are adopting teachings supporting and recognizing same-sex marriages.

Some religious marriages between same-sex couples are recognized within the church but not by the secular government. This presents a quandary: If the government believes in the sanctity of marriage and refuses to recognize same-sex marriage because of certain religious teachings, why does that position not violate the Establishment Clause of the First Amendment?

On February 21, 2006, the United States Supreme Court issued a decision in *Gonzales v. O Centro Espirita Beneficente Uniao Do Vegetal, et al.*[37] The case involved the Religious Freedom Restoration Act of 1993 (RFRA).[38] That statute prohibits the government from interfering with the exercise of religion unless the government "demonstrates that application of the burden to the person represents the least restrictive means of advancing a compelling government interest."[39]

The case involved a religious group that used a sacramental tea in their ceremonies. The government believed the tea violated the Controlled Substances Act.[40]

A religious group can challenge the government's action if it can show that the sincere exercise of the religious ceremony is substantially burdened. The government may rebut by showing that the burden results from the protection of a compelling government interest.

The RFRA does not apply to the states.[41] But questions arise as to whether the federal DOMA would withstand a challenge under RFRA. What would happen if a religious denomination that recognized same-sex relationships challenged DOMA as creating an unreasonable burden on the practice of religion? Could an argument be made that the government's refusal to recognize same-sex marriages, sanctified by a church, results in that church and its religious beliefs being treated differently from other churches that agree with DOMA? Does DOMA's intent to prohibit same-sex marriages rise to the level of a compelling government interest such that a person's religious beliefs can be burdened? And if such a challenge were successful, would that be the impetus for Congress to pass a constitutional amendment banning recognition of same-sex relationships? The RFRA adopted a strict scrutiny test—a much higher hurdle than the rational basis test currently used to determine same-sex marriage cases.

The Supreme Court, in the *Gonzalez* decision, stated, ". . . Congress had a reason for enacting RFRA, too. Congress recognized that 'laws "neutral" toward religion may burden religious exercise as surely as laws intended to interfere with religious exercise,' and legislated the 'compelling interest test' as the means for the courts to 'strik[e] sensible balances between religious liberty and competing prior government interests.'"[42]

This decision may lend support to the argument that DOMA violates the United States Constitution.

P. Alternatives to Traditional Marriages and "Family"

A London-based think tank, Ekklesia, has a different idea about how to resolve the marriage issue. In June 2006, the organization proposed that governments abolish civil marriage while continuing to allow church marriages.[43] But the government would also permit couples to register civil partnerships.

Right now, people must apply for a marriage license before their marriage is legally recognized. State statutes grant the authority for clergy to officiate over legally recognized marriages. The key is the state's authority to recognize marriage. This is a civil, not a religious, act. Ekklesia's proposal would do away with civil marriages and only recognize civil partnerships. Couples would continue to be free to seek a religious marriage, but their relationship would be legally recognized only if they also registered their civil partnerships.

The group argues that establishing civil partnerships and religious marriages will remove the emotional issues from the marriage debate. According to the group's report, the proposal allows the "[m]utually beneficial disentangling of the roles, interests, and practices of church and state. Religious communities are entitled to have their own ideal of marriage, which they offer to the wider society. But requiring others to accept this definition by law benefits no one. It is confusing and counterproductive."

The report also stated, "What is called 'marriage' today is essentially a civil contract which can be dissolved or re-entered as many times as necessary. Superimposed on that is a Christian ideal of lifelong fidelity which many accept as 'a nice idea,' but which is not necessarily what they are really choosing, and whose basis in a community of faith they often do not understand or accept."

Governments grant secular rights to their citizens, and it is inappropriate to use religion as a basis for granting these rights. Introducing civil partnerships permits those who register to obtain all the secular rights granted to committed couples.

Today, no one is required to be married in a religious ceremony, and the state authorizes religious personnel to officiate at these ceremonies and requires them to submit the government-required license in order for the marriage to be legally recognized. People who are married in a religious ceremony but who do not obtain a marriage license are not legally married. Civil partnerships make a clear distinction between religious and civil ceremonies.

There is also a movement afoot to redirect the focus from same-sex marriage to an acceptance of relationships other than marriage. In April 2006 a group of LGBT activists began discussing the politics of marriage and family. The product is *Beyond Same-Sex Marriage: A New Strategic Vision for All Our Families and Relationships.*[44]

A basic premise of this document is that marriage is "not the only worthy form of family or relationship, and it should not be legally and economically privileged above all others." As the statement points out, most people do not live in married relationships. The mix of relationships is as varied as the imagination can conjure—single parents, elderly couples, friends sharing a house, adult children living with their parents, etc.

Beyondmarriage.org intends to reframe the debate. And the 2006 Washington Supreme Court decision gives reason to believe that may be a preferred stance.

Families are no longer defined merely by a marriage certificate. The scope of "family" has expanded to include myriad forms that are not part of our tradition or history. Yet they are families nonetheless. Statutory rights, legal and economic recognition of relationships can no longer be limited to the marital model. Every family has the right and is entitled to expect equal protection under the laws of every state, regardless of whether marriage is part of the formula.

A new definition of family is required. What constitutes a "legitimate family"? Is it one where there is a mother and a father, and they are married? What about the grandparents raising their grandchildren? What about uncles and aunts raising nieces and nephews? No one is talking about this changing face of the family. The government's refusal to recognize the new face of family in this country does a disservice not only to the adults involved, but also to the children. And the government is constantly claiming to be concerned with the welfare of children.

The Beyond Marriage coalition sees the agenda of the right wing as one that will not benefit the most people. According to their report, "The purpose is not only to enforce narrow, heterosexist definitions of marriage and coerce conformity, but also to slash to the bone governmental funding for a wide array of family programs, including childcare, healthcare and reproductive services, and nutrition, and transfer responsibility for financial survival to families themselves."

Among their goals, Beyond Marriage seeks:

- Legal recognition of a wide range of relationships;
- Separation of benefits and recognition from marital status;
- Separation of church and state in all matters; and
- Access to all government support programs.

These are but a few of the principles set forth in the report. The list of signatories is growing. To add your name, visit the Web site, www.beyondmarriage.org.

If successful, the discussion will go beyond marriage and include all relationships. This does not include the weird and irrational "relationships" dreamed up by the conservative right wing, but real people in real relationships with real needs.

Q. Starting a Relationship

Most couples starting a new relationship never think about what happens if it ends. Lesbians and gay men are no different. But what happens at the end of a same-sex relationship can be less traumatic if certain precautions are taken at the beginning.

Whether one calls it a "living together agreement," a "domestic partnership agreement," or a "prenuptial agreement," most lesbian and gay couples will benefit from reducing their intentions to writing. When either or both own real estate, taking the time to consider the future will bode well should the honeymoon end. As with all legal documents, it is important to take extra care in drafting.

> **Practice Tip**
>
> Construct the agreements clearly to relay the parties' intentions. If the state restricts recognition of same-sex relationships, consider labeling the agreements as investment or business arrangements. A title alone can change how the document is perceived.

Another issue crops up if only one partner owns real estate and both intend to live in "her" house. If both parties intend to contribute to the mortgage, maintenance, and upkeep of the house, they may want to address those responsibilities. One partner may earn more than the other. A 50-50 split is not always equitable. Likewise, any increase in equity or value of the house would benefit the titleholder. The other partner would not be entitled to recover any money paid into the kitty. Any interest in real estate must be in writing to comply with the Statute of Frauds.

Money can be the bane of a successful relationship. It behooves a couple to consider their financial relationship at the start. Writing down each person's respective obligation concerning money will reduce the likelihood of future disputes. The agreement can be revisited on a regular basis or when one partner's financial situation changes. The issues to consider include rent or mortgage payments, property taxes, entitlement to the tax deduction, insurance, maintenance, cleaning, etc.

When only one partner's name is on the house, the other partner should be encouraged to purchase renter's insurance to cover her possessions. The homeowner's policy usually will not cover the belongings of anyone whose name is not on the title. Some couples believe there will be no problem, as the owner will claim all the contents as her own. But this is a dicey stance to take. The couple will not know if it works until after disaster hits—and then it is too late. Renter's insurance is inexpensive and worth the peace of mind.

It is also important to be clear on the ownership. When one partner owns the house, the I.R.S. may consider the housing to be a gift to the other partner unless he is paying rent. The homeowner-partner can charge rent and keep accurate records. The rent record, even if never actually paid, can be based on $12,000 per year. That amount may be gifted from one person to another without incurring any gift tax liability. If the rent is listed as $1,000 or less per month, there is no gift and no liability. Convincing clients to keep good records is essential. Helping them set up a record-keeping system is time well spent.

Couples must also be careful about transferring an interest in real estate to each other. Often, this happens and then the couple tells their lawyer. It is better to confer with a lawyer *before* the transfer takes place. A transfer may trigger gift tax liability or, if there is a mortgage, the "due on sale" clause inherent in every mortgage. That comes into play when an interest in the property is transferred without the mortgage holder's approval.

Because of dower and curtesy rights, married couples do not risk pulling the "due on sale" clause trigger. But unmarried couples can be caught up in them. Once the clause is triggered, the mortgagee can call in the note. This will usually create significant financial distress for the mortgagor. Most people do not understand what their mortgage requires, let alone the varied nuances of real estate titles and gift tax liability.

Instead of holding title to real estate jointly with rights of survivorship, a couple may want to consider holding title as "tenants in common." This allows an unequal division of the interest in the property. It is a more flexible way to hold title, but there is no automatic transfer of interest when one of the title-holders dies. One way to address that particular issue is to couple a tenants in common title with a revocable living trust. That allows the parties to hold unequal shares in the real estate and yet provides for the transfer of the property on the death of one party. Making the living trust revocable allows the parties to terminate the trust if the relationship ends.

Also, transferring assets into a living trust avoids probate. It can be difficult to contest a trust; therefore, this may be another tool to discuss with clients. There is no one opinion about living trusts. Some lawyers swear by them and others swear *at* them. Revocable living trusts can be a godsend for some clients and a viper pit for others. The trust itself is not the problem; it is the way the trust is written, whether it is funded, and whether it meets the clients' needs.

Depending on the relative financial positions of both partners, a trust may be used to grant the surviving partner a life estate in the residence. There is no post-death transfer of interest in the property; the surviving partner continues to live in and maintain the residence, and upon her death the property transfers to someone else. If the parties jointly own the property, a survivorship deed is preferable. The surviving partner avoids probate.

Any agreement the parties enter into can address what happens should the relationship end. It is wise to include either an arbitration or mediation clause. In some cases the parties may want to include both, starting with mediation and moving to arbitration. These processes are often cheaper than full-blown litigation.

Language can be included that addresses the issues of support and the tax consequences of paying it. A possible clause is:

> We understand that a division of any joint assets between us (when dissolving this relationship) may result in tax consequences to one or both of us. We agree to take into consideration any possible tax consequence when dividing our joint assets. We also agree to share any tax payment (consequence) on a pro rata basis. We intend for each of us to pay a percentage of the total tax bill. The percentage will be equal to our individual proportional share of any assets that we hold jointly. Any tax payment will be deducted from the assets we will divide. We have described and listed those jointly held assets in this document. We will update this agreement whenever we accrue other jointly held assets. If we fail to formally update this agreement, all jointly held assets, whenever accrued and wherever situated, will be subject to this agreement.

It is also important for the parties to consider any tax liability when agreeing to pay support after the relationship ends. These considerations must take place *before* signing any agreement. Once signed, if adequate and valuable consideration is given, the promise is an enforceable contract. Consider the following support clause language:

> We understand that any support one of us pays the other may not be tax-deductible. We also understand that whoever receives the support will be required to pay income tax on it. We understand that any support paid or received is not treated as alimony in a legally recognized marriage. We both agree to consider any tax liability when agreeing to an amount to be paid for support. It is our intent that any support to be paid will not result in an unreasonable or inequitable tax burden on the one paying support. If we are unable to agree on a support amount, we will calculate support in the following manner: _____.
> We will also consider the tax consequences involved with any support calculation method.

The method used to calculate a support amount varies by couple. This language is only a suggestion to start the discussion. Rather than use impersonal pronouns—"parties," etc.— it is better to use first names or second-person pronouns. This makes the document easier to read and understand. That results in fewer disputes about what each party intended.

Domestic Partnership Issues to Consider

1. How long has the relationship existed before signing the agreement?
2. Acknowledge the future uncertainty of same-sex marriage; indicate how the agreement will be interpreted if the law changes. What happens if the agreement is not recognized or enforceable? Determine if the agreement is a contract or some other type of writing.
5. Children: Are both partners legally recognized as parents? Include language concerning the parties' intentions about the children.
6. What happens to the agreement if the couple moves to another state? Which state law applies to the interpretation and enforcement of the contract?
7. Specify the parties' intentions in the body of the document.
8. How will the parties end their relationship? Will either party have responsibility of notifying the other if they intend to end the relationship? What form is notice to take? How should it be delivered? Format for dividing property.

9. Describe each partner's rights, responsibilities, and obligations under the Agreement as to each other, their property, children, etc.
10. Include an arbitration and/or mediation clause.
11. List property each person is bringing into the relationship and its relative value; income of each party at the start and pro rata division of expenses.
12. Address tax issues.
13. If parties jointly hold any real estate, it is important to discuss how the property will be divided. This includes appraisals, right of first refusal to buy/sell, listing price, listing agent, etc. What about division of increase in value/equity?
14. What happens if either party reneges on her obligations under the agreement?
15. Any consideration to the partner who is not on the house title but contributed toward the mortgage/property taxes, and the equity/value of the house increased during the relationship.
16. Will there be a provision for future support?

If children are involved, a parenting agreement is very important. That may be made part of the domestic partnership agreement or as a separate agreement and incorporated into the other. In any agreement dealing with children, custody, visitation, and support, include a reference to the applicability of the Uniform Child Custody Jurisdiction Enforcement Act (UCCJEA) and the Parental Kidnapping Protection Act (PKPA). These are federal laws, enforceable in all states, that protect children from being swiped by one parent and taken to another state. (See Chapter 4 on Children.)

Even without a formal written agreement, lesbian and gay couples must be cautious when setting up their household. Creating joint property ownership may trigger an immediate taxable gift. If the value is over the annual exclusion amount, currently at $12,000, the person making the gift must file a gift tax return. The amount over the annual exclusion will be charged against the individual's $1 million lifetime amount.

The Internal Revenue Service has found no gift tax liability if there was no "donative intent." This can occur if the parties created the joint tenancy to expedite transfer on death or to avoid probate. The parties' action resulted in nominal joint ownership and there was no gift. The individual facts will control not the transfer itself.

When setting up joint bank accounts, the gift occurs only when the co-owner withdraws the original owner's money. If the parties open a joint account together, it is wise to develop a system to track each person's deposits into that account. The I.R.S. will increase gift tax audits against lesbian and gay couples when one dies.

Some couples may find that using "payable on death" or "transfer on death" accounts are better than joint accounts for estate-planning purposes. Of course, most couples use joint accounts to simplify their lives, and they are not thinking about what happens after death.

A couple may want to establish a joint account for household purposes and maintain separate accounts for personal use. This would make it easier to track deposits made by both parties. This is especially true if the individual's employer allows automatic deposits.

The couple may make annual gifts to each other in order to reallocate their individual assets. Such action also allows a wealthier partner to reduce his potential taxable estate.

Couples need to consider who will make charitable contributions for the year and take the deduction. The same is true for mortgage and property tax deductions. Working with an experienced tax preparer is money well spent for many lesbian and gay couples.

When children are involved, the parents need to determine who will claim "head of household" and who will claim the children as dependents. Using the I.R.S. definition of dependent is crucial in making this determination. In particular, if one partner is not legally recognized as the child's parent, the situation becomes more complex. Any support paid when there is no legal obligation to support may be considered a taxable gift by the I.R.S. if it exceeds the annual exempt amount.

The Employee Retirement Income and Security Act (ERISA) does not apply to same-sex couples. But, lesbian and gay couples must keep their beneficiary designations up to date. Naming a beneficiary is a good way to manage an estate and may reduce any minimum distribution requirements from qualified plans. Doing so allows the plan to continue to accumulate on a tax-deferred basis.

Both parties should invest in long-term care insurance, term life insurance, and disability insurance. Long-term care insurance may help a person qualify for Medicaid if his home state participates in a Partnership Program. These programs involve allowing a person to qualify for Medicaid if he or she has a specific amount of long-term care insurance. Details about a given state's participation can be obtained from the state's Medicaid office. This insurance is even more crucial when the parties have children.

With life insurance, each will initially own his policy and then assign it to the other and have that person become responsible for all premiums.[45] This is necessary if the parties cannot establish an insurable interest in their partner's life. Doing so removes the proceeds from the insured's estate.[46] An umbrella insurance policy is another one to consider. And if either party works from home, discussing a business insurance policy with the agent is important.

Can One Partner Be the Dependent of the Other?

Five tests must be met in order for one partner to claim the other as a dependent.

1. Support: Is one partner supplying at least 50% of the other's total support during the year? This includes food, shelter, clothing, medical and dental care, education, entertainment, etc.
2. Citizen or resident: The person being supported must be a U.S. citizen, resident alien, or a citizen of either Canada or Mexico.
3. Income: The supported person cannot have taxable income over $2,900. Nontaxable income such as nontaxable Social Security benefits, gifts, or welfare benefits do not count. But be careful with welfare and Social Security; household income may be considered for eligibility purposes.
4. Relationship: A person living in the home for the entire year may be considered a dependent provided the relationship does not violate local law. Even if local law prohibits unmarried cohabitation, fornication or similar acts, those laws are questionable and subject to a successful challenge. Worst-case scenario is the I.R.S. will reject the dependency claim and recalculate the return.
5. Unmarried person: If the dependent person is married and files a joint tax return with his or her spouse, there can be no claim of dependency.

R. The Party's Over

Gay divorce is a growing niche in the practice of family law. Civil unions, marriages, and domestic partnerships are becoming more prevalent, and lawyers must address the unique issues presented by lesbian and gay couples as they end their relationships.

In many respects, these relationships are no different from others. There are the same issues to be considered: property division, child custody, support, and visitation. However, there are few provisions for an equitable division of property or family rights. In fact, a judicial resolution may not be possible because the courts will decline to exercise jurisdiction. Attorneys and their clients must remember that the marital laws in most states do not apply to same-sex couples. Virginia even has a law that prohibits contracts between same-sex couples. It is probably not constitutional, but the law exists and the courts in Virginia are likely to enforce it at the lower levels.

Couples married in Massachusetts can get divorced there. Vermont and New Jersey residents in a civil union can file for dissolution. Check for residency requirements. In Vermont, there is a one-year residency requirement. Connecticut and California have procedures for dissolving a domestic partnership. Washington allows same-sex couples to use the state's divorce laws unless either party shows it would be unfair. Same-sex couples are allowed to divorce in Washington but not allowed to marry.

In the other states, couples may not have any specific procedure. Most claims will be construed as an action in contract. That will take care of the property, but will do nothing to address the issues concerning any children the parties may be raising.

The courts are beginning to address issues affecting children when there is no second-parent adoption and the non-biological parent wants, or does not want, any rights, obligations, or responsibilities concerning the child. The issues include "psychological parents," "de facto parents," intentions of the parties, rights of surrogates, and similar issues. This is a new and expanding area of law. The rules are still being written, and there are few road maps to follow. It is an exciting, frustrating, challenging, and heart-breaking time to enter into this area.

Having a parenting agreement may be helpful, but it is not a panacea. Florida refuses to honor those agreements when same-sex couples are involved. An agreement involving children must include evidence of the parties' intentions concerning the children. Also, include language stating that the birth or adoptive parent voluntarily waives her right to invoke any federal or state constitutional rights to the children. This did not work in Florida, but a parent should be able to voluntarily waive such rights when deciding to raise a child with her partner.

Several states have Parent Coordinator statutes.[47] Parent coordinators have authority to take over many daily child-rearing decisions if the parents are unable to agree. Some of the states that have these statutes also recognize the rights of same-sex parents. A parent coordinator may provide another way to deal with same-sex parents who let their adult issues interfere with their parental responsibilities. The process takes the children out of the middle.

Many parent coordinators are mental health professionals. The parents pay the coordinators an hourly fee. There may be couple and individual sessions involved. The goal of a parent coordinator is to help parents negotiate their own decisions about the children.

The concept of parent coordinators originated in Colorado in 1998. By August 2006, 17 states had some sort of formal parent coordinator program. In states like Colorado, Kansas, Idaho, and Minnesota, there are statutes that specify the procedures for appointing a parent coordinator. The statutes also spell out the coordinator's responsibilities.

Other states, such as Arizona, California, New Jersey, and Vermont, have less specific statutes and programs. But they allow courts to appoint a coordinator with the authority to make binding post-custodial decisions. Parent coordinators can prevent long-running custody battles because they have the authority to make the decisions the parents cannot or will not make.

Parent coordinators cannot change custody or make decisions concerning religion or relocation. In California, both parents must consent to a general delegation of judicial power.[48] Even with limitations on their authority, parent coordinators can be helpful in mediating parental conflicts and helping the combatants to see how their actions hurt their children. And if that is not working, the parent coordinator may step in and take the decision-making out of the parents' hands.

Most people who entered into civil unions in Vermont live outside the state. When the parties end their relationship, they run into difficulties in their home states. The courts in those states refuse to grant a divorce because the relationship is not recognized.

Lawyers can provide a means by which the parties can resolve their differences. The problem remains whether any agreement can be enforced in a court of law.

Massachusetts, Vermont, Connecticut, New Jersey, and California are among the states that have some legal mechanism for ending a same-sex relationship. Connecticut recognizes civil unions and domestic partnerships entered into outside the state. It does not recognize Massachusetts' same-sex marriages. Washington, by court order, is applying state divorce laws to same-sex couples dissolving their relationship.

In 2005, an Iowa judge granted a divorce to a lesbian couple. A lawsuit challenging the court's jurisdiction was rejected the lawsuit because the plaintiffs had no standing to challenge the court's jurisdiction. The divorce stands.

States that do not recognize a couple's relationship will also not recognize its termination. After all, how can one terminate something that does not exist? This is where lawyers come into the picture. Given the volatile nature of the entire concept, a good lawyer can assist a couple in terminating their relationship and seek court approval of any agreement. Another possibility is to have the parties accept binding arbitration with an understanding that the arbitrator's decision is enforceable in court.

Courts like arbitration, and it may be easier to enforce an agreement entered into by the parties than to make new law by filing a lawsuit. One party may object (often the one with the most to lose) to the court's jurisdiction and cite the state DOMA law in support.

When children are involved, a lawyer can often persuade the parties to make the dissolution amiable. This is in the child's best interests and, in the long term, also benefits the adults involved. Each party should have his or her own lawyer. No lawyer should ever attempt to represent both parties. This opens the lawyer to myriad charges of undue influence, malpractice, and duress.

Dividing a couple's property may also present problems. It is necessary to consider whether any gift tax liability exists for either or both partners. There may be such liability unless the exchange was either for valuable consideration or to pay support under a court order. Since same-sex couples do not qualify as spouses, absent a court order awarding support to one partner, any payments will qualify as a gift. If the amount exceeds the annual exemption amount (currently $12,000), the payor will be obligated to file a gift tax return.

Assuming the transfer involved valuable consideration, the I.R.S. will determine whether there was "adequate and full consideration in money or money's worth."[49] One way to avoid any gift tax is to dissolve the relationship through a contested court action. A court order dividing the parties' property would not be subject to DOMA and would qualify as a gift tax exemption. Also, any transfers that can qualify as repayment of a past loan are not considered gifts.

Divorces by their nature are difficult, and a plethora of laws exist to govern the process. There is no similar established protocol for ending a lesbian or gay relationship.

S. Termination Protocol

There are ways to resolve differences even where there is no established legal or informal mechanism in place. A post-separation agreement will help the parties dissolve their relationship in a civilized manner.

Post-separation Agreement Issues
1. Determine what issues need to be resolved. How will they be resolved?
2. Establish a time line for the parties.
3. Discuss using arbitration (binding or not), mediation, lawsuits.
4. Identify all assets; who holds title; any jointly owned property.
5. Determine existence of any written agreements.

> 6. Option to engage a therapist to assist in the emotional issues. Some family law lawyers require clients to be in therapy during the divorce. The lawyer deals with the legal issues and the therapist with the emotional detritus of the breakup.
> 7. Have the parties agree to work together without interference from families or friends.
> 8. Close all joint accounts and divide the money. This seems easy except when one person claims to have deposited more than the other. Without records, it may be impossible to determine who deposited what money or who paid what bills.
> 9. Determine what to do with joint credit cards. If accounts are to be left open, change to require joint authorization for all purchases, advances, etc.
> 10. Review all the bills and determine who is responsible for what. Arrange to keep payments current while the process is ongoing.
> 11. Divide all personal property, furniture, etc.

When a couple separates, they are best served by taking specific action. This means locating and copying critical documents including bank records, deeds, insurance policies, credit card statements, wills, trusts, advance directives, and powers of attorney. Both partners should secure their personal property, especially the items of either monetary or sentimental value.

Closing joint accounts and credit card accounts is an important step to take. It is important for this to take place even when the parties cannot agree who will be responsible. One of them must take action. If these accounts are left open, either party can continue to make withdrawals and charges.

The parties must determine who will live where, including who moves out of the residence they currently share. A time line for moving out is also important. If the parties intend to continue living together, they must resolve any joint accounts they maintain. Neither party should continue to put money into any joint accounts. By their nature, these accounts are accessible by both partners.

The parties should also decide how expenses will be handled while they live together. Reviewing bills and arranging payments is important to preserve the credit rating of each individual. A preliminary division of property is advisable.

If domestic violence is an issue, encourage the party at risk to move as quickly as possible. Provide information about shelters and other social services available to victims of domestic violence.

> **Practice Tip**
>
> Some homeless shelters and domestic violence shelters will not accept lesbians or gay men. Be prepared to argue the client's case for admittance.

When a relationship ends, emotions run high. Resolving disputes may be difficult. If the parties executed a domestic partnership agreement, the process for resolving disputes may be included. Both parties should look to their agreement when the situation becomes tense.

Rental agreements must be revised. Removing one person's name from the lease requires the acquiescence of the landlord. If that is not possible, both parties remain liable for the rental payments. When both parties jointly own real estate, one person may buy out the other's interest in the property. If the parties cannot arrive at a mutually agreeable resolution, it may be necessary to sell the home and divide the proceeds. Too often the parties will execute quitclaim deeds to achieve a quick resolution. This is not advisable, because the person quitclaiming his interest will be left with little or no negotiating room after the deed is recorded. This is another reason to retain counsel.

A lesbian or gay couple with children makes the safety and welfare of the children a priority. Maintaining an amicable separation is in the children's' best interests. Unfortunately, the non-legal parent may have no rights or obligations concerning the children.

The parents must work out a plan for the benefit of the child. The child's interests are of paramount concern. Therapy for all parties may be needed to help the child through the separation and termination period.

Avoiding a custody battle is equally important. The parents need to remember to do what is best for child. Their individual problems with each other must take a back seat to protecting the child. Arranging visitation and physical custody in an amiable manner will save the child a great deal of emotional trauma and anguish. It is morally wrong to deny a child the right to visit or maintain contact with the other parent. Even when that person's legal status is unclear, the child has a relationship with the person. Children do not know or care about the legalities. They just want to be secure in their relationships with the adults in their lives. It is important for adults to do the right thing where children are concerned.

The termination process becomes more problematic when children are involved. How to address these issues will be discussed in Chapter 6.

T. Update

On May 9, 2007, Oregon became the first state to enact laws allowing domestic partnership and prohibiting discrimination based on sexual orientation and gender identity.

The non-discrimination law codified the 1998 Oregon Court of Appeals decision in *Tanner v. Oregon Health Sciences University*.[50] The court's decision dealt with extending discrimination bans to include sexual orientation. The case involved partnership benefits for employees of a state medical school.

The Oregon domestic partnership law is virtually identical to the civil union laws of Vermont, Connecticut, and New Jersey. The legislature compromised on the name for political reasons. The new law grants same-sex couples the same rights and responsibilities of heterosexual married couples and provides for inheritance rights, child-rearing and custody, state taxes, and property ownership. The effective date of the new law is in limbo. Opponents are gearing up to place the issue on the ballot in hopes of repealing it.

Colorado's governor, Bill Ritter (D), signed an LGBT antidiscrimination law on May 25, 2007. This law applies only to employment discrimination and adds sexual orientation and religion to the categories of protected classes in employment. The law defines sexual orientation broadly to include bisexuals, transsexuals (actual or perceived), and everyone else based on their sexual orientation. With that language, a gay-owned company could not discriminate against heterosexuals because of their sexual orientation.

The law excludes religious organizations from coverage, with a caveat. Any such organization, "supported in whole or in part by money raised by taxation or public borrowing" is not exempt. The law goes into effect the day after the deadline for submitting a referendum petition. That makes the effective date August 8, 2007, unless the opponents successfully file the petitions.

Iowa also has a new law protecting LGBT persons in that state. On May 25, Governor Chet Culver (D) signed the law barring discrimination based on sexual orientation or gender identity. The law applies to housing, employment, credit, public accommodations, and education. Religious organizations may discriminate based on sexual orientation if required "for a bona fide religious purpose." But the religious exemption does not apply to if the organization owns or operates property for commercial purposes. The legislature also provided that the law does not require recognition of same-sex marriages.

New Hampshire joins other New England states with its Civil Union Act. The law goes into effect January 1, 2008, and grants same-sex couples in civil unions all the right, benefits, obligations, and responsibilities given to heterosexual married couples. The law also requires New Hampshire to recognize same-sex unions formed in other jurisdictions if legal where formed. New Hampshire state employees in civil unions will be entitled to the same spousal benefits as their married counterparts.

On January 1, 2008, 27 states and the District of Columbia will have laws banning sexual orientation discrimination in employment. Most of those states also ban discrimination in housing and public accommodations. Some of them include education and credit. Thirteen of these states protect gender identity (see Appendix).

Oregon, New Hampshire, Vermont, Connecticut, New Jersey, and California grant same-sex couples all marital rights. Maine, Washington, and Hawaii provide fewer rights to same-sex couples. And Massachusetts remains the only state that allows same-sex couples to marry.

U. Conclusion

As with all relationships, there is a great deal of emotion involved. Unlike heterosexual couples, lesbian and gay couples face a daily barrage of negativism that may adversely affect their relationships. Providing a modicum of rational and reasonable advice goes a long way to alleviate the client's stress.

Lawyers who recognize and validate their clients' relationships will find themselves involved in an exciting and evolving field of law. This remains one of the few areas of law where creativity, innovation, and personal investment are hallmarks of the practice.

Notes

1. Defense of Marriage Act, Pub. L. No. 104-199, 110 Stat. 2419 (Sept. 21, 1996); 28 U.S.C. § 1738C.
2. 440 Mass. 309 (2003).
3. GL c. 207, §§ 11 and 12.
4. Cote-Whitacre v. Dep't of Pub. Health, SJC 09436 (March 30, 2006).
5. *Id.*
6. VA. CODE § 20-45.3.
7. Baker v. Vermont, 170 Vt. 194, 744 A.2d 864 (1999).
8. Pawelski et al., *The Effects of Marriage, Civil Union and Domestic Partnership Laws on the Health and Well-Being of Children*, 118:1 PEDIATRICS 349-64 (July 2006) (doi:10.1542/peds.2006-1279).
9. Many European countries do not grant religious personnel any authority to establish civil marriages. Most couples are married in a civil ceremony and follow up with a religious one. Only civil marriages are considered legal and require a license signed by the civil authorities.
10. 28 U.S.C.A. § 1738C.
11. Rep. John Lewis (D-GA), leader of black civil rights movement, in *Boston Globe*, Nov. 25, 2003.

12. Loving v. Virginia, 388 U.S. 1 (1967).
13. Zablocki v. Redhall, 434 U.S. 374 (1978).
14. Hernandez v. Robles, 26 A.D.3d 98, 805 N.Y.S.2d 354, 2005 N.Y. slip. op. 09436 (July 6, 2006).
15. *Id.*, at 6.
16. Anderson v. King County, 158 Wash. 2d 1, 138 P.3d 963 (Wash. July 26, 2006) (No. 75934-1, 75956-1).
17. Bowers v. Hardwick, 478 U.S. 186 (1986), *overruled,* Lawrence v. Texas, 539 U.S. 558 (2003).
18. *Bowers, supra* at 199.
19. 188 N.J. 415, 908 A.2d 196, N.J. Oct. 25, 2006 (No. A-68 Sept. 2005).
20. 1997 GAO Study on Marriage Rights, www.gao.gov/archive/1997/og97016.pdf.
21. GAO Report No. 04-353R, Jan. 2, 2004; www.gao.gov/new.items/d04353r.pdf.
22. P.L.R. 9111018.
23. Consol. Omnibus Budget Reconciliation Act, 29 U.S.C. § 1162, et seq.
24. *Hernandez*, 26 A.D.3d 98.
25. Loving v. Virginia, 388 U.S. 1 (1967).
26. "Equal Rights, Fiscal Responsibility: The Impact of A.B. 205 on California's Budget," M.V. Lee Badgett, Ph.D., Dept. of Economics, Univ. of Mass and R. Bradley Sears, J.D., Williams Project, UCLA School of Law, Univ. of Calif., Los Angeles, May 2003.
27. "Supporting Families, Saving Funds: A Fiscal Analysis of New Jersey's Domestic Partnership Act," Badgett and Sears with Suzanne Goldberg, J.D., Rutgers School of Law, Newark, N.J., Dec. 2003.
28. Alaska Civil Liberties Union v. State, 122 P.3d 781 (Alaska 2005).
29. 122 P.3d 781 (Alaska 2005).
30. 159 P.3d 513 (Alaska, Dec. 19, 2006) (No. 5-12480).
31. 133 N.M. 579, 66 P.3d 948 (2003).
32. 36 Cal. 4th 824 (2005).
33. Civ. Code § 51.
34. 25 A.D.3d 90, 802 N.Y.S.2d 476 2005 slip. op. 07495 (N.Y.A.D. 2 Dept. Oct. 11, 2005) (No. 2003-04702, 11618/02).
35. 539 U.S. 558 (2003).
36. Hawaii Act 383 (1997).
37. 546 U.S. 418, 126 S.Ct. 1211 (2006).
38. 42 U.S.C. § 2000bb, et seq.
39. 42 U.S.C. § 2000bb-1(b).
40. 21 U.S.C. § 801, et seq. (2000 ed. and Supp. 1).
41. City of Boerne v. Flores, 521 U.S. 507 (1997).
42. Gonzales v. O Centro Espirita Beneficente Uniao Do Vegetal, et al., 546 U.S. 418, 126 S.Ct. 1211 (2006); *also see* 42 U.S.C. § 2000bb(a)(2), (5).
43. http://www.ekklesia.co.uk/content/article_abolishmarriage.html
44. *Beyond Same-Sex Marriage: A New Strategic Vision for All Our Families and Relationships,* www.beyondmarriage.org.
45. I.R.C. § 2042(1) and Treas. Reg. § 20.2042-1(b)(1).
46. I.R.C. § 2042(1), (2) and Treas. Reg. § 20.2042-1(b)(1).

47. Arizona, California, Colorado, Florida, Idaho, Kansas, Kentucky, Massachusetts, Minnesota, New Jersey, Ohio, Oklahoma, Oregon, Texas, Vermont, and Wisconsin.
48. Ruisi v. Thieriot, 53 Cal. App. 4th 260 (1997).
49. I.R.C. § 2512(b).
50. 971 P.2d 435 (Or. Ct. App. 1998).

CHAPTER THREE

LGT Families

"Traditional family." It is a term heard frequently in society, but the definition has changed over time. In the past, it meant marrying for money, consolidating power, preserving a dynasty, or ensuring an available labor force. There is no such thing as a "traditional family" today, at least not one that matches the picture painted by those who continue to see it as Mom, Dad, and 2.5 children.

This book discusses issues facing LGT families in America today. It is not intended as the definitive statement on these issues. Due to the rapidly changing nature of the legal landscape, such a work is beyond the scope of any contemporary publication. Rather, this book will be a guide—a road map to what is happening in the realm of legal rights for children and their parents who happen to be lesbian, gay, or transgender.

Former Supreme Court Justice Sandra Day O'Connor said, "[T]he domestic unit in early 21st Century America has become a crazy quilt of one-parent households, blended families, singles, unmarried partnerships and same-sex unions."[1] Justice O'Connor recognized that the "traditional family" is quite different from the 1950s stereotype. Ozzie and Harriet have become Ozzie and Harry, and the Beaver now lives with his grandmother, because June and Ward are nowhere to be found.

> **Webster's[2] definition of "family"**
> 1. A group of individuals living under one roof and usually under one head;
> 2a. A group of persons of common ancestry (clan);
>   b. a people or group of peoples regarded as deriving from a common stock (race);
> 3a. A group of people united by certain convictions or common affiliation (fellowship);

> b. the staff of a high official (as the President);
> 4. A group of things related by common characteristics;
> 5a. The basic unit in society traditionally consisting of two parents rearing their own or adopted children; also any various social units differing from but regarded as equivalent to the traditional family (a single parent);
> b. spouse and children.

That definition comes from a general dictionary. The term is also found in Black's Law Dictionary.[3] The legal definition of family is: "[M]ost commonly refers to a group of persons consisting of parents and children; father, mother and their children; immediate kindred, constituting a fundamental social unit in civilized society."

It seems significant that these definitions refer to parents and children in addition to "father, mother and their children." Under this definition, "family" could be interpreted to include same-sex partners and their children.

There is an ongoing battle in society concerning the legitimacy of lesbian and gay families. There are parents. There are children. Using the above definitions, there is no other requirement to constitute a family.

Justice Sandra Day O'Connor addressed the issue of changing family structure in *Troxel v. Granville*. She wrote, "The demographic changes of the past century make it difficult to speak of an average American family. The composition of families varies greatly from household to household."[4]

Nevertheless, attacks on families that do not meet the "traditional family" ideal are growing. According to the right-wing fundamentalist view, the only "true" families are those with a mother, father, and children. Other entities that do not fall within these parameters are not families.

This conservative definition of family leaves out couples who cannot bear children; people who remarry late in life and are beyond childbearing years; younger couples who choose not to have children; and lesbian and gay couples who make a considered decision to share their love with a child.

Historically, there is a link between marriage and childbearing. That link is weakening due to the availability of contraceptives, abortion, and the rise in the numbers of unmarried parents. Statistics show that one-third of all births are to unmarried mothers.

The days of "Ozzie and Harriet," "Leave It to Beaver," and "Father Knows Best" are gone. The 2000 U.S. census indicated that only 25% of households surveyed reflect the traditional "nuclear family." Four out of 10 children are being raised in homes where their parents are unmarried and cohabiting.

In addition to moms and dads raising children, there are grandparents raising grandchildren, aunts and uncles raising nieces and nephews, and older siblings raising younger ones.

The key is to ensure a loving, safe, and secure home environment for children. The quality of a family relationship should be more important than its form or structure.

A. Issues Facing Lesbian and Gay Families

Federal and state courts are actively determining the rights of lesbian and gay families in these and other areas. Private and public employers are also facing these issues. However, private employers are recognizing that their LGT employees are assets in need of protection rather than liabilities that they need to be protected from.

New York Governor George Pataki signed legislation that gives domestic partners, same- and opposite-sex couples, the right to make decisions about funerals for their partners. In most states, only blood relatives have the right to make these decisions. Biological families often take control of funeral arrangements and interment and exclude the surviving partner. Often, the arrangements made do not reflect the wishes of the decedent. Surviving partners are prevented from attending the funeral or visiting the grave.

Legal Areas Important to Lesbian and Gay Families

1. Parental rights
2. Custody
3. Adoption
4. Child support
5. Visitation
6. Housing discrimination
7. Employment rights
8. School discrimination and harassment
9. Reproductive rights
10. Public benefits
11. Estate planning
12. Public and private pension plans
13. Transgender rights
14. Recognition of relationships
15. Taxes
16. Marriage
17. Advance directives
18. Immigration
19. Conflict of laws
20. Rights to make funeral decisions

Under New York law, people are permitted to designate a person to carry out their wishes for the disposition of their remains. It also gives domestic partners the same priority, under the law, as that enjoyed by surviving spouses. A form called a "death care proxy" authorizes the appointment of an agent and provides for additional instructions. Two people must witness the form. When there is no signed proxy, the law specifies a list of persons with the right to control the disposition of remains. The list includes domestic partners.

Maryland is considering limited rights for same-sex couples. The pending legislation requires people to list advance directives on a state registry. These directives would include how to treat end-of-life decisions. This legislation would apply to both married and unmarried couples. The Maryland Department of Health and Mental Hygiene would manage the registry.

Many legislative and judicial reactions to legal claims raised by the LGT community are based on prejudice and ignorance rather than a carefully considered legal analysis. In *Lawrence v. Texas*,[5] Justice O'Connor wrote, "We have never held that moral disapproval, without any asserted state interest, is a sufficient rationale under the equal protection clause to justify a law that discriminates among groups of persons." These decisions result in substantial harm to an identifiable group of American citizens.

The United States Supreme Court, in *Romer v. Evans*,[6] struck down the Colorado Amendment because it lacked a relationship to any legitimate state interest. According to the Court, Amendment Two ". . . classifies homosexuals not to further a proper legislative end but to make them unequal to everyone else."[7]

The effort by the states and the federal government to undermine lesbian and gay families merely because some people do not like them does not bear any rational relationship to a legitimate state interest.

Sources of U.S. Family Law

1. Common, statutory, and constitutional laws in each state.
2. United States Constitution.
3. The small but growing body of federal law concerning family law issues.
4. Federal and state laws that use marital status, dependency, and family configuration to determine entitlement to benefits.
5. Local laws, regulations, and ordinances, including those restricting cohabitation in residential property to those persons related by affinity or consanguinity or restrict the number of unrelated adults/children who can live in one residence.

B. Family Law

Historically, the individual states have been the sole purveyors of family laws in this country. The U.S. Supreme Court addressed this issue in *Rose v. Rose*[8]: ". . . [t]he whole subject of domestic relations of husband and wife, parent and child, belongs to the laws of the States and not to the laws of the United States."

In an earlier case, *DeSylva v. Ballentine*,[9] the Court took a similar stand: ". . . [t]here is no federal law of domestic relations, which is primarily a matter of state concern."

Marriage has lost the monopoly status it once enjoyed. A growing number of people do not marry. Many people marry multiple times. And some states recognize variations on the marriage theme, including covenant marriages, civil unions, and domestic partnerships.

Marriage is not a viable option for some; namely, senior citizens. Marriage between two seniors can adversely affect a person's continued eligibility to receive a pension or Social Security benefits. This is one reason some states, such as California, permit heterosexual persons over the age of 62 to enter into domestic partnerships. Since those relationships do not equate to marriage, there is no danger of losing needed benefits.

States are "free to experiment" in the development of innovative social regulation to address the changing needs of society within each state.[10]

Equal protection under the law is a hallmark of American jurisprudence. Present that question to the average American and the response will be universal—the law should apply equally to everyone. Over the past 230 years, the United States judicial system has struck down state and federal laws that discriminate on the basis of gender, race, and illegitimacy.[11]

Many right-wing conservatives shout "judicial activism" when a court's decision is not in lockstep with their beliefs. Yet historically, the courts have often been seen as the great levelers. The courts often protect minority interests from the tyranny of the majority. "The majority may not use the power of the State to enforce its views," including popular notions of morality.[12]

So, the question that lawyers and the rest of society must address is whether non-traditional intimate relationships, such as those of same-sex couples, will be granted full constitutional protection for their families.

Family relations have long been considered a fundamental liberty in this country. All aspects of family relationships, including procreation, marriage, and living arrangements, are protected under the federal Constitution. *Griswold v. Connecticut* held that state interference with family relationships require significantly greater judicial scrutiny than non-fundamental rights.[13]

The government must have a rational basis before depriving a person or group of their liberty. The government must also show that it is meeting a legitimate state interest. This is the conundrum in which lesbian and gay persons and same-sex couples find themselves.

When opposing same-sex marriage, government lawyers usually argue that procreation is the primary reason for marriage. Since there has never been a requirement that married couples produce children, this is a specious and disingenuous argument that is losing favor with judges and government lawyers.

Griswold dealt with the right of married couples to use birth control. *Griswold* presented a monumental change in how people viewed their personal rights. This change came through judicial activism, yet few now argue that the Court was wrong.

Five years after *Griswold*, the United States Supreme Court issued its decision in *Eisenstadt v. Baird*.[14] This case dealt with the rights of unmarried couples to use birth control. The Court held:

> If the right of privacy means anything, it is the right of the individual, married or single, to be free from unwarranted governmental intrusion into matters so fundamentally affecting a person as the decision whether to bear or beget a child.

As with the *Griswold* decision, few people are interested in changing the Court's decision that restricts the government's ability to interfere with their right to use contraceptives.

The American family has evolved into different forms, and persons constituting those families are entitled, under our federal Constitution, to privacy. This is an inherent right of substantive due process supported by the United States Supreme Court.[15]

The Court has also weighed in on issues involving changes in family life and recognized social conventions.[16] However, even without social acceptance, privacy concerns are protected when individual interests are significant.[17]

No state has undertaken a comprehensive review of its individual family laws. No state has made an effort to develop a modern code of family law. Until the states adopt such a family code and recognize the changing face of the family, lesbians and gay men will continue to face a patchwork of judicial decisions and state laws.

State laws affecting families presume the existence of a marriage. The laws have not kept up with advances in reproductive technology and adoption.

Second-parent adoptions are comparable to stepparent adoptions, yet the former are not recognized in most states. Many judges considering second-parent adoptions refuse to consider the reasons for permitting stepparent adoptions and apply the same logic to the former.

C. LGT Legal Documents

Lesbian and gay families are trying, through legal documents, to provide legal protection for their families. However, in states that do not recognize same-sex relationships, there is a chance that those documents may be ignored.

The documents lesbian and gay couples typically execute include Domestic Partnership Agreements, Parenting Agreements, Designation of Agent, Durable Power of Attorney for Finances, Advance Directives, and Pre-Pregnancy Donor Agreements.

These documents are comparable, in some ways, to marital contracts. There are three categories of marital contracts:

1. Antenuptial or prenuptial agreements: entered into before marriage and addressing issues of death or divorce;
2. Contracts entered into during marriage; used to set the terms for continuing the marriage or "reconciliation agreements"; and
3. Separation agreements.

LGT couples may use these documents to memorialize their relationships. These are contracts, and traditional contract considerations must be met, that is, intent, consideration, capacity, etc. If the parties intend the contract to last longer than a year, the Statute of Frauds, requiring a written contract, may come into play.

Most states recognize antenuptial or prenuptial agreements. The contractual agreements signed by same-sex partners are comparable to those marriage-related contracts. The major difference is the court in which a party may seek enforcement. In most states, family court will not entertain an action to enforce a same-sex couple's contracts. Enforcement will be limited to the courts of general jurisdiction and the grounds will lie in contract law. As with all contracts, evidence of fraud, coercion, or duress will affect the enforceability of the contract.

Agreements made during a marriage also result in the creation of legal duties. The contracts entered into by same-sex couples also create enforceable legal rights. The major question arises when a co-parenting agreement exists. But parents have the authority to waive their constitutional rights to raise their children. They can enter into contracts that provide for another person to develop a relationship with their child. Such contracts can be enforceable absent fraud, duress, or coercion.

In 2004, Virginia enacted a law that prohibits contracts between same-sex couples. A 2005 Maine commission recommended that same-sex couples be given no legal rights or recognition. Is it possible for any state to restrict or prohibit the contractual rights of its citizens? And have those restrictions been upheld in a court of law? Does the concept of equal protection and due process enter into the equation? These legal questions must still be answered.

D. Families Moving to Another State

American society is mobile. Families move frequently within and between states. Unlike their heterosexual counterparts, lesbian and gay families must consider the legal consequences of any move before they make it. Protections granted a family in one state may not exist in another; in fact, the laws of a new state may be diametrically opposite those of the parties' home state. Therefore, lesbian and gay families must be conscious of what can happen when they come under the jurisdiction of a new state's laws.

It is important for these families to understand that some states are refusing to give full faith and credit to court orders issued by other states. This includes court decrees granting adoptions, custody, and visitation orders and legal recognition of the parents' relationship.

For lesbian and gay families, moving can be more complicated than remembering which boxes contains the sheets and blankets.

Before moving, parents should take the following steps:

- Check with lawyers in the new state to find out what the law is before moving.
- Check Web sites of lesbian and gay organizations and gather information about the new state.[18]
- Be prepared to execute new legal documents (Wills, Trusts, Advance Directives, Durable Power of Attorney for Finances, and authority granted to the non-legal parent).
- Inform school officials and teachers about the family's situation.

E. Conclusion

When addressing family law issues for LGT families, lawyers may need to argue novel theories. Analogize their case to existing law. What was the reason for the law in the first place? Research the legislative history to discover what was on the minds of the legislature when discussing the law. It is time to convince judges and legislatures to expand the view of what it means to be a "family."

Most people know of families that do not meet the usual definition. Most people know of divorced parents, single parents, and orphaned children being raised by grandparents or other relatives and stepparents who have adopted their spouse's children from a prior marriage. Family law makes it personal. People identify with families. They identify with children. No rational person believes it is right to punish a child for the actions of the parent.

But the arguments must be made, and the time may be right to make them.

Notes

1. Siobhan Morrissey, *The New Neighbors: Domestic Relations Law Struggles to Catch Up with Changes in Family Life*, A.B.A. J., March 2002, at 37-38.
2. Merriam-Webster's Collegiate Dictionary, 10th Ed.
3. Black's Law Dictionary, 8th Ed.
4. 530 U.S. 57, 63, 120 S. Ct. 2054, 147 L. Ed. 2d 49 (2000).
5. Lawrence v. Texas, 539 U.S. 558 (2003).
6. 517 U.S. 620 (1996).
7. Lawrence v. Texas, 539 U.S. 558, 636 (2003).
8. 481 U.S. 619 (1987).
9. 351 U.S. 570 (1956).
10. Santosky v. Kramer, 455 U.S. 745 (1982) (Rehnquist, J., dissenting).
11. Orr v. Orr, 440 U.S. 268 (1979); Loving v. Virginia, 388 U.S. 1 (1967); Levy v. Louisiana, 391 U.S. 68 (1968).
12. Lawrence v. Texas, 539 U.S. 558 (2003).
13. Griswold v. Connecticut, 381 U.S. 479 (1965) (birth control).
14. Eisenstadt v. Baird, 405 U.S. 438 (1972).
15. Troxel v. Granville, 530 U.S. 57 (2000); Planned Parenthood of Southeastern Pa. v. Casey, 505 U.S. 833 (1992).
16. Moore v. City of East Cleveland, 431 U.S. 494 (1977); Michael H. v. Gerald D., 491 U.S. 110 (1989).
17. Lawrence v. Texas, 539 U.S. 558 (2003).
18. Human Rights Campaign (www.hrc.org); Lambda Legal Defense and Education Fund (www.lambdalegal.org); National Center for Lesbian Rights (www.nclrights.org).

CHAPTER FOUR

Children

The "gayby boom" started in the late twentieth century. The Human Rights Campaign (HRC), a national lesbian/gay/bisexual/transgender (LGBT) organization, estimates that one of every three lesbian couples and one of every five gay male couples are raising children. HRC estimates there are between one and nine million children in the United States being raised by same-sex couples.

The 2000 census counted almost 600,000 same-sex couples.[1] Of this number, nearly 25% of same-sex couples are raising children—34.3% of lesbian couples and 22.3% of gay male couples. By comparison, 45.6% of married heterosexual couples and 43.1% of unmarried heterosexual couples are raising children.

The census figures show the South with the highest percentage of same-sex couples raising children—36.1% of lesbian parents and 23.9% of gay male parents. Mississippi has the highest percentage of lesbian parents, 43.8%. Alaska has the highest percentage of gay male parents at 36%. Over 40% of same-sex couples who are raising children have been together for five years or more, while only 19.9% of heterosexual unmarried couples reach that same level of commitment.

More than 60% of the children being raised by same-sex parents live in the states that prohibit second-parent adoption. In those states, a significant number of children are living in families that do not enjoy the same benefits as children in "traditional families."

The number of states granting second-parent adoptions is growing.[2] Some states permit second-parent adoptions by statute, others by trial or appellate decisions. At last count, 26 states permitted second-parent adoptions, either statewide or in specific jurisdictions.[3]

Appellate courts in Ohio, Utah, and Wisconsin issued decisions against granting second-parent adoptions.[4]

Children raised in nontraditional families are treated differently than children in traditional ones. In most states, nontraditional families and the children in them are penalized by the state. They have limited or no access to health care, Social Security benefits, and inheritance rights. These children also lack the security of knowing the adults in their lives are recognized legally for their parental role.

Making parenting difficult adversely affects the children involved. Denying same-sex parents legal rights ultimately hurts the child and is not in the child's best interest.

Lesbians and gay men become parents in myriad ways. These include the use of assisted reproductive technology, surrogacy, and adoption. Some same-sex families are composed of children from former heterosexual relationships, and both the lesbian or gay parent and the former spouse continue to be involved with the children.

The issues facing lesbian and gay parents are similar to those faced by any parent. The primary difference, however, involves the laws that govern children. Most of these laws predate the reproductive technology that is available today. Most states have no laws governing parental rights when a surrogate is used. Too often, the rights of the adults trump the best interests of the children involved. The United States continues to view children, for the most part, as the property of their parents and not as individuals with independent legal rights.

Attorneys working with lesbian and gay couples are compelled to discuss the legal documents needed and ensure that clients understand there are no guarantees on the enforceability of those documents. As opposed to relying solely on precedent or established procedure, this is an attorney's best guess about what will work. But an important aspect is the parties' intentions concerning the begetting and raising of the child.

Most family law statutes in the United States do not reflect the changing nature of the American family. The days of mom, dad, and 2.5 kids within a marriage have given way to families headed by single parents, grandparents, aunts, uncles, foster parents, and, in some cases, legal strangers. Rather than looking at ways to serve the interests of these families, state legislatures are concentrating on limiting the rights of gay and lesbian families. This is a myopic view that does not reflect the status quo.

The general rule, when dealing with children, is to make a decision that is in the best interests of the child. However, the child's best interests are not a simple determination. Some courts find that the parent's rights are the primary factor in deciding cases involving their children.

Consider, for example, the U.S. Supreme Court's plurality decision in *Troxel v. Granville*,[5] where the Court decided that the state visitation statute unconstitutionally infringes on a parent's fundamental right to rear his or her children. In *Troxel*, the Court decided that the Washington Superior Court could not order more visitation than the children's mother wanted to give. *Troxel* is often cited in custody and visitation cases involving lesbian and gay parents who have ended their relationship. The biological/adoptive/legal parent uses *Troxel* to prevent or restrict access between the children and their former partners.

Terminating or limiting contact between a child and a de facto or psychological parent with whom the child has a significant relationship can be detrimental to the long-term interests of the child. Yet this is a common result in many courts, even when the evidence shows the child will be harmed by the decision.

A. No Difference Between Straight and Gay Parents

Over the last 30 years, research has been conducted on children raised by lesbian parents. The research fails to show any difference between the health and psychological or emotional development in children raised by lesbian mothers and those of heterosexual mothers.[6]

The research also indicates there is no difference between the gender identity or sexual orientation of children raised by lesbians and gay men and those raised by heterosexual families.[7]

This research can be helpful to lawyers representing lesbian or gay male parents in court. Opponents of these parents often use pseudo-science to support their biases. However, established scientific data is far superior in convincing a court of the client's preference to continue parenting a child. Essentially, a child does better in a loving and stable family relationship without regard to the parents' sexual orientation. There is more security in such a situation than in one where the child fears for her future and that of her parents.

> **Emily**
> My name is Emily and I have three moms. It's normal for me. It is also normal for me to tell kids in my class that I have three moms and no dad. They don't care so I don't feel different. I get to do a lot of different things. They are all different, so I get to do different stuff with them.
>
> I have a lot of love and a lot of people taking care of me. There is nothing bad about having more than one mother.
>
> If someone I know had the same kind of family as me and they were being teased, I would say there is nothing wrong with her family.

> And then I would say, "what if someone was teasing you about your family, how would you feel?" Then I might tell a teacher or an adult.
>
> I tell people I have three moms and that I don't have a dad. Sometimes people ask why I don't have a dad and I tell them I have a donor. I tell them a donor is a man who helps women who don't want to get married to a man have a baby. When they ask why I have so many mothers, I say, "two were with me ever since I was born and one came in when I was four."
>
> I don't feel different. My friends don't really care that I don't have a dad.

B. Let's Start a Family

Lesbian and gay couples must discuss the legal, emotional, and psychological ramifications of their decision to have children. Family-related laws in the United States reflect a long-past time when men were considered the owners of their wives and children. And those states that updated their laws to reflect societal changes in the 20th century encompass a model that is "mommy"-centered. Few states have amended their laws to reflect the changing face of the family. And most states are not keeping up with technological advances in childbearing, let alone with changes in the family structure.

Any parenting document drafted must include a recitation of each parent's duties, responsibilities, and obligations toward the child. The non-legal parent is well served if the biological or adoptive parent clearly establishes his intent to have his partner considered the child's parent for all legal matters. This reflection of his intention to jointly parent may enable the non-legal parent to succeed if his parental status is challenged should the couple terminate their relationship. If the legal parent objected later, citing his constitutional right to raise his child, an argument can be made that he also has the authority to voluntarily waive that right.

There is an inherent conflict between the parties to this agreement, and the legal parent must be advised of the possible effect of the intention clause. Therefore, it is advisable for both parties to seek an attorney's advice. This will avoid accusations of undue influence or malpractice on the part of either party later on. The couple must realize the significance of their actions: they are deciding to bring a child into their world.

There are federal and state statutes that govern custody and visitation: the Parental Kidnapping Prevention Act (PKPA)[8] and the Uniform Child Custody

Jurisdiction Enforcement Act (UCCJEA). The National Conference of Commissioners on Uniform State Laws drafted the UCCJEA to correct discrepancies between the old UCCJEA and PKPA. The two are now compatible in relation to the child custody orders and their enforcement. As of June 1, 2006, 43 states adopted the UCCJEA.[9]

1. *Artificial Reproductive Technology*

Technology today is becoming more commonplace and sophisticated with respect to reproductive technology. Artificial Reproductive Technology (ART) includes:

- artificial insemination
- donation of ovum
- donation of embryos
- *in vitro* fertilization (including intracytoplasmic sperm injection)
- embryo transfer

Occasionally the use of ART methods can result in fragmented parentage. For example, a child born following ART may have five different "parents": sperm donor, egg donor, surrogate/gestational host, and two non-biologically-related individuals who will raise the child. The contracts entered into before the ART process begins are vitally important to avoid problems after the birth.

The fragmented parentage of the child may cause legal issues that challenge the intended parents' rights. The surrogate, gestational host, egg donor, embryo donor, and sperm donor may all claim parental rights. The parties' contract may resolve some or all of these issues. Not all states have statutes addressing the issues that arise, however.

> **Melissa Brisman**
> For same-sex couples, artificial reproductive technology is most often the only option available to them to start their families. The most common questions I hear from my same-sex clients are, "Who will be named on the birth certificate?" and "Will I have to adopt my own child?"
>
> The advances in reproductive technology have far surpassed the current legislation in most states that can leave same-sex parents in a precarious and unpredictable situation when they are going through the process of trying to create their "legal" family. The legal issues surrounding these arrangements vary greatly and differ in male versus female relationships.

> In most cases, the non-biological parent will have to adopt the child, and some states, recognizing this need of same-sex couples, have streamlined the process. Same-sex male couples face a further challenge of the possibility of having to terminate maternal rights, even when the child is not biologically related to the birth mother.
>
> It is a good idea for same-sex couples, upon learning of a pregnancy, to have some form of agreement in place stating the intention of both the biological and non-biological parent so it is clear from the beginning that both partners plan to be the legal parents of their child and agree to accept the rights and obligations that flow therefrom.
>
> Attorneys specializing in reproductive law are working every day to shape the ever-changing landscape of this area of the law. Reproductive attorneys must make a continuing effort to stay on top of new case law and legislation that can affect the legal rights of their clients in order to offer them the best possible representation.
>
> ---
>
> Melissa B. Brisman is licensed to practice law in New York, New Jersey, Massachusetts, and Pennsylvania. Her address is: 77 Market Street, 2nd Floor, Park Ridge, New Jersey 07656, (201) 505-0078, or info@reproductivelawyer.com. Her Web site is www.reproductivelawyer.com.

2. Surrogacy

Using a surrogate or gestational host is an artificial reproductive method commonly used by gay men. This process involves the intended parents (gay couple), the surrogate, her spouse (if married), the egg donor, and, possibly, a sperm donor.

A case pending in Pennsylvania illustrates the potential problems.[10] James Flynn and his fiancée, Eileen Donich, signed a surrogacy contract with Danielle Bimber. The egg donor, Jennifer Rice, of Texas, also signed a contract with the couple to furnish eggs for implantation in a surrogate.

The children, triplets, were born in November 2003. They were born prematurely and remained in the neonatal intensive care unit for some time after their birth. Bimber discouraged the intended parents, Flynn and Donich, from calling or attending the pre-birth doctor appointments. She also failed to tell them she had decided to have a C-section or the date of the procedure. Flynn and Donich learned of the birth from hospital personnel.

After the birth, Bimber decided the intended parents were unfit. The hospital administration released the children into Bimber's custody without telling Flynn. Bimber placed her husband's name on the children's birth certificates. This is when the legal fireworks began.[11]

A trial court in Pennsylvania awarded physical, full-time custody to Bimber and her husband; Flynn was awarded visitation; the surrogacy contract was declared void; the egg donor's parental rights were terminated; and Bimber was declared the children's "legal mother" and Flynn the "legal father." That was only the beginning of the litigation that spanned Pennsylvania and Ohio.

A fair share of litigation took place in Ohio because Flynn and Donich lived there. Flynn sought to have his rights determined in Ohio. The Ohio Ninth District Court of Appeals ruled in Flynn's favor.[12] The court held that full faith and credit did not control the Pennsylvania trial court decision. The court decided this because Pennsylvania did not include Rice, the egg donor, in the action.

The Ohio court found that the Pennsylvania court's determination of legal parentage rested on the terms of the contract it had voided. The Ohio court noted, ". . . deeming a contract void but then relying on that contract in the ensuing analysis is legally questionable." The Ohio court found it odd that Bimber was named the children's mother despite having no genetic relationship to them.

Now, back to Pennsylvania. On appeal, a Pennsylvania Superior Court panel overturned the trial court's decision.[13] The court reversed the trial court's decision to void the surrogate contract because the contract's validity was not at issue. Therefore, the court had no authority to void the contract *sua sponte*. Further, the egg donor, Jennifer Rice, was an indispensable party to the action and the court did not include her—even though it terminated her parental rights.

Lastly, the Pennsylvania Superior Court held that Bimber had no standing to bring any action in the matter because, ". . . there is no law in this Commonwealth that accords standing to a surrogate with no biological connection to the child she seeks to take into her custody."

The genetic parents of the children are Rice and Flynn. At no time did either of them authorize Bimber to take the children. Bimber plans to appeal.

This is an important case on several levels. First, it shows what can happen despite the best-laid plans. The parties executed a surrogacy contract. Flynn and Donich executed a contract with the egg donor. Both Rice and Bimber agreed to relinquish any rights they might have to any children born. Bimber agreed that she would not establish a parent-child relationship.

Bimber received $20,000 from Flynn under the contract. She also received an additional $4,000 from Flynn when her doctor ordered four months of bed rest. She refused to return any of that money to Flynn and sought child support. So, she breached the contract agreement and filed litigation in Pennsylvania. The contract was to be enforced under Ohio's laws.

Second, this case is also important because the court rulings set forth the requirements for establishing parentage in these types of cases. Ohio's Ninth District Court of Appeals stated, "State courts and legal scholars have developed four different approaches for determining maternity in gestational surrogacy arrangements: (1) intent-based theory (California, Nevada, New York); (2) genetic contribution theory (Ohio); (3) gestational mother preference theory (North Dakota, Arizona); and (4) the "best interest of the child" theory (Michigan, Utah)."[14]

Surrogacy is an unsettled area of law. California, however, is one state with a progressive view of surrogacy cases, including those involving lesbian and gay couples. One particular case worth noting is *K.M. v. E.G.*[15] K.M. and E.G. terminated their long-term lesbian relationship in 2003. During their relationship, K.M., at E.G.'s insistence, donated eggs for an IVF procedure. They also used an anonymous sperm donor. E.G. served as a gestational host and gave birth to twins. The twins were five years old when their mothers separated.

At the time of the donation, K.M. signed the standard egg donor document relinquishing all parental rights to any children born. However, the couple agreed to have children together. During the course of litigation, E.G. insisted that K.M. had no legal right to be considered the children's mother. The California Supreme Court disagreed in its August 22, 2005 decision. The court held that the standard language in the egg donor contract did not apply to K.M. She was, in fact, a co-parent with E.G. of the two children. This landmark decision came down the same day as two other cases involving lesbian parents, *Kristine H. and Elisa B.*[16]

In *Kristine H.*, the California couple had a child through artificial reproduction technology. California allows intended parents to seek a determination of maternity before the child is born. Kristine and Lisa obtained such an order declaring them both to be the child's mother. But when the couple separated a few years later, Kristine challenged Lisa's rights and prevented her from seeing their child. The California Supreme Court ruled that Kristine was barred from challenging the court order she sought before the child's birth.

Elisa B. presents a somewhat different situation. Elisa and her partner, Emily, had twins. One of the children was diagnosed with Down's syndrome and requires constant care. The couple separated, and Elisa stopped visiting the children and supporting them financially. The California Supreme Court held that Elisa is a parent of the twins and is required to pay child support. This decision is especially important because the court ruled that same-sex couples that use artificial reproductive technology to have children are both legal parents. The court stated the parties' gender, sexual orientation, or marital status does not matter with respect to the determination of legal parentage.

These cases have helped to establish equity in parenting and family law cases involving same-sex couples and their children.

3. Surrogacy Considerations

Gay male clients who are thinking about using a surrogate or gestational host must be aware of all the pitfalls. Thus, a surrogacy contract is extremely important. Gay men may want to consider contracting with an egg donor rather than using the surrogate's eggs. With this approach, the gestational host has no genetic connection to the child. The child or children would be genetically connected to the intended parents and the egg donor. The couple might also want to consider both men contributing semen for the IVF process. This further establishes the couple's joint intention to become parents.

Existing case law to date in this area involves lesbian couples engaged in situations where the adoptive or biological mother attempts to use existing family law to prevent her former partner from having further contact with the children. Case law dealing with gay male couples and their children is virtually nonexistent.

As is too often true in heterosexual divorces, the children's interests are ignored. The differences in these situations between gay male parents and lesbian parents could make an interesting study.

Given the current political climate, gay male couples will want to take all precautions to prevent the gestational host from changing her mind once the child is born. In terms of avoiding potential problems, a stranger may prove to be a better surrogate than a known host. But there is no absolute way to carry out this process, as most states do not address surrogacy contracts or the children born as a result.

This creates a more manageable situation for the intended parents. Insurance issues can be addressed before the child's birth and the judgment can establish the legal rights of the intended parents to the custody, care, and control of the child from birth.

Most other states are not as progressive as California.[17] A recent Ohio decision is a case in point. *Nemcek v. Paskey*[18] involves two married couples who are friends. Ms. Paskey agreed to serve as the gestational host for the Nemceks' child because Ms. Nemcek could not conceive and carry a child. Ms. Paskey was implanted with an egg harvested from Ms. Nemcek. Mr. Nemcek's sperm was used to fertilize the egg.

The parties filed a complaint for judgment declaring the donors to be the parents of the unborn child. They also sought an order that the child's birth certificate reflect their status as parents. Paskey waived service and consented to judgment.

The Ohio Probate Court dismissed the complaint because the court lacked subject-matter jurisdiction. The judge decided that Probate Court has no jurisdiction to determine parentage of an unborn child. He suggested the legislature take up the issue.

The surrogacy contract is extremely important to the entire process. Unfortunately, not all states will recognize or enforce the contract. A court, without statutory guidance, may be reluctant to use strict contract law to construe the document's provisions. Some courts may object to these contracts as violating the state's public policy.

Such arguments can be rebutted. Public policy is set by the legislature, not by the courts. Courts have equitable jurisdiction and the authority to determine a child's best interests. When the parties to the contract agree, equity should control the outcome. That does not always happen, but the argument is available.

C. Contracts

Some states restrict surrogacy contracts or find them illegal. Gay and lesbian couples seeking to use this process must be aware of the applicable law. Clients and their lawyers must also consider the jurisdictional law with respect to the state where the surrogate lives, the state where the children will be born, and the state where the family will live. As with the *Flynn* case, different state laws may apply—even if the contract designates the controlling state law. The essential parties to these contracts include the intended parents, the surrogate (and her spouse), and the egg donor, if one is used.

Some egg donors, like sperm donors, are anonymous, because there is no direct interaction between the intended parents and the donors. This type of situation can simplify matters by reducing the number of known persons involved. A separate contract between the intended parents and an egg donor is advisable if the donor is known. This contract must include a waiver of all parental rights on the part of the donor.

In a surrogacy situation, the contract must specify the intended parents' legal rights and terminate all parental rights of the surrogate. The lawyer drafting the contract will want to specify who will be the legal parents. The *Flynn* case demonstrated what happens when this is left out. In that case, the contract did not specify the legal mother.

In all surrogate situations, independent counsel must represent each party to the contract. This avoids a claim from the surrogate or her husband that the intended parents pressured them into signing or that they did not understand the contract. Independent counsel must also represent any donors. The parties must also address who pays the legal fees.

Surrogacy Contract Clauses

(Note: This list is not exhaustive. Include any additional provisions required in individual situations.)

- Financial issues: compensation to surrogate, attorney fees, use of trust account
- Medical and psychological screening within designated parameters
- Health and life insurance: who pays, and contingencies if the insurance lapses
- Delineation of parental rights, obligations, and responsibilities toward any children
- Termination of the surrogate's parental rights and those of her husband
- Provision addressing multiple births, including whether selective reduction will apply
- Reference to the egg or sperm donor contract if one exists
- The parties' intentions regarding parental rights[19]
- Complete financial responsibility of the intended parents for the child(ren)Intended parents' financial responsibility if the child is born/becomes disabled
- Legal and medical consent forms, include HIPAA language
- Who must be tested for sexually transmitted diseases (including HIV and AIDS)
- Confirmation that the surrogate is physically able to conceive and carry the child to term
- Surrogate's agreement to refrain from sexual relations during specified periods
- Attachment of all applicable laws from all states involved
- Description of specific responsibilities of all parties, during and after the pregnancy
- Surrogate agreement to not establish a parent-child relationship and not interfere with the parental rights of the intended parents
- Provision for individual and group therapy for the surrogate

> **Egg/Sperm Donor Contract Clauses**
> - Explicit relinquishment of all parental rights by donor
> - Voluntary and informed legal and medical consent
> - Financial responsibility of the intended parents for all expenses
> - Compensation, if any, due the donor
> - Description of full legal custody and parental rights of intended parents
> - Who must be tested for sexually transmitted diseases, including HIV and AIDS
> - Medical examination of donor to determine suitability
> - Financial responsibility for the use, storage, and disposal of excess embryos
> - Description of responsibilities and privacy or confidentiality concerns of all partiesSpecification of laws that will govern the contract and its terms
> - Provision reflecting the intentions of the parties
> - Donor agreement to assist the intended parents in obtaining any court orders needed to establish their parental rights and responsibilities
> - Donor agreement not to file any legal action to gain custody or parental rights with the child
> - Donor agreement not to attempt to establish a parent-child relationship (may not apply where a gay male couple and lesbian couple agree to co-parent children)

1. Egg/Sperm Donor Contracts

A contract between the intended parents and the egg/sperm donor is also needed if a known donor is used. No similar contract is required with anonymous donors.

Egg donation consists of the removal of the donor's eggs, fertilization by the intended father's sperm, and transfer to the intended recipient mother or to a surrogate. Sperm donation is similar: it involves the use of a donor's sperm to fertilize the egg of either the intended mother or an egg donor. It is possible for a couple to use donors for both sperm and egg as well as a gestational host.

A parenting arrangement between a lesbian and gay couple is more common than one may think and is a situation requiring considerable thought and planning on the part of all parties involved.

2. Egg Donation from One Lesbian Partner to the Other

There is another situation that lawyers may see with lesbian couples. One partner donates her eggs for implantation into her partner's womb. That causes both women to have a biological connection to the child, one as the genetic mother and the other as the gestational mother. Under some state laws, the child will be biologically related to both mothers.

Jamie[20] and her former partner, Becky, decided to start a family in the mid-1990s while they were together. Jamie donated the eggs and Becky bore the child, Kelly, after being artificially inseminated. The father is known; he is the former partner's brother. Kelly is genetically related to both women. The father, under a donor agreement, waived all parental rights to the child.

Kelly is now 10 and enjoys a healthy and loving relationship with both parents and Jamie's partner, Sam. The parents do not identify the birth mother to outsiders, as they believe it invalidates the other parent. Neither party is worrying about her respective legal rights because they are committed to raising Kelly as a family, albeit a nontraditional one. This is a relationship where the adults agree that their child's interests are their primary responsibility.

In any event, including the parties' intentions in this situation will help everyone understand each person's rights and responsibilities. These contracts are not "boilerplate"; they must be drafted with the interests, responsibilities, rights, and remedies that are unique to each situation.

D. Best Friends

A gay male couple, Glenn and Bill, after seven years together, decided to start a family. They did not, however, want to go through a lot of legal rigmarole. They knew their best friends, Ellen and Virginia, were also considering starting a family. Ellen and Virginia found the idea of an anonymous sperm donor very impersonal. Glenn and Bill did not like the idea of an anonymous egg donor and a gestational host, as that was too "sci-fi-ish" for them. So, over a period of several months, the two couples[21] discussed whether they could start a family between them. Neither couple consulted a lawyer during the process. They spent many hours discussing the technical aspects of the situation. Finally, after much soul-searching, both couples decided to cooperate and make a baby.

Ellen and Virginia decided that Virginia should carry the child, with an egg donated by Ellen. Bill and Glenn planned to provide a mix of semen from both to fertilize the egg. Both couples were present when Ellen introduced the sperm to Virginia's uterus.

Nine months later a beautiful baby boy, Nathaniel Richard, was born. Due to the existing law in their home state, only Virginia's name could be listed as the mother; no father's name was added.

At first, all was well between the parents. Shortly before Nathan was six months old, Ellen and Virginia decided they no longer wanted Bill and Glenn involved with "their" child. Then the lawyers became involved.

Ellen and Virginia argued that Glenn and Bill were just sperm donors. They never intended that the men should be involved in raising their child. As there was no contract or any type of documentation, the case came down to a situation of "she/he/they said."

Nathan is now three years old. DNA testing established Glenn as Nathan's father, and he is entitled to parenting time with his son. Ellen's legal relationship to the child is murky; her egg did result in the child, but existing laws do not address this situation. Is she just an egg donor, or does the existence of her DNA make her a biological mother? Is Virginia merely the "gestational mother," or does she also have legal rights to the child? Only Bill is a legal stranger to the boy, with no legal right to custody or visitation.

The parents continue to litigate the situation, with funds that could be used to start a college fund for Nathan.

Moral of the story: Put your intentions in writing. A decision such as this is far too important to rely on friendship and good intentions. A contract is evidence of the parties' intent. Conforming to basic contractual requirements puts everyone on notice that the matter is serious and warrants their attention. A contract will set forth each party's rights, responsibilities, and obligations. The document can also protect the child's interests if the adults become irrational.

If a question arises about the potential enforceability of such a contract, most courts will consider the child's best interests. And the model existing in most states does not envision a situation like the one above. But the parties, through the contract, will evince their intentions; they will agree to be bound by the terms of the contract, and the court may be persuaded to allow the parties to enforce that contract and its terms.

A written agreement is powerful evidence, and the parties to it may decide it is best to abide by it than risk bankruptcy in the courts. Including a mediation clause in the contract may help. But where children are concerned, the court's primary authority over their well-being may usurp any rights guaranteed by the contract.

One thing is sure: Without a contract, the non-legal parents may be hard-pressed to gain any recognition.

E. Parental Rights

A legal parent is the one granted the right to live with and control the child, bear legal responsibility for the child's financial support, and exercise legal authority over the child. Anyone attempting to interfere with a parent's legal prerogatives concerning their children will find it a difficult task.

Under the Uniform Parentage Act (UPA), a sperm donor, with the intent to be a parent, is a parent without regard to the parents' marital status.[22] Generally, an anonymous sperm donor has no intent to be a parent, so the definition would not apply.

The UPA is designed to provide full equality for all children in their legal relationship with their parents. The UPA's primary concern is the right of the child in situations involving child-parent relationships. As of 2003, 20 states had adopted the UPA. Other states adapted the Act and inserted it into their state law.

In 1996, the United States Supreme Court ruled, in *M.L.B. v. S.L.J.*,[23] that ". . . the interest of parents in their relationship with their children is sufficiently fundamental to come within the finite class of liberty interests protected by the 14th Amendment."

This type of language raises the bar in family law cases involving same-sex couples. Absent second-parent adoptions or other legal recognition, former partners may find themselves expending significant sums of money to fight over who gets the kids.

In *Troxel v. Granville*,[24] the U.S. Supreme Court admitted there is a balancing act even in cases involving a fit parent. The balance involves consideration of the child's best interests. A parent's interest in the child must be given "special weight" when deciding whether limitations will be placed on that interest and its accompanying rights.

Lately, the Supreme Court has seemed reluctant to take cases that involve gay parental rights. On May 15, 2006, the Court denied certiorari in *Britain v. Carver*.[25]

The *Britain* case originated in Washington state and involves Sue Ellen Carver's efforts to be legally recognized as one of the child's parents. The Washington Supreme Court agreed that Carver has standing to pursue the case and remanded the matter back to the trial court.[26]

These cases illuminate the problems inherent in lesbian and gay families when only one partner is recognized as the child's legal parent. Should the couple terminate their relationship, the non-legal parent, in many states, has no legal recourse to maintain the parent-child relationship. This, by all indications, is detrimental to the health and well-being of the child. Many times, it seems the courts do not recognize that aspect of the case.

Throughout their practice, lawyers will see lesbian and gay couples both with and without documentation reflecting their parental responsibilities and obligations. Oddly, in some states it does not matter whether the couple entered into an agreement. Some courts enforce the agreements, while others do not.

Amy and her partner were together almost eight years. During their relationship, they agreed to start a family. Amy's former partner is their son's biological parent. The women executed wills and advance directives to provide for their son. They did not enter into a parenting agreement, although they discussed it. Three years ago, Amy and her partner separated. Initially, the birth mother told Amy she would never see the boy again because he was not Amy's son. The child was five years old at the time. Amy now has regular visitation with the child. Her former partner is in another relationship, and they just had a child. Amy supports her son financially and pays the tuition for a private school, summer camp, extracurricular activities, and clothing. Amy's son once told her that he never got to say goodbye when Amy left; his mother would not let him say goodbye.

1. Illegitimacy

The U.S. Supreme Court has issued more than 30 rulings on the issue of illegitimacy. Most significant is *Stanley v. Illinois*,[27] in which the Court ruled that unwed fathers have custody rights. The Court's rulings on this issue are based on the Equal Protection and the Due Process Clauses of the United States Constitution. Illegitimacy is treated as a "quasi-suspect class" under the Equal Protection Clause. Any discrimination because of a person's illegitimacy is presumptively unconstitutional. While not all discrimination against illegitimacy has been removed, the Court has ruled that dissimilar treatment is allowed only when it is substantively related to a public interest.

The Court's ruling in *Lehr v. Robertson*[28] might give same-sex couples some comfort. The Court said, "... the mere existence of a biological link..." between a parent and a child does not, on its own, give rise to any constitutional protection.[29] This case can give hope to the parent without a legally recognized relationship to the child. The concepts of "psychological parent" and "de facto parent" can be founded on the Court's ruling in *Lehr*.

2. Adopted Children

When lesbian and gay couples who are raising children terminate their relationship, many issues are raised directly involving their children in the ensuing turmoil. The issues do not fit neatly into existing laws dealing with families, and that requires creative arguments from counsel. Courts throughout the country are beginning to address these scenarios, and not always in a pro-LGBT family light.

In 2006, the Kentucky Supreme Court issued a decision against the non-biological parent of a six-year-old child.[30] The parties in that case were involved in an eight-year relationship. During the relationship, Brenda Fawbush and Teresa Davis decided to adopt a child. They decided that Davis would be the adoptive parent because they believed Kentucky law did not permit second-parent adoptions. The parties separated in 2003 and Davis moved out with the couple's child. Following the separation, Davis denied Fawbush visitation and custody rights.

Fawbush filed a lawsuit in Jefferson Family Court seeking a determination of her rights. She argued that she was the child's "de facto custodian." The trial court dismissed the action, finding that Fawbush did not meet the statutory definition of "de facto custodian." Evidence presented at the trial showed that Davis was the primary caregiver of the child, including washing, feeding, clothing, and teaching the child.

The Kentucky statute, Ky. Rev. Stat. 403.270, defines "de facto custodian" as:

> [a] person who has been shown by clear and convincing evidence to have been the primary caregiver for, and financial supporter for, a child who has resided with the person for a period of . . . one (1) year or more if the child is three (3) years of age.

The Kentucky Supreme Court agreed with the trial court, finding that Fawbush did not qualify as the child's "de facto custodian" because she was not the primary caregiver despite the fact that she participated ". . . substantially in the support and rearing of the child for a significant period of time."

Same-sex couples adopting a child in states that do not expressly recognize or permit second-parent adoptions run the risk of protracted litigation when their relationship ends. In many cases, the biological or adoptive parent seeks to deny the former partner any contact with the child or children. The biological parent's opposition to continued contact is often used by courts to deny the former partner any parental status.

F. Benefits of Families

Stability is extremely important to children. It promotes the child's well-being and is, as supported by all the evidence, in the child's best interests. Yet many children being raised by same-sex parents are denied the protection of state and federal laws.

While the family is often looked upon as the foundation of society, children of lesbians and gay men are prohibited, in most states, from enjoying that status. The lack of legal protection results in these children experiencing legal, economic, and familial insecurity. They are subject to heterosexist laws that condemn their parents and, by extension, the children.

Existing laws deny lesbians and gay men custody and visitation rights enjoyed by their married and unmarried heterosexual counterparts. Most states treat the children of lesbian and gay parents differently even though they are similarly situated to children of heterosexual parents. Their constitutional rights to equal protection are regularly and systematically denied by a legal system that cannot see past their parents' sexual orientation and their own biases and prejudices.

The paramount consideration must be the health, safety, and well-being of the children. It makes no sense to deny these benefits to a child merely because some people do not like the nature of the parents' relationship. That is not in the child's best interests.

The American Academy of Pediatrics notes that "[c]hildren's optimal development seems to be influenced more by the nature of the relationships and interactions within the family unit than by the particular structure it takes."[31]

With a divorce rate of 40% to 50%,[32] millions of children are subjected to the whims of their parents. Yet there is evidence that even children whose parents are divorced are best off when their parents are living with a partner and maintain a positive and friendly relationship with the other parent.[33] This is important for lawyers representing the biological or adoptive parent in custody and visitation disputes with a former partner.

The same does not take place when children enjoy a positive and loving family unit. A negative relationship between the legal parent and her former partner, who also has a parent-child relationship, can wreak havoc on a child's self-esteem and psychological well-being. Anyone practicing family law sees the effect on the children of a combative relationship between the parents during a divorce. All efforts must be made to reduce the destructive pattern so many parents engage in when a relationship ends.

Children deprived of a legally recognized family unit are harmed far more than is first apparent. A child can be denied the protection of a second parent should that parent die or become incapacitated. Legal recognition of both parents also protects the child's legal right to enjoy an unencumbered relationship with them. Should the legal parent die or become incapacitated, that parent's biological family could come and remove the child, thereby depriving that child of the only other parent she has. Without that protection, the child might be at risk of losing both parents if one is lost.

Legal recognition also guarantees a continued parent-child relationship with both parents should the couple separate. Both parents would have the right to petition for custody and visitation. The child may be legally entitled to financial support from both parents. Without legal recognition, the child may lose healthcare benefits if the legally unrecognized parent provides them.

Lawyers can only do so much. Legal documents can be prepared that include a co-parenting agreement, domestic partnership agreement, last will and testament, a trust, guardianship, and authorization to provide medical care for the minor child. However, there is no guarantee those documents will be enforceable in court.

For example, in January 2006, the First District Court of Appeals in Florida ruled that a co-parenting agreement was unenforceable.[34] The parties, a lesbian couple, signed the agreement after the birth of their two children. The couple later separated after 15 years together. The plaintiff filed suit to enforce the agreement, but the trial court sided with the birth mother.

The court held, "The Florida Supreme Court has held that, under the privacy provision of the Florida Constitution, a third party, even a grandparent, cannot be granted by statute the right to visitation with minor children, because, absent evidence of a demonstrable harm to the child, such a grant unconstitutionally interferes with a natural parent's privacy right to rear his or her child."[35]

The court based its decision on chapter 61, Florida Statutes, claiming the law does not allow non-parents to seek custody or visitation. "By its explicit provisions, section 61.13, Florida Statutes (2004), concerns only the parents' custody, support and visitation."[36]

The appellate court also held that ". . . Florida courts have held that agreements granting visitation rights to a non-parent are unenforceable."[37] According to the Florida court, an individual does not have the right to enter into an enforceable contract with another person establishing parental rights, responsibilities, and obligations. However, the court did include language from a previous decision that seems to reflect a certain hesitancy by the court.

> There is an inherent problem with utilizing a best interest analysis as the basis for government interference in the private lives of a family, rather than showing demonstrable harm to the child. It permits the state to substitute its own views regarding how a child should be raised for those of the parent. It involves the judiciary in second-guessing parental decisions. It allows a court to impose its own notion of the children's

best interests over the shared opinion of these parents, stripping them of their right to control in parenting decision.[38]

This case reflects a concern that lawyers must discuss with their clients. Even though both parties agree to co-parent, without legal recognition of their status, a court may refuse to honor their agreement. This is particularly true when the legal parent objects to enforcing an agreement. This type of discussion will place the non-legal parent in the unenviable position of signing an agreement with the knowledge that her loving partner may one day seek to have it declared a nullity.

A 2006 decision by the Oklahoma Court of Civil Appeals[39] illustrates how courts in different states, with similar fact patterns, can arrive at diametrically opposed conclusions. Renee Hays and Sharon Taffs were partners for over 15 years. They took a newborn into their home and agreed that Sharon would adopt the child because of her better employment.

Sharon adopted the child and encouraged, fostered, and nurtured a parent-child relationship between Renee and their child.

When Renee and Sharon ended their relationship, they entered into a visitation and property settlement agreement. The agreement stated that Hays would have visitation and pay child support. In August 2004, Taffs terminated visitation. The trial court dismissed Hays's complaint, finding that the agreement ". . . is unenforceable as against public policy." The appellate court held that the agreement did not violate any public policy ". . . known to this court." The court decided that the contract is a ". . . mutual obligation . . . [and] provides sufficient and valid consideration to support the agreement."

The legal mother in this case argued that her parental rights were paramount and that only she could determine what was best for her child. The appellate court, however, held to the contrary. ". . . [w]e know of no reason why this constitutionally protected right cannot be voluntarily waived or curbed, like any other constitutional rights, or be made subject to a contractual agreement." The court continued with, ". . . there is nothing in Oklahoma law to prevent the making of a contract for the benefit of the child, and we believe the agreement . . . is a contract that benefits the child." This court also found that the child, as a beneficiary to the agreement, has an interest in its performance, enforcement, modification and termination.

Sharon moved to Boston, Massachusetts, and is living with her new partner and the child. The appellate court remanded the case to the trial court. Following that hearing, Renee and the court-appointed guardian ad litem traveled to Boston to visit the child. On arriving, Renee discovered the child was terrified of her. Two years of hearing nothing but negative comments from Sharon had taken its toll. The child did not want to see or visit with Renee. Renee decided to end her quest for visitation, even with court approval, because she did not want to subject her child to more stress.

In July 2006 the American Academy of Pediatricians (AAP) released a paper, *The Effects of Marriage, Civil Union and Domestic Partnership Laws on the Health and Well-Being of Children.*[40] This study addresses the effects of statutes and laws on children with gay or lesbian parents. The study reflects the AAP's core philosophy, ". . . that the family is the principal caregiver and the center of strength and support for children."

The study talks about civil marriage providing ". . . a context for legal, financial and psychological well-being, an endorsement of interdependent care and a form of public acknowledgment and respect for personal bonds."[41]

Unlike heterosexual couples that are allowed to marry, lesbian and gay parents must execute a plethora of documents and hope they are sufficient. The documents these parents may execute carry no guarantee they will be enforceable. This is particularly true if the challenge comes from a couple's extended birth family. Still, it is important for the couple to carry their documents with them when traveling.

In 2004, the Congressional Budget Office (CBO) issued a report addressing the potential effect of same-sex marriages on the federal budget.[42] According to the CBO, federal tax revenues would increase $400 million annually to 2010. Medicaid and Supplemental Security Income expenditures would decrease. The CBO estimates the net savings to be almost $1 billion dollars annually.

The AAP study cited similar results from the Williams Institute at the University of Los Angeles School of Law.[43]

Numerous organizations have arrived at the same conclusions established by the AAP's analysis.[44] These organizations also support civil marriages for lesbian and gay parents as the best way to protect children absent a nationwide acceptance of same-sex marriage.

G. Canada Started 2007 Right: Three Legal Parents

On January 2, 2007, Canada's highest court, the Court of Appeal for Ontario, decided that a five-year-old boy could have three legal parents.[45] Due to privacy concerns, the court used initials rather than the parties' names. D.D. is the little boy who lives with his two moms, A.A. and C.C. His biological father, B.B., is also an integral part of his life. D.D.'s mothers are his primary caretakers.

In 2003, Superior Court Judge David Aston dismissed A.A.'s application to be declared the boy's legal parent because he believed he had no jurisdiction to issue a ruling. Judge Aston told *The Canadian Press* he would have ruled in

A.A.'s favor had he thought he had jurisdiction.[46] The Court of Appeal ruled in favor of A.A.'s application to be deemed D.D.'s legal parent.

A.A. did not seek to adopt D.D. because that would terminate the parental rights of the child's father, B.B. Instead, the parental trio sought a legal determination of their joint status. Canada's Children's Reform Act did not support their efforts. As the Appeals Court found, the "[L]egislature did not foresee for the possibility of declarations of parentage for two women, but that is a product of the social conditions and medical knowledge at the time. The Legislature did not turn its mind to that possibility, so that over 30 years later the gap in the legislation has been revealed."[47]

The court also decided that depriving the child, D.D., of the legal recognition of one of his parents is contrary to his best interests. According to the court, the Children's Reform Act, while progressive when first enacted, did not contemplate the situation of a child born into a relationship of two mothers, two fathers, or two mothers and a father. Nor did the Act reflect on the disadvantages that a child might suffer in these situations. The court found a gap in the law and decided to close it, using the child's best interests as its guiding rule. In so doing, the court recognized that this one child is lucky enough to be loved by three loving parents.

In the *A.A.* decision, the court referred to an affidavit written by a 12-year old and filed in another, similar case."I just want both of my moms recognized as my moms. Most of my friends havenot had to think about things like this—they take for granted that their parentsare legally recognized as their parents. I would like my family recognized the same way as any other family, not treated differently because both my parentsare women."It would help if the government and the law recognized that I have two moms.It would help more people to understand. It would make my life easier. I wantmy family to be accepted and included, just like everybody else's family."*M.D.R. v. Ontario (Deputy Registrar General)*, [2006] O.J. No. 2268 (S.C.J.).

H. Conclusion

These are dicey times for lesbian and gay parents. The law is not keeping up with the changing face of the family. And there are strong forces seeking to restrict parenting by lesbians and gay men.

As in so many family law cases, lawyers representing lesbian and gay families will be faced with confrontations over custody, support, and visitation. Lawyers representing the biological or adoptive parent often use the heterosexist laws that prohibit the former partner from maintaining a parent-child relationship. Existing laws are used to thwart the parties' intentions at a better time in the relationship.

Ultimately, the laws used to prevent a non-legal parent from continuing the relationship causes great harm to the child. The best interests of the child frequently take a back seat to adult needs. Until the courts truly look at the child's best interests, these cases will continue to interfere with a parent-child relationship whose development the legal parent allowed and encouraged.

Children deserve, and have the right to demand, legal recognition of their families. Anything less is an affront to the child and an insult to "family values." No child should learn that her family is less important than that of another merely because her parents lack a piece of paper.

Notes

1. www.census.gov.
2. *See* Appendix D, LGBT Adoption Laws.
3. *See id.*
4. *In re* Adoption of Doe, 719 N.E.2d 1071 (Ohio Ct. App. 1998); *In re* Adoption of Luke, 640 N.W.2d 372 (Neb. 2002); *Interest of* Angel Lace M., 516 N.W.2d 678 (Wis. 1994).
5. 530 U.S. 57 (2000).
6. Flaks, Ficher, Masterpasqua & Joseph, *Lesbians Choosing Motherhood: A Comparative Study of Lesbian and Heterosexual Parents and Their Children*, 31 DEV. PSYCHOL.105-114 (1995); Green, Hotvedt, Gray & Smith, *Lesbian Mothers and Their Children: A Comparison with Solo Parent Heterosexual Mothers and Their Children*, 15 ARCH. SEX BEHAV. 167-84 (1986).
7. Bailey, Bobrow, Wolfe & Mikach, *Sexual Orientation of Adult Sons of Gay Fathers*, 31 DEV. PSYCHOL. 124-29 (1995); Gottman, *Children of Gay and Lesbian Parents*, 14 MARRIAGE & FAM. REV. 177-96 (1989).
8. Parental Kidnapping Prevention Act, 28 U.S.C. Sec. 1738A.
9. See Appendix for complete list of state statutory citations; Indiana, Missouri, Louisiana, Massachusetts, South Carolina, and Vermont have not adopted the UCCJEA; Puerto Rico also has not adopted it.
10. J.F. v. D.B., 2006 Pa. Super. 90, No. 221 WDA 2005 (April 21, 2006).
11. J.F. v. D.B., 66 Pa. D.&C. 4th 1 (Apr. 2, 2004); Rice v. Flynn (Oct. 29, 2004), Summit C.P. No. 2004-04-1561; Rice v. Flynn, 9th Dist. No. 22416, 2005-Ohio-4667; Flynn v. Bimber (Jan. 7, 2005), 70 Pa. D.&C. 4th 261.
12. J.F. v. D.B., 165 Ohio App. 3d 791, 2006-Ohio-1175 (March 15, 2006).
13. J.F. v. D.B., 2006 Pa. Super. 90, No. 221 WDA 2005 (April 21, 2006).
14. Larkey, Court citing, *Redefining Motherhood: Determining Legal Maternity in Gestational Surrogacy Arrangements*, 51 DRAKE L.REV. 605, 622 (2003); *see also* Coleman, *Gestation, Intent and the Seed: Defining Motherhood in the Era of Assisted Human Reproduction*, 17 CARDOZO L.REV. 497, 505-29 (1996).
15. 37 Cal. 4th 130, 117 P.3d 673 (2005).
16. Kristine Renee H. v. Lisa Ann R. (2005), 37 Cal. 4th 156; Elisa Maria B. v. Super. Court (2005), 37 Cal. 4th 108, 117 P.3d 660.

17. Wisconsin, Virginia, Pennsylvania, Maryland, Florida, Colorado, Nevada, Illinois, and Connecticut also allow pre-birth determinations.
18. 137 Ohio Misc. 2d 1, 2006-Ohio-2059 (April 6, 2006).
19. Johnson v. Calvert, 5 Cal. 4th 84, 19 Cal. Rptr. 2d 494, 851 P.2d 776 (1993).
20. The situation is true, the names are fictitious.
21. The situation is based on fact. The names used are fictitious. Any similarity to similarly named persons is strictly coincidental.
22. Drafted by the National Conference of Commissioners on Uniform State Laws, 1973; amended 2002.
23. 519 U.S. 102 (1996).
24. 530 U.S. 57 (2000).
25. No. 05-974 (May 15, 2006).
26. *In re* Parentage of L.B., 155 Wash. 2d 679, 122 P.3d 161 (Wash. S. Ct., Nov. 3, 2005).
27. Stanley v. Illinois, 405 U.S. 645 (1972).
28. 463 U.S. 248 (1983).
29. *Id.* at 261.
30. B.F. v. T.D., 2005-SC-000557-DG (Ky. S. Ct., June 15, 2006).
31. Ellen C. Perrin, M.D. and the Committee on Psychosocial Aspects of Child and Family Health, Am. Acad. of Pediatrics, *Technical Report: Coparent or Second-Parent Adoption by Same-Sex Parents*, 109:2 PEDIATRICS 341 (Feb. 2002).
32. www.cdc.gov/nchs/data.nvsr/nvsr53/nvsr53_19.pdf.
33. S.L. Huggins, *A Comparative Study of Self-Esteem of Adolescent Children of Divorced Lesbian Mothers and Divorced Heterosexual Mothers*, 18 J. HOMOSEX.123-35 (1989).
34. Wakeman v. Dixon, 921 So. 2d 669, Fla. App. 1 Dist., 2006.
35. *Id.* at p. 6.
36. *Id.* at pp. 9-10.
37. *Id.* at p. 7, cite omitted.
38. *Id.*
39. Hays v. Taffs, No. 101, 540 (Okla. Ct. of Civ. App., March 28, 2006), *cert. denied*, Okla. Sup. Ct.
40. 118:1 PEDIATRICS 349-64 (July 2006) (doi: 10.1542/peds.2006-1279).
41. *Id.* at 356.
42. The Potential Budgetary Impact of Recognizing Same-Sex Marriages, *available at* www.cbo.gov/showdoc.cfm?index=5559&sequence=0.
43. www.law.ucla.edu/williamsinstitute/publications/Policy-Econ-index.html.
44. The American Psychoanalytic Association, the National Association of Social Workers, the American Academy of Child and Adolescent Psychiatry, and the American Medical Association.
45. A.A. v. B.B., 2007 Ont. Ct. App. 2 (20070102).
46. *Canadian Boy Can Have Two Moms and a Dad, High Court Rules*, THE CANADIAN PRESS, Jan. 3, 2007.
47. A.A. v. B.B., 2007 Ont. Ct. App. 2, [38] (20070102).

CHAPTER FIVE

Adoption

To understand the issues faced by lesbian and gay individuals and couples in adoption, it is necessary to understand the concept of adoption. Adoption creates a new parent-child relationship that is equivalent to a biological parental relationship.

Adoption is a statutory creature. It does not exist in common law. The basic principle of adoption is that it extinguishes all ties to an existing family and creates a new family.

> **Common Statutory Adoption Requirements**
> 1. Consent of certain parties (e.g., natural parents, court-appointed guardians)
> 2. An agency-generated home study of the prospective adoptive parents
> 3. A judicial determination that adoption is in the child's best interests
> 4. A cutoff provision that requires both parents to surrender all legal rights and responsibilities to the child; or, the court terminates those rights

The cutoff provision is the most common statutory obstacle to lesbian and gay adoptive parents. In most states, lesbian and gay non-biological/legal parents cannot adopt their partner's children without the partner terminating all parental rights.

The cutoff provision does not interfere with traditional stepparent adoptions. A same-sex couple seeking to adopt the same child is similarly situated except they cannot marry. The law allows stepparent adoptions but assumes the stepparent is a person of the opposite gender from the biological parent.

Many courts consider this an issue the legislature must address. However, some courts have used a statutory construction to overcome the cutoff provision. Adoption laws are, in many states, ambiguous.

A general rule is to not construe any statutory ambiguity in a way that produces an absurd or unjust result. Courts regularly resolve ambiguities in statutory language to meet the core values of the individual statutes. No statute is drafted or intended to address every possible scenario.

Applying the cutoff provision to same-sex couples violates the rule against construing a statute to produce absurd results. Terminating the rights of the biological parent who agrees to the adoption and wants to raise a child with her partner in a committed relationship is an absurd result. This is particularly true when the evidence shows that the adoption is in the child's best interest. Upholding the cutoff provision in adoptions involving same-sex couples makes no sense.

By their nature, adoption laws are to be liberally construed. The courts are empowered by the legislatures to apply the adoption laws to meet the child's best interests. Furthermore, there is no evidence that any legislature intended the cutoff provision to apply in any adoption where the natural parent is a party to the adoption.[1]

Under *In re Jacob*,[2] the District of Columbia Court of Appeals decided the cutoff provision was ". . . [d]esigned as a shield to protect new adoptive families and was never intended as a sword to prohibit otherwise beneficial intrafamily adoptions by a second parent."

As a practical matter, state legislatures did not consider same-sex couples when enacting adoption laws. There is no specific intent in these adoption laws to prevent or prohibit an interpretation that would permit second-parent adoptions in same-sex couples. Only Florida specifically prohibits lesbians and gay men from adopting children. Mississippi law is comparable. In Utah, unmarried persons are not permitted to adopt.

Courts often interpret statutes to apply in situations never anticipated by the legislatures. A statute's legislative history is rarely a clear-cut explanation of what the legislature intended. And an omission by the legislature is not synonymous with a legislative intent to address the specific issue before the court.

Adoptions are intended to benefit children. A commitment to promote the child's best interests is the paramount reasoning behind adoption laws. Legislatures enacted adoption laws and delegated the responsibility for decisions under those laws to the courts. The courts are empowered to make a case-by-case decision of what is in the child's best interests.

The courts are also empowered to act in family law issues involving custody, support, and visitation. It is well established that judges are in the best position to determine what will benefit an individual child in a specific case. Even an appellate court will not overturn a trial court's decision in these cases unless there is an abuse of discretion.

There are an estimated 1.5 million adopted children in the United States.[3] Exact numbers are unknown because states are not required to report adoptions to a central database.

The National Center for State Courts (NCSC) first began compiling adoption statistics in 1992. The NCSC estimates that 126,951 children were adopted through foster care, domestic, and international agencies and by stepparents. According to the estimates, 42% of all adoptions were by stepparents and 15% were through foster care.[4]

In 2003, according to the U.S. Department of Health and Human Services' Adoption and Foster Care Analysis Reporting System (AFCARS), the number of adoptions reported by the states was 50,362.[5] These numbers constitute an actual count by all 50 states and differ dramatically from the estimates of years past. For example, the NCSC estimated there were over 127,000 adoptions in the United States in 1999.

Children can be adopted in different ways:

- **Foster Care:** Children are in a state's care and reunification with their birth parents is not possible. Adoptions are arranged by state or county welfare agencies. Private agencies with state contracts also arrange adoptions of children in foster care. Relatives, foster parents, and legal strangers may adopt foster children. Federal law requires states to find permanent homes for foster children in a timely manner.
- **Private Adoptions:** Private agencies can be nonprofit or for-profit. Children can also be placed through an independent adoption. This takes place directly between the adoptive parents and the birth parents. Attorneys or other types of facilitators can assist with private adoptions.
- **International Adoptions:** Adoption agencies arrange these adoptions of children from other countries by U.S. citizens. The adoptions are finalized in the child's birth country. Once back in the United States, the adoptive parents must take action to formalize the adoption here.
- **Transracial Adoptions:** Children are placed in an adoptive family of another race or ethnicity. This is often considered a separate category because of the cultural issues faced by the families and children involved. The National Adoption Information Clearinghouse estimates that 15% of the children adopted from foster care in 1995 were transracial or transcultural.[6]

Most children adopted through international avenues are under five years old. Most children adopted from foster care are over five years old.

Placement decisions are based on several factors, including:

1. Is the person or couple caring, nurturing, and sensitive to others?
2. Do they have qualities needed to parent a child?
3. What are their individual strengths and weaknesses?
4. How do their strengths and weaknesses complement the needs of the child?
5. Do they have the capacity to nurture a child not born to them?

> **Practice Tip**
>
> When dealing with lesbian and gay prospective parents, other questions need to be considered by them and the agency. These include: 1. Do the prospective parents have a positive self-image with being gay? 2. Do they have a stable relationship and a commitment to each other? 3. Do they own a home, share finances, have a will and other such documents?

A placement agency also considers a variety of factors when processing an application for adoption. No single factor determines suitability. The agency is seeking a family for the child. Sexual orientation is a separate issue from the ability to nurture. Placement decisions are usually made on the basis of the strengths and needs of the individual child as well as the perceived abilities of the prospective parents to meet those needs. Often, children viewed by someone else as less desirable are placed with unmarried couples, individuals, and lesbian and gay applicants. These children are often older or with special needs.

While all prospective parents ought to be given equal consideration, the preference is still for white, married, upper-middle-class couples. These applicants usually do not want an older or special needs child.

There continues to be a bias against lesbian and gay prospective adoptive parents. This is often expressed as a belief that a child placed in a gay or lesbian home will become gay. Agencies consider whether it is fair to the child to place her in a lesbian or gay home and expose her to society's prejudices. However, heterosexual parents do not guarantee heterosexual children.

In Boston, Massachusetts, Catholic Charities terminated its adoption placements because they refuse to comply with the state's nondiscrimination laws with regard to lesbian and gay prospective parents. The governor of Massachusetts attempted, without success, to exempt this church-based organization from being bound by the non-discrimination laws in the commonwealth.

A 2004 Harris Interactive Poll (December 2004) posed questions to heterosexuals on issues of gay equality. On the issue of adoption, the majority (55%) favored equal federal adoption assistance for lesbian and gay parents.

A. Private Adoptions

Private domestic adoptions occur through for-profit or nonprofit agencies or directly between the birth parents and adoptive parents. These types of adoptions deal with U.S.-born infants. The number of annual private adoptions is not readily known because states are not required to maintain records.

State laws govern private adoptions. The states license the adoption agencies, which charge fees to prospective adoptive parents. The agencies also provide pre- and post-adoption services. Most states permit independent adoptions; a few even allow unlicensed intermediaries, such as attorneys, to assist birth parents in finding an adoptive parent.

B. International Adoptions

International adoptions constitute a significant number of infant adoptions in the United States. Most of the children adopted are girls, and Asia is the preferred location for these adoptions. The U.S. Department of State maintains records on the number of visas issued to children being adopted from other countries.

> **Practice Tip**
>
> The State Department issues two types of visas for foreign adopted children. The laws of the child's birth country determine which visa is used. 1. IR3 visas are used for orphans who are adopted in their birth country and then emigrate to the United States. 2. IR4 visas are issued to children whose adoptions are finalized in the United States after they emigrate from their country of origin.

Adoptions from China are illustrative. China has a one-child rule for families, and because boys are more highly valued, their families abandon the girls, which explains the large number of girls being adopted from that country.

> **Practice Tip**
>
> **Chinese Adoptions**
> China has instituted new regulations that will adversely affect lesbian and gay prospective adoptive parents—individuals and couples. The Chinese government agency responsible for overseeing foreign adoptions will no longer allow the following people to adopt: 1. Unmarried individuals. 2. Obese individuals (body mass index of no more than 40). 3. Anyone who is taking medication for psychiatric conditions, including anxiety and depression. 4. Persons over the age of 50. 5. Anyone with a severe facial deformity. Prospective parents must be between the ages of 30 and 50. People up to age 55 will be considered if they adopt children with special needs. The new rules took effect May 1, 2007.

C. Second-Parent Adoptions

Since 2000, 21 states have granted second-parent adoptions. Five states and the District of Columbia allow second-parent adoptions following appellate court decisions. Among the states permitting second-parent adoptions are: Connecticut, California, Illinois, Massachusetts, New Jersey, New York, Pennsylvania, Vermont, and the District of Columbia. An appellate court in Indiana recently approved of second-parent adoptions.[7] The Indiana Attorney General plans to appeal that decision to the Indiana Supreme Court.

Second-parent adoption procedures allow the biological parent's same-sex partner to adopt a child without terminating the rights of the biological or adoptive parent. Second-parent adoption is also called "co-parent adoption." This type of adoption is comparable to a "stepparent adoption," except both parties are the same gender.

Joint adoption allows a same-sex couple, with no biological or legal relationship to the child, to simultaneously adopt. The fact that both adoptive parents are of the same gender is not an issue in joint adoptions.

Adopted children enjoy numerous advantages, including legal security. Adopted children are entitled to financial benefits from both parents. They also enjoy inheritance rights and Social Security benefits from both parents.

Children being raised by same-sex parents are at a disadvantage if there is no legal relationship between the children and both parents. For example, the child's biological parent may not have health insurance to cover the child, but the non-legal parent does. Further, employers that offer domestic partnership benefits may not cover the non-legal child of the employee.

Likewise, if the non-legal parent dies, the child cannot receive surviving dependent benefits from the Social Security Administration. This can place the child in a difficult financial position if the deceased parent was the family's primary wage earner.

Without a legal relationship to the parent, children have no standing to bring a wrongful death action or receive tort benefits for the loss of that parent.

When same-sex couples break up, the children are affected because they may be denied a continuing relationship with the non-legal parent. Further, the child may be denied financial support from the departing parent. As with other situations mentioned above, the child's financial position may be significantly impaired because of the parent's departure from the relationship.

This need for adoption rights is becoming more obvious given the rise in litigation between former partners over custody, visitation, and support rights.

The Delaware Supreme Court ruled on a case involving two former partners and the non-legal parent's rights to continue a relationship with their three children. However, the court stated that its decision is limited to the unique facts of the case.[8]

The women, Erica Smith and Sheila Smith (pseudonyms), were involved in a nine-year relationship. During that time, Erica gave birth to triplets. The trial court held that the non-legal parent, Sheila, is a de facto parent and entitled to joint custody.

Erica appealed the case but also filed a claim for retroactive child support. Sheila was ordered to pay $721 per month. The high court used that action by Erica to uphold the trial court's decision. The court ruled that Erica, by seeking and accepting child support payments, acknowledged Sheila's de facto parent status.

Had Sheila been allowed to adopt the children, there would have been no need for litigation to determine the relative rights of the parties to have contact with the children.

The National Center for Lesbian Rights[9] originated the concept of second-parent adoptions in the 1980s. A San Francisco court granted the first second-parent adoption in 1986.[10] Other states have ruled on gay adoptions either through statute and appellate court[11] or trial court decisions.[12]

Courts in Colorado, Nebraska, Ohio, and Wisconsin have ruled that second-parent adoptions are not allowed.

> **Practice Tip**
>
> **Adoption Practice Points**
> 1. Research your state law on second-parent adoption.
> 2. Can your clients qualify under the stepparent adoption law?
> 3. What was the legislative intent in passing the adoption laws?
> 4. Adoption should be pursued in states that recognize civil unions, domestic partnerships, or same-sex marriage. Otherwise, parental rights may be lost if the couple breaks up.
> 5. If adoption is not possible, draft a co-parenting agreement for the clients to sign.
> 6. Consider whether the adoption will be recognized in other states.
> 7. Advise clients to carry adoption papers when traveling.
> 8. Even if adoption is unnecessary in your state (i.e., children born during a civil union/domestic partnership/same-sex marriage are considered "of the" relationship), adoption may be necessary to obtain a court order to gain recognition in other states.

D. Adoption Costs

The National Adoption Information Clearinghouse (NAIC) provides the following estimates of the costs involved in different types of adoptions:

> Foster Care Adoptions: $0 - $2,500
> Licensed Private Agency Adoptions: $5,000 - $ 40,000+
> Independent Adoptions: $8,000 - $40,000+
> Facilitated/Unlicensed Adoptions: $5,000 - $40,000+
> International Adoptions: $7,000 - $30,000+

The costs vary because of the unique factors inherent in every adoption. Prospective parents should investigate the types of adoptions and ask questions.

E. Adoptions by Lesbian and Gay Individuals and Couples

Lesbian and gay individuals and couples face many hurdles when adopting children. Florida is the only state that bans lesbians and gay men from adopting.[13] However, the Florida law does not apply to lesbians and gay men who want to become foster parents.

A gay male couple unsuccessfully challenged the Florida ban in federal court.[14] In *Lofton v. Secretary of Dept. of Children and Family Services*, the Eleventh Circuit ruled that adoption is based on state, not common, law. The parties stipulated that there is no fundamental right to adopt or to be adopted. They also stipulated that adoption is a privilege created by statute and not by common law. (¶ 35)

According to *Lofton*, ". . . [t]he state can make classifications for adoption purposes that would be constitutionally suspect in many other arenas." (¶ 29) In Florida, the classification in question prohibits gay men and lesbians from being allowed to adopt.

The court went to great lengths spelling out Florida's duties concerning children. ". . . [I]n the adoption context, the state's overriding interest is the best interests of the children whom it is seeking to place with adoptive families. Florida, acting as parens patriae . . . bears the high duty of determining what adoptive home environments will best serve all aspects of the child's growth and development." (¶ 28)

The court also concluded that the United States Supreme Court decision in *Lawrence v. Texas*[15] did not create a new fundamental right to "private sexual intimacy."

The Eleventh Circuit ultimately decided that the issue of whether lesbians and gay men should be able to adopt must be resolved in the state legislature. "Thus, any argument that the Florida legislature was misguided in its decision is one of legislative policy, not constitutional law. The legislature is the proper forum for this debate, and we do not sit as a super legislature 'to award by judicial decree what was not achievable by political consensus.'" (Citation deleted.) (¶ 88)

The court, however, found nothing wrong with Florida's practice of naming lesbian and gay individuals as foster parents or guardians. This practice, according to the court, ". . . has its foundation in state law and contractual arrangements." (¶ 27)

The decision, read in its entirety, is a convoluted exercise in relative rational thinking that seeks to justify an implausible outcome. Its twists and turns would evoke laughter if the outcome were not so sad and disturbing. At the end, the ones most affected by the decision are the children languishing in foster homes until they "age out" and enter a world with no family and no support.

Utah[16] and Mississippi[17] prohibit lesbian and gay couples from adopting. Alabama's Supreme Court ruled against gay adoptions. New Hampshire adopted a ban in 1987 and repealed it in 1999.

A number of states have introduced or plan to introduce legislation banning lesbians and gay men from adopting children or serving as foster parents. The Ohio House speaker declared that state's proposed legislation "dead on arrival." The speaker, Jon Husted, was adopted.

Many lesbians and gay men face opposition to their adoption petitions specifically because of their sexual orientation.

Linda Kaufman is an Episcopal priest who also happens to be a lesbian. She faced off against the commonwealth of Virginia in her effort to adopt a foster child from the District of Columbia. Kaufman, a resident of Virginia, adopted her first child in Virginia in 1992. That child also came from the D.C. foster care system.

Officials in the District of Columbia approved the adoption. Those officials decided that Kaufman, who lives in Arlington, Virginia, would provide a stable and loving home for the child.

Virginia officials opposed the adoption solely because Kaufman is a lesbian. Lawyers with Lambda Legal Defense and Education Fund represented Kaufman[18] and filed a lawsuit on her behalf in December 2001. Kaufman argued that the child's best interest, not the adoptive parent's sexual orientation, is the controlling factor when evaluating a prospective adoption.

In 2003, the commonwealth of Virginia settled the case and agreed to proceed with Kaufman's adoption application. The settlement requires Virginia's Department of Social Services to send an adoption directive to its local departments and agencies. The directive governs consideration for adopting out-of-state children. Consideration of such applications "will be limited to whether the proposed placement is contrary to the interests of that child." The directive also states there are "no absolute barriers" to adoptions. This will rebut Virginia's previous stance not to consider any applications from gay men or lesbians.

The laws of each state vary on who may adopt and whether joint or second-parent adoptions are available. Lesbian and gay couples need the guidance of an experienced and sympathetic lawyer to achieve their goal of adopting a child to complete their family.

F. Developing Law

On May 19, 2006, the U.S. District Court for the Western District of Oklahoma struck down the Oklahoma Adoption Invalidation Law. This law, passed in 2004, states that Oklahoma "shall not recognize an adoption by more than one individual of the same sex from any other state or foreign jurisdiction."[19]

On August 3, 2007, the 10th U.S. Circuit Court of Appeals upheld the lower court's decision declaring that Oklahoma's Adoption Invalidation Law is unconstitutional.[20]

Lambda Legal Defense and Education Fund (Lambda Legal), representing the plaintiffs, argued that the law is unconstitutional under the federal Constitution's guarantees of equal protection, due process, right to travel, and the Full Faith and Credit Clause.

Six same-sex couples and their families are plaintiffs in the action. The families include children adopted while the parents were living in other states. One of the plaintiff couples, Ann Magro and Heather Finstuen, adopted their twin girls while living in New Jersey. Magro teaches at the University of Oklahoma. The new Oklahoma law threatens the legal adoption between Finstuen and the twins.

Another of the couples is Ed Swaya and Greg Hampel and their three-year-old daughter, Vivian. The couple lives in Washington state. They adopted Vivian after her birth in Oklahoma. The Oklahoma State Department of Health initially refused to issue an amended birth certificate that reflected both men as the child's legal parents after a Washington court approved the adoption. Since then, the Department of Health has issued the revised birth certificate. However, they fear the new Oklahoma law may interfere with them traveling to Oklahoma to visit Vivian's birth mother.

The court ordered the state to issue birth certificates for children involved and list the names of both parents. The court also ordered the state to not enforce the law in the future. An appeal is expected.

In 2005, the Virginia Supreme Court issued a decision that state law does not preclude the Registrar of Vital Records and Health Statistics from issuing amended birth certificates listing same-sex parents.[21]

The case involved three sets of adoptive parents. The Superior Court of the District of Columbia issued final decrees of adoption for the children involved. All the children were born in Virginia. The Virginia Registrar refused to issue new birth certificates reflecting the names of both adoptive parents.

In holding against the State Registrar, the court held, "... there is nothing in the statutory scheme that precludes recognition of same-sex parents as 'adoptive parents.' [T]he statute ... refers only to the undefined terms of 'adoptive parents' and 'intended parents.'"

There is no indication, at this time, that the Virginia Legislature intends to introduce legislation to change the outcome of this case.

On the foster parent front, the Arkansas Supreme Court issued a decision June 29, 2006,[22] declaring a state regulation unconstitutional. Regulation 200.3.2 stated that no one could be a foster parent "[i]f any adult member of that person's household is a homosexual."

The Child Welfare Review Board adopted the regulation in 1999. Before that, lesbian and gay couples regularly received approval to serve as foster parents. The court noted that lesbian and gay individuals could continue to be foster parents *after* the regulation took effect.

The court decided that ". . . testimony demonstrates that the driving force behind adoption of the regulation was not to promote the health, safety and welfare of foster children, but rather based upon the Board's view of morality and its bias against homosexuals."

It is not often that a court will explicitly cite a party's bias when deciding a case involving lesbian and gay issues. The court decided the regulation was designed to "[e]xclude a set of individuals from becoming foster parents based on your morality and bias."

Board members testified at trial that they considered same-sex relationships wrong. They viewed homosexual behavior as a sin, and homosexuality violated their religious convictions.

The court also held that the board exceeded its mandate by trying to legislate public morality. That, of course, gives opponents of lesbian and gay parenting rights an opening. The Arkansas Legislature will, undoubtedly, be asked to legislate the regulation into law. The only people who are hurt by such action are the foster children who will not have a chance for a loving home.

G. Conclusion

Adoption is an issue of significance to lesbian and gay couples. Some states are banning the use of alternative reproductive technologies for unmarried women. This is nothing more than an effort to prevent lesbians from having children. Many lesbian and gay couples want to raise children. Adopting a child or children is a way to provide that child with a loving and supportive home and the couple with an opportunity to parent. The goal should be to find homes so that no child is left behind.

Notes

1. *In re* M.M.D., 662 A.2d 837 (D.C. Ct. App. 6/30/1995).
2. 86 N.Y.2d 651, 660 N.E.2d 405 (1995).
3. Jason Fields, *Living Arrangements of Children,* U.S. Census (Apr. 2001).
4. Nat'l Adoption Info. Clearinghouse, *How Many Children Were Adopted in 2000 and 2001* (August 2004).
5. www.ndacan.cornell.edu/NDACAN/Datasets/UserGuidePDFs/118_AFCARS_2003v1_Supplement.pdf.
6. Nat'l Adoption Clearinghouse, Transracial Adoption Fact Sheet, www.calib.com/naic/pubs/trans.htm.

7. *In the Matter of* Infant Girl W, Ind. Ct. App., No. 55A01-0506-JV-289 (April 13, 2006).

8. Smith v. Smith, No. 232, 2005 (Del. Sup. Ct., March 7, 2006).

9. www.nclrights.org

10. *In re* Adoption Petition of N., Case No. 18086 (Cal. Super. Ct., San Francisco Cty., filed March 11, 1986).

11. California, Connecticut, District of Columbia, Illinois, Indiana, Massachusetts, New York, New Jersey, Pennsylvania, and Vermont.

12. Alabama, Alaska, Delaware, Hawaii, Iowa, Louisiana, Maryland, Michigan, Minnesota, Nevada, New Mexico, Oregon, Rhode Island, Texas, and Washington.

13. FLA. STAT. ch. 63.042(3) (West 1985 & Supp. 1995).

14. Lofton v. Sec. of Dept. of Children and Family Servs., 358 F.3d 804 (11th Cir. 2004).

15. Lawrence v. Texas, 539 U.S. 558 (2003).

16. UTAH CODE ANN. § 78-30-1(3)(b).

17. MISS. CODE ANN. § 93-17-3(2).

18. Linda Kaufman v. Va. Dep't of Social Servs. (unreported) (case settled 2003).

19. Finstuen v. Edmondson, 497 F. Supp. 2d 1295, 2006 WL 1445354 (W.D. Okla. May 19, 2006) (No. CIV.-04-1152C) *affirmed in part and reversed in part by* Finstuen v. Crutcher, 496 F.3d 1139 (10th Cir. (Okla.) Aug. 3, 2007).

20. Finstuen v. Crutcher, 496 F.3d 1139 (10th Cir. (Okla.) Aug. 3, 2007) (No. 06-6213, 06-6216).

21. Davenport v. Little-Bowser, 269 Va. 546, 611 S.E.2d 366 (2005).

22. Dept. of Human Services, et al. v. Howard et al., ___ S.W. 3d ___, 367 Ark. 55, 2006 WL 1779467, Ark. June 29, 2006 (No. 05-814).

CHAPTER SIX

Parenting Rights

Relationships end. The end of a relationship becomes more complicated when children are involved. There is no shortage of case law addressing the needs of children following their parents' divorce. Children are often the focus of divorces, but not out of a concern for their well-being. Too often, parents use the children as battering rams against each other. This can also be the case when lesbian and gay couples break up. This chapter deals with custody, visitation, and support orders.

There is a growing body of case law dealing specifically with the legal issues facing lesbian and gay parents when the relationship ends. Lesbian and gay couples deal with the "legal parent v. non-legal parent" dichotomy.

As we discussed previously, most children raised by lesbian and gay couples find themselves with only one legally recognized parent. This creates problems for the non-legal parent when she tries to gain recognition of her parent-child relationship. The couple may have a co-parenting agreement, yet in most states there is no guarantee a court will honor that agreement.

The contested custody and visitation cases being reported revolve around the legal parent's desire to prevent the former partner from having any contact with the child. All too often, the legal parent is successful.

The face of family law is changing, albeit slowly, around the country. Unfortunately, as in many heterosexual divorces, the needs and concerns of the children often take a back seat to the wants and needs of the adults involved.

The concepts of "intended parenthood," "*in loco parentis,*" "psychological parent," "parent by estoppel" and "de facto parent" are raised by the unrecognized parent in many cases.

Anytime lawyers deal with custody or visitation cases involving a lesbian or gay parent, it is time to bring out those dusty old law books and look for creative ways to maintain parent-child relationships, even when there is no specific statutory authority to do so.

This chapter addresses ways to convince a court to recognize alternative definitions of "parent," consider whether the legal parent waived his or her constitutional rights, and reiterate the primacy of the child's best interests. The judge is empowered with great discretion in these matters, but it is the lawyer's job is to persuade, convince, and influence the court to arrive at a fundamentally fair and reasonable decision benefiting the child.

A. Applicable Laws Establishing Parenting Rights

1. Parental Kidnapping Prevention Act[1] (PKPA)

The PKPA requires states to give full faith and credit to child custody determinations from other states. Once a court properly exercises jurisdiction to determine custody, no other court can issue an order. The PKPA provides that:

> (c) A child custody determination made by a Court of a State is consistent with the provisions of this section only if -
> (1) such court has jurisdiction under the law of such State; and
> (2) one of the following conditions is met:
> (A) such State (i) is the home State of the child on the date of the commencement of the proceeding, or (ii) had been the child's home State within six months before the date of the commencement of the proceeding and the child is absent from such State because of his removal or retention by a contestant or for other reasons, and a contestant continues to live in such State;
> (B) (i) it appears that no other State would have jurisdiction under subparagraph (A) and (ii) it is in the best interest of the child that a court of such State assume jurisdiction because (I) the child and his parents, or the child and at least one contestant, have a significant connection with such State other than mere physical presence in such State, and (II) there is available in such State substantial evidence concerning the child's present or future care, protection, training and personal relationships;
> (C) the child is physically present in such State and (i) the child has been abandoned, or (ii) it is necessary in an emergency to protect the child because he has been subjected to or threatened with mistreatment or abuse;

(D) (i) it appears that no other State would have jurisdiction under subparagraph (A), (B), (C) or (E), or another State has declined to exercise jurisdiction on the ground that the State whose jurisdiction is in issue is the more appropriate forum to determine the custody of the child, and (ii) it is in the best interest of the child that such court assume jurisdiction; or

(E) the court has continuing jurisdiction pursuant to subsection (d) of this section.

(d) The jurisdiction of a court of a State that has made a child custody determination consistent with the provisions of this section continues as long as the requirement of subsection (c)(1) of this section continues to be met and such State remains the residence of the child or any contestant.

(e) Before a child custody determination is made, reasonable notice and opportunity to be heard shall be given to the contestants, any parent whose parental rights have not been previously terminated and any person who has physical custody of a child.

(f) A court of a State may modify a determination of the custody of the same child made by a court of another State, if -

(1) it has jurisdiction to make such a child custody determination; and

(2) the court of the other State no longer has jurisdiction, or it has declined to exercise such jurisdiction to modify such determination.

(g) A court of a State shall not exercise jurisdiction in any proceeding for a custody determination commenced during the pendency of a proceeding in a court of another State where such court of that other State is exercising jurisdiction consistently with the provisions of this section to make a custody determination.

The significance of this statute is shown in *Miller-Jenkins v. Miller-Jenkins*.[2] The PKPA played an integral role in contesting the decision issued by the Virginia trial court. That decision was in direct contradiction of the earlier Vermont decision. The final verdict: The Vermont decision prevails, and Janet Jenkins is entitled to regular visitation with the parties' daughter.

2. Uniform Child-Custody Jurisdiction and Enforcement Act (UCCJEA)[3]

> **Practice Tip**
>
> The National Conference of Commissioners on Uniform State Laws (NCCUSL) approved the UCCJEA in 1997. This uniform law replaced the Uniform Child-Custody Jurisdiction Act adopted in 1968. By June 2006, 43 states had adopted the 1997 Act. The only states that have not adopted the UCCJEA are Indiana, Missouri, Louisiana, Massachusetts, South Carolina and Vermont. Puerto Rico also has not yet adopted the Act.

The UCCJEA tailored its requirements to those of the PKPA. It provides exclusive continuing jurisdiction in child custody and visitation cases to courts in the child's home state. The "home state" is defined as the state where the child lived with a parent for six consecutive months before the proceeding began. For children under the age of six, the home state is the one where the child lived since birth.

The provisions establishing a court's jurisdiction under the UCCJEA are consistent with those in the PKPA. The UCCJEA governs a court's jurisdiction to make an original custody/visitation order or modify an existing order. It is intended to avoid custody battles between competing states. It also promotes uniformity in jurisdiction and enforcement of custody orders. The UCCJEA does not apply in child support cases.

While it is not a substantive custody statute, it is designed for adoption by all 50 states and Puerto Rico to ensure interstate enforceability of court orders affecting children.

State courts, exercising jurisdiction under the UCCJEA and the PKPA, are entitled to have their orders enforced under full faith and credit by other states. The UCCJEA and PKPA also give the original court continuing jurisdiction as provided in the Acts. Eliminating interstate custody battles is a stated purpose of the Acts.

One goal of the UCCJEA is to avoid protracted custody litigation. Children are adversely affected when they are subjected to such litigation. Their sense of security can be irreparably damaged by their parents' actions. The UCCJEA is also intended to avoid "self-help recovery" by parents unhappy with a court's decision.

This is what happened in the 2003 case, *Miller-Jenkins v. Miller-Jenkins*.[4] The birth mother initiated a dissolution case in Vermont and sought a custody and support order. She did not like the Vermont decision and filed a second case in Virginia. This case is pending in both Vermont and Virginia and will likely end up in the United States Supreme Court.

Under the UCCJEA, courts have continuing jurisdiction over permanent, temporary, initial, and modification orders. The Act requires states to recognize and enforce custody orders from other states when the original order conforms to the UCCJEA's standards.

The UCCJEA does not apply to American Indian children when the Indian Child Welfare Act applies.[5]

Under the UCCJEA, there are two requirements for making or modifying a custody order: (1) the court must have a basis for jurisdiction, and (2) the parties to the proceeding must have notice and an opportunity to be heard. But personal jurisdiction over the child or a party is not required.

There are four bases for initial jurisdiction:

1. Home state;
2. Significant connection;
3. More appropriate forum; and
4. Vacuum jurisdiction.

Home state jurisdiction is given priority by the Act in initial proceedings. Courts have discretion to decline jurisdiction if they believe another court is better suited to exercise it.

Original jurisdiction continues until one of the following occurs:

1. The original court loses significant contact jurisdiction; or
2. Neither the child, parents, nor anyone acting as a parent lives in the state.

The original state court has sole authority to determine whether a significant connection remains. Another state's court cannot make that determination.

The original state court retains continuing jurisdiction even if the child and the custodial parent move to another state. This usually occurs when the non-custodial parent remains in the original state.

The original court may decline to exercise jurisdiction if it determines that retaining jurisdiction is inconvenient or because of unjustifiable conduct. The latter may arise if a non-custodial parent removes the child from the custodial parent without justification.

The UCCJEA includes a registration procedure for out-of-state custody and visitation orders. This is not required, but it can serve to avoid future problems. Registration can be a pretest of enforceability; it places the courts of another state on notice of its existence. Registration limits defenses against enforcement, and a registered order is deemed a local order as of the date of registration.

> **Practice Tip**
>
> The UCCJEA registration process is simple.
> 1. The registering party sends copies of the order and a request for registration to a court in another state. Other information may also be required.
> 2. The receiving court files the order as a foreign judgment and notifies the parent who received custody or visitation.
> 3. The recipient parent has 20 days to request a hearing to contest the validity of the order.
> 4. If no hearing is requested, the order is confirmed and is then enforceable as a local order.

The UCCJEA also includes authority for enforcement of custody and visitation orders by local public officials.[6] The provisions are based on a successful program in California that uses district attorneys to enforce custody and visitation orders. Section 315(a) of the UCCJEA provides statutory authority for prosecutors to use the court to enforce an existing order. The prosecutor represents the court, not one of the parties.

Prosecutors have authority if:

- there is a prior custody determination;
- a court requests the prosecutor's assistance in a pending proceeding;
- there is a reasonable belief that a criminal statute has been violated; or
- there is a reasonable belief that a child has been removed or retained in violation of the Hague Convention.

> **Practice Tip**
>
> There are only three defenses available to an order seeking registration:
> 1. The court making the order lacked jurisdiction;
> 2. The person contesting the order did not receive notice of the underlying custody proceeding; and
> 3. The custody determination has been vacated, stayed, or modified.

Prosecutors have authority to enlist the assistance of local law enforcement. In addition, prosecutors and law enforcement agencies are permitted to recover their costs from the non-prevailing party.

The UCCJEA and PKPA work only with the commitment of knowledgeable lawyers, uniform interpretation by courts, and use of the laws by prosecutors and law enforcement. Custody disputes always affect the children involved. When parents refuse to acknowledge that fact, lawyers, courts, and public officials must take action to protect the children.

This federal law applies in all states in all cases involving children and interstate jurisdiction. It is important for lesbian and gay parents to understand it because, as shown by the *Miller-Jenkins* case, *supra*, the UCCJEA can prevent one parent from removing the child to a new jurisdiction to avoid compliance with a court order.

3. Uniform Parentage Act (2002)[7]

The National Conference of Commissioners on Uniform Law (NCCUL) originally addressed the issue of parentage in the United States in 1973. The Uniform Parentage Act (UPA) in 1973 was revolutionary in its scope. It involved determination of parentage, paternity actions, and child support. In particular, the 1973 UPA, for the first time, made children of unmarried parents a focal point.

In the 1960s and 1970s, the United States Supreme Court resolved the discriminatory treatment of illegitimate children. The Court determined that illegitimacy could not be a legal barrier to a child enforcing his legal rights in a variety of areas. Before the UPA (1973) came into existence, an illegitimate child had no right to support from her father, and the unmarried father had no right to custody. He also had no obligations under common law.

The 1973 version of the UPA sought to correct this injustice. It provided: "The parent and child relationship extends equally to every child and every parent, regardless of the marital status of the parent."[8] The UPA devoted itself to determining paternity and identifying the child's biological father. Section 15 of the UPA authorized a support determination in a paternity action.

Over the years, the NCCUL dealt with a variety of parentage issues. In 1988, the Commission implemented the Uniform Status of Children of Assisted Conception Act, which established rules governing children conceived by alternative insemination techniques. It addressed birth by biological and surrogate mothers. The NCCUL also implemented the Uniform Putative and Unknown Fathers Act. This allowed for the identification of putative and unknown fathers and the subsequent termination of their parental rights.

In 2000, the NCCUL revised the UPA; it was subsequently amended in 2002 following concerns raised by the American Bar Association. The 1988 Acts are now incorporated into the UPA.

The UPA contains seven articles:

- Art. 2, Parent-Child Relationships;
- Art. 3, Voluntary Acknowledgment of Paternity;
- Art. 4, Registry of Paternity;
- Art. 5, Genetic Testing;
- Art. 6, Proceeding to Adjudicate Parentage;
- Art. 7, Child of Assisted Conception; and
- Art. 8, Gestational Agreement.

Under the 2002 amended UPA, a mother can be the woman who gives birth to the child or the woman determined by a court to be the legal mother or an adoptive mother. A woman who donates her eggs is not considered a legal parent. A legal mother can also be one determined by a gestational agreement. The significance is that the adjudicated mother, adoptive mother, or the mother named in an agreement are not the women who birthed the child.

Under the amended UPA, the legal father may be one of the following:

1) The presumed father married to the birth mother at conception;
2) The presumed father who lived with the child for the first two years of life and treated the child as his own;
3) A man who acknowledged paternity;
4) An adjudicated father following a paternity action;
5) An adoptive father;
6) A man who consents to assisted reproduction; and
7) An adjudicated father under the terms of a gestational agreement.

The first four fathers may be genetically related to the child and the legal father; the last three are not necessarily the child's genetic father but may be considered the child's legal father.

Article 8 of the UPA (2002) deals with gestational agreements. This type of agreement is between a couple and an individual woman who agrees to carry the child for the intended parents. This involves an assisted conception (e.g., *in vitro* fertilization, artificial insemination). The woman who carries the child is not the legal mother. The legal rights, obligations, and responsibilities of the parties are set out in the agreement. Some states that adopted the UPA did not adopt Article 8. Other states do not recognize these agreements. The surrogate's husband must consent to the agreement; otherwise he may have parental rights to the child.

Under the UPA (2002), a court must validate gestational agreements to make them enforceable. A hearing is held to determine the intended parents' qualifications. The surrogate has the right to terminate the agreement and to receive payment for expenses.

The UPA (2002) attempts to reconcile the rights, responsibilities, and obligations of parents against the technical background that exists for conceiving children. The issues are complicated and made more so by technology.

No state has adopted the UPA (2002) in its entirety. All states[9] that adopted the concepts presented in the UPA, either the 1973 or 2002 version, made changes to reflect their individual predilections. Delaware, Texas, and Washington adopted the 2002 version several years ago. North Dakota and Utah adopted that version in 2005. Wyoming adopted it in 2003 and made changes in 2005.

The UPA serves as a model for states to update their parentage laws to stay abreast of the evolving issues of parental rights.

The UPA blends the Uniform Interstate Family Support Act (UIFSA [1996] and UIFSA [2001]) and the Uniform Child Custody Jurisdiction and Enforcement Act (UCCJEA [1997]). Its provisions are consistent with these other Acts.

When dealing with custody or visitation cases, it is imperative that the parties and their lawyers understand how these federal laws affect custody and visitation. Court decisions concerning custody and visitation in one state must be honored in other states. These federal laws are designed to avoid competing jurisdictions and court decisions that can wreak havoc with a child's life.

B. *Miller-Jenkins v. Miller-Jenkins*[10]

The *Miller-Jenkins* case highlights the problems when a custody/visitation order is issued in one state and a sister state refuses to enforce it. The states involved are Vermont (original jurisdiction) and Virginia.

Janet and Lisa were in a committed relationship for five years. They lived together in Hamilton, Virginia, until 2002. In 2002, they entered into a civil union in Vermont. After the birth of their daughter in July 2002, they moved to Vermont because they did not want to raise their child in Virginia. The couple separated in September 2003 and Lisa returned to Virginia with their child.

Lisa initiated legal proceedings in Vermont in November 2003. She sought to dissolve the civil union and obtain a custody and child support determination. Lisa described the child as a biological/adoptive child of the civil union. Vermont recognizes both parties as parents of children born to a same-sex couple involved in a civil union.

The Rutland County Family Court issued a decision in June 2004. The court awarded custody to Lisa and granted Janet visitation with the child in Virginia and Vermont.

Lisa, apparently unhappy with the Vermont decision, filed legal action in circuit court in Frederick County, Virginia, in July 2004. She asked the Virginia court for an order awarding her sole custody and denying Janet visitation and any other parental rights. The Virginia court issued that requested order.

On July 1, 2004, the Virginia Affirmation of Marriage Act[11] took effect. This law prohibits the recognition of out-of-state civil unions. This statute not only prohibits civil unions, it also states that ". . . partnership contract or other arrangement entered into by persons of the same sex in another state or jurisdiction shall be void in all respects in Virginia and any contractual rights created thereby shall be void and unenforceable."

Vermont found Lisa in contempt of court for refusing to comply with its order. In November 2004, the Vermont court awarded Janet all legal rights of any parent of any child born into a marriage.

Janet challenged Virginia's jurisdiction under Virginia, Vermont, and federal law. This includes the UCCJEA and the PKPA. Virginia adopted the UCCJEA[12] and is bound by the provisions of the PKPA as well. Janet's position is that once Vermont took jurisdiction over her child's custody, Virginia could not assert jurisdiction. She also argues that Virginia is required to enforce the Vermont orders.

Lisa selected the original forum for the custody determination. She did so within a month after moving back to Virginia. Her forum shopping exercise is improper under both Virginia and federal law.

But Virginia's Judge Prosser does not see it that way: "[P]ublic policy in Virginia is that civil unions are void in all respects. One could make the argument that nothing has taken place in Vermont that would preclude this court from determining jurisdiction."

Apparently, Judge Prosser is unaware of the provisions of Va. Code Ann. § 20-146.1, *et seq.* The other theory expressed by Judge Prosser is more disturbing. Prosser ruled that Virginia's legislature intended the Affirmation of Marriage Act to overrule the custody laws. He also ruled that the Affirmation of Marriage Act is more powerful than the laws of Virginia, Vermont, and any federal law.

On August 4, 2006, the Vermont Supreme Court issued its decision in the *Miller-Jenkins v. Miller-Jenkins* case.[13] The court held in favor of Janet Miller-Jenkins, the Vermont resident, on all issues. The court stated:

> We conclude the civil union between Lisa and Janet was valid and the family court had jurisdiction to dissolve the union. Further, we decide the family court had exclusive jurisdiction to issue the temporary cus-

tody and visitation order under both the Uniform Child Custody Jurisdiction Act (UCCJA), 15 V.S.A. §§ 1031-1051, and the Parental Kidnapping Protection Act (PKPA), 28 U.S.C. § 1738A (2000). We affirm the family court's determination that Janet is a parent of IMJ, the resulting visitation order, and the order of contempt issued against Lisa for her failure to abide by the visitation order.

Lisa appealed the Vermont decision to the United States Supreme Court. The Court denied her petition for certiorari on April 30, 2007.[14]

On November 28, 2006, the Virginia Court of Appeals rejected Lisa's contentions and held that the Vermont court order is controlling over Virginia law.[15] Lisa petitioned the Virginia Supreme Court to hear her appeal of the appellate decision. The court dismissed her petition on May 8, 2007,[16] and refused her petition for a rehearing on June 22, 2007.

> **Virginia Court of Appeals**
> On November 26, 2006, the Virginia Court of Appeals issued its decision in *Miller-Jenkins v. Miller-Jenkins*. The court held "... [t]hat the trial court erred in failing to recognize that the PKPA barred its exercise of jurisdiction. Accordingly, we vacate the orders of the trial court and remand this case with instruction to grant full faith and credit to the custody and visitation orders of the Vermont court." The court found that Lisa Miller-Jenkins placed herself before the Vermont court by filing her Complaint for Civil Union Dissolution with that court. Since Lisa initiated the Vermont proceeding, she could not deny the jurisdiction of that court. The Virginia court's decision is a solid confirmation that Vermont has jurisdiction and had properly exercised it. The court also came down squarely against any exercise of jurisdiction by Virginia. The court held: "By filing her complaint in Vermont, Lisa invoked the jurisdiction of the Vermont court. She placed herself and the child before that court and laid before it the assertions and prayers that formed the bases of its orders. By operation of the PKPA, her choice of forum precluded the courts of this Commonwealth from entertaining countervailing assertions and prayers."

C. Changing Ways to Become a Parent

Reproductive technology provides a growing number of people with the opportunity to become parents. This technology includes artificial insemination, *in vitro* fertilization, ova and sperm donations, traditional surrogacy, and surrogacy combined with ova donation. These procedures, in addition to adoption, are some of the ways in which gay and lesbian couples become parents.

Gay men are more limited in the resources available to them that would allow them to become parents. They can adopt children, use traditional surrogacy methods, or surrogacy with ova donation. Lesbians may be less apt to use a surrogate because of their ability to bear children.

In traditional surrogacy, the intended father artificially inseminates the surrogate with his sperm. The other type of surrogacy involves an egg and sperm donor. This technique may appeal to gay male couples who want to become parents. One partner donates the sperm, and the other recruits a female relative to donate the ova. This results in both partners being genetically related to the child. The surrogate has the role of gestational host. One advantage of taking this approach is to further restrict any genetic relationship between the gay couple and the surrogate. For example, using an unrelated ova and sperm donor with a surrogate gestational host results in children with no parents by traditional genetic or legal standards.

As reproductive technologies become more advanced, people who might otherwise not have children are becoming parents. Likewise, more people are becoming responsible for children to whom they are unrelated by consanguinity or affinity.

D. Who Is a Parent?

Defining who is a parent is changing with the advances in medical reproductive technologies, adoptions, and the proliferation of family relationships that do not match the heterosexual marriage model. Lesbian and gay couples and their children are in the forefront of developments in this area. They face legal hurdles that do not exist for married or unmarried heterosexual couples with children.

There are significant issues that must be addressed when these couples end their relationships. While the trend toward acknowledging a person as a legal parent without requiring a biological or adoptive connection is growing, there is no universal model.

Courts have slowly begun to recognize that the long-held precedents do not necessarily apply to the changing face of American families. More states and courts are offering legal protections to same-sex couples and the children they are raising.[17]

Some courts are also overturning previous decisions on issues such as second-parent adoptions to conform to advances in legal thought and parenting realities.[18]

Historically, courts have tried to balance a parent's right to raise his or her child with a concern for the child's best interest. In the past, courts awarded custody to the mother, especially when the child involved was of "tender years." The rationale was that young children were best served by being placed with their mothers. That precedent has been replaced, for the most part, with gender-neutral decisions. Courts now look at the child's relationship with the parents and may be less concerned with other factors like lifestyle, religion, and finances.

Still, the laws the courts use to make decisions are based on a heterosexual, married, man-woman/husband-wife model. The issues faced by lesbian and gay parents are different. In most states, there are no laws that allow these couples to formalize their relationships or address the children they are raising. This situation requires them to maneuver through the heterosexual-based legal system and hope the courts cobble together a result that meets the best interests of the children in these alternative family arrangements.

Courts are also wrestling with the concept of non-parents seeking custody and visitation with children following divorce or termination of a relationship. These cases are not limited to same-sex couples. Stepparents and grandparents are also seeking legal determinations of their rights in custody and visitation cases.

In 2000, the United States Supreme Court addressed some of these issues in *Troxel v. Granville*.[19] This comment by Justice O'Connor is oft repeated to confirm the changes in American families: "The demographic changes of the past century make it difficult to speak of an average American family. The composition of families varies greatly from household to household."[20]

In *Troxel*, the Court affirmed a Washington state Supreme Court decision that the Washington state law[21] permitting "any person" to seek visitation rights with children is unconstitutional. The Washington court held, *inter alia,* that section 26.10.160(3) unconstitutionally infringes on parents' fundamental right to rear their children. Still, the court could not completely agree on the outcome of this case, or the reasons for it. That is evident from the varying opinions issued by the Justices.

Justices O'Connor, Rehnquist, Ginsburg, and Breyer concluded that section 26.10.160(3), as applied to Granville and her family, violated her due process right to make decisions concerning the care, custody, and control of her daughters. Justices Souter and Thomas filed concurring opinions. Justices Kennedy, Stevens, and Scalia filed dissenting opinions.

The Court recognized the changes in American families, but also found the Washington state law to be overbroad in permitting interference with parental decisions. Since that decision, states have dealt with requests by relatives and non-relatives seeking visitation with children when the parents object.

Yet, courts around the country are recognizing that a child's best interests are well served by continuing a parent-child relationship between a non-legal parent and the child. This is particularly true when the child's legal parent encourages the development of such a relationship.

Defining who is a parent for purposes of custody and visitation is necessary to protect parent-child relationships and to meet the child's best interests. One party in a gay or lesbian relationship may not be considered the child's legal parent, and that interferes in custody and visitation cases. Not all states permit second-parent or joint adoptions, and artificial reproduction techniques often result in only one partner being the legal parent. This prevents the non-adoptive or biological parent from achieving a legal parent-child status.

Courts are developing a body of case law addressing the rights of the non-legal parent. These persons are classified as "de facto" parents, "psychological" parents, or acting *in loco parentis*.[22]

Some states have case law that prevents courts from recognizing a non-legal parent. In 1991, New York's highest court issued its decision in *Alison D. v. Virginia M.*[23] The court held that a lesbian co-parent lacks standing to petition for visitation rights. The court cited New York's Domestic Relations Law in denying Alison any rights because she did not fall within the meaning of "either parent" under the law. The majority wrote, "[T]raditionally, in this State, it is the child's mother and father who, assuming fitness, have the right to the care and custody of their child, even in situations where the non-parent has exercised some control over the child with the parents' consent."[24] The court determined it had no authority to make an exception without legislative action.

Wisconsin's Supreme Court took a similar tack in 1991.[25] But the court reversed itself in 1995 when it issued the decision in *In re Custody of H.S.H.-K.*[26]

In the former case, the court held that a lesbian co-parent could not seek parental rights because she had no standing to do so. Four years later, the court reversed itself and held that the lesbian former partner could seek visitation under the court's equitable authority. The court applied the "best interests standard" in the case. The former partner lacked standing under the state's marital laws, but could obtain standing by proving the existence of a parent-child relationship.

The court concluded that the circuit court had "equitable power to hear a petition for visitation when it determines that the petitioner has a parent-like relationship with the child and that a significant triggering event justifies state intervention in the child's relationship with a biological or adoptive parent."

In its decision, the Wisconsin Supreme Court created a four-prong test a petitioner must meet to establish a parent-child relationship. This test is similar to those adopted by other state courts in similar situations.

To demonstrate the existence of the petitioner's parent-like relationship with the child, the petitioner must prove four elements: (1) that the biological or adoptive parent consented to, and fostered, the petitioner's formation and establishment of a parent-like relationship with the child; (2) that the petitioner and the child lived together in the same household; (3) that the petitioner assumed obligations of parenthood by taking significant responsibility for the child's care, education and development, including contributing towards the child's support, without expectation of financial compensation; and (4) that the petitioner has been in a parental role for a length of time sufficient to have established with the child a bonded, dependent relationship parental in nature.[27]

The court also stated:

To establish a significant triggering event justifying state intervention in the child's relationship with a biological or adoptive parent, the petitioner must prove that this parent has interfered substantially with the petitioner's parent-like relationship with the child, and that the petitioner sought court-ordered visitation within a reasonable time after the parent's interference. The petitioner must prove all these elements before a circuit court may consider whether visitation is in the best interest of the child.[28]

This case did not recognize the petitioner as a "parent" but did allow her to petition for visitation rights.

In 2000, the New Jersey Supreme Court established a test, based on the Wisconsin case, to determine who is a "psychological parent." According to the New Jersey court, "the legal parent must consent to and foster the relationship between the third party and the child; the third party must have lived with the child; the third party must perform parental functions for the child to a significant degree; and most important, a parent-child bond must be forged."[29]

The petitioner met the requirements and obtained a visitation order.

The supreme courts in Massachusetts, Rhode Island, Pennsylvania, and Maine and an appellate court in New Mexico issued similar decisions.[30]

Under the Pennsylvania case, the court defined *in loco parentis* as "a person who puts oneself in the situation of a lawful parent by assuming the obligations incident to the parental relationship without going through the formality of a legal adoption."[31] The court also found that the rights and liabilities from an *in loco parentis* relationship are the same as between parent and child.[32] On remand, the court granted visitation.

This case is interesting on several fronts. The Pennsylvania Supreme Court declared T.B. the child's co-parent in 2001[33] and remanded the case to the trial court for a decision on visitation. The hearing officer determined that T.B. was fit to exercise partial custody and visitation. L.R.M. appealed that decision to the trial court. The trial court agreed with the hearing officer but also found that L.R.M. through "carefully calculated efforts successfully alienated the child against T.B." The trial court then ruled, "Because of [L.R.M.'s] persistent attitude and conduct, I can envision nothing but emotional and psychological turmoil for the child if the visits were to be forced, even in a 'therapeutic setting,' as recommended. . . . [L.R.M.] would, I believe, continue her efforts to thwart visitation if . . . ordered. . . . [M]y concern for the child's well-being will not permit me to order visits. I believe it would be to the child's benefit to have a relationship with [T.B.], but only if [L.R.M.] discontinued her efforts to thwart that relationship, which will obviously not happen."[34] The trial judge then vacated the visitation order and T.B. appealed. By this time, T.B. had not seen the child in eight years, despite being awarded visitation in 1997 and 2004.

In footnote 5 of the majority opinion, Judge Joyce wrote:

> It is inconceivable that an embittered spouse who successfully estranges the children from the other spouse, to the point where the other spouse is unknown to the children, should be rewarded by a determination that it shall be in the best interest of the children not to have any relationship at all with the alienated spouse because of the custodial parent's feelings. The preposterousness of this scenario is equally applicable to the case at bar, despite Appellant's non-traditional status.

In June 2006, the Kentucky Supreme Court issued a decision finding that a lesbian former partner did not qualify as a "de facto custodian" as defined by a state statute.[35] In that case, the parties were involved in an eight-year relationship. During the relationship, they decided to adopt. T.D. was the adoptive parent. The couple did not know if Kentucky permitted joint adoption. The couple ended their relationship when the child was six years old. T.D. and B.F. did not execute any documents recognizing B.F. as the child's guardian or custodian. B.F. asserted that she is, in fact, a de facto custodian. The trial court, however, determined that she did not meet the statutory requirements for de facto custodians. The Kentucky Court of Appeals affirmed that decision, and B.F. appealed to the Supreme Court.

Kentucky law[36] defines "de facto custodian" as "a person who has been shown by clear and convincing evidence to have been the primary caregiver for, and financial supporter of, a child who has resided with the person for a period of . . . one (1) year or more if the child is three (3) years of age."

At every level, Kentucky courts determined that B.F. did not meet the requirements set forth in the statute. The evidence showed that T.D. was the child's primary caregiver. Since there can only be one primary caregiver, B.F. did not qualify as a de facto guardian.

One odd part of this case involved verbal assurances given to B.F. by the trial court that she could raise common-law custody issues. Even though the court gave these assurances, it subsequently refused to hear any additional arguments and dismissed the case. The trial judge acknowledged its promise but determined that since B.F. failed to qualify as a de facto custodian, she lacked standing to raise any other claims.

The high court also noted that Kentucky law is more restrictive about who may attain standing in custody cases.[37] In Kentucky, the state's statutes control custody standing.[38]

Despite the significant parent-child relationship, the court held she had no legal right to visitation.

The decision in *Carvin v. Britain* out of Washington[39] is significant for several reasons. First, the Washington Supreme Court took great pains in defining "*in loco parentis,*" "psychological parent," and "de facto parent." Second, the court invoked its equitable authority to issue a decision that did not fit neatly into any state statute. Third, the court recognized the changing realities of families in America. Last, the United States Supreme Court declined certiorari in this case without comment. Whether the Court declined because the issue was not important enough or because it is continuing a course of not reviewing cases involving gay litigants is unknown. What is known is that the Washington Supreme Court's decision in the *Carvin* case is final.

The Washington Supreme Court adopted, in a footnote, the following definitions of parents in an attempt to resolve the confusion that exists. Practitioners representing lesbian and gay families will find these definitions helpful.

For purposes of our review, we adopt the following general definitions:

- *In loco parentis:* Latin for "'in the place of a parent," this term is temporary by definition and ceases on withdrawal of consent by the legal parent or parents. While some legal responsibility often attaches to such a relationship, Washington courts and statutes have never considered the same actual parents or akin to actual parents. (Cites omitted.)

- *Psychological parent:* Psychological parent is a term created primarily by social scientists but commonly used in legal opinions and commentaries to describe a parent-like relationship which is "based . . . on [the] day-to-day interaction, companionship, and shared experiences" of the child and adult. As such, it may define a biological parent, stepparent, or other person unrelated to the child. A person who, on a continuing and regular basis, provides for a child's emotional and physical needs. In Washington, psychological parents may have claims and standing above other third parties, but those interests typically yield in the face of the rights and interests of a child's legal parents. Courts have, nevertheless, recognized and relied on a person's characterization as a "psychological parent" in supporting their decisions. (Cites omitted.)

- *De facto parent:* Literally meaning "parent in fact," it is juxtaposed with a legally recognized parent . . . defining de facto as "[a]ctual; existing in fact; having effect even though not formally or legally recognized." We are asked in this case to define the parameters of this term and in doing so, find that it describes an individual who, in all respects, functions as a child's actual parent, meeting the criteria suggested herein. (Cites omitted.)[40]

In discussing the case, the Washington Supreme Court stated, "Our legislature has been conspicuously silent when it comes to the rights of children like L.B., who are born into nontraditional families, including any interests they may have in maintaining their relationships with the members of the family unit in which they are raised."

The court adopted the test set forth by the Wisconsin Supreme Court in 1995:[41]

To establish standing as a de facto parent we adopt the following criteria, delineated by the Wisconsin Supreme Court and set forth in the Court of Appeals opinion below: (1) the natural or legal parent consented to and fostered the parent-like relationship, (2) the petitioner and the child lived together in the same household, (3) the petitioner assumed obligations of parenthood without expectation of financial compensation, and (4) the petitioner has been in a parental role for a length of time sufficient to have established with the child a bonded, dependent relationship, parental in nature.

The court also held that "[a] de facto parent is not entitled to any parental privileges as a matter of right, but only as is determined to be in the best interests of the child at the center of any such dispute."

In addition to the categories of parents defined in the Washington case, the American Law Institute (ALI) describes a new category: "parents by estoppel." According to the ALI's 2002 publication, *Principles of the Law of Family Dissolution: Analysis and Recommendations*,[42] "parents by estoppel" are "afforded all of the privileges of a legal parent." This would include having standing to bring an action for custody or visitation. A person can be deemed a "parent by estoppel" by meeting many of the requirements established for de facto and psychological parents. These include living with the child, accepting full parental responsibilities, and having a co-parenting agreement with the legal parent.[43] The child's best interests also come into play, as they should.

A 2006 Massachusetts case reflects what happens to parenting rights when a state formally recognizes same-sex relationships. The case is *A.H. v. M.P.*[44] The case involved an attempt by the birth mother's former partner to establish her parental rights. She based her case on the concepts of "parent by estoppel" and "judicial estoppel." It is important to note that this case, and the couple's relationship, predates the Massachusetts Supreme Judicial Court decision establishing same-sex marriage.

The women began their relationship in 1995. In 1998, they joined in the purchase of a house. The couple discussed starting a family and, according to the evidence, both women intended to bear a child. In 2000, M.P. initiated fertility treatment at a Boston facility. M.P. and A.H. completed paperwork listing themselves as "Parent 1" and "Parent 2," respectively. Their son was born in January 2001. Shortly after the birth, the couple discussed a second-parent adoption with an attorney. M.P. completed all the necessary paperwork immediately. A.H. did nothing. Over the next few years, M.P. tried to get A.H. to sign the paperwork. A.H. considered these constant requests comparable with "nagging" and refused to comply. A.H. testified at trial that she considered the adoption paperwork to be a mere "formality" that would be necessary only in a "worst-case scenario."

After the child's birth, M.P. became a stay-at-home mom and A.H. took a three-month maternity leave—a leave that actually lasted only two months. During those two months, A.H. contributed to the child's caretaking, but M.P. did so as well and was the "final arbiter" concerning the child's care. Following the birth, A.H. attempted to reduce her workload, but financial problems at her nonprofit agency required her full-time attention. A.H. also found time to train for and complete triathlons and a half-marathon. The judge in the case was not impressed with A.H.'s extracurricular activities.

Less than a year after the child's birth, A.H. asked M.P. to return to work. They hired a nanny to care for their son and M.P. began working part-time from home. All of these plans were for naught. When the couple separated in April 2003, their son was 18 months old. A.H. had never signed the paperwork to complete the second-parent adoption. M.P. destroyed the adoption papers and three years of litigation began.

A.H. filed a complaint in July 2003 seeking joint legal and physical custody, visitation, recognition as the child's "de facto parent," custodial rights and a child support order. M.P. also sought child support and a formal visitation schedule. M.P.'s request was granted in 2003.

The trial judge assigned two guardians ad litem to investigate whether the child's best interests would be served by continuing contact with A.H. The judge did not instruct the guardians to look into the custody issue.

In 2004, M.P. filed a motion to vacate the child support order. The court granted that motion in 2005 following the reasoning in *T.F. v. G.L.*[45] In that case, the Massachusetts Supreme Judicial Court refused to impose a child support order on the former same-sex partner who was neither the biological nor adoptive parent of the child. Following the trial court's decision, M.P. returned $9,000 in support payments to A.H.

The case went to trial in July 2006. The trial judge dismissed all of A.H.'s claims and awarded sole legal and physical custody to M.P. The judge ruled that A.H. failed to prove that she had achieved "de facto parent" status during the relationship. The judge based her decision on several findings. Primary among these was that the child's best interests would not be served by allowing visitation with A.H. The judge also decided that the child would not suffer irreparable damage by not having visitation.

As expected, A.H. appealed to the Massachusetts Appeals Court. That court upheld the trial court's decision. On transfer to the Supreme Judicial Court, the chief justice noted that the issues presented were matters of first impression for the court.

The court declined to "[e]rase the distinction between biological and adoptive parents . . . and de facto parents . . . and to apply estoppel principles to intrude into the private realm of an autonomous, if non-intact, family in which the child's bests interests are appropriately taken into consideration."

On the issue of "parent by estoppel,"[46] the court cited the ALI Principles concerning that concept. Those principles contemplate "parent by estoppel" only in those jurisdictions where adoption is either not possible or legally unavailable.[47] A formal co-parenting agreement is crucial in attempts to invoke the "parent by estoppel" concept. The Massachusetts Supreme Judicial Court held that this principle is ". . . [a] most dramatic intrusion into the rights of fit parents to care for their child as they see fit." The court cited *Troxel v. Granville*[48] in support of its position. Massachusetts does not recognize parenthood by contract and refused to adopt an estoppel theory to support A.H.'s claim.

This case is important, because the court recognized that non-biological parents have the right to adopt their partner's child. Since A.H. refused to do so, she could come to the court later and seek an equitable resolution to the matter over M.P.'s objections. The case also points out how difficult it is for the non-biological parent to qualify under the ALI Principles, given their emphasis on caretaking. Non-biological parents who are the family's primary breadwinner are at a distinct disadvantage in qualifying for parental rights. This is true even though fathers in heterosexual households historically have qualified under similar circumstances.

Same-sex couples must finalize adoptions, in states that permit them, in order to preserve the parental rights of the non-biological or non-adoptive parent. If a state permits same-sex couples to adopt or enter into legally recognized relationships, it is imperative they take advantage of those advances. Failure to do so will place them in the same position as unmarried heterosexual couples. And is that not what the LGBT community is seeking?

In states that do no recognize second-parent adoptions, a written co-parenting agreement addressing all pertinent issues, including the parties' intent to raise the children together, is essential. While parenthood by contract may not be recognized, a co-parenting agreement will establish the parties' intentions concerning the children. Most important, it will establish the intent of the biological or adoptive parent to raise the child with his or her partner. This is the type of paper trail same-sex couples must establish to protect their individual and joint rights.

E. Co-parenting Agreements

One way to establish that a couple is serious about their parenting responsibilities is to draft and execute a co-parenting agreement (also called a shared parenting agreement) (see Appendix). Attorneys representing the couple need to know, and communicate to clients, that while these agreements may not be enforceable in court, they are very important documents. These are largely uncharted waters for lesbian and gay parents. While the legal consensus on these matters is improving, there are still far too many states that seek to declare lesbian and gay families to be against public policy.

For practitioners, it is most important to include a clause reflecting the parents' intentions about the agreement. This language will assist the non-legal parent if the couple ends their relationship and that partner wants to enforce the agreement.

The agreement should discuss the parties' process in arriving at the decision to become parents. The legal parent's decision to include her partner in raising the child is an important part of the agreement.

The Delaware Supreme Court found the agreement dispositive when a legal parent objected to her former partner's attempt to maintain the parent-child relationship.[49] The court held that the biological mother's actions precluded her challenging her former partner's status as a parent. These actions also included the biological mother's decision to seek, receive, and accept child support. The couple also executed a parenting agreement. The court found that the biological mother's receipt of benefits under the agreement estops her from challenging her former partner's standing.

The key to a co-parenting agreement is the child's best interest. This is not about the adults involved; it is about the child.

Courts, from the United States Supreme Court on down, have made custody decisions in gay and lesbian parent cases dependent upon the legal parent's constitutional right to be free of unwarranted government interference.[50] These decisions make it necessary for any co-parenting agreement to include a waiver of those rights. The decisions are premised on the historically based heterosexual concept of family and parenting. The laws have not kept pace with the changes in family form or substance.

A specific clause reflecting the legal parent's intent to waive any constitutional rights to unfettered access to her children may be used later should a court try to thwart a co-parent's attempt to maintain the parent-child relationship.

But in *Wakeman v. Dixon*, the Florida court refused to consider that the legal parent had voluntarily waived her constitutional rights when voiding the parenting agreement signed by both parties. For practitioners, it is important to include a reference to both the state and federal constitutions when including this waiver.

Practice Tip

Consider including the following provisions in the parenting agreement:
1. Appointment of the non-legal parent as the child's co-parent.
2. Intent of the parties to raise the child jointly, to financially support the child together, and to jointly provide for the child's emotional, psychological, and physical needs; and for custody, visitation, and support if the couple ends their relationship.

3. Non-legal parent's authority to approve medical treatment for the child. A separate Power of Attorney for Medical Treatment of a Minor is another format. These agreements can include co-parenting clauses that provide for the care of the child.
4. The biological/adoptive parent acknowledges and waives any constitutional parental rights.
5. A clause acknowledging the detrimental effect on the child of denial of continued access to the non-biological/non-adoptive parent.
6. Acknowledgment by the legal parent that he/she encourages and fosters a parent-child relationship between the other partner and the child and believes it is in the child's best interests to have a relationship with the other parent.
7. The legal parent consents to adoption by his/her partner if it becomes available.
8. List the people who should not visit with the child.
9. If the family includes multiple children with different biological/adoptive parents, acknowledge the harm to the other children if they are separated or prevented from maintaining a relationship.
10. The non-biological/adoptive parent acknowledges her/his obligations to support the child and maintain the parent-child relationship.
11. Provide for resolution of any disputes concerning visitation or child support through mediation rather than litigation.
12. Guardianship clause: interim and testamentary. Include alternate guardians. This provides that a guardian is immediately appointed for the child if the legal parent dies.
13. Include Health Insurance Portability and Accountability Act (HIPAA) language.
14. Express who the child should not be placed with—for example, grandparents who disapprove of the legal parent's same-sex relationship.

Include a provision in the legal parent's will clearly stating her position concerning parental rights. Consider the importance of such a provision when naming the co-parent as the child's prospective guardian.

> **Practice Tip**
>
> Practitioners may add a provision stating that any future domestic partnership registration or civil union is considered a "marriage" for purposes of interpretation. The clause could also reflect the parties' intentions to have their relationship perceived to comply with future changes in the law as if they formalized it themselves.

There is a concern within the LGBT legal community that using the word "partner," "committed relationship," or similar terms may violate a state's constitutional amendment banning same-sex marriage. Unless the state of residence permits same-sex marriage, the term "marriage" must not be used. It has legal significance and could complicate the administration of an estate.

Given the language being included in state constitutional amendments, using the word "marriage" may violate these amendments. An argument could be made that the word seeks to give the parties' relationship the look of a marriage and that is against the state's strong public policy. These mini-DOMAs and constitutional amendments are new and have not yet been subjected to judicial review. Whether the language in these laws will be applied to individual legal documents, including wills, is unknown. Practitioners must be wary of these amendments and mini-DOMAs.

> **Practice Tip**
>
> When representing a lesbian or gay client in a heterosexual divorce, delete the cohabitation prohibition. This may prevent a future controversy should the former spouse enter into a same-sex relationship. Deleting this clause may affect spousal support provisions. This reflects the importance of understanding clients and their underlying issues.

This action would have prevented the result in *Burns v. Burns*.[51] In that case, the parties divorced in December 1995. The Georgia court awarded the husband custody and the wife visitation. A modification of the original order included a cohabitation provision. The mother entered into a civil union in Vermont in July 2000. The father filed a contempt motion alleging violation of the court's order prohibiting cohabitation.

The trial court ruled that a civil union was not a marriage because Vermont law does not bestow the status of civil marriage on civil unions. Under Georgia's mini-DOMA[52] there are no contractual rights, and no Georgia court has jurisdiction to rule on any rights arising out of or in connection with that type of relationship.

The appellate court, in reviewing the modified order, held, "If Susan wanted to ensure that her civil union would be recognized in the same manner as a marriage, she should have included language to that effect in the consent decree itself."[53]

Of course, that raises the issue of whether the court could recognize a civil union, considering the restrictions under Georgia law. In any case, the court upheld the order limiting visitation as valid and enforceable.

Another area that must be covered in these agreements deals with the parties' intent concerning the financial support of the child. Where one parent is more financially stable than the other, this may have enormous importance in the future. Financial inequity may adversely affect the children involved if the issue is not adequately addressed in the agreement. Further, by addressing these issues, the parties are expressing their intentions concerning the child they intend to jointly parent.

Intent is a major component of any co-parenting agreement. Having the legal parent express the intention to co-parent helps establish the future rights of the non-legal co-parent. Fostering the relationship between the non-legal co-parent and the child, and expressing the intent to do so, may limit the legal parent's ability to contest a former partner's action to enforce the agreement.

Attorneys drafting these agreements for lesbian and gay clients must consider the current state of law in their respective states as well as around the country. Clients must be fully informed that these agreements may not be enforced. When agreements are first drafted, couples are not considering the end of their relationship. But because a lawyer's obligation is to consider what might happen, and this is a contract, it is wise to cover all bases. All lawyers know that any contract may be challenged. This is also true where co-parenting agreements are concerned and the parties no longer like each other. The underlying basis of the agreement is, however, to ensure that the child's best interest, health, welfare, and safety are protected.

F. Same-Sex Parenting Case Law

The following cases are not inclusive of the evolving body of case law on this subject. The cases noted are intended to help practitioners focus on what courts have held thus far. Additional research is required to present an adequate argument in the lawyer's forum state.

All 50 states have visitation statutes relating to non-parents. Lawyers may refer to *Troxel v. Granville*[54] for a list of these statutes.

1. Colorado

In 2004, the Colorado Court of Appeals applied a strict scrutiny analysis to determine if infringement of the adoptive parent's due process rights was warranted.[55]

The Colorado case involved a lesbian couple, together for years, who decided to adopt a child from China. After the adoption, they obtained a court order awarding joint custody of the child to both women. Later, the adoptive mother petitioned to change the child's name to include the co-parent. Their relationship ended a few years later. The trial court found that the relationship ended because the adoptive mother, Cheryl Clark, objected to the close relationship between her partner, Elsey McLeod, and the child. The women were granted joint custody of the child.

The adoptive mother took the child and gradually reduced visitation, with the intent to end it altogether. Clark had apparently become a devout Christian, and McLeod worried about anti-gay religious rhetoric.

Clark challenged the validity of the joint custody order. She convinced a magistrate that the order was void because the court lacked jurisdiction. The trial judge determined that the joint custody order was valid and awarded joint parental responsibility to McLeod and Clark. But the court provided that Clark would have sole responsibility for religion and dental care. The court ordered Clark to refrain from exposing the child to any "homophobic" teachings. Clark appealed.

A three-judge panel heard the appeal. *The court decided that legal parents have a fundamental right concerning decisions and control of their children.* There must be a compelling state interest before there could be circumvention of that right. The panel found that McLeod's deep bond with the child presented the basis for such a compelling interest. The state is concerned with avoiding psychological or physical harm to children.

The panel also found a long history in Colorado of finding that terminating a child's contact with a "psychological parent" may significantly harm the child. The panel affirmed the joint parenting order.

But the court did not stop there. The appellate court was troubled by the "homophobic" restriction placed on Clark. There was no evidence in the record to support the restriction. The court remanded the case to the trial court with instructions for additional fact-finding before issuing a final decision.

2. West Virginia

West Virginia's Supreme Court weighed in on the concept of "psychological parent" in *In re Clifford K.*[56] This case involves the death of the biological mother and the successful attempt by her surviving partner to be named the child's parent.

In 2002, Christina, the child's mother, and her partner, Tina, were involved in an automobile accident. Christina was killed. While Tina was recovering from injuries suffered in the crash, the child's maternal grandfather assumed physical custody of the couple's son, Z.B.S., and then was named the boy's guardian.

Clifford K. had assisted the couple in producing their son. After his birth in December 1999, he resided with Christina and Tina in their home.

Clifford and Tina filed a joint petition for custody of the boy. Following a hearing, Tina and Clifford were granted visitation and Paul S., the grandfather, was awarded custody. After psychological evaluations, the court determined that Tina had standing to seek custody as the child's "psychological parent." The Family Court then awarded Tina primary custody of her son based on her status as the child's second parent. The grandfather appealed to the Circuit Court, which reversed the custody award. The Circuit Court also found that Tina did not have legal standing to seek custody because she was not the child's legal parent. The court awarded custody to Paul S. and visitation to Tina. On remand, the Family Court awarded primary custody to Clifford K. as the child's biological father and gave visitation to Paul S. and Tina. Paul appealed, and the Circuit Court again reversed the Family Court. It ordered the Family Court to determine custody between Clifford and Paul, advising that Tina had no standing in the matter. But wait, it's not over!

While this was going on, Tina appealed to the West Virginia Supreme Court from the First Order of Remand issued in 2003. That one directed the Family Court to determine custody between Clifford and Paul. The Supreme Court granted the petition, stayed the Circuit Court's December 2003 and May 2004 orders, and reinstated the Family Court's July 2003 order awarding primary custody to Tina. No one said these cases were easy.

The only issue before the West Virginia Supreme Court is whether Tina is authorized by statute to seek custody of her son. On the issue of determining whether a person is a child's psychological parent, the court stated:

> [we] find that the most crucial components of the psychological parent concept are the formation of a significant relationship between a child and an adult who may be, but is not required to be, related to the child biologically or adoptively.

. . . Accordingly, we hold that a psychological parent is a person who, on a continuing day-to-day basis, through interaction, companionship, interplay, and mutuality, fulfills a child's psychological and physical needs for a parent and provides for the child's emotional and financial support. The psychological parent may be a biological, adoptive, or foster parent, or any other person. The resulting relationship between the psychological parent and the child must be of substantial, not temporary, duration and must have begun with the consent and encouragement of the child's legal parent or guardian. (Cites and footnotes omitted.)[57]

The court also stated that this decision does not mean that the existence of a psychological parent relationship automatically permits intervention by that parent in a custody proceeding. The court held:

In the law concerning custody of minor children, no rule is more firmly established than that the right of a natural parent to the custody of his or her infant child is paramount to that of any other person; it is a fundamental personal liberty protected and guaranteed by the Due Process Clauses of the West Virginia and United States Constitutions.[58]

3. New Jersey
Heading north to New Jersey, the Essex County Superior Court decided that a lesbian co-parent, in a recognized domestic partnership, is a legal parent and entitled to have her name listed on the child's birth certificate.[59] Kimberly Robinson and Jeanne LoCicero registered as domestic partners in 2003 while living in Brooklyn, New York. In 2004, they married in Niagara Falls, Ontario, Canada. Following their wedding, they moved to Essex County, New Jersey, where they bought a house.

The couple decided to start a family and that Kimberly should be the birth mother. Kimberly became pregnant following artificial insemination with sperm from an anonymous donor. When she was eight months pregnant, the couple filed a petition to have both of them declared the child's legal parents.

The couple wanted to use New Jersey's statute concerning artificial insemination that provides for the husband of a woman inseminated with donor sperm to be considered the legal father. They argued that the statute should be construed in gender-neutral terms, should recognize their domestic partnership, and should declare Jeanne a legal parent.

New Jersey permits second-parent adoptions. It also recognizes domestic partnerships entered into outside of New Jersey.

The couple did not want to pursue an adoption because of the time and expense involved. They were concerned that their child would be adversely affected by any delay in a determination of their joint legal parental status. Their case raised Equal Protection constitutional issues, as they claimed that refusal to grant their request would deny their child the rights and privileges that accrue to similarly situated children of heterosexual parents.

The judge referred to New Jersey's long-standing policy of emphasizing the child's best interests. The judge found that although the New Jersey Domestic Partnership law is distinct from marriage, there is no reason for it to "preempt or diminish any rights that may be available through the Artificial Insemination statute."

While their Canadian marriage is not yet recognized in New Jersey, it did reflect their commitment to each other and the relationship.

The judge ruled, "The Court is unable to discern any State's interest that would preclude LoCicero from the protection of the statute. We have a child born within the context of a marriage with two spouses, the non-birth mother wishes to have legal responsibility; the State, as a threshold matter, would not have the responsibility for the care of the child."

The court declared Jeanne LoCicero to be Vivian's parent and made the decision retroactive to April 30, 2005, so the child would have two legal parents from the date of birth.

This case reflects creative lawyering at its best. It also reflects a determination by a state court judge to decide what is truly in a child's best interest. Courts repeatedly state that a child is best served with two parents. This New Jersey judge brings that theory into reality.

Lesbian and gay parents also face the prospect of losing custody of children from a prior heterosexual marriage. A gay or lesbian parent's sexual orientation is often used in an attempt to prejudice a court in custody cases. But discrimination based on a parent's sexual orientation is happening less frequently. Most courts admit, that absent any evidence of adverse impact on the child, a parent's sexual orientation is irrelevant.

4. Tennessee

A Tennessee appellate court made that position known when reversing a lower court's decision in a custody case.[60]

Christy and Lester married in 1996, a month after birth of their son, Stephen. The couple filed for divorce in 2000. The court awarded the couple joint custody of Stephen, with Christy as the primary caretaker. Christy informed Lester that she was a lesbian. Lester remarried in 2001, after which he underwent a religious conversion. He then decided that it was wrong for Stephen to live with Christy. He filed his custody action in 2004.

The chancellor issued a decision in June 2004 changing custody to Lester. The chancellor based his decision on "the mother's sexual preference, her 'openly gay lifestyle' and the child's exposure to that lifestyle." He did not find any demonstrable harm to the child but claimed that "undoubtedly he will have to deal with his mother's sexuality and the controversy associated with that sexuality as he matures."

Christy appealed, and the appellate court reversed. The court cited *In re Parsons*[61] as precedent. That decision held that a parent's sexual orientation "does not control the outcome of the case absent evidence of its adverse effect on the child." There was nothing in the lower court's decision reflecting such adverse impact. The appellate court reversed and remanded the case with instructions that the 2001 joint custody agreement controls the situation.

5. Pennsylvania

Pennsylvania's Superior Court affirmed a lower court ruling awarding custody to the former lesbian partner of the children's mother.[62] The court decided that the children's best interest outweighed their maternal ties. The former partner developed a strong connection to the two children. Their mother engaged in a pattern of conduct that convinced the court she was unfit to have custody of her children.

Patricia Jones and Ellen Boring Jones began their relationship in 1988. Ellen gave birth, following artificial insemination, to twin boys in 1996. The couple separated in 2001. Ellen filed a support action against Patricia but also tried to eliminate contact between Patricia and the boys.

The traditional approach in Pennsylvania in disputes between biological parents and legal strangers is to favor the parents. A parent's rights would be infringed only upon a showing of unfitness. The Quaker State has evolved over the years and has departed from this traditional stance in cases involving stepparents. In the *Jones* case, the court was prepared to extend these considerations to same-sex couples.[63]

Pennsylvania courts adopted an *in loco parentis* standard for persons who have bonded with a child and established a close parent-child relationship. Those persons could petition for custody of that child without proving the biological parent unfit. The burden is on the "intended parent" to prove by clear and convincing evidence.

Patricia proved, to the court's satisfaction, that the children's interests were best served by awarding her custody.

The court's decision to treat same-sex partners in the same way as stepparents is a huge step forward. It further chips away at the reluctance of courts to view gay and lesbian families as just families.

6. California

A triumvirate of California cases rounds out this chapter. On August 22, 2005, the California Supreme Court issued three cases that significantly changed the status quo in that state. They are: *Elisa B. v. Superior Court*,[64] *K.M. v. E.G.*,[65] and *Kristine J. v. Lisa R.*.[66] The Supreme Court also instructed its official reporter as to the sequence in which the cases were to be issued. They are listed in that order here.

All three cases deal with family issues and lesbian couples. All three decisions came down squarely in favor of recognizing these family relationships.

In *Elisa B. v. Superior Court*, the court ruled that a lesbian parent, not biologically related to the child, is liable for child support. Elisa and her former partner started a family. Through artificial insemination, Elisa's partner gave birth to twin boys. One of the twins has Down's Syndrome and requires medical care.

After the couple separated, Elisa continued to support the twins. Although she never adopted the children, she undertook this responsibility. After Elisa lost her job, she stopped providing any financial support for the boys. The birth mother, Emily, was forced to apply for public assistance. The county then turned to Elisa for contributions.

The trial judge found that Elisa was a co-parent and responsible for supporting the children. He also found that Elisa and Emily intended to become parents and to raise the children jointly. The appellate court reversed. The supreme court reinstated the trial court decision. The court, citing the Uniform Parentage Act, decided that both women intended to become parents; the children born could have two mothers and California law presumes both parties to be parents to children born during the relationship.

"Having helped cause the children to be born, and having raised them as her own, Elisa shall not be permitted to later abandon the twins simply because her relationship with Emily dissolved."[67]

K.M. v. E.G. involves a complex set of facts. This lesbian couple also decided to start a family. K.M. donated her ova to her partner, who did not produce enough eggs to succeed in becoming pregnant. E.G. then became pregnant and delivered twins in December 1995. Only E.G. was listed on the birth certificate.

The couple raised the children together until their relationship ended in 2001. K.M. then filed legal action to establish her parental rights.

The court record reflects the parties' agreement that K.M. would not reveal her genetic connection with the children. E.G. claimed she never intended to jointly raise the children with her partner. K.M., on the other hand, stated she only donated her ova because she understood they would raise the children jointly.

One key aspect of this case lies in the donor agreement K.M. signed. The standard donor agreement contained a waiver of all parental rights. Based on this, the trial judge dismissed the case and the appeals court affirmed the dismissal.

The Supreme Court, however, disagreed, finding that a preconception waiver could not determine the outcome of this particular case. The lower courts believed the California sperm donor statutes applied to K.M. The Supreme Court held the sperm donor analogy did not apply, "under the circumstances of this case in which K.M. supplied ova to impregnate her lesbian partner in order to produce children who would be raised in their joint home." The court focused on the biological connection between K.M. and the twins. Also, anonymous sperm donors do not intend to become parents of the children that may result from their donation. They, unlike the parties in this case, make their deposit and take their leave.

This case has caused dissent in the lesbian and gay community. Some think, as did the dissenting Justice, that the case creates a "lesbian exception" to the sperm donor statute. Another concern arises from K.M.'s statement that she received the donor agreement just minutes before the procedure. E.G. claims the papers were given to K.M. long before the procedure date.

Either way, whatever the parties actually intended, the Supreme Court has held that K.M. has parental rights even over E.G.'s objections.

The last case in this trilogy is *Kristin H. v. Lisa R.* The couple sought and obtained a pre-birth stipulated judgment decreeing that they were both legal parents of the forthcoming child. They used the judgment to put both names on the birth certificate and establish parentage from the date of birth.

As with the other two cases, the women ended their relationship two years after the child's birth. Kristin filed legal action to have the declaration deemed invalid and to terminate her former partner's parental rights. The trial judge denied the motion. The court of appeals reversed, holding the trial judge could not accept "the parties' stipulation as the basis for entering the judgment of parentage." The court believed that parentage is a legal issued to be decided by the court and not by the prospective parents.

This decision created great fear around the state of California that it would invalidate thousands of adoptions and parental rights determinations.

California Supreme Court Justice Moreno, writing for the court, found it inappropriate to permit Kristine to attack the judgment she once sought. The judgment was based on Kristine's affirmation that Lisa would be the child's mother. It was also clear to the court that Lisa relied on Kristine's statements in developing a relationship with the child.

Justice Moreno wrote, "Estoppel long has been utilized to prevent a party from contesting the validity of a judgment that was procured by that party . . . [we] hold only that Kristine may not now challenge the validity of the judgment."

By invoking estoppel as the basis for the decision, the court alleviated the concern expressed by others in California. This decision effectively precludes anyone from returning years later to seek to invalidate a stipulated judgment.

7. *Canada*

Canada's highest court started off the new year right by ruling that five-year-old D.D. can have three legal parents.[68] The justices decided that depriving the child of all three parents was not in his best interests. Canada's Children's Reform Act (CRA) does not provide for this scenario. But that did not stop the Superior Court judge. The court determined there is a "gap" in the CRA. The Canadian legislature would have provided for the circumstances presented by A.A., B.B., and C.C. if they had thought about it. As it is, the CRA was quite progressive when initially enacted, and Canada's highest court has just made it even more progressive. Now, if only judges in the United States would take the same bold action to protect a child's right to enjoy the love of multiple parents.

This 2007 case involves a small child and three loving parents: Mom, Mom, and Dad. The moms live together with the child. Dad, and his children from his marriage, visit for weekly dinners and is an integral part of his son's life. This is the way the parents—all three of them—want it. The non-biological mother, A.A., cannot legally adopt her son without terminating Dad's parental rights. So, the next best thing is to petition the court for an order declaring all three adults to be D.D.'s legal parents. Sound far-fetched? Not to the courts in our neighbor to the north.

G. Conclusion

There will continue to be changes in the law involving children of lesbian and gay parents. The form those changes will take is yet to be determined. Some of those changes will not bode well for lesbian and gay clients and their children.

To protect clients and their families, lawyers must be willing to look outside the lines of accepted arguments and reach deeper into the underlying reasons that courts seek to protect children. Creativity and ingenuity are needed to achieve the goals of clients and their children. It may be prudent to have clients execute agreements in which they define their intentions and expectations concerning their relationship and children. Providing for mediation as the sole basis to resolve differences is another possibility. No one is required to go to court to resolve their differences. It is often better to resolve problems between the parties without abdicating that responsibility to a judge who will enforce laws that do not contemplate the uniqueness of same-sex couples and their children.

Lawyers have a duty to educate judges and legislatures about how existing laws affect their clients. The law does not operate in a vacuum, nor should it. Especially in the area of family law, where people are at the fore, lawyers must seek out the best possible result for these situations.

Whether drafting co-parenting agreements or advising clients on custody, artificial reproduction techniques, or ending a relationship, lawyers must be counselors as well as advocates, social workers as well as advisers. Lawyers must be confident that their clients understand the stakes and present the legal consequences clearly. There is always a risk that a client will walk out and not return. This is the cost of honesty and ethical behavior. But being honest and forthright with a client is far better than realizing that failure to do so resulted in pain to another person—especially if it is a child.

In co-parenting agreements, have the parties specifically express their intent to co-parent. Ensure that the legal parent specifically acknowledges the intent to waive any state or federal constitutional protections that inure to the benefit of legal parents.

Lesbians and gay men become parents after careful consideration, because there is no easy way for them to achieve that goal. All competent scientific and psychological evidence shows that children raised by same-sex parents are as stable, healthy, and wonderful as those raised in heterosexual families. In some ways, the children of lesbian and gay parents are more thoughtful, accepting, and diverse than children raised by heterosexual parents.

You need a license to catch a fish[69] but not to parent a child. Lesbians and gay men need the benefit of a lawyer's knowledge, skill, and experience to provide for themselves and their families.

Notes

1. 28 U.S.C. § 1738A.
2. 912 A.2d 951 (Vt. 2006), *cert. denied,* No. 06-1110, 2007 WL 444487, 75 U.S.L.W. 3440 (Apr. 30, 2007); 49 Va. App. 88, 637 S.E.2d 330 (Nov. 28, 2006) (Virginia's Supreme Court declined to hear an appeal from that ruling).

3. Uniform Child-Custody Jurisdiction and Enforcement Act (1997), 9 (1A) U.L.A. 657 (1999); *available at* www.nccusl.org.

4. Miller-Jenkins v. Miller-Jenkins, 912 A.2d 951 (Vt. 2006), *cert. denied*, No. 06-1110, 2007 WL 444487, 75 U.S.L.W. 3440 (Apr. 30, 2007); 49 Va. App. 88, 637 S.E.2d 330 (Nov. 28, 2006) (Virginia's Supreme Court declined to hear an appeal from that ruling).

5. 25 U.S.C. § 1901, et seq.; UCCJEA, § 104 (Application to Indian Tribes).

6. §§ 315-317.

7. www.nccusl.org; electronic version: www.law.upenn.edu/bll/uld/ulc_frame.htm; also, www.law.cornell.edu/uniform/vol9.html.

8. § 2.

9. Alabama, California, Colorado, Delaware, Hawaii, Kansas, Minnesota, Missouri, Montana, Nevada, New Jersey, North Dakota, New Mexico, Ohio, Oklahoma, Rhode Island, Texas, Utah, Washington, and Wyoming. Illinois and Maine are considering adoption.

10. 912 A.2d 951 (Vt. 2006), *cert. denied*, No. 06-1110, 2007 WL 444487, 75 U.S.L.W. 3440 (Apr. 30, 2007); 49 Va. App. 88, 637 S.E.2d 330 (Nov. 28, 2006) (Virginia's Supreme Court declined to hear an appeal from that ruling.), No. 070355, *dismissed* 5/7/07; *pet. for reh'g den.*, 6/22/07.

11. VA. CODE ANN. § 20-45.3

12. VA. CODE ANN. § 20-146.1, et seq.

13. Miller-Jenkins v. Miller-Jenkins, 912 A.2d 951 2006, 2006 WL 2192715 (Vt., Aug. 4, 2006).

14. No. 06-1110, 2007 WL 444487, 75 U.S.L.W. 3440.

15. 49 Va. App. 88, 637 S.E.2d 330 (Nov. 28, 2006).

16. No. 070355, *dismissed* 5/7/07; *pet. for reh'g den.*, 6/22/07.

17. *See* National Center for Lesbian Rights, *Marriage, Domestic Partnerships and Civil Unions: An Overview of Relationship Recognition for Same-Sex Couples in the United States,* www.nclrights.org/publications; Lambda Legal Defense and Education Fund, *Partial Summary of Domestic Partnership Registry Listings*, www.lambdalegal.org; *50 State Rundown on Gay Marriage Laws*, www.stateline.org

18. *In re* Adoption of M.M.G.C., 785 N.E.2d 267 (Ind. Ct. App. 2003) (court reversed denial of second parent adoption).

19. 530 U.S. 57 (2000).

20. 530 U.S. 57, 63 (2000).

21. WASH. REV. CODE § 26.10.160(3).

22. *In loco parentis:* of, relating to, or acting as a temporary guardian or caretaker of a child, taking on all or some of the responsibilities of a parent. BLACK'S LAW DICTIONARY, 2d Pocket Ed. (2001).

23. 77 N.Y.2d 651, 569 N.Y.S.2d 586, 572 N.E.2d 27 (1991) (per curiam).

24. Alison D. v. Virginia M., 572 N.E.2d 27, 29-30 (1991).

25. In the Interest of Z.J.H., 162 Wis. 2d 1002, 471 N.W.2d 202 (1991).

26. 193 Wis. 2d 649, 533 N.W.2d 419 (1995).

27. *In re* Custody of H.S.H.-K., 193 Wis. 2d 649, 533 N.W. 2d 419 (1995).

28. *In re* Custody of H.S.H.-K., 533 N.W.2d 419, 436 (1995).

29. V.C. v. M.J.B., 163 N.J. 200, 222 (2000).

30. E.N.O. v. L.M.M., 429 Mass. 824, 711 N.E.2d 886 (1999); Rubano v. DiDenzo, 759 A.2d 959 (R.I. 2000); T.B. v. L.R.M., 567 Pa. 222, 786 A.2d 913 (2001); C.E.W. v. D.E.W., 2004 ME 43, 83 A.2d 1146 (Me. 2004); A.C. v. C.B., 113 N.M. 581, 829 P.2d 660 (Ct. App. 1992).

31. T.B. v. L.R.M., 567 Pa. 222, 786 A.2d 913, 916 (2001).

32. *Id.* at 913, 917 (2001).

33. T.B. v. L.R.M., 786 A.2d 913 (Pa. 2001).

34. *Id.* at ¶ 5.

35. B.F. v. T.D., 2005-SC-0005570DG (June 15, 2006).

36. KY. REV. STAT. § 403.270.

37. KY. REV. STAT. § 403.260.

38. KY. REV. STAT. § 403.420 and 403.270.

39. *In re* Parentage of L.B., 155 Wash. 2d 679, 122 P.3d 161 (Wash. 2005), *cert. denied* by U.S. Supreme Court 2006.

40. *In re* Parentage of L.B., 155 Wash. 2d 679, 122 P.3d 161, 168 (Wash. 2005), *cert. denied* by U.S. Supreme Court 2006.

41. *In re* Custody of H.S.H.-K., 193 Wis. 2d 649, 533 N.W.2d 419 (1995).

42. AM. LAW INST., PRINCIPLES OF THE LAW OF FAMILY DISSOLUTION: ANALYSIS AND RECOMMENDATIONS (2002), § 2.03 cmt. b.

43. *Id.* § 2.03(1)(b)(iii) & (iv).

44. SJC-09815, official cite pending, decided Dec. 8, 2006.

45. 442 Mass. 522 (2004).

46. "Parent by estoppel": contemplates the situation of two cohabiting adults who undertake to raise a child together, with equal rights and responsibilities as parents. Adoption is the clearer, and thus preferred, legal avenue for recognition of such parent-child relationships, but adoption is sometimes not legally available or possible, especially if one of the adults is still married to another, or if the adults are both women, or both men. Neither the unavailability of adoption nor the failure to adopt when adoption would have been available forecloses "parent by estoppel" status. However, the failure to adopt when adoption is available may be relevant to whether an agreement was intended. ALI PRINCIPLES, § 2.03, cmt. b(iii) at 114.

47. ALI PRINCIPLES, § 2.03(1)(b): ". . . obligated to pay child support . . . or (iii) lived with the child since the child's birth, holding out and accepting full and permanent responsibilities as parent, as part of a co-parenting agreement with the child's legal parent . . . to raise a child together each with full parental rights and responsibilities, when the court finds that recognition of the individual as a parent is in the child's best interests"; § 2.03, cmt. b(iii) at 115, 114.

48. 530 U.S. 59 (2005).

49. Erica Smith v. Sheila Smith, 893 A.2d 934, Del. Supr. March 7, 2006 (No. 232, 2005).

50. Wakeman v. Dixon, 921 So. 2d 669, Fla. App. 1 Dist., 2006).

51. 253 Ga. App. 600, 560 S.E.2d 47 (Jan. 23 2002).

52. O.C.G.A. § 19-3-3.1(6).

53. 253 Ga. App. 600, 560 S.E.2d 47, 49 (Jan. 23 2002).

54. 530 U.S. 57 (2000).

55. *In re* E.L.M.C., a Child, 100 P.3d 546, 2004 WL 1469410, 124 A.L.R. 5th 731 (Colo. Ct. App. 2004), *cert.denied*, 2004 WL 2377164 (Colo. 2004), and *cert. denied*, 125 S. Ct. 2551, 162 L. Ed. 2d 287 (U.S. 2005).

56. *In re* Clifford K., 217 W. Va. 625, 619 S.E.2d 138 (2005).

57. *In re* Clifford K., 217 W. Va. 625, 619 S.E.2d 138, 157 (2005).

58. *Id.*

59. *In re:* Child of Kimberly Robinson, Doc. No. FD-07-6312-05-A (Essex Cty. Sup. Ct. May 23, 2005).

60. Berry v. Berry, 2005 WL 1277847 (May 31, 2005).

61. 914 S.W.2d 889 (Tenn. Ct. App. 1995).

62. Jones v. Boring Jones, No. 271 EDA 2005, 2005 Pa. Super. 337 (Pa. Super. Ct. Sept. 30, 2005).

63. Charles v. Stehlik, 744 A.2d 1255 (Pa. 2000), stepfather given primary custody of child without showing that the biological father was unfit.

64. 37 Cal. 4th 108, 33 Cal. Rptr. 3d 46, 117 P.3d 660 (2005).

65. 37 Cal. 4th 130, 33 Cal. Rptr. 3d 61, 117 P.3d 673 (2005).

66. 37 Cal. 4th 156, 33 Cal. Rptr. 3d 81, 117 P.3d 690 (2005).

67. Elisa B. v. Superior Court, 37 Cal. 4th 108, 33 Cal. Rptr. 3d 46, 117 P.3d 660, 669 (2005).

68. A.A. v. B.B., 2007 Ont. Ct. App. 2.

69. Author's note: In Ohio it is a 4th-degree misdemeanor to fish without a license. You can be arrested and jailed for not having a license. In Ohio, a 4th-degree misdemeanor is one step below a felony.

CHAPTER SEVEN

LGBT Students and Schools

Representing lesbian, gay, and transgender clients may also include helping their children. Providing a safe school environment is the job of the school administration. Ensuring that the administration does its job can become the responsibility of a student and his or her parents.

Gender-nonconforming students face myriad problems in school. These students may or may not identify as lesbian, gay, bisexual, or transgender. They may be subjected to bullying and harassment simply because they do not meet a stereotypical standard set by society.

School administrators and faculty may fail or refuse to protect at-risk students from bullying, harassment, and/or assault. Adolescence is difficult enough without students having to worry about their personal safety while attending school. Students who face these situations often have nowhere to turn.

Not all states have laws that protect students, and not all school districts have policies that include sexual orientation or gender identity in their nondiscrimination policies. Some states considering these laws are met with opposition from those who do not want sexual orientation or gender identity included in the laws or school policies.

Unfortunately for school districts that do not protect nonconforming students from bullying and harassment, juries in several states are holding them liable for damages suffered by students. This is a cautionary tale for those districts and one of optimism for students facing the abuse.

This area of family law will involve heterosexual, lesbian, or gay parents with gender-nonconforming children. The emphasis is on protecting the child from an abusive school situation.

> **What Did You Say?**
>
> In November 2006, William Scherfel, vice president of the Ambridge Area School Board, allegedly referred to students in the high school's Gay-Straight Alliance as "faggots." Pennsylvania's code of conduct for teachers prohibits sexual orientation discrimination.
>
> Scherfel explained his comments by saying he grew up in a different time when such words were acceptable when speaking of gays. At least two school board members, including the president, are defending the vice-president and downplaying the incident.
>
> The Gay, Lesbian, Straight Education Network (GLSEN) of Pittsburgh is calling for an apology and demanding that the entire school board attend a workshop dealing with the effect of anti-gay behavior and bias in the schools.
>
> But since the school board seems to see nothing wrong with Scherfel's comments, it seems unlikely those demands will be met.

A. Definitions

To understand what students face, it is important to understand the terms being used. These terms are taken from the collaborative project mentioned in section III of this chapter.

- **Gender identity:** a person's internal, deeply felt sense of being either male or female or something other.
- **Gender expression:** an individual's characteristics or behaviors; for example, appearance, dress, mannerisms, or speech patterns.
- **Transgender:** an umbrella term for gender expression that is non-conforming and/or gender identity that is different from that assigned at birth; the individual may or may not identify as lesbian, gay, bisexual, transsexual or queer; the term includes transsexuals, cross-dressers, transvestites, drag queens, butch lesbians, feminine gay men, and generally women with masculine characteristics or men with feminine characteristics.
- **Transsexual:** someone who transitions from one gender to another; may include necessary medical care, hormone therapy, counseling, and/or surgery; this is a medical condition, treated by physicians to improve the patient's quality of life.

- **Gender nonconforming:** someone perceived to have gender characteristics or behaviors that do not conform to traditional or societal expectations.
- **Gender queer:** a person who does not identify themselves as male or female; one who may or may not identify as transgender.
- **Sexual orientation:** a person's emotional and sexual attraction to others based on the gender of the other person; persons identify as heterosexual, lesbian, gay, bisexual, or queer.
- **LGBTQ:** lesbian, gay, bisexual, transgender or questioning (someone who is unsure of his or her sexual orientation or gender identity).
- **Female/male cross-dressers:** a person who occasionally wears opposite-sex clothing; perceived conflict with his anatomical gender structure.
- **Drag queens/kings:** cross-dressers who are lesbian, gay, or bisexual.

B. Harris Interactive and GLSEN Study

In 2005, Harris Interactive and the Gay, Lesbian and Straight Education Network (GLSEN) conducted a survey of students and teachers concerning the school climate for LGBT students.[1] The study found that perception of a person's sexual identity is just as applicable as actual characteristics. The study also found there is a distinct link between a student's academic performance and being in a harassing and unsafe learning environment. Based on the study results, it is clear that harassment is not rare. The statistics and information in this section come from the GLSEN study.

Of the students surveyed, 65% reported physical or verbal harassment because of their appearance, gender, sexual orientation, gender expression, race/ethnicity, disability, or religion. It is important to note that harassment is not limited to sexual orientation; other factors come into play. However, it appears that race/ethnicity, disability, or religion are viewed as unacceptable bases for harassment, while anything dealing with sexual orientation or gender is considered fair game.

Thirty-three percent of the students surveyed reported being harassed because of their actual or perceived sexual orientation. While 36% of students believe bullying and harassment are serious problems, 53% of the teachers classify the problem as serious. And students who openly identify as LGBT have more problems than those who do not.

Ninety percent of LGBT students report being verbally or physically harassed or assaulted, while 62% of non-LGBT students report these problems.

The two most common reasons for bullying are appearance and actual or perceived as being LGBT.

One interesting aspect of the study is the difference between how often teachers and students see intervention by faculty when they hear racist, sexist, or homophobic remarks. Sixty-five percent of the teachers claim to intervene, but only 40% of the students agree that teachers step up.

Twenty percent of LGBT students report feeling unsafe at school. Consider the number of students at the local high school, then calculate 20%. This gives a clearer focus concerning the number of students potentially involved.

Another frightening statistic from this study is that 20% of private and public school teachers believe they have no obligation to ensure a safe and supportive learning environment for LGBT students. The study did not ask if the teachers believe they have an obligation to intervene when a student is being harassed, bullied, or assaulted.

C. GSA/Transgender Law Center/NCLR Report

To assist students who do not conform to any gender norm, it is necessary to understand the problem.

In 2004, a collaborative project of the Gay-Straight Alliance Network (GSA), the Transgender Law Center, and the National Center for Lesbian Rights (NCLR) produced a report addressing issues faced by students in U.S. schools.[2] The report also provides tools that students, parents, and school districts can use to resolve problems and develop policies and procedures to ensure a safe learning environment. This section includes information from that collaborative project.

"Gender nonconforming" relates to a person whose gender expression or outward appearance does not follow a traditional or stereotypical gender role. The term includes students who engage in activities thought to be the exclusive province of the opposite sex. For example, girls who play sports or work on cars are often seen as tomboys or unladylike. Boys may be called "sissy" or "faggot" if they dance ballet, for instance.

Gender-nonconforming students are often thought to be gay, lesbian, or bisexual. This is not always the case, because some students might simply be dressing or acting in an unconventional manner. A student's dress or conduct does not always reflect his or her sexual orientation. High school is a time for young people to challenge the status quo by dressing or behaving in a manner their elders find irritating. Thus the premise that one "can't tell a book by its cover."

"Transgender youth" is an umbrella term used to define anyone whose gender identity is different from the sex assigned at birth and/or whose gender expression is nontraditional. This includes students who do not dress in a stereotypical manner or who are transsexual.

Examples of discrimination faced by gender-nonconforming students include schools refusing to permit students to wear clothing that fits their gender identity and denying access to school activities because of the student's actual or perceived gender identity or expression. An example of the last is restricting girls to home economics classes and prohibiting them from taking shop; likewise, doing the same to boys—in reverse.

Harassment can come in many forms: name-calling, threats of violence, sexual harassment, or physical assaults.

Junior high school and senior high school present difficult territory for students who look or act "different." For gender-nonconforming students, the situation can be murky and dangerous. These students are often thought of as gay or lesbian even when they are not. And the problem does not always stop with high school. Students who are perceived to be lesbian or gay may find problems continuing into college. A recent incident involved a gay male student at a very conservative college. After he came out on his MySpace.com Web page, the school expelled him.

The National Center for Lesbian Rights represented a former member of the women's college basketball team in federal district court. According to the player, the University of Pennsylvania women's basketball coach forced her off the team because the coach thought she was a lesbian. The woman was one of the top scorers on the team but was nonconforming in her appearance—according to the coach.

The plaintiff is not a lesbian but still lost her place at the university because of the coach's perception. The coach has been quoted as saying lesbians do not play on her teams. The plaintiff now plays for a college in Virginia. The parties entered into a confidential settlement in the case. In mid-2007, the coach resigned from her position with the University of Pennsylvania.

Transgender students, those who do not conform to their birth sex, have particular problems in school. The biggest issue seems to revolve around restrooms. Transgender students are often prevented from using a restroom that conforms to their gender identity.

Consider a transgender student, a biological female, who identifies and appears as a male. He cannot use the women's restroom because he looks like a male; yet he cannot use the men's restroom because physically he is a female. There is a risk of assault by or confrontation with other students. Many transgender students deal with the situation by deciding not to use the restroom while at school. Doing so can cause emotional and physical problems for the student involved.

Restrooms are not the only gender-segregated locations in a school. Locker rooms also create an unsafe space for gender-nonconforming students.

Many schools fail to understand their legal duty to stop harassment. This duty exists under federal law even if state law is silent. California protects students under the Student Safety and Violence Prevention Act of 2000 (AB 537).

D. Handling Discrimination and Harassment

Students facing harassment and/or discrimination in school have avenues available to seek recourse. Many school districts fail or refuse to acknowledge their responsibility to all students. This malfeasance on the part of school districts can be an expensive mistake.

> **Practice Tip**
>
> It is important to *document all incidents in detail*, including names of all witnesses. Written statements from the witnesses will also be helpful, although they may be difficult to obtain because of the general reluctance of students to become involved. It is also important to write down the names of any faculty member or administrator who witnessed the incident.

Written documentation of all incidents and the action taken by the student and the administration is an important part of developing the case. Whenever possible, *involve the student's parents or guardian* in the process. It is in the student's best interest to have the parents involved as soon as possible. This may not always be possible, because teens are often reluctant to admit to having problems at school. However, the student's health and safety may be at risk in situations involving harassment and/or discrimination. Having a parent in the student's corner will help in the end.

Filing a written complaint with the principal is the next step. A written complaint is important because oral complaints can be easily denied. A written complaint leaves a paper trail that will support any necessary legal action. The successful lawsuits in this area rely on the knowledge of the administration concerning complaints about harassment or discrimination. The school district will raise lack of knowledge as a defense to any lawsuit seeking damages for injuries suffered by a student. Federal law requires a showing that school officials knew about the problem and failed to take any corrective action in order for the plaintiff to succeed.

> **Suicide of a 14-year-old**
>
> In January 1997, 14-year-old Robbie Kirkland saw no option other than to commit suicide. He was a freshman at St. Ignatius High School.
>
> St. Ignatius is a male-only Jesuit preparatory school on Cleveland's near west side. It is known for its academics and its football prowess. But Robbie Kirkland was no football player. He was a slight, gentle young man who wrote poetry. He was also gay, and that was leading to trouble on the high school campus. His best friend went to Ignatius, and he knew the secret. Robbie told two other classmates and then, as is common in high school, the news spread.
>
> Robbie, by all accounts, did not fit into the male, macho hallways of St. Ignatius. He knew from an early age that he was different. By the third grade, the other kids teased him.
>
> He was seeing a therapist and was unhappy with being gay. He knew what it meant. Unlike many other lesbian and gay kids, Robbie's parents were supportive. But for this young man, death was the only option that would offer him any peace.
>
> Perhaps what is most telling about Robbie Kirkland's death is the school's reaction. The school administration declined an offer by Robbie's mother to speak to the students. Instead, a mass would be celebrated with the focus on suicide. Even with Robbie's death and knowing why it happened, this Christian school could not address the issue of homophobia in its own student body.

The student and her parents should *file a police report* any time physical violence is involved or whenever the student fears for her safety. Often, when this type of incident is reported to schools, there is pressure to keep the police out of the picture. Doing so only benefits the school, not the student. File the police report and let law enforcement authorities take the necessary action. This also forces the school district to respond to the situation.

When meeting with school officials, the student and her parents are well advised to make notes of comments made by administration officials about the complaint(s). This is particularly important if the administration promises to take corrective action, refuses to acknowledge that a problem exists or, as has happened, blames the student for the harassment. These contemporaneous notes will also help the parents later if the situation continues and/or the school refuses to take action. The parents may also want to tape the meetings. Placing a tape recorder on the table may cause school officials to understand the seriousness of the problem. Of course, any taping must be conducted with the consent of the other party. Have the tape running when the school official gives that consent. It might also help to offer a copy of the tape to the official. That may prevent challenges to the tape's authenticity later.

If the principal's response is inadequate, file a written complaint with the school district superintendent. Attach copies of the complaints filed with the principal and the notes taken during any meetings. Filing with the superintendent should take place within a reasonable time. Some states that have laws dealing with these issues may include specific time limits that must be met. The superintendent may identify another district employee responsible for addressing the complaint.

Most important is for action to be taken within a reasonable time. Neither the parents nor the student need wait months for a response or corrective action. Often, it is apparent whether the school or district will take any action. If none is forthcoming, the student's parents may want to consider retaining legal counsel.

Providing the district with citations to the pertinent case law may encourage a quicker resolution. The following are some of the leading cases involving harassment and/or discrimination of students.

1. *Flores, et al. v. Morgan Hill Unified School Dist.*[3] involved the harassment of six students because of their real or perceived gender and sexual orientation. The harassment included threats of and actual physical violence. The Ninth Circuit found that the school district had an obligation, under the Equal Protection Clause, to deal with complaints of harassment and discrimination based on sexual orientation. The district settled the case in 2004 for over $1 million dollars.
2. In *Massey v. Banning Unified School Dist.*,[4] the school prohibited an eighth grade lesbian from attending gym class because of her sexual orientation. The district paid the student $45,000 after settling the case in 2004.
3. The *GSA Network & Loomis v. Visalia Unified School Dist.*[5] concerned verbal harassment of a student by fellow students *and* teachers. The school put the student involved on independent study and subjected the student to sexually suggestive touching. That district settled the case in 2002 for $130,000 in damages.

4. The first notable case in this area is *Nabozny v. Podlesny.*[6] The court found that the school's failure to protect a gay student from harassment violated the Equal Protection Clause of the federal Constitution. The district had a duty to protect Nabozny to the same extent as other students who were protected from harassment. The school failed to do so because of the student's gender and sexual orientation. The student initially reported the problem to school administration officials. The administrator told Nabozny and his parents that he should expect the harassment because he was openly gay. The school district settled, on the eve of trial, for nearly $1 million.

E. What Does the Law Say?

Federal and state courts cite Title IX of the federal Education Amendment Act of 1972 and the Equal Protection Clause of the United States Constitution as the basis for requiring schools to protect students from harassment and discrimination. All students have a right to be protected, and schools have a duty to guarantee that protection. A brief discussion of the applicable laws follows.

1. Title IX[7]

Title IX prohibits sex discrimination in educational programs and all activities receiving federal assistance. One form of prohibited conduct is discrimination based on gender nonconformity. Title IX does not explicitly prohibit discrimination based on sexual orientation. But Title IX does apply if an LGBT student is sexually harassed, and the harassment is severe and pervasive enough to adversely affect that student's participation in educational opportunities or activities.

Although Title IX does not prohibit discrimination on the basis of sexual orientation, sexual harassment directed at gay or lesbian students that is sufficiently serious to limit or deny a student's ability to participate in or benefit from the school's program constitutes sexual harassment prohibited by Title IX under circumstances described in this guidance.[8]

Name-calling is one form of discrimination that violates Title IX. For example, calling a boy by girls' names because he is perceived to be effeminate, as happened in *Montgomery v. Independent School District No. 709*, may be a violation if the school fails to take corrective action.[9]

The *Montgomery* court stated: "We are unable to garner any rational basis for permitting one student to assault another based on the victim's sexual orientation, and the defendants do not offer us one."

Section III of the Title IX Guidance provides: "[g]ender-based harassment, which may include acts of verbal, nonverbal, or physical aggression, intimidation or hostility based on sex or sex-stereotyping, but not involving conduct of a sexual nature, is also a form of sex discrimination to which a school must respond...."[10]

A school district can be held liable for damages caused by sex- or gender-based harassment if it knew about the problem and failed to take corrective action. Telling a teacher will probably not be enough to trigger the knowledge requirement. Parents must tell someone with the authority to take corrective action to ensure there is not a "lack of knowledge" defense.[11] This could be the principal, vice-principal, or district official. Again, waiting a reasonable time before moving up the administrative food chain may be necessary. But "reasonable" depends on the situation. A reasonable time to correct a name-calling problem will be dramatically different from one where physical violence is present.

Title IX permits private lawsuits for money damages in federal court.[12] An aggrieved party may also file a complaint with the Office of Civil Rights (OCR) of the U.S. Department of Education. An OCR investigation may result in the termination of a school's federal funding. The OCR has negotiated settlements in cases involving LGBT students based on gender identity or sexual orientation harassment. If a student decides to contact the OCR, it is important to note the time constraints involved and how a complaint filed with the OCR affects any future litigation.

Schools receiving federal funds are required to have a non-discrimination policy in effect. They are also required to notify all employees, students, and parents of elementary and secondary school students of the policy.[13] The school must also adopt and publish grievance procedures for resolving complaints.[14] At least one employee must be designated the Title IX coordinator and be responsible for ensuring compliance with the law.[15]

2. Equal Protection Clause

Everyone has a federally protected constitutional right to equal protection under the law. This is a cornerstone of the United States Constitution. All students, therefore, have a right to be protected from harassment and discrimination. The schools have a duty, under the Constitution, to protect all students. Schools cannot excuse their failure or refusal to protect students because they believe the student's actual or perceived gender or sexual orientation caused the problem.

A transgender student, for example, has a constitutional right to be treated in the same manner as other students of the same gender identity. This situation arose in *Doe v. Yunits*.[16] The school required a male-to-female transsexual to conform to a dress code different from biological females. The court held that the school discriminated against the student because it applied its rules in a discriminatory fashion.

3. The First Amendment and the Due Process Clause

The First Amendment and the Due Process Clause of the United States Constitution also protected the student in the *Yunits* case. According to the court, students have a First Amendment right to speech and expression. The school had no authority to censor the student's dress without a compelling reason. The court also held that students have a protected interest in their personal appearance under the Due Process Clause.

4. State Laws

The District of Columbia, California, Connecticut, Massachusetts, Minnesota, New Jersey, Vermont, Washington and Wisconsin have state laws prohibiting discrimination based on sexual orientation in educational facilities.[17]

Laws in California, Minnesota, and New Jersey also prohibit gender identity discrimination.

F. Gay-Straight Alliances (GSAs)

Harassment and discrimination are not the only issues facing students today. Schools are also dealing with student-led efforts to establish gay-straight alliances. These efforts have come under fire because some people believe they are covers for sex clubs. Parents and administrators alike express displeasure with the idea of LGBT students forming these organizations. Students see GSAs as a group that provides a safe place to meet and a forum to promote a positive view of differences in sexual orientation, gender identity, and similar issues.

School districts and others who oppose these groups have tried to prevent their existence. A court decision in Kentucky addressed this issue. Students in Boyd County, Kentucky, boycotted classes because the school allowed a GSA to meet. As a result, the school reversed itself and decided the club could not meet. Litigation ensued. The court rejected the district's argument that the GSA would cause a significant disruption to the school environment. The judge held that negative reaction by other people cannot be the basis to prevent the club from meeting. The judge said: "A school may not deny equal access to a student group because student and community opposition to the group substantially interferes with the school's ability to maintain order and discipline."[18] Some districts go so far as to prohibit all non-academic student organizations and all extracurricular activities. Fortunately for students seeking to start a GSA, there is a federal law that supports them.

In 1984, Congress passed the Equal Access Act (EAA).[19] This federal law applies to all public secondary schools that receive federal funding. Under this statute, schools that permit *any* student-initiated, non-curriculum-related clubs to meet on school grounds must allow *all* such groups to meet. The schools cannot discriminate against any club, even those that present an unpopular viewpoint.[20] The statute's original intent was to protect meetings of student religious clubs.

The United States Supreme Court held in 1969 that opposition to the expression of unpopular ideas is not sufficient to suppress speech.[21]

The federal judge in *Colin v. Orange Unified School District*[22] said:

> The Board Members may be uncomfortable about students discussing sexual orientation and how all students need to accept each other, whether gay or straight. . . . [But] [school officials] cannot censor the student's speech to avoid discussions on campus that cause them discomfort or represent an unpopular viewpoint. In order to comply with the Equal Access Act, . . . the members of the Gay-Straight Alliance must be permitted access to the school campus in the same way that the District provides access to all clubs, including the Christian Club and the Red Cross/Key Club.

The judge also explained that a school can deny access only if the club's own members are engaging in disruptive activities that interfere with the school's order and discipline.

The EAA requires schools to treat GSAs in a manner equal to all other similarly situated groups. School officials cannot discriminate against GSAs or the student members.[23] To act in a discriminatory fashion is a violation of the EAA and may violate the First Amendment and Due Process Clause of the federal Constitution. But, the statute also allows schools to "[m]aintain order and discipline on school premises, and to protect the well-being of students and faculty."[24]

The students have a right under the First Amendment to name the group and define its mission. Schools cannot require the students to change the group's name to one that is less confrontational.[25] The *Colin* court[26] held:

> A group's speech and association rights are implicated in the name that it chooses for itself. The board is not allowed to require the student group to change its name merely because the Board finds that it would

be less "divisive." . . . [The students] testified that these name changes would attack the very core reason for having the club. . . . [One student] said that the use of the word "Gay" in the title is important to announce that "being gay or homosexual is not bad, it's who you are." . . . [Another student] said that taking the word gay out would take the focus away from the issues people face and would imply that there's something wrong with the word "gay." . . . For all of the reasons that [the students] mentioned when talking about being forced to change the club's name, the Board's suggested name change clearly infringes on profound expressive meaning that the group attaches to its name.

The United States Supreme Court defined a "curriculum-related group" as one "that has more than just a tangential or attenuated relationship to the courses offered by the school. [A] student group directly relates to a school's curriculum if the subject matter of the group is actually taught, or will soon be taught, in a regularly offered course; if the subject matter of the group concerns the body of courses as a whole; if participation in the group is required for a particular course; or if participation in the group results in academic credit."[27] Clubs for languages (French, Spanish, German, etc.), Chemistry Club, Geometry Club, and Science Club are examples of curriculum-related groups.

The Court defined a non-curriculum-related club as one "that does not directly relate to the body of courses offered by the school."[28] Examples of this type of club are the juggling club, the ski club, and the Christian club.

In Texas, the Lubbock Independent School District successfully argued an EAA exception that allowed the district to deny access to a GSA.[29] The exception is based on a "materially and substantial interference with the orderly conduct of educational activities within the school." The school district is one that has a strict abstinence-only policy and the GSA planned to discuss safe-sex issues. The case is on appeal.

In December 2006, the White County School District in Georgia agreed to settle a federal lawsuit brought by students in the district.[30] The American Civil Liberties Union represented the students, who sought to establish a Gay-Straight Alliance group at the high school. The plaintiffs also succeeded in getting the school district to enact an anti-bullying policy in the schools. Perhaps most sobering part of the case for the school district occurred when it agreed to pay the plaintiffs $10,000 and the ACLU $168,000 for legal fees. The school district's refusal to permit the GSA to meet on campus violated the federal Equal Access Act. As with so many other school boards and school districts, this error in judgment proved costly to the Georgia taxpayers.

G. Harassed Students and What They Did About It

1. In May 2004, a Kansas teen, Dylan Theno, sued the Tonganoxie Unified School District because of persistent homophobic harassment.[31] Dylan claimed the harassment began in junior high school and continued until he dropped out of high school in his junior year. Dylan's classmates believed, erroneously, that he was gay. According to Dylan, school officials knew about the harassment and did nothing to stop it.

    After the judge denied the school district's motion for summary judgment, the case proceeded to trial. A jury found in favor of Dylan and awarded him $250,000. The court found that the district's behavior constituted deliberate indifference to the severe harassment experienced by Dylan. The judge decided that the district's action violated Title IX of the United States Code.

    The school district appealed the jury's decision, and a judge ordered the case to a federal mediator. On December 22, 2005, the school district settled the case for $440,000—$190,000 more than the jury awarded.

2. A high school student in Orange County, California, filed a lawsuit against the Garden Grove Unified School District claiming violations of her right to privacy, free expression, and the Equal Protection Clause. The student was disciplined and then forced to transfer from Santiago High School because she was seen hugging and kissing another student on school grounds. Ordinarily, teenagers hugging and kissing would not create a scene, unless, as in this case, the teens involved were both women.

    Charlene Nguon, an "A" student in the top 5% of her class, was singled out for disciplinary action after being charged with a public display of affection involving her girlfriend. The principal, Ben Wolf, also "outed" Charlene to her mother. Charlene was denied admission into the National Honor Society because of the disciplinary action taken against her. She was then suspended for one week for hugging her girlfriend.

    The school demanded that either Charlene or her girlfriend transfer to another school. Charlene's transfer to Bolsa Grande High School turned a four-block walk to school into a nine-mile round-trip bike commute. Her grades suffered because of the harassment.

    After the American Civil Liberties Union of Southern California sent a letter to the school district, Charlene was allowed to return to Santiago High School. But the school took no action to improve the campus climate or to ensure that Charlene would not again experience discrimination.

Charlene, her parents, and the GSA Network filed a federal lawsuit against the school district. In an initial proceeding, the judge denied the district's motion to dismiss the privacy claim. The judge ruled that students have a right of privacy, including the right to decide what highly personal information will be released to their parents. The case is currently pending in U.S. District Court.

3. Lambda Legal filed a lawsuit on behalf of a lesbian student in New Jersey.[32] The plaintiff suffered through verbal harassment and physical attacks for over two years at Holmdel High School. The school administration knew of the attacks and took no action to end them. The administration also rejected pleas for help from the student and her parents.

   The plaintiff, Nancy Wadlington, left school during her junior year for her protection. During her time at Holmdel High School, other students threw bottles at her, pushed her down a flight of stairs, and stole or destroyed her personal belongings, including urinating in her backpack.

   Because of the attacks and constant harassment, Nancy stopped using the school restrooms. She stopped using the locker rooms for gym class and stopped walking in the halls between classes (she walked outside to get to the next class)—all because she is a lesbian.

   The lawsuit claims a violation of the New Jersey Law Against Discrimination prohibiting sexual orientation discrimination in schools. Based on the precedent set in other cases, the Holmdel Township Board of Education may find itself responsible for paying Nancy a significant sum of money.

4. In *Ramelli v. Poway Unified School District*,[33] a jury awarded two students $300,000 because school officials did not take action to correct gay harassment complaints.

   Joseph Ramelli and Megan Donovan dropped out of school in their senior year because of the harassment. They completed high school through independent study programs. Both are now attending community colleges in California.

   This case is an example of how letters to school administrators are often not enough to get action. The two students were shunned by classmates, spat upon, and called derogatory names.

   The plaintiffs' case was helped with testimony from another former student with a similar story—harassment, reporting to the administration, no action taken, dropping out of school.

The jury awarded Ramelli $175,000 and Donovan $125,000 and determined that the harassment deprived both students of an education.

5. Students are not the only ones engaging in harassing, discriminatory, and bullying behavior. Sometimes the student's worst enemy is a teacher. An assistant principal in Arkansas condoned a teacher's harassment of a student. The assistant principal disciplined the student and ordered him to stop talking about his sexual orientation. The administrator also informed the student's mother that he was gay. The mother—and her son—sued the school. The district settled for $25,000.[34] In this case, the school knew about the harassment and condoned it. When the student complained, the school took disciplinary action against him but not the teacher.

6. Derek Henkle sued a Reno, Nevada, school district in 2000 following years of harassment and physical attacks at various high schools.[35] Before filing suit, Derek transferred to three different high schools and an adult education program. He dropped out of the adult education program because, at 16, he was not old enough to take the G.E.D. exam and did not have enough high school classes to qualify for a diploma.
He experienced constant harassment because of his sexual orientation. This included being lassoed around the neck. Derek reported the abuse to the school principal, who told him to stop acting like a "fag." He filed a criminal complaint against one student, who was charged with a hate crime.

After losing on different motions to dismiss, the school district settled the case in August 2002 for $451,000. The district's insurance policy had a $1 million limit. A trial could have resulted in a verdict exceeding the policy limits.

The district also agreed to introduce new policies to protect LGBT students from harassment and discrimination. The policies will include grievance and reporting procedures.

Lawyers representing students in gender-identity or sexual orientation discrimination cases can also use *Price Waterhouse v. Hopkins*[36] to support their clients' position. The Supreme Court held that sex stereotyping in the workplace is illegal. It is a short distance to extend that holding to schools.

There are cases stating that sex-specific distinctions are allowed if they reflect community standards, morals, or values. For example, schools may prohibit boys from wearing earrings if to do so conforms to community values.[37]

The 1980 decision in *Fricke v. Lynch*[38] held that a same-sex couple could not be excluded from a school dance. The court wrote, "The First Amendment does not tolerate mob rule by unruly school children."

H. Conclusion

The National Center for Lesbian Rights (NCLR) and the Gay, Lesbian and Straight Education Network (GLSEN) published *Fifteen Expensive Reasons Why Safe Schools Legislation Is In Your State's Best Interest*.[39]

This document, published in 2004, provides a brief synopsis of 15 cases that "[h]ave been brought against school districts for failing to protect students from discrimination on the basis of sexual orientation." According to the report, the cases, some of which have been discussed in this chapter, reflect awards ranging from $40,000[40] to $1.1 million.[41]

For lawyers researching these issues, the NCLR and GLSEN provide an invaluable resource. There is a growing number of cases that address issues of harassment, discrimination, and abuse in schools. Most of these cases deal with harassment and discrimination based on sexual orientation or gender identity. School district counsel also need to be aware of how the courts, federal and state, are deciding these cases. In these times, when school funding is never enough, it is advisable for school districts to be aware of their potential liability.

All students are entitled to a safe learning environment. No student can be expected to tolerate a poisonous atmosphere. There is no room for discrimination, harassment, violence, or bullying in schools. The cases set forth in this chapter will help students, parents, and their lawyers persuade school districts and administrators that protecting all students is in the district's best (financial) interest.

Notes

1. Harris Interactive and GLSEN, From Teasing to Torment: School Climate in America, A Survey of Students and Teachers (2005).
2. Stephanie Cho et al., Beyond the Binary: A Toolkit for Gender Identity Activism in Schools (2004).
3. 324 F.3d 1130 (9th Cir. 2003).
4. 256 F. Supp. 1090 (C.D. Cal. 2003).
5. GSA Network & Loomis v. Visalia Unified School Dist., U.S. Dist. Ct., Consent Decree & Order (August 2002).
6. 92 F.3d 446 (7th Cir. 1996).
7. 20 U.S.C. § 1681(a).
8. O.C.R. Revised Guidance, § III.
9. Montgomery v. Indep. Sch. Dist. No. 709, 2000 WL 1233063 (D. Minn. 2000); Miles v. New York Univ., 979 F. Supp. 248 (S.D.N.Y. 1997).

10. U.S. Dept. of Education, Office of Civil Rights, Revised Title IX Guidance (January 2001).
11. Davis v. Monroe County Sch. Dist., 526 U.S. 629 (1999); Gebser v. Lago Vista Ind. Sch. Dist., 524 U.S. 274 (1998).
12. Franklin v. Gwinnett Cty. Public Schs., 503 U.S. 60 (1992).
13. 34 C.F.R. § 106.9.
14. 34 C.F.R. § 106.8(b).
15. 34 C.F.R. § 106.8(a).
16. 2000 WL 33162199 (Mass. Super. 2000).
17. Conn. Gen. Stat. § 10-15c; D.C. Code 1981 § 1-2520; Mass. Gen. Laws ch. 76, § 5; Minn. Stat. § 363.03, sub. 5; N.J. Stat. § 10:5-12f(1); N.J. Stat. § 10:5-5(l); N.J. A.B. 1874 (effective Sept. 6, 2002) (supplementing ch. 37 of Title 18A of the New Jersey Statutes); 16 Vt. Stat. § 565; Wash. Rev. Code §§ 28A.320, 28A.600; Wis. Stat. § 118.13.
18. Boyd Cty. High School Gay Straight Alliance v. Bd. of Educ. of Boyd Cty., 258 F. Supp. 2d 667, 690 (E.D. Ky. 2003).
19. 20 U.S.C. § 4071(a),(b).
20. Board of Educ. of Westside Community Sch. v. Mergens, 496 U.S. 226 (1990).
21. Tinker v. Des Moines Indep. Cnty. Sch. Dist., 393 U.S. 503, 508-09 (1969).
22. 83 F. Supp. 2d 1135, 1148 (C.D. Cal. 2000).
23. *Mergens*, 496 U.S. at 271 (1990); Prince v. Jacoby, 303 F.3d 1074 (9th Cir. 2002).
24. 20 U.S.C. § 4071(f).
25. Latino Officers Ass'n v. City of New York, 196 F.3d 458 (2d Cir. 1999); Hurley v. Irish-American Gay, Lesbian & Bisexual Group, 515 U.S. 557 (1995); Gay Activists Alliance v. Lomenzo, 31 N.Y.2d 965 (1973).
26. 83 F. Supp. 2d 1335, 1147-48.
27. *Mergens*, 496 U.S. at 238 (1990).
28. *Id.* at 239.
29. Caudillo v. Lubbock Indep. Sch. Dist., 311 F. Supp. 2d 550 (N.D. Tex. 2004).
30. White County High School Peers Rising in Diverse Education (PRIDE) v. White County School District, Case 2:06-cv-00029-WCO, filed 7/14/2006 (U.S. Dist. Ct., N. Dist. of Ga., Gainesville Div.).
31. Theno v. Tonganoxie Unified Sch. Dist., 377 F. Supp. 2d 952 (D. Kan. 2005).
32. Wadlington v. Holmdel Twp. Bd. of Educ., Super. Ct. of Monmouth Cty., N.J.
33. June 8, 2005, Super. Ct., San Diego Cty., Calif., Judge Steven R. Denton.
34. McLaughlin v. Bd. of Educ. of Pulaski Cty. Special Sch. Dist., 296 F. Supp. 2d 960 (E.D. Ark. 2003).
35. Henkle v. Gregory, 150 F. Supp. 2d 1067 (D. Nev. 2001).
36. 490 U.S. 228 (1989).
37. Oleson v. Bd. of Educ. of Sch. Dist. No. 228, 676 F. Supp. 820 (N.D. Ill. 1987); Hines v. Caston Sch. Corp., 651 N.E.2d 330 (Ind. App. 1995); Jones v. W.T. Henning Elem. Sch., 721 So. 2d 530 (La. App. 1998); *but also see* Doe v. Brockton Sch. Comm., 2000 WL 33342399 (Mass. App. Ct. Nov. 30, 2000).
38. 491 F. Supp. 387 (D.R.I. 1980).
39. http://www.nclrights.org/publications/15reasons.htm
40. Iverson v. Kent (settled in 1998).
41. Flores v. Morgan Hill Unified Sch. Dist., 324 F.3d 1130 (9th Cir. 2003).

CHAPTER EIGHT

Representing Transgender/Transsexual Clients

Representing transgender and transsexual clients may present a challenge to lawyers unaccustomed to dealing with people whose gender identity does not correspond to stereotype. Transgender and transsexual individuals face myriad forms of discrimination.

The Transgender Law Center[1] is an excellent resource for attorneys representing transgender clients. The Center's primary focus is on legal issues concerning the transgender individual's status. The issues they most often deal with are discrimination, identity documentation, immigration, family law, and employment. Lambda Legal Education and Defense Fund[2] and the National Center for Lesbian Rights[3] are other sources of assistance and information.

It is important to understand the terminology involved. There are differences between sexual orientation and gender identity. The terms "transsexual" and "transgender" are not synonymous. Persons who are "gay," "lesbian," or "bisexual" are not necessarily transsexuals.

Sexual orientation refers to a person's relationships with and attractions to others. Gender identity refers to a person's deep-seated understanding of himself or herself as a man or a woman. The terms "asexual," "homosexual," "heterosexual," and "bisexual" relate to a person's sexual orientation. "Gender identity" refers to a person's sense of himself or herself—that the person believes "I am male" or "I am female."

Gender Identity Disorder (GID) is defined in the American Psychiatric Diagnostic and Statistical Manual of Mental Disorders IV (DSM IV, 1994). The DSM lists five criteria that must exist before a person will be given a diagnosis of Gender Identity Disorder (302.85). These are:

1. Evidence of a strong and persistent cross-gender identification;
2. Cross-gender identification must be more than a mere desire for the perceived cultural advantages of the other sex;
3. Evidence must exist of either a persistent discomfort with or a sense of inappropriateness in the gender role of one's assigned sex;
4. The person must not have a concurrent physical intersex condition; and
5. Evidence must exist of clinically significant distress or impairment in social, occupational or other important areas of functioning.

Gender disorders that do not fall within the framework of these criteria are included in the diagnosis of Gender Identity Disorder Not Otherwise Specified (GIDNOS, 302.6) within the DSM-IV.

Transgender healthcare experts recommend a three-pronged therapeutic response to gender identity disorder, sometimes called "triadic therapy": a real-life experience in the desired gender role, hormone therapy, and sex reassignment surgery.[4] The prevailing medical standards of care recognize that all elements of triadic therapy will not be necessary for every person with GID.

Dr. Virginia Prince first used the term "transgender" in the 1970s. She developed the term to differentiate between people who wanted to live as the sex opposite of their birth gender without surgery and those who wanted surgery. Transsexuals are individuals who desire to undergo physical gender transition. "Transgender" is now viewed as an umbrella term for anyone whose gender identity is at odds with his birth gender; the term is sometimes used even more broadly to include those who challenge gender stereotypes, including masculine women, feminine men, and cross-dressers.

The "transgender" umbrella includes numerous gender identifications. These include pre- and post-operative transsexuals, cross-dressers, and transvestites.

Often transsexuals are confused with cross-dressers. A cross-dresser is a person who dresses in clothing usually reserved for the opposite sex, but whose identity as a man or a woman conforms to societal expectations. Transsexuals, on the other hand, have a deeply felt internal gender identity that does not match the sex assigned at birth.

Gender dysphoria refers to the persistent distress that transsexuals feel toward the gender assigned to them at birth.

The usual prescribed treatment[5] is:

1. Hormone therapy;
2. Living as a member of the opposite sex (real life experience); and
3. Sex reassignment surgery.

Transsexualism affects both sexes. Many transsexuals become aware of their situation at an early age. Untreated, the condition causes severe depression and, in some profound cases, leads to suicide.

Sex reassignment surgery is expensive and, in the case of female to male transsexuals, can be cost-prohibitive. It is still the norm for private health insurance policies to exclude coverage for these procedures, deeming them "experimental" or "cosmetic." Medicaid coverage varies from state to state. As a result, many transsexuals cannot afford sex reassignment surgery and live in accordance with their gender identity without surgical interventions.

A. Representing Transgender Clients

First, there is no fundamental difference between representing a transgender or transsexual person and anyone else. It is important to consider training and educating your support and other professional staff members to ensure that your clients are in a comfortable environment.

The legal issues or problems bringing the individual to your office may have nothing to do with his or her gender identity. Your ability to focus on the real issue also helps the client maintain focus.

Do not make assumptions about the person's gender. If in doubt, ask how the client wants to be addressed. This may be an uncomfortable and new experience, but that may also be true for the client. Many lesbians, gay men, and transgender people do not seek legal assistance because they are afraid of how they will be treated. If you treat the client with respect, you will discover an untapped market for your services.

The primary areas of law affecting transgender and transsexual persons because of their status are immigration, employment, family law, housing, healthcare, and criminal justice issues. Transgender and transsexual youths also face discrimination and harassment in schools, foster care, and youth offender programs.

Most employment cases involve an interpretation of Title VII of the Civil Rights Act of 1964 or analogous state laws.

Representing a transgender or transsexual client can present different challenges for the lawyer. Office and court staff as well as opposing counsel, opposing parties, and the judge may need education in order to keep everyone's attention on the case rather than on your client's identity.

Clients who are transitioning during a trial may present other issues. It is important for the court to understand what is happening. Jury trials will pose greater problems. Voir dire gives you an opportunity to raise the issue and determine which members of the panel are best able to handle the situation. Your client's case should be judged on its merits, not on the appearance of your client or the prejudices of the jury.

You may want to use affidavits from physicians and mental health professionals to assist the judge with his or her preconceptions about transgender persons. Such evidence will be important in marriage cases if the issue concerns your client's legal sex.

Network with lawyers who are representing transgender and transsexual individuals in court. Often you may find yourself presenting a case of first impression. Other lawyers in other jurisdictions may have ideas on presenting the case. Use all the resources available to you. Networking also will help you avoid creating bad law because you do not understand the issues or how to argue them. Remember that your ego must be subordinated to the client's interests.

It is important to use the correct name in all correspondence, court papers, and settlement papers. Be sure to use the proper name and pronoun—do not make assumptions about what pronoun your client prefers. In some cases, you might decide that it is strategically wise to use the client's former name. Take the time to discuss your thoughts with your client. Communication is important; it fosters understanding and trust between client and lawyer. One way to reference the client's former name is through a footnote in the pleading.

Ask opposing counsel, staff, and the judge to use the client's correct name. You may be respectful, but firm. Your client will expect you to do so and appreciate your efforts. It may not make you popular, but it will make you right!

Transgender clients will appreciate a polite and professional staff and accessible restrooms based on gender identity. If possible, provide gender-neutral restrooms, as some transgender and gender nonconforming people feel safest in that setting. Amend your intake forms to allow the client to note, "Also known as . . . ." And educate your staff on the basics of transgender terminology and identity. Your local LGBT Community Center will be able to help in this area. That, in turn, will let them know you are a lawyer to whom it can refer clients.

If, however, there is any chance you will be unable to treat the client with respect and dignity, do everyone a favor and refuse the case. This is especially true if you or your staff will not diligently and competently prepare the client's case and represent his or her interests. That is the fastest way to a malpractice or disciplinary complaint.

B. Statutory Protections

There are no explicit protections for transgender individuals under federal law. Most states also do not include transgender persons or gender identity in their state non-discrimination laws.

The Rehabilitation Act of 1973[6] and the 1997 Americans with Disabilities Act[7] (ADA) explicitly exclude transsexualism and gender identity disorders from coverage. These are considered disorders not arising from physical impairments.

Contrary to those laws, the Social Security Act does allow a disability determination based on transsexualism. In *Manago v. Barnhart*,[8] the court ruled that a transsexual woman was entitled to disability benefits based on her "inability to work because of suffering from severe depression, anxiety and post-traumatic stress secondary to gender identity disorder/transsexualism."

The question in this case was not whether Manago was disabled; rather, it concerned whether the onset of disability was outside the eligibility date. Since Social Security disability benefits are available only for a limited time, based on a person's work history, the administrative law judge ruled that her disability began in the 1980s. He denied the disability claim because too much time had elapsed between her work history and the decision. The court rejected that decision and ruled that Manago was entitled to disability benefits back to 1990.

Some states follow the Rehabilitation Act and the ADA and exclude gender identity disorder and transsexualism.[9] Some state courts have held that transsexualism is not a protected disability.[10]

Other states, like New Jersey, Washington, and Massachusetts, protect transsexuals under state law.[11] There are also administrative rulings protecting transsexuals in Oregon, Florida, Illinois, Massachusetts, and New Hampshire.

The federal First, Second, Sixth, and Ninth Circuit courts have all issued decisions favorable to transsexuals.[12] These decisions are based on recent United States Supreme Court decisions[13] expanding the scope of Title VII of the Civil Rights Act of 1964. A few federal district courts also issued decisions protecting the rights of transsexuals.[14]

Based on several cases, it seems that state discrimination claims are currently the most viable venue to seek redress for transsexual clients.[15] But there is a growing pattern of success under Title VII sex discrimination claims.

California, Minnesota, New Mexico, Illinois, Washington, Maine, and Rhode Island have employment discrimination statutes that explicitly protect transgender and transsexual persons.[16] In 1993, Minnesota became the first state to enact this legislation. Minnesota defined sexual orientation to include "having or being perceived as having a self-image or identity not traditionally associated with one's biological maleness or femaleness."[17]

But Minnesota's Supreme Court has also ruled that employers may require employees to use the bathroom for their biological sex.[18] The case involved a transsexual undergoing a male-to-female transition. She wanted to use the women's restroom and management insisted that she use the men's room. Since she dressed as and presented herself as a woman, using the men's restroom posed a serious problem for her. Restroom issues are often the underlying reason for employment discrimination claims.

To counter an employer's argument, practitioners can argue that the transsexual plaintiff altered her biological sex by undergoing sex reassignment surgery. Where the employee has not undergone sex reassignment surgery, counsel can point out that a common-sense approach requires the employee to use the restroom that corresponds with the gender he or she identifies with and presents as.

Illinois, Maine, Minnesota, Rhode Island, Hawaii, Washington, California, and New Mexico also include protection for transgender and transsexual persons in their non-discrimination laws.[19]

The Rhode Island non-discrimination statute includes "gender identity or expression" as a protected category.[20] The statutory definition is: "A person's actual or perceived gender, as well as a person's gender identity, gender-related self-image, gender-related appearance or gender-related expression; whether or not that gender identity, gender-related self-image, gender-related appearance, or gender-related expression is different from that traditionally associated with the person's sex at birth."[21]

New Mexico amended its human relations law in 2003.[22] The statute prohibits discrimination because of "gender identity." The statute defines gender identity as "[a] person's self-perception or perception of that person by another, of the person's identity as a male or female based upon the personal appearance, behavior or physical characteristics that are in accord with or opposed to the person's physical anatomy, chromosomal sex or sex at birth."

California's Government Code section 12926 clarified the definition of "sex." The law now includes the following language: "[a] person's actual or perceived sex, including a person's identity or appearance, whether or not that identity or appearance is different from that traditionally associated with that person's sex at birth." This language is intended to codify anti-transgender discrimination in California.

The National Gay and Lesbian Task Force and the Transgender Law Center published an overview of transgender legislation.[23] Attorneys representing transgender clients may find it a useful reference when preparing their cases.

C. Family Law Issues

Transgender individuals face obstacles when it comes to marriage and parenting. One issue concerns whether the person transitioned during the marriage, before the marriage, or after the divorce. Case law is starting to evolve in this area.

Where the transition occurred before marriage, some state courts have invalidated a marriage because one partner is transgender. The Kansas Supreme Court did so in *In re Estate of Gardiner*,[24] where the surviving wife transitioned years *before* the marriage. Yet the court decided the marriage was invalid because Kansas does not recognize marriages between two men. In the court's opinion, both parties to the marriage were men. The court's opinion included the following:

A traditional marriage is the legal relationship between a biological man and a biological woman for the discharge to each other and the community of the duties legally incumbent on those whose relationship is founded on the distinction of sex.

The stated purpose of K.S.A. 2001 Supp. 23-101 and K.S.A. 2001 Supp. 23-115 is to recognize that only traditional marriages are valid in this state. A post-operative male-to-female transsexual is not a woman within the meaning of the statutes and cannot validly marry another man. Pursuant to K.S.A. 2001 Supp. 23-101, a marriage between a post-operative male-to-female transsexual and a man is void as against public policy.

J'Noel Gardiner had sex reassignment surgery in Wisconsin and obtained an amended Wisconsin birth certificate. This is allowed under Wisconsin law, as in most states. The Kansas court refused to accept her argument that the federal Full Faith and Credit Clause required Kansas to recognize the amended birth certificate. J'Noel had sex reassignment surgery in 1994. She and Michael Gardiner were married in September 1998. Michael was fully aware before the marriage that J'Noel was transgender and suffered from gender dysphoria.

The case started when Michael's estranged son, Joe, sought letters of administration and alleged that J'Noel waived her spousal rights. When J'Noel objected, he amended his pleadings to argue the marriage was void because J'Noel is transgender. That would make Joe the sole heir to his father's estate.

The Kansas court stated: "We view the legislative silence to indicate that transsexuals are not included. If the legislature intended to include transsexuals, it could have been a simple matter to do so. We apply the rules of statutory construction to ascertain the legislative intent as expressed in the statute."

So many courts use the language, "if the legislature intended to include . . . it could have been a simple matter to do so." Yet most legislatures never considered transsexuals, gay men, or lesbians when passing any of the statutes involved. Just because these various groups are not *included*, however, does not mean they are *excluded*.

Courts have the authority to interpret legislative language. Looking at the reason for the statute is often just as important as the language involved.

Before the Kansas Supreme Court heard of J'Noel Gardiner, Texas was dealing with *Littleton v. Prange*.[25] The Texas court, in a case involving an estate, defined the issue as: "[C]an a physician change the gender of a person with a scalpel, drugs and counseling, or is a person's gender immutably fixed by our Creator at birth?"[26] Since this is Texas, one can presume this is a rhetorical question.

Littleton involved a medical malpractice case. As in the Kansas case above, *Littleton* involved a male-to-female transsexual wife married to a male husband. Another similarity is that Christie Littleton, the wife, transitioned to a female years before marrying her husband. The couple married in 1989 and lived together as husband and wife until John Littleton's death in 1996.

The defendants in the medical malpractice case alleged that Christie had no standing to bring suit because the underlying marriage was void. The Texas court concluded that Christie was born a male, had male chromosomes, and she was a male, period, end of story. The court also concluded that psychology, surgery, and medical diagnoses could not change the fact that Christie Littleton was a man and could not marry another man. The court concluded, "There are some things we cannot will into being. They just are."

The Texas court could not see past the chromosomes. It refused to accept the expert testimony that Christie Littleton was psychologically and physically a woman and had lived in a marriage for seven years.

A contrary view is presented in *M.T. v. J.T.*,[27] a 1976 New Jersey case involving a husband who did not want to pay alimony. To support his position, the husband argued his marriage was void because his wife was not a woman. The issue before the court, and similar Kansas and Texas cases, was whether the marriage of a post-operative male-to-female transsexual and a male was a lawful marriage between a man and a woman. The New Jersey court found that it was a valid marriage.[28]

Although there are similarities with the Kansas and Texas cases, there are also significant differences, including the outcome. The New Jersey court refused to accept the husband's argument that his marriage was void. The *M.T.* court also stated:

> In this case the transsexual's gender and genitalia are no longer discordant; they have been harmonized through medical treatment. Plaintiff has become physically and psychologically unified and fully capable of sexual activity consistent with her reconciled sexual attributes of

gender and anatomy. Consequently, plaintiff should be considered a member of the female sex for marital purposes. It follows that such an individual would have the capacity to enter into a valid marriage relationship with a person of the opposite sex and did so here. In so ruling we do no more than give legal effect to a *fait accompli*, based upon medical judgment and action which are irreversible. Such recognition will promote the individual's quest for inner peace and personal happiness, while in no way disserving any societal interest, principle of public order or precept of morality.[29]

An issue unique to the *M.T.* case concerned the husband's contribution to his wife's male-to-female transition process. The wife transitioned to female after meeting her husband. He paid for the surgery. The couple lived together since 1964 and was married for two years. He then refused to support her after deserting her. In the end, the court ordered the husband to pay support to his wife. The court also found the underlying marriage valid.

In *Kantaras v. Kantaras*,[30] a Florida trial court, in an 800-page opinion, found the Kantaras marriage to be valid. Michael Kantaras, the husband, is a female-to-male transsexual. The trial court also awarded custody of the couple's two children to Michael Kantaras. Mrs. Kantaras appealed the decision.

The Florida 2nd District Court of Appeals reversed, stating that one's gender at birth cannot be changed for a marriage to be valid under Florida law. The court decided that was an issue for the Florida Legislature to address. The appellate court reversed the decision recognizing the couple's marriage. The court remanded the case for a determination of parental rights and responsibilities.

Michael adopted the older child and is listed as the father on the younger child's birth certificate. The couple settled the parenting matter, and Michael retains all parental rights and responsibilities for his children as well as primary custody.

Kantaras is an exception to the general rule that transgender people and transsexuals are discriminated against in custody and visitation cases. If the validity of a marriage can be successfully challenged, the transsexual spouse's parental status and rights are often jeopardized.

This is made clear in *In re Marriage of Simmons*,[31] an Illinois case involving a female-to-male transsexual, a marriage, and children. The trial court denied Sterling Simmons's petition to dissolve the marriage. The court declared the marriage *void ab initio* and awarded sole care and custody of the minor child to the mother, Jennifer Simmons. The court also held that Sterling Simmons had no standing under Illinois law to seek custody or visitation of the child and terminated his parental rights.

The child was born in July 1992 following artificial insemination. Sterling is listed as the father on the child's birth certificate. The father and child have a longstanding parent-child relationship. Reading the court's decision, however, it appears the existence of this relationship had no effect on the judges.

In fact, the court cited an earlier Illinois case, involving a lesbian couple, to support its decision. *In re Visitation With C.B.L.*[32] involved a long-term lesbian relationship and a minor child. When the couple ended their relationship, the non-legal parent sought visitation with the minor child. She argued she had standing as a *de facto* parent or as one *in loco parentis*. The court held that Illinois' Marriage Act was the only authority for granting visitation. Since the petitioner had no standing under that Act, she had no standing to seek visitation with the child.

The court considered its hands tied on the matter: "Finally, this court is not unmindful of the fact that our evolving social structures have created nontraditional relationships. This court, however, has no authority to ignore the manifest intent of our General Assembly. Who shall have standing to petition for visitation with a minor is an issue of complex social significance. Such an issue demands a comprehensive legislative solution. That solution is provided, by our General Assembly, within [the Marriage Act]."[33]

An interesting aspect of the *Simmons* case involved the fact that Sterling Simmons had undergone some surgical procedures to alter his anatomy (a hysterectomy) but not others. Surgical procedures for female-to-male transsexuals can be more complex and expensive than for their male-to-female transsexual counterparts. At least one doctor testified that Sterling's hysterectomy was not a part of his gender transition.

Despite the recognition by transgender healthcare experts that the elements of transition are individualized for each transgender person, the *Simmons* court concluded that Sterling had not fully transitioned and still required extensive surgical procedures to complete the process. Reading the decision, it sounds like the court believed his process was less than convincing, as if Sterling did not really intend to transition to a male, despite the fact that he had lived as a male for decades.

One aspect missing from these cases is the psychological effect on the children involved. While a strict interpretation of a statute is often necessary, it is not always appropriate with issues concerning a child. The cases do not seem to consider what happens to the child when a person with whom the child has a close and loving relationship is suddenly no longer there.

There is nothing "activist" about protecting a child's relationship with a loving parent—even when that parent does not rate a place in the legislation-passed hierarchy of parents. When a biological, adoptive, or other legal parent introduces another adult into a child's life, both adults assume responsibilities. Those responsibilities include doing nothing to hurt that child. Yet the children seem to be left behind in all these discussions.

Some parties have used estoppel to prevent a spouse from challenging the validity of the marriage. When a person knowingly enters into a marriage with a transsexual person, they should be estopped from later challenging the marriage's validity. One way to approach the issue is with something akin to having both parties sign an informed consent, acknowledging that the husband/wife is a transsexual.

There is always the chance a court will refuse to allow another adult to willingly, knowingly, and voluntarily agree to waive certain legal rights. Courts are notorious for wanting to protect people from themselves. The *Simmons* court held that estoppel did not apply because the wife could not confer the right of standing on Sterling. The court ignored Mrs. Simmons' actions in bearing a child with her husband, placing his name on the birth certificate, and joining with him in raising the child. She should be estopped from challenging a status in which she willingly joined.

Courts are in a better position to respond to changing social situations. Legislatures, through their legislative enactments, provide statutory guidance to the courts. However, the legislature cannot and will not consider every possible nuance under every piece of legislation. Therefore, the courts are in a position to use the legislative history, if any exists, and apply the thought process of the legislature to a case of first impression.

Whenever children are concerned, judges must be willing to do what is right and best for the minors involved rather than walking in lockstep with a statute written decades earlier. Some call this making law rather than interpreting it. But children cannot wait for a legislature to attain the level of intestinal fortitude needed to protect their interests. They rely on judges to make a decision.

Cases involving children are in the present. Legislative activity is in the future. And each case involving a child is decided on its own merits. Why can't a judge, looking at the facts, make a decision? Unless a statute specifically *excludes* a certain decision, the judge has the authority to interpret the law to serve a child's best interests.

Some courts understand their responsibilities. In *Marriage of D.F.D.*,[34] the Montana Supreme Court reversed a decision awarding sole custody to the mother and restricting the father's visitation. The trial court ordered restricted visitation because the father cross-dresses in private. A Minnesota Court of Appeals also awarded custody to a cross-dressing father.[35]

In 1985, a New York court prevented a female-to-male transsexual from denying his parental responsibilities and did so without considering the validity of the marriage.[36] An unpublished decision in Minnesota[37] affirmed a custody award to a transsexual father.

For sexual orientation, transgender, or transsexual status to be relevant in a parental rights and responsibilities scenario, there must be a showing of actual harm to the child. The Colorado Court of Appeals refused to change custody granted to a transsexual parent.[38] After her first marriage ended, the mother transitioned to a male. He then married a woman. The court decided that the mother's subsequent transition to a man and marriage to a woman did not justify a change of custody.

1. Terminating Parental Rights

Not all judges treat transgender parents appropriately. The Nevada Supreme Court proves this point. In *Daly v. Daly*,[39] a husband admitted being a transsexual to his wife during the marriage. Shortly after, the parties divorced. The mother received custody of the parties' daughter. During a visitation, the child's father confided in her his plan to transition to a female. He asked his daughter to say nothing to either her mother or grandmother. When the mother noticed the child becoming more withdrawn after each visit and inquired as to the reason, the child told her of the father's plans.

A psychologist warned the mother that it was dangerous to permit the child further visits with the father. The mother filed legal action seeking to terminate the father's parental rights. This same psychologist testified at trial that the child would not be damaged if she never saw her father again. The child told the judge and psychologist that she did not want to see her father again. The court stated, "Such considerations are further complicated by the apparent degree of Mary's revulsion over Suzanne [formerly Tim] and the irretrievable loss of Suzanne's former relationship with Mary as a parent-father."[40]

The court blamed the situation on Suzanne.

> The future prospects for emotional family stability are also dimmed by Suzanne's indication that Mary should know lesbians, homosexuals and transsexuals and "be a part of their lives" if "they are my [Suzanne's] friends."
>
> Suzanne, who admitted that many of her friends are to be found among the aforementioned groups, has thus postured herself in a position of recurring conflict with the child's mother and the "traditional" upbringing enjoyed by Mary during her formative years. The resulting

equation does not bode well for the emotional health and well-being of the child. This Court can perceive no basis for such disruption of Mary's life. Nor do we see the necessity for inflicting a continuing sense of instability and uneasiness on this child.

As noted previously, when Mary reaches the age of majority she can decide whether to reinstate a relationship with Suzanne. In the meantime, given the circumstances concerning Mary's view of Suzanne and the extent of her opposition to further ties with a vestigial parent, it can be said that Suzanne, in a very real sense, has terminated her own parental rights as a father. It was strictly Tim Daly's choice to discard his fatherhood and assume the role of a female who could never be either mother or sister to his daughter.[41]

The court then ruled that Suzanne's parental rights should be terminated. It also mentioned that Suzanne had not paid support in over a year, nor had she attempted to visit with the child. The court was very opposed to Suzanne's solution of requiring psychological counseling for the child to help her accept the transition. The court did not think the child needed to undergo counseling to deal with a situation created solely by her father. It is worth noting that some aspects of this father's behavior are problematic. For example, he asked the child to keep a secret. Nevertheless, the court's transphobic dicta are uncalled for.

In 1997, an appellate court in Missouri reversed an award of custody to a transsexual parent. The court imposed a moratorium on visitation because the child found it emotionally confusing to see the father as a woman.[42] In 1992, a New York court refused to grant overnight visits to a cross-dressing father because of the possible effect on his children.[43]

2. Marriage

One legal issue affecting transsexual spouses arises with attempts to collect survivor benefits, inheritance claims against the decedent's estate, or tax benefits that are limited to married couples. Employers may challenge the marriage to exclude the transsexual surviving spouse from qualifying for health insurance or other company-provided benefits. Even if the employer does not object, the insurance company may. If there is a denial, issues of standing are raised that may preclude a surviving spouse from filing or succeeding in a lawsuit.

Inheritance claims may be particularly difficult when the decedent dies intestate.

A memorandum of understanding between the spouses, in which both acknowledge the transsexual spouse's status, may help preserve the marriage's validity. The applicable legal principle is that the validity of a marriage is determined at the time it is created. Once a valid marriage exists, nothing but death or divorce dissolves it. In cases involving a transsexual spouse who transitioned after the marriage, this legal principle applies and the marriage is valid. But the transsexual spouse may have difficulty establishing or retaining parental rights.

Courts in California and New Jersey[44] have declared marriages valid where there is one transgender spouse. Florida, Illinois, Kansas, Ohio, and Texas, however, have taken the opposite view. Those courts decided that a person's sex is determined at birth and any subsequent marriage is void *ab initio* because both parties are of the same sex. In Ohio, an appellate court refused to honor a female-to-male transsexual's Massachusetts birth certificate showing his sex as male.[45]

Divorce is often the catalyst for raising issues that adversely affect a transsexual spouse. The other spouse may threaten to publicly reveal the other's transgender status to avoid custody, support, or alimony contests.

Some spouses may claim their spouse is a cross-dresser. In some states, a court might mistakenly assume that cross-dressing is per se harmful to children.

Opposing counsel may try to rely on outdated and questionable data to undermine the transsexual spouse's position. Unfortunately, many family law judges listen to these myths and base decisions on them. These same judges refuse to acknowledge widely accepted scientific, psychological, and medical opinions that clearly refute the junk science proffered by opponents. Appeals are expensive, and the client's best shot is at the trial level.

Lawyers representing the transsexual spouse in divorce, custody or visitation cases must research, understand, and present the latest data to the court. Recruiting experts early in the process will serve the lawyer and the client well. The lawyer will be responsible for educating the judge about the law, the data, and the realities of transsexualism.

The National Center for Lesbian Rights, Lambda Legal, and the Transgender Law Center are excellent resources for lawyers to tap into for experts and legal advice. These organizations will provide myriad forms of assistance when asked.

3. Estate Planning

When assisting a married couple in developing their estate plan, it is best to address the transgender spouse's status. This can be done in the last will and testament, durable power of attorney for finances, advance directives, and any prenuptial agreement.

The latter is a personal relationship agreement that includes a detailed account of each spouse's rights and responsibilities concerning a plethora of issues that is entered into before marriage. These include property, finances, support, children, and other equally important issues. The document can include language reflecting the awareness of each spouse concerning the transgender status of one spouse. Doing so may later help the transgender spouse avoid claims of fraud or deception. This may also help protect the parties if the marriage is challenged. At the very least, it will prevent the non-transgender spouse from denying knowledge of the other's status.

These agreements can also provide for inheritance rights even if their marriage is declared invalid later. Marriage is a contract subject to contract law. Attorneys must make sure any agreement meets the six basic elements of a contract: offer, acceptance, consideration, intent, capacity, and subject matter. Whether the parties enter into marriage through a religious or civil ceremony, the essence of a marriage lies in the contract.

D. Employment

The rights of transgender and transsexual persons in employment situations are being developed in the courts. The Sixth Circuit Court of Appeals determined that Title VII of the Civil Rights Act of 1964 protects transgender workers.[46]

In the *Smith* case, the court decided that a transsexual firefighter was pressured into resigning after informing her superiors of her transition. Jimmie Smith was a lieutenant in the Salem, Ohio, Fire Department. After being diagnosed with gender dysphoria, she began feminizing her appearance and dress. Perceiving Jimmie as an effeminate male, her co-workers began commenting that she was not "masculine enough," and that is when Smith informed her superiors. She asked that the information be kept confidential, but her supervisor immediately informed city officials. The fire department and city officials began a campaign to get rid of Smith by demanding a series of psychological tests with the expectation that Smith would refuse and then be fired for insubordination. The city's safety director informed Smith of the plan and called it a "witch hunt."

Smith retained counsel and filed a discrimination complaint with the Equal Employment Opportunity Commission. He was then charged with a policy infraction, later found to be without merit.

Smith's lawsuit alleged Title VII sex discrimination, constitutional and state law violations, and invasion of privacy. The trial judge dismissed the lawsuit, finding that Title VII did not prohibit discrimination against transsexuals. In her appeal, Smith argued that the trial court's reasoning was superseded by the

U.S. Supreme Court decision in *Price Waterhouse v. Hopkins*.[47] In that case, the Supreme Court held that sex stereotyping is a form of sex discrimination that Title VII prohibits.

The Sixth Circuit decision held the trial judge erred in concentrating on Smith's transsexual status rather than the reasons for the discrimination. According to the court, Title VII addresses "prohibited grounds" that include sex discrimination. The court found that this interpretation relates to the 1998 Supreme Court decision in *Oncale v. Sundowner Offshore*.[48] In that case, the Supreme Court ruled that a complainant discriminated against because of sex has standing even if the harassers were of the same gender.

Judge Cole, writing for the Sixth Circuit panel, wrote: "Sex stereotyping based on a person's gender-nonconforming behavior is impermissible discrimination, irrespective of the cause of that behavior. A label such as 'transsexual' is not fatal to a sex discrimination claim where the victim has suffered discrimination because of his or her gender non-conformation." Cole went on to say, "[B]y definition, transsexuals are individuals who fail to conform to stereotypes about how those assigned to a particular sex at birth should act, dress, and self-identify. Ergo, identification as a transsexual is the statement or admission that one wishes to be the opposite sex or does not relate to one's birth sex. . . . Thus, if an individual suffers discrimination because he or she is transgendered, such discrimination violates Title VII's ban on sex discrimination."

The Ninth Circuit Court of Appeals allowed a transgender woman in prison to sue under the federal Violence Against Women Act.[49] The court noted that earlier decisions dismissing employment discrimination claims by transsexuals were superseded by the *Price Waterhouse* decision. The same court also ruled that homophobic harassment violated Title VII if the complainant could show that the harassment was based on gender nonconformity.[50]

A day after the Sixth Circuit released the *Smith* decision, an Arizona federal district court judge issued a similar ruling in *Kastl v. Maricopa County Community College*.[51] This decision also upheld a Title VII discrimination claim brought by a transsexual plaintiff. The plaintiff, however, recently lost on summary judgment.

The Fifth Circuit issued a decision in 1981 finding no violation under the federal Equal Protection Clause for a transsexual fired for refusing to wear men's clothing to work. The firing occurred after the employer learned the plaintiff was having sex reassignment surgery.[52]

In 2005, the New York Appellate Division refused to overturn a decision allowing a landlord to refuse to renew a commercial lease. The plaintiff, the

Hispanic AIDS Forum, sued its landlord, Bruno, because of the non-renewal. The landlord wanted the Forum to require its transgender clients to use the "appropriate" restroom. When they refused, Bruno refused to renew their lease. The plaintiffs filed their lawsuit two years before New York City amended its Human Rights law to protect transgender persons. The court ruled that the new law did not apply to the case. According to the court, the landlord's decision to designate restrooms based on "biological gender" and not "biological self-image" was not discrimination under the laws in existence in 2000. Even if state or city nondiscrimination laws did protect transgender people, the behavior of the landlord was not a violation because requiring restroom usage based on birth-assigned sex is not discriminatory. This is similar to the holding in *Goins*.[53] The court dismissed the case.[54]

One potential way around the restroom issue is to cite Occupational Safety and Health Administration (OSHA) regulations that require employers to provide restrooms for all employees.[55] The downside of citing OSHA regulations is that employers are not prohibited from requiring employees to use the restrooms that match their gender identity. Many transgender employees find that careful educational strategies are the best route to assuaging employers' fears about restroom access. Outside trainers can also be brought in to address managers' concerns.

> **Cole Thaler, Attorney, Lambda Legal Transgender Law Project, Atlanta, Georgia**
> As Lambda Legal's national transgender rights attorney and a transgender man, my work affords me a rare perspective on the concerns of the transgender community. As I talk with transgender people throughout the country about their legal problems, I have noticed a clear pattern of vulnerability.
>
> First, Lambda Legal gets more calls about workplace discrimination than any other transgender issue. Supervisors of Jimmie Smith, a transgender firefighter, tried to drive her out of her position by subjecting her to a series of invasive psychological examinations. Transgender employees should take heart from Jimmie's victory: the Sixth Circuit ruled in 2004 that Title VII, the federal sex discrimination law, protects transgender employees. Many Lambda Legal callers report difficulty obtaining identity documents, like driver's licenses, bearing the appropriate gender designation. One transgender man I spoke with was threatened with physical violence when someone behind him in line noticed that his driver's license listed his sex as "female." Some judges even refuse name changes for transgender petitioners who cannot

> present evidence of surgery. When challenged, these judges recognize that they cannot hold transgender people to a higher legal standard. But the pattern persists.
>
> Discrimination is not neutral in its application. Low-income transgender people are more likely to encounter sex-segregated spaces, like homeless shelters, that exclude or mistreat them. Transgender prisoners are vulnerable to many forms of abuse; Lambda Legal's *Sundstrom* case challenges a Wisconsin law prohibiting transition-related health care for transgender inmates. As more attorneys around the country become involved in litigation and advocacy on behalf of the transgender community, I am hopeful that protections will increase and the pattern of vulnerability will fade into memory.

1. Disability Laws

Neither the Rehabilitation Act of 1973[56] nor the Americans with Disabilities Act (ADA)[57] permits claims by transgender persons. In fact, both statutes explicitly exclude transsexualism and "gender identity disorders" that do not result from physical impairments.

Iowa, Indiana, Louisiana, Nebraska, Ohio, Oklahoma, Texas, and Virginia also have explicit exclusions of transsexuals from their state laws that are similar to the Rehabilitation Act and the ADA.

Some state courts have ruled that state disability statutes do not protect transsexuals even when those statutes do not specifically exclude them.[58] Given the advances in understanding the medical and psychological aspects of transsexualism, these decisions may not hold up if the issue is raised and pursued.

There is case law holding that disability laws protect transsexuals.[59] State agencies are also issuing decisions finding that state discrimination laws cover transsexuals.[60]

In 1996, Oregon's Bureau of Labor and Industry decided that a transsexual woman, fired because of her status, was protected under the Oregon disability law. The Oregon Legislature responded by amending the state law as follows: "[a]n employer may not be found to have engaged in an unlawful employment practice solely because the employer fails to provide reasonable accommodation to a person with a disability arising out of transsexualism."[61] The statute, however, does not exclude transsexuals from being fired or discriminated against because of their transsexual status. The reasonable accommodation issue may arise around bathroom concerns.

2. Federal Laws

In the 1970s and 1980s, federal courts were reluctant to hold that transsexuals were protected from employment discrimination under Title VII. The prevailing position was summarized by *Ulane v. Eastern Airlines, Inc.*[62] The Seventh Circuit held in that case that "Title VII does not outlaw discrimination against a person who has a sexual identity disorder." The seeds for a reversal of that trend were planted by the 1989 Supreme Court decision in *Price Waterhouse v. Hopkins*. After *Price Waterhouse*, a growing number of state and federal courts acknowledged that the "sex stereotyping" form of sex discrimination applied to transsexual employees as well as to others who failed to conform to employers' gender stereotypes. With the decisions by the Sixth and Ninth Circuits, it will be interesting to see if the Court takes the next opportunity to resolve the differences between the circuits. The City of Salem, Ohio, did not appeal the Sixth Circuit's decision. The State of Ohio unsuccessfully sought certiorari in a later case that affirmed *Smith*.[63] Perhaps, like Eastern Airlines, the Seventh Circuit decision will no longer fly.

Decisions similar to the *Ulane* case came out of the Eighth Circuit and the District courts in Kansas and Maryland.[64] But two of these cases were pre-*Price Waterhouse*.

Since the U.S. Supreme Court is taking a more expansive view of Title VII, the early cases denying protection to transsexuals should not be considered viable.

In *Rosa v. Park West Bank & Trust Co.*,[65] the First Circuit reinstated the claim filed by a transsexual under the federal Equal Credit Opportunity Act.

A glaring exception to the pattern is found in *Oiler v. Winn-Dixie*,[66] where the District Court upheld the firing of an employee who wore women's clothing *off the job*. The court decided that this employee did not have Title VII protection.

The district court in Utah also decided against a transsexual plaintiff's claims of discrimination. In *Etsitty v. Utah Transit Authority*,[67] the plaintiff was a bus driver for the local transit authority. She was fired for using the women's restroom even though she was in a pre-operative transition stage. The trial judge granted summary judgment against the plaintiff. The judge held that Congress never intended to include transsexuals under Title VII. He found a "huge difference" between a woman who is not feminine enough and a man changing his sex. "Such drastic action cannot be fairly characterized as a mere failure to conform to stereotypes."

An interesting postscript to the *Etsitty* case is that the employer claimed that she is eligible to be rehired after completing her surgical transition. *Etsitty* is being appealed to the 10th Circuit Court of Appeals.

Title IX is usually considered a sports-related statute, but it is also being used successfully by transsexuals. In *Miles v. New York University*,[68] the court decided that the transsexual plaintiff did have a Title IX action. This suit involved sexual harassment. In 2001, the New Hampshire District Court found that harassing someone because of "sex-typed stereotypes" is actionable under Title IX.[69]

When a public education institution is involved, using Title IX as a basis for any discrimination lawsuit is advisable. This includes educational institutions at all levels. If the school receives federal funds, Title IX will apply. Contrary to popular belief, it is not limited to actions involving sports.

In 1990, the Department of Veteran Affairs (previously Veterans Administration) Office of General Counsel issued an opinion on determining veterans' benefits when a marriage involved a transsexual veteran. The question answered in the opinion was: "Is a transsexual veteran, who undergoes sexual reassignment surgery and then marries a member of the veteran's original gender, entitled to the additional VA benefits normally provided on account of a spouse?" The General Counsel, interpreting Texas law (where the marriage took place), held: "Under Texas law, where a veteran has anatomically changed his/her sex by undergoing sexual-reassignment surgery and has thereafter legally married a member of his/her former sex, his/her marriage partner may be considered the veteran's spouse for the purpose of determining entitlement to additional vocational rehabilitation allowance payable on account of a dependent spouse."[70]

E. Sex Reassignment Surgery

The federal Medicaid law does not exclude sex reassignment surgery from coverage. But many state Medicaid statutes do exclude sex reassignment surgery (SRS). Illinois, Pennsylvania, and Alaska are some examples.[71] On the other hand, there is case law holding that states cannot categorically exclude SRS from coverage.[72]

In the best of circumstances, it is difficult to get Medicaid reimbursement for SRS. The problem starts with Medicaid staff, who may automatically deny the claim because they believe it is not covered. The staff may also view SRS as cosmetic or an experimental procedure that is not covered. However, internationally accepted treatment protocols recognize that sex reassignment surgery is not cosmetic, but is effective and necessary treatment for gender dysphoria.

The claims often fail to include adequate documentation supporting the medical necessity of the procedure. Some advocates and attorneys for transsexuals fail to adequately represent their client's interests due to ignorance, prejudice, or inability to find the required information. Even if Medicaid covers the procedure, many healthcare providers that perform SRS do not accept Medicaid for payment.[73]

The federal Medicare program does not exclude coverage for SRS.[74] The same policy holds for the Civilian Health and Medical Program of the Uniformed Services (CHAMPUS).[75]

After SRS, transsexuals often find it difficult to obtain proper medical treatment appropriate for their new sex. A Massachusetts Superior Court decided that a male-to-female transsexual could not be denied medically necessary breast reconstruction surgery.[76] In this case, a transsexual woman who transitioned 25 years earlier required reconstructive breast surgery. She sued after Medicaid denied the procedure because she was transsexual.

Sex reassignment surgery is not performed in VA medical centers or under VA auspices.[77]

Many private insurers also specifically exclude SRS from coverage under their health plans. Contract law governs private health insurance. If the policy does not contain a specific exclusion, the transsexual insured may be covered for SRS.[78]

Even when the policy specifically excludes SRS, the insured may be able to successfully appeal the exclusion. This is where it is essential that all information relating to the medical necessity of the procedure be provided.[79]

Some private health insurers try to avoid paying anything involving a transsexual insured's healthcare. They construe all healthcare as related to the gender transition and deny coverage. This includes regular medical care routinely covered for non-transsexual insureds.

Some insurers object to payment on the grounds these are experimental procedures. To the contrary, physicians have performed sex reassignment surgeries for decades.

There have been a few lawsuits attempting to require an employer to offer equal health benefits.[80] In *Mario*, a female-to-male transsexual sued his employer under the Employee Retirement Income Security Act of 1973 (ERISA). The plaintiff lost because he failed to establish that SRS was medically necessary.

In the insurance claims arena or civil litigation, the burden is on the plaintiff to prove the case. Most cases are lost because the plaintiff did not meet the burden of proof. Failing to provide sufficient credible evidence to support the claim makes it easier for judges and other entities to dismiss.

Contrary to popular belief, there is not one single sex reassignment surgery. In fact, physical gender transition may involve a variety of surgical interventions. Regardless of which surgeries are at issue, the cost can be prohibitive and beyond the means of most transsexuals. Some courts have refused to recognize discrimination against a transsexual who has not undergone multiple forms of sex reassignment surgery.[81]

F. Transsexuals in Prison

Prison officials have a duty to protect inmates from violence. An official's "deliberate indifference" may result in liability under the Eighth Amendment to the federal Constitution prohibiting cruel and unusual punishment.

Transsexuals are at great risk in prison settings. A transsexual who has not completed genital surgery will be classified by his or her birth sex. For example, male-to-female transsexuals are typically placed in men's prisons. This often leads to abuse from other inmates and corrections officers.

In 1994, the United States Supreme Court weighed in on the subject of prison officials' liability to transsexual inmates.[82] A pre-operative male-to-female transsexual prisoner was brutally beaten and raped by her cellmate two weeks after entering the facility. The Supreme Court, in a unanimous ruling, stated that prison officials are liable only if they knew of the situation and disregarded the excessive risk to the transsexual prisoner.

In its decision, Justice Souter, writing for the Court, wrote: "We hold instead that a prison official cannot be found liable under the Eighth Amendment for denying an inmate humane conditions of confinement unless the official knows of and disregards an excessive risk to inmate health or safety; the official must both be aware of facts from which the inference could be drawn that a substantial risk of serious harm exists, and he must also draw the inference."

The Court discussed the application of protections under the Eighth Amendment and stated, "The question under the Eighth Amendment is whether prison officials, acting with deliberate indifference, exposed a prisoner to a sufficiently substantial 'risk of serious damage to his future health.'" (Cite omitted.) The Supreme Court remanded the case for consideration of evidence showing violation of the Eighth Amendment.

Since the Court imposed a subjective test, it is important for lawyers who represent transsexual defendants to notify prison authorities of possible danger to their clients. Many transsexuals are placed in segregation for their protection. While this may appear to resolve the potential for violence, it is punitive and restricts the transsexual inmate's activities.

Segregation may involve remaining in one's cell for 23 hours of every day. Lawyers representing transsexual inmates are in a bind because adequate protection may involve a very restrictive setting, and less protection may result in severe injury or death to the inmate. Lawyers must discuss this Hobson's choice with their clients and prison officials.[83] A legal notice to prison officials advising them of their constitutional obligation to treat the inmate humanely and notifying them of his or her transgender status places the matter on the record. Counsel should bear in mind that the federal Prison Litigation Reform Act requires inmates to exhaust internal grievance procedures as a prerequisite to filing suit. Grievance and litigation time lines may be tight, so counsel is well advised to seek consultation from experienced prison litigators.

Transsexual persons in jail may be unable to make rational decisions about plea-bargaining. This may be caused by fear, harassment, and misclassification or trying to avoid sexual assaults in jail. Transsexuals exist in a state of fear and distress in a jail environment. Lawyers representing a transsexual client must consider these factors when evaluating the case and the client's ability to cooperate.

During trial, especially during voir dire, it is important to broach the transsexual issue and its effect on prospective jurors. Will the individual juror be able to weigh the evidence against the defendant without prejudice or bias?

When getting a job is a condition of probation, the court must acknowledge, *on the record*, that a transsexual may have greater difficulty fulfilling that requirement. The court and the court liaison must acknowledge that failure to obtain employment because of discrimination will not cause a revocation of the defendant's probation. The same official acknowledgment is required if the defendant is sentenced to a halfway house or a shelter. In those situations, it is important for the court to instruct the residence of the defendant's transgender status. One caveat: It is important to consider whether such notification is in the defendant's best interests. Consider whether the defendant is post-transition but not "out" in other contexts.

The court must also instruct the residence officials that the defendant is transitioning and is not required to revert to his/her birth gender.

When imposing a probation requirement of substance abuse counseling, defense counsel must ask the court to notify the substance abuse program about the defendant's transgender status, as any accompanying guilt may be manifested as substance abuse issues. The transgender probationer must be treated with respect in his or her new gender presentation.

A transsexual inmate's right to hormone therapy and sex reassignment surgery while incarcerated has been the subject of much litigation. Most courts recognize that transgender inmates have a serious health condition that requires some form of treatment.[84] Most prisoners are unsuccessful in convincing prison officials or the courts to provide the necessary medical treatment[85] because courts generally leave the contours of that treatment up to each prison's healthcare providers. Courts have denied inmates' healthcare requests for a variety of reasons: because health insurance would not pay *(Maggert)*; no right to estrogen therapy *(Long)*; and no Equal Protection Clause claim *(Brown)*.

The public is generally unconcerned with the lives of prison inmates. But raise the issue of taxpayers paying for sex reassignment surgery or other medical procedures and there will be an avalanche of protest. Still, some courts have allowed transsexual inmates to access medical treatment for their condition.[86]

The *DeLonta* case provides a good basis for understanding what happens when appropriate medical care is denied or withdrawn. DeLonta is a pre-operative transsexual incarcerated in Virginia since 1983. Prison doctors diagnosed her with gender identity disorder and provided her with estrogen therapy beginning in 1993. The treatment stopped in 1995 following release of a new prison policy:

> It is the policy of the Department of Corrections that neither medical nor surgical interventions related to gender or sex change will be provided to inmates in the management of [GID] cases.
>
> If an inmate has come into prison and/or is currently receiving hormone treatment, he is to be informed of the department['s] policy and the medication should be tapered immediately and thence discontinued.
>
> Inmates presenting with [GID] should be referred to the institution[']s mental health staff for further evaluation.

The prison medical staff immediately terminated DeLonta's hormone treatment. They did not follow the policy that required a tapering of the medication. This resulted in DeLonta experiencing nausea, depression, and itching. She also began mutilating her genitals. The trial court dismissed her complaint against all named defendants. The Fourth Circuit reversed the dismissal and remanded the case. The court stated:

> ... [w]e conclude that it does not appear beyond doubt at this early stage of the litigation that DeLonta cannot prove facts sufficient to support her claim that she has not received constitutionally adequate treatment to protect her from her compulsion to mutilate herself. We therefore reverse the district court order dismissing DeLonta's suit and remand to the district court for further proceedings. In so doing, we make no comment on

the merits of any issues not yet addressed by the district court, and we specifically make no comment on the type of treatment, if any, to which DeLonta is entitled.[87]

In *Kosilek*,[88] the district court in Massachusetts found the plaintiff's gender identity disorder to be a severe medical need. Likewise, the Ninth Circuit decided that the termination of a plaintiff's hormone treatment when she was transferred to a new facility constituted a violation of the Eighth Amendment.[89]

In a case from the Eastern District of Pennsylvania,[90] the prison officials were found to be deliberately indifferent to the plaintiff's plight. In Michigan, the court granted the plaintiff's request for a preliminary injunction. The court distinguished between refusing to pay for sex reassignment surgery and taking action that reversed the effect of years of medical treatment.[91]

These cases illustrate the arguments lawyers may make on behalf of transsexual clients. Although prisons are often particularly reluctant to provide sex reassignment surgery, transgender inmates have had more success in the realm of hormone therapy. This is especially true if the inmate was on hormone therapy before entering prison.

Lawyers must also be familiar with whether their jurisdiction has anti-cross-dressing statutes. In the past, cities have used these laws to punish transsexuals. An early case out of Texas held the Houston cross-dressing ordinance unconstitutional as ". . . applied to individuals undergoing psychiatric therapy in preparation for sex-reassignment surgery."[92]

Discrimination against transsexuals and transgender people is ongoing, and some public officials or law enforcement officers may use outdated laws to harass transsexuals. Lawyers must be aware of any charges being brought and ensure that the laws are still valid.

Lawyers advocating on behalf of transgender prisoners that placement decisions should be in accordance with gender identity should remember that male-to-female transsexuals no more belong in men's prisons than other female inmates do. At least one county jail (King County, Washington) has adopted a policy that considers gender identity for transgender inmates when making placement determinations.

In the prison context, there is often no precedent readily apparent. Fortunately, a number of resources are available to lawyers who represent transsexuals and transgender people.

These issues present unique conditions that require creativity by the lawyer in helping the court devise a sentencing scheme that serves society's need to punish the wrongdoer and protects a person who does not fit the usual profile.

One judge refused to sentence a pedophile because the man was too short to survive prison. Immigration authorities sometimes refuse to deport convicted felons because it is too dangerous to return them to their native countries. Perhaps similar consideration is due a person suffering from a medically accepted condition: gender dysphoria.

G. Identification

Transgender persons often have difficulties obtaining accurate identification, which is a critical part of everyday life. Their driver's license may not reflect the gender to which they are transitioning. This creates many headaches, and those will become migraines with the propensity for states and the federal government to pass legislation requiring identification for various purposes. Changing the sex designation on one's birth certificate often facilitates access to other government identification, such as driver's license, state ID, passport, etc.

Virtually every state permits general corrections to birth certificates. Most states will reissue a birth certificate that reflects the new sex designation.[93] These states acknowledge it is legally possible to change one's sex. In *Matter of Helig*,[94] the Maryland court stated that courts have jurisdiction to enter an order declaring the legal sex of a transgender person who is born in another state but residing in Maryland. There are three exceptions: Tennessee, Idaho, and Ohio.[95]

Tennessee's statute specifically prohibits transgender persons from amending their birth certificates, declaring it against the state's strong public policy. However, transgender activists in Tennessee are actively working to repeal this misguided statute.

Some states have general statutes that do not address the situation.

1. Determining a Person's Legal Sex

There is a common misconception that individuals have a single, easily determined "legal sex." To the contrary, people possess a patchwork of documents and records—driver's licenses, birth certificates, passports, and Social Security records—each bearing a gender designation. Those designations sometimes conflict. Also, different public entities routinely designate gender: public benefits offices, prisons and jails, the clerk's office that issues marriage licenses. Changing the sex listed on your documentation or undergoing medical transition might or might not lead a state or local entity to decide that your sex designation should be changed in its records.

Unfortunately, most judges ignore the scientific literature on the subject. They generally take one of three approaches to their decision-making:

1. Judges believe it is matter of public policy, and that falls under the authority of the state legislature.
2. Too many judges rely on religious beliefs and rhetoric when rendering a secular decision; "Almighty God sets a person's gender at birth."
3. Some refer to *Webster*'s definitions of "male" and "female" to find a basis for their decision.

None of these methods rely on sound scientific, psychological, or medical information.

Lawyers involved in these cases need to present a complete picture to the court. That picture includes the science and the law, and how the transgender plaintiff fits into it. It is important to personalize the situation. Make the judge understand that the issue involves a person, not an idea. Show how the decision will affect the individual. This is personal. These are not rhetorical cases or law school hypotheticals. That needs to be hammered home during the proceedings.

2. Birth Certificates

There is little constitutional law and little history in the states involving birth certificates and transsexuals. Some states allow administrative agencies to reissue corrected birth certificates without a court order declaring the person a member of the new gender. Others, like California, require such a court order.

States such as Florida have general statutes. A Florida attorney general's opinion in 1976 authorized use of that statute by transsexuals to obtain a reissued birth certificate.[96] In Connecticut, a federal district court judge permitted a transsexual to use the state's general statute to have a birth certificate reissued.[97]

Some people are U.S. citizens but were born outside the United States. These people have a birth certificate issued by the U.S. Department of State. Foreign-born transsexuals can change their names and gender markers on U.S. Department of State birth certificates. To do so, one must obtain a legal name change and submit a certified or original copy of the order. In addition, the applicant must submit the original birth certificate and a letter from the surgeon who performed the sex reassignment surgery. The information is sent to:

U.S. Dept. of State
1111 19th St. NW, Ste. 510
Washington, D.C. 20502-1705
202-955-0307

The State Department issues a new birth certificate, not an amended one. It takes 60 to 90 days to complete the process. Applicants may contact the State Department's Web site for information on current fees.[98]

3. *Name Changes*

Changing one's name is usually a simple process. Name changes are freely granted unless the intent is to defraud. But some judges refuse to grant the request when the listed name is commonly associated with the opposite sex. This is a problem often encountered by transsexuals.

Changing one's name without changing the gender designation on one's government-issued identification prohibits transgender people from living fully as a member of the gender with which they identify. For this reason, changing the name and sex designation on identity documents are tandem concerns.

The federal government has no specific regulation concerning changing one's gender marker. Requests for changes are made to the Social Security Administration, Department of State (passports), Department of Homeland Security (Immigration and Citizenship Enforcement), and the Department of Defense. Only the Social Security Administration and the State Department (passports) have uniform policies. It is necessary to contact the other agencies for their policies on the matter.[99]

Social Security's system for changing one's name is simple. A court order is not needed, although it is easier with one.[100] Getting a corrected Social Security card requires some documentation:

- one document (court order) showing *both* the old and new name;
- one document showing the new name (health insurance card);
- one document showing the old name (driver's license);
- documents showing the person's age, date of birth, and/or parent's names;
- photograph;
- legal document/court order showing name change (divorce, marriage, etc.) (not required but very helpful).

The name on the new Social Security card must match the person's new name.

The U.S. State Department is responsible for issuing passports. The passport agency recognizes common-law name changes, but the new name must be used over a lengthy time. With the recent focus on terrorism, however, changing one's name on an existing passport may prove difficult.

Most people use a birth certificate when applying for a passport. Transsexuals will have difficulty if they do not yet have a reissued birth certificate. Their identification documents will conflict. That, in turn, will raise flags at the agency.

The official name change policy of the passport agency requires a certified copy of the court order or evidence of the public and exclusive use of the name over a lengthy period. The "lengthy time" has been defined as five years.

The passport agency issued a Passport Bulletin (No. 92-22) that addresses the pre-operative applicant. A letter from the applicant's surgeon or attending physician that outlines the person's medical history and diagnosis of gender identity disorder is required with the application. The letter should include information about the applicant's psychological and hormonal treatment, current stage of treatment, and the approximate date for SRS.

Post-operative applicants submit the appropriate medical documents from their attending surgeon or hospital. These documents will indicate the dates on which the sex reassignment surgery took place.

Passports issued for pre-operative transsexuals are good for one year. Because this type of passport will be issued only once, lawyers may want to advise their clients to get the passport only if surgery is imminent.

The Department of Defense has no consistent policy concerning name changes, but it does not permit name changes on a service member's DD-214 (discharge papers) or the historic record. A veteran should be able to effect a name change for VA purposes. As mentioned above, a letter from the attending physician or the surgeon is required to change the gender marker.

H. Conclusion

Representing transsexual and transgender clients in cases involving their transgender status can be emotionally and professionally challenging. This area of law is too often grounded in prejudice and fear rather than sound legal and scientific analysis. Lawyers representing transsexuals will find themselves serving as educators as much as advocates.

Many people are uncomfortable with transsexual and transgender persons. Most people are unfamiliar with anyone who is transgender or transsexual. This can and does result in discrimination and abuse directed toward the transsexual or transgender person.

Transsexuals and transgender persons are a minority. Their lives and issues are frequently misunderstood and derided. Transgender clients deserve the best legal assistance available. The attorney's reward is realizing the difference made in the life of one person—with the potential for precedent that can affect many more.

Remember that there is no need to go it alone. There are multiple organizations available to assist lawyers taking on these cases. There is case law—some good, some bad; but it is there, and attitudes are slowly changing. References to these organizations are included in the Appendices.

Notes

1. www.transgenderlawcenter.org.
2. www.lambdalegal.org.
3. www.nclrights.org.
4. WORLD PROFESSIONAL ASS'N FOR TRANSGENDER HEALTH, STANDARDS OF CARE FOR GENDER IDENTITY DISORDERS, www.hbigda.org.
5. WORLD PROFESSIONAL ASS'N FOR TRANSGENDER HEALTH, STANDARDS OF CARE FOR THE DIAGNOSIS AND TREATMENT OF GENDER IDENTITY DISORDERS (6th ed., Feb. 2001), Harry Benjamin; www.hbigda.org.
6. 29 U.S.C. § 705 (20)(F)(i).
7. 42 U.S.C. § 12211(b)(1).
8. 321 F. Supp. 2d 559, 98 Soc. Sec. Rep. Serv. 323 (E.D. N.Y. 2004).
9. Indiana, Iowa, Louisiana, Nebraska, Ohio, Oklahoma, Oregon, Texas, and Virginia.
10. Holt v. Nw. Pa. Training P'ship Consortium, Inc., 694 A.2d 1134 (Pa. Commw. Ct. 1997); Dobre v. Nw. R.R. Passenger Corp. (AMTRAK), 850 F. Supp. 284, 2 A.D. Cas. (BNA) 1567, 63 Fair Empl. Prac. Cas. (BNA) 923, 63 Empl. Prac. Dec. (CCH) P 42735 (E.D. Pa. 1993); Sommers v. Iowa Civil Rights Comm'n, 337 N.W.2d 470, 1 A.D. Cas. (BNA) 442, 47 Fair Empl. Proc. Cas. (BNA) 1217, 33 Empl. Proc. Dec. (CCH) ¶ 34260 (Iowa 1983).
11. Enriquez v. West Jersey Health Sys., 342 N.J. Super. 501, 777 A.2d 365, 11 A.D. Cas. (BNA) 1810, 86 Fam. Empl. Proc. Cas. (BNA) 197 (App. Div. 2001); Lie v. Sky Pub. Corp., 15 Mass. L. Rptr. 412, 2002 WL 31492397 (Mass. Super. Ct. 2002); Doe *ex rel.* Doe v. Yunits, 15 Mass L. Rptr. 278, 2001 WL 664947 (Mass. Super. Ct. 2001); Doe v. Boeing Co., 121 Wash. 2d 8, 846 P.2d 531, 2 A.D. Cas. (BNA) 548, 61 Empl. Prac. Dec. (CCH) ¶ 42220 (1993).
12. Rosa v. Park West Bank & Trust Co., 214 F.3d 213 (1st Cir. 2000); Schwenk v. Hartford, 204 F.3d 1187 (9th Cir. 2000); Smith v. City of Salem, Ohio, 378 F.3d 566 (6th Cir. 2004).
13. Price Waterhouse v. Hopkins, 490 U.S. 228 (1989); Oncale v. Sundowner Offshore Servs., Inc., 523 U.S. 75 (1998).
14. Miles v. New York Univ., 979 F. Supp. 248 (S.D. N.Y. 1997); Snelly v. Fall Mountain Reg'l Sch. Dist., 2001 DNH 57, 2001 WL 276975 (D. N.H. 2001).
15. *Enriquez, supra* note 3; *Lie, supra* note 3; *Yunits, supra* note 3; Rentos v. Oce-Office Systems, 23 A.D.D. 508, 72 Fair Empl. Prac. Cas. (BNA) 1717 (S.D.N.Y. 1996); Maffei v. Kolaeton Indus., Inc., 164 Misc. 2d 547, 626 N.Y.S.2d 391, 68 Fair Empl. Prac. Cas. (BNA) 1039 (Supp. 1995); McGrath v. Toys "R" Us, Inc., 409 F.3d 513 (2d Cir. 2005).

16. CAL. GOVT. CODE §§ 12916(p), 12940, 12955; CAL. PENAL CODE § 422.76; MINN. STAT. ANN. § 363.01(45); N.M. STAT. ANN. § 28-1-2(Q); R.I. GEN. LAWS § 11-24-2 (2001).

17. MINN. STAT. ANN. §363.01(45) (1996).

18. Goins v. West Group, 635 N.W.2d 717 (Minn. 2001).

19. 775 ILL. COMP. STAT. 5/1-102; 5 MINN. REV. STAT. ANN. § 4552, § 3.5 MINN. REV. STAT. ANN. 4553, sub. § 9(c) (2005), § 2.5 MINN. REV. STAT. ANN. § 4553, sub. § 6-A § 3.5 MINN. REV. STAT. ANN. 45534.5, MRSA 4553, sub. § 3.5 MINN. REV. STAT. ANN. 455310-E; MINN. STAT. §§ 363A.02, sub. § 1(3), 363A.03, subd. 44; R.I. STAT. § 28-5-7; N.M. STAT. § 28-1-7; HAW. REV. STAT. §§ 515-7, 378-1-3, 489-2-3; WASH. REV. CODE §§ 49.60-130, 175, 176, 180, 190, 200, 215, 222-225; WASH. ADMIN. CODE § 356-09-020.

20. R.I. GEN. LAWS § 11-24-2 (2001).

21. R.I. GEN. LAWS § 11-24-2 (a)(8) (2001).

22. N.M. STAT. ANN. § 28-1-2(Q) (2003).

23. www.thetaskforce.org/ourprojects/tcrp/index.cfm; www.thetaskforce.org/ndlaws/ngltf/pichart.pdf

24. *In re* Estate of Gardiner, 273 Kan. 191, 42 P.3d 120 (2002).

25. Littleton v. Prange, 9 S.W.3d 223 (Tex. App. San Antonio, 1999), *cert. denied*, 531 U.S. 872 (2000).

26. *Id.* at 224.

27. M.T. v. J.T., 140 N.J. Super. 77, 355 A.2d 204, *cert. denied*, 71 N.J. 345 (1976).

28. M.T. v. J.T., 140 N.J. Super. 77, 90, 355 A.2d 204, *cert. denied*, 71 N.J. 345 (1976).

29. M.T. v. J.T., 140 N.J. Super. 77 at 89-90, 355 A.2d 204, *cert. denied*, 71 N.J. 345 (1976).

30. Kantaras v. Kantaras, 884 So. 2d 155 (Fla. Dist. Ct. App. 2d Dist., 2004), *rev. den.*, 898 So. 2d 80 (Fla. 2005).

31. *In re* Marriage of Simmons, 355 Ill. App. 3d 942, 292 Ill. Dec. 47, 825 N.E.2d 303 (1st Dist. 2005).

32. *In re* Visitation With C.B.L., 309 Ill. App. 3d 888 (1999).

33. *Id.* at 894-95.

34. Marriage of D.F.D., 862 P.2d 368 (Mont. 1993).

35. *In re* V.H., 412 N.W.2d 389 (Minn. Ct. App. 1987).

36. Karin T. v. Michael T., 484 N.Y.S.2d 780 (N.Y. Fam. Ct. 1985).

37. *In re* Custody of T.J., 1988 Minn. App. LEXIS 144 (Minn. App., Feb. 2, 1988) (unpublished).

38. Christian v. Randall, 516 P.2d 132 (Colo. Ct. App. 1973).

39. Daly v. Daly, 715 P.2d 56 (Nev. 1986).

40. *Id.* at 59.

41. Daly v. Daly, 715 P.2d 56, 59 (Nev. 1986).

42. J.L.S. v. D.K.S., 1997 Mo. App. LEXIS 377 (March 11, 1997).

43. B. v. B., 184 A.2d 609 (N.Y. Div. 1992).

44. M.T. v. J.T., 355 A.2d 204 (N.J. App. Div. 1976).

45. *In re* Application of Nash and Barr, Ohio Ct. App. No. 2002-T-1049 (Dec. 13, 2003).

46. Smith v. City of Salem, Ohio, 378 F.3d 566 (6th Cir. 2004).

47. Price Waterhouse v. Hopkins, 490 U.S. 228 (1989).

48. Oncale v. Sundowner Offshore, 523 U.S. 75 (1998).

49. Schwenk v. Hartford, 204 F.3d 1187 (9th Cir. 2000).
50. Nichols v. Azteca Restaurant Enters., Inc., 256 F.3d 864 (9th Cir. 2001); Rene v. MGM Grand Hotel, Inc., 305 F.3d 1061 (9th Cir. en banc, 2002), *cert.denied*, 538 U.S. 922 (2003).
51. CIV-02-1532 PHX SRB (June 2, 2004) (not for publication).
52. Kirkpatrick v. Seligman, 636 F.2d 1047 (5th Cir. 1981).
53. Goins v. West Group, 635 N.W.2d 717 (Minn. 2001).
54. Hispanic AIDS Forum v. Bruno, No. 02399, 2005 N.Y. App. Div. LEXIS 3247 (N.Y. App. Div. 3/29/05).
55. OSHA, 29 C.F.R. § 1910.141(c)(1)(i) (2002); Standards and Interpretation and Compliance Letters, April 6, 1998; "Interpretation of 29 C.F.R. § 1910.141(c)(1)(i): Toilet Facilities,"; *but see* DeClue v. Central Ill. Light Co., 223 F.3d 434 (7th Cir. 2000).
56. Rehabilitation Act of 1973, 29 U.S.C. § 706 (8)(F)(i) (as amended, 1997).
57. Americans with Disabilities Act, 42 U.S.C. 1221 (b)(1) (1997).
58. Holt v. Nw. Pa. Training P'ship Consortium, Inc., 694 A.2d 1134 (Pa. Commw. 1997); Dobre v. Nat'l R.R. Passenger Corp. (AMTRAK), 850 F. Supp. 284 (E.D. Pa. 1993); Somers v. Iowa Civil Rights Comm'n, 337 N.W.2d 470 (Iowa 1983); Conway v. City of Hartford, 1997 Conn. Super. LEXIS 282 (Feb. 4, 1997); Underwood v. Archer Mgmt. Servs., Inc., 857 F. Supp. 96 (D.D.C. 1994).
59. Enriquez v. West Jersey Health Sys., 2001 N.J. Super. LEXIS 283 (N.J. Super. 2001); Lie v. Sky Publishing Co., 2002 Mass. Super. LEXIS 402 (Mass. Super. Oct. 7, 2000); Doe v. Yunits, 2001 WL 664947 (Mass. Super. Feb. 26, 2001).
60. Smith v. City of Jacksonville Correctional Inst., 1991 WL 833882 (Fla. Div. Admin. Hrgs. 1991); Evans v. Hamburger Hamlet & Forncrook, 1996 WL 941676 (Chi. Comm'n on Human Rel., 1996); Jette v. Honey Farms Mini Market, 2001 Mass. Comm. on Discrim., LEXIS 50 (Oct. 10, 2001); Jane Doe v. Electro-Craft Corp., No. 87-B-132 (N.H. Sup. Ct. 1988).
61. Or. Rev. Stat. § 659.439 (1997).
62. Ulane v. Eastern Airlines, Inc., 742 F.2d 1081 (7th Cir. 1984), *cert. denied*, 471 U.S. 1017 (1985).
63. Barnes v. Cincinnati, 401 F.3d 729 (6th Cir. 2005), *cert. denied*, 126 S. Ct. 624 (2005).
64. Somers v. Budget Marketing, 667 F.2d 748 (8th Cir. 1982); James v. Ranch Mart Hardware, Inc., 881 F. Supp. 478 (D. Kan. 1995); Powell v. Reads, Inc., 436 F. Supp. 369 (D. Md. 1977).
65. Rosa v. Park West Bank & Trust Co., 214 F.3d 213 (1st Cir. 2000).
66. Oiler v. Winn-Dixie, 2002 U.S. Dist. LEXIS 17417 (E.D. La. Sept. 16, 2002).
67. Etsitty v. Utah Transit Auth., 2005 WL 1505610 (D. Utah, June 24, 2005).
68. Miles v. New York Univ., 979 F. Supp. 248 (S.D.N.Y. 1997).
69. Snelling v. Fall Mountain Reg'l Sch. Dist., 2001 WL 276975 (D.N.H. 2001).
70. Veterans Admin. Gen. Counsel, Dep't of VA, Benefit Determination Involving Validity of Marriage of Transsexual Veterans, 1990 WL 605201 (Vet. Off. Op. Gen. Couns. Prec. 15-9, May 25, 1990), *available at* http://www.index.va.gov/search/va/va_search.jsp?QT=transsexual+veterans.
71. Ill. Admin. Code tit. 89, § 140.6(1); 55 Pa. Code § 1163.59(a)(1); Alaska Admin. Code tit. 7, § 43.385(a)(1).

72. Pinneke v. Preisser, 623 F.2d 546 (8th Cir. 1980); J.D. v. Lackner, 80 Cal. App. 3d 90 (Cal. Ct. App. 1978); Doe v. State, 257 N.W.2d 816 (Minn. 1977); *contrary decisions*: Smith v. Rasmussen, 249 F.3d 755 (8th Cir. 2001) (SRS not covered by Iowa); Rush v. Parham, 625 F.2d 1150 (5th Cir. 1980).

73. Kari Hong, *Categorical Exclusions: Exploring Legal Responses to Health Care Discrimination Against Transsexuals*, 11 COLUM. J. GENDER & L. 88 (2002).

74. Medicare Program: National Coverage Dec., 54 Fed. Reg. 34,555, 34,572 (Aug. 12, 1989).

75. 32 C.F.R. § 199.4(e)(7).

76. Beger v. Div. of Med. Assistance, 2000 Mass. Super. LEXIS 126.

77. Ch. 11, "Gender Reorientation" (Sex Change); Dep't of Veterans Affairs, Veterans Health Admin. Manual, M-2, "Clinical Programs," Part XIV, "Surgical Service" (Nov. 17, 1993).

78. Davidson v. Aetna Life & Casualty Ins. Co., 420 N.Y.S.2d 450 (N.Y. Sup. Ct. 1979).

79. Kari Hong, *Categorical Exclusions: Exploring Legal Responses to Health Care Discrimination Against Transsexuals*, 11 COLUM. J. GENDER & L. 88 (2002).

80. Mario v. P & C Food Markets, Inc., 2002 U.S. App. LEXIS 26433 (2d Cir. 2002).

81. *See* Etsitty v. Utah Transit Auth., 2005 WL 1505610 (D. Utah, June 24, 2005).

82. Farmer v. Brennan, 511 U.S. 825 (1994).

83. Darren Rosenblum, *Trapped in Sing Sing: Transgendered Prisoners Caught in the Gender Binarism*, 6 MICH. J. GENDER & L. 499 (2000).

84. Merriweather v. Faulkner, 821 F.2d 408 (7th Cir. 1987), *cert. denied*, 484 U.S. 935 (1987).

85. Maggert v. Hanks, 131 F.3d 670 (7th Cir. 1997); Long v. Nix, 86 F.3d 761 (8th Cir. 1996); Brown v. Zavaras, 63 F.3d 967 (10th Cir. 1996); White v. Farrier, 849 F.2d 322 (8th Cir. 1988); Cuoco v. Mortisugo, 222 F.3d 99 (2d Cir. 2000).

86. DeLonta v. Angelone, 330 F.3d 630 (4th Cir. 2003); Kosilek v. Maloney, 221 F. Supp. 2d 156 (D. Mass. 2002); South v. Gomez, 211 F.3d 1275 (9th Cir. 2000); Wolfe v. Horn, 130 F. Supp. 2d 648 (E.D. Pa. 2001); Phillips v. Mich. Dept. of Corrections, 731 F. Supp. 792 (W.D. Mich. 1990).

87. DeLonta v. Angelone, 330 F.3d 630, 635-36 (4th Cir. 2003).

88. Kosilek v. Maloney, 221 F. Supp. 2d 156 (D. Mass. 2002).

89. South v. Gomez, 211 F.3d 1275 (9th Cir. 2000).

90. Wolfe v. Horn, 130 F. Supp. 2d 648 (E.D. Pa. 2001).

91. Phillips v. Mich. Dept. of Corrections, 731 F. Supp. 792 (W.D. Mich. 1990).

92. Doe v. McConn, 489 F. Supp. 76 (S.D. Tex. 1980).

93. Alabama, Arkansas, Arizona, California, Colorado, Connecticut, Delaware, District of Columbia, Florida, Georgia, Hawaii, Illinois, Indiana, Iowa, Kansas, Kentucky, Louisiana, Massachusetts, Maryland, Michigan, Minnesota, Mississippi, Nebraska, New Hampshire, New Jersey, New Mexico, North Carolina, North Dakota, Oklahoma, Oregon, Pennsylvania, Rhode Island, South Carolina, South Dakota, Texas, Utah, Virginia, Vermont, West Virginia, Wisconsin, and Wyoming.

94. Matter of Helig, 2003 Md. LEXIS 31 (Md. Ct. App. Feb. 11, 2003).

95. TENN. CODE ANN. § 68-3-203(d); IDAHO CODE § 39-250; OHIO REV. CODE ANN. § 3705.15; *In re* Declaratory Relief for Ladrach, 513 N.E.2d 828 at 832 (Ohio Misc. 1987); *In re* Bonfield, 780 N.E.2d 241 (Ohio 2002).

96. Fla. A.G. Op. 076-213 (1976); *see also* 1975 Mass. A.G. Op. 62.
97. Darnell v. Lloyd, 395 F. Supp. 1210 (D. Conn. 1975).
98. www.state.gov
99. http://www.nctequality.org/Issues/Federal_Documents.asp
100. 20 C.F.R. § 422.10.

CHAPTER NINE

Lesbian, Gay, and Transgender Elders

Let's talk about the largest segment of American society—the baby-boomers. The first of that generation, born in 1946, are turning 60. This generation represents a huge number of people: 76,957,164,[1] or 26.75% of the population. By 2030, baby-boomers will be between the ages of 66 and 84 and will make up 20% of the U.S. population.

More than 50% of all boomers live in nine states: California, Texas, Florida, New York, Ohio, Pennsylvania, Illinois, Michigan, and New Jersey. Seventeen states have boomer populations of over 30%.[2]

Boomers are more likely to vote than younger people. In the 2000 presidential election, 59% of those folks voted. They have a higher education level than any preceding generation, and they are not known for their patience with unreasonable government policies.

Estimates put the number of lesbian, gay, and transgender elders at 2.9 million people over the age of 55. This number is expected to grow to 3.3 million by 2010.[3] By 2030, one in five Americans will be 65 or older, and 4 million of those will be lesbian, gay, bisexual, or transgender.[4]

This is a significant percentage of older Americans and a largely untapped client base for lawyers, especially those practicing in the field of elder law.

There is a mistaken belief that gay men and lesbians are independently wealthy. Gay men earn 13% to 32% less than heterosexual men do; lesbians earn the same or slightly less than heterosexual women. Lesbian couples, however, earn less than married heterosexual couples.[5]

Same-sex couples do not receive the same tax benefits as married couples. For example, employers can offer health insurance that includes the spouse.

The cost of the health insurance is not counted as income to the employee. An employee in a same-sex couple is taxed on those same benefits. This results in same-sex couples paying more for the same product by being taxed at a higher amount and being less able to save for retirement.

Lesbian, gay, and transgender (LGT) elders face other unique issues as well. There are four primary areas of concern for LGT elders: (1) access to affordable and sensitive healthcare; (2) non-recognition of same-sex relationships; (3) affordable housing; and (4) "coming out" as a senior citizen and what that entails.

Due to historic discrimination and the current political climate, many LGT elders do not have access to the same level of social services provided to their heterosexual counterparts. Most social service agencies do not consider offering services to this demographic. Many LGT elders have lived their lives in the closet and are fearful of the response if they are open about their sexuality at a point in their lives when they are more vulnerable. Others who have lived openly as lesbians, gay men, or transsexuals return to the closet as they get older in order to avoid being harassed—or denied services at all.

LGT elders, fearing homophobia or transphobia, will avoid seeking healthcare, affordable housing, and similar services. They prefer to remain silent rather than risk being verbally, physically, or emotionally abused.

Since same-sex partnerships are not legally recognized in most jurisdictions, LGT elders are concerned that they will be unable to participate in healthcare decisions involving their life partners or visit their partners in the hospital. They fear they will be excluded or barred from their partners' funerals. They wonder if they will be allowed to live together, as a couple, in a retirement facility.

Transgender elders face even greater discrimination because of their gender identity. Most people do not understand gender dysphoria or gender identity disorder.[6] Fear often results in discrimination. Some transgender elders find themselves evicted from nursing homes or treated as "disturbed" when they dress in gender-nonconforming clothing.[7]

Forty states have no laws prohibiting housing and public accommodation discrimination based on sexual orientation. Most states do not prohibit sexual orientation discrimination by nursing homes, assisted living facilities, or senior housing complexes. It is illegal to discriminate based on age (Age Discrimination in Employment Act) but not because of sexual orientation.

Many lesbian, gay, and transgender elders do not have a social support network comparable to that of heterosexuals. Many LGT elders have no one to contact in emergencies. They must rely on public services, and those may be withheld because the staff lacks training or is overtly homophobic.

The Joint Commission on Accreditation of Healthcare Organizations (JCAHO)[8] provides one bright spot in an otherwise depressing landscape. JCAHO bans sexual orientation discrimination in the accreditation process for assisted-living facilities and nursing homes. Complaints may be filed on the JCAHO hotline, 1-800-994-6610, when there is noncompliance.

A state's Long-Term Care Ombudsmen Program may also be contacted when there are questions concerning an elder-care facility's compliance.[9] Some of these offices may provide nursing home and assisted-living facilities with staff training on LGT issues.

Lawyers representing LGT elders must be aware of the myriad issues faced by this generation. Social Security, Medicaid, Medicare, health insurance, long-term care insurance, retirement and pension plans, federal and state estate tax laws, and housing are just some of the subjects that apply differently to LGT elders than to their heterosexual contemporaries.

A. "Out & Aging: The Metlife Study of Lesbian and Gay Baby Boomers"[10]

Zogby International conducted an online survey that included a random sample of 1,000 LGBT Americans ages 40-61. Zogby invited more than 34,000 people, gay and straight, to participate. Among those invited, 4%-6% were estimated to be gay and 1% of that group self-identified as LGBT. This is the first national survey of LGBT boomers ever conducted.

Among the questions presented was whether health-care providers, pharmacists, and social service providers would discriminate against LGBT seniors. Would these providers claim religious reasons for refusing to care for or provide services to them? Twenty-seven percent of the respondents fear discrimination as they age, and 12% have "absolutely no confidence that they will be treated respectfully."

While 47% want end-of-life care in their current residence or in hospice, 16% want their care in their own home without hospice. Lesbians and bisexual women are less financially prepared for the end of life and less likely to have long-term care insurance and wills. Plus, they are more fearful of outliving their finances.

Less than 50% of LGBT boomers have a will or other estate plan in place, including advance directives. This is an astonishing figure and further establishes the need for lawyers to market to this community. The need is there, and it is not being met.

Eighty percent of respondents expect to serve as caregivers at some point. They may be caring for their partners, elderly parents and siblings, or all of the above.

There are serious misunderstandings about financing their care. This is probably not unique to the LGBT community, but it does raise the bar about the need for more education to an aging population.

- 50% believe health insurance will pay all expenses;
- 48% will rely on personal savings;
- 47% will trust in Medicare;
- 25% plan to use long-term care insurance;
- 15% actually purchased long-term care insurance;
- 20% plan to qualify for Medicaid;
- 12% will seek the assistance of their families; and
- 31% have no plans at all or are unsure about what to do.

Lesbians and gay men in civil unions, domestic partnerships, or same-sex marriages are more concerned about discrimination because they are more obvious. Most of those responding have discussed end-of-life issues with another person, and most of them are in committed relationships. Significantly fewer discussed these issues with their doctor, lawyer, financial planner, children, therapist, or spiritual adviser.

Given all that, the study shows that 74% are afraid of being unable to care for themselves, and 56% are concerned about becoming dependent on others. Seventy-five percent of respondents believe someone else will serve as their caregiver.

B. Older Americans Act (OAA)

The Older Americans Act,[11] originally enacted in 1965 and reauthorized in 2000, provides services for Americans over 60. The reauthorization extends the Act's programs through fiscal year 2005.

According to the Administrative Office on Aging, 44 million Americans are age 60 or older. The OAA is the primary vehicle for the organizing, coordinating, and providing of community-based services for older Americans and their families.

A variety of services are provided under the Act, including home-delivered meals, health screenings and counseling, abuse protection, volunteer guardians, and legal services. In addition, eligible seniors may be able to get help with minor home repairs, yardwork, housekeeping, and respite care.

The reauthorized Act includes a new program, the National Family Caregiver Support Program (NFCSP). This is designed to help family caregivers of older adults who are ill or who have disabilities. Two-thirds of non-institutionalized persons rely on family and friends for assistance with daily living activities. One quarter of those people supplement family care with services from paid providers.

The NFCSP provides grants to state agencies on aging to work with Area Agencies on Aging and service and community organizations to provide support services. These services include:

- Information to caregivers about available services;
- Assistance in gaining access to services;
- Counseling, support groups, and caregiver training;
- Respite care; and
- Supplemental services to complement the care being given.

The Act also maintains the original objectives to preserve the rights and dignity of older Americans. There are provisions for low-income minorities and an added focus on older individuals living in rural areas.

This Act can be a source of assistance for lesbian and gay elders who remain in the community. Clients who need assistance, or their caregivers, should contact their local Area Agency on Aging for more information. They can also contact the U. S. Administration on Aging at www.aoa.gov.

In 2001, the federal Office on Aging recognized that lesbian and gay elders in the United States are underserved through the Older Americans Act. While that recognition is significant, to date Congress is not considering any legislation that will remedy the situation.

Lawyers can check the Web site, www.benefitscheckup.org, to determine a client's eligibility for federal and state benefits. The National Council on Aging, a nonprofit group in Washington, D.C., set up this site in June 2001.

The Eldercare Locator, at 1-800-677-1116, is a national toll-free service designed to help find appropriate community resources. The U.S. Office on Aging provides this service.[12]

C. Social Security

The Old Age, Survivors and Disability Insurance program (OASDI)[13] contains language that specifically addresses eligibility for survivor benefits. This program includes retirement benefits, disability benefits, and Supplemental Security Income (SSI).

SSI is a federal income supplement program funded by general tax revenues, *not* Social Security taxes. It is designed to help blind and disabled people age 65 and older who have little or no income, and it provides cash to meet basic needs for food, clothing, and shelter.

42 U.S.C. 416(h)(1)(A) presents an interesting question for lawyers. The section reads as follows:

(h) Determination of family status

(1)(A)(i) An applicant is the wife, husband, widow, or widower of a fully or currently insured individual for purposes of this subchapter if the courts of the State in which such insured individual is domiciled at the time such applicant files an application, or, if such insured individual is dead, the courts of the State in which he was domiciled at the time of death, or, if such insured is or was not so domiciled in any State, the courts of the District of Columbia, would find that such applicant and such insured individual were validly married at the time such applicant files such application or, if such insured individual is dead, at the time he died.

(ii) If such courts do not find that such applicant and such insured individual were validly married at such time, such applicant shall, nevertheless be deemed to be the wife, husband, widow, or widower, as the case may be, of such insured individual if such applicant would, under the laws applied by such courts in determining the devolution of intestate personal property, have the same status with respect to the taking of such property as a wife, husband, widow, or widower of such insured individual. (emphasis added by author)

The key language in subsection (1)(A)(ii) raises the following questions: If an applicant of the insured individual was entitled to the insured's intestate property under state law, and the state law considers the partner to be a "spouse," is the applicant eligible to apply for benefits? How should the conflict between this statute and the federal Defense of Marriage Act be resolved? Which law has priority? Is there an equal protection argument? State rights? Due process?

Vermont's civil union statute provides for intestate succession for lesbian and gay couples who registered a civil union. These couples are treated, under Vermont law, the same as a heterosexual married couple under the state's intestacy statute. Could a Vermont same-sex couple apply for OASDI benefits under title 42 of the United States Code?

California also recognizes the intestate inheritance rights of domestic partners in the same manner as those of heterosexual married couples. Another aspect of California law, which makes it even more interesting, is that heterosexuals over the age of 60 can register their domestic partnerships.

Massachusetts also addresses these issues, since it recognizes same-sex marriages. In Massachusetts, married couples are viewed as spouses, and they would be covered under the plain language of the statute.

Connecticut has a Domestic Partnership law, passed by the legislature, that provides the benefits of marriage. And Connecticut recognizes civil unions and domestic partnerships from other states.

While the questions posed here have not been answered, keep in mind that the federal statute relies on the law of the insured's domicile to determine family status. Since state law controls, a state that grants intestate inheritance rights to LG couples would appear to also make those couples eligible for OADSI benefits under title 42.

It is clear that Social Security treats same-sex couples differently from heterosexual married couples. Lesbian and gay couples are discriminated against in retirement, disability, and survivor benefits. And their children are denied survivor benefits from the account of the parent who is not legally recognized by the government.

Under Social Security retirement, an individual receives benefits based on his or her earnings history. Married individuals are also entitled to have their benefits calculated on their own *and* their spouse's record. A wife could receive benefits on her account and up to 50% of the amount based on her husband's earnings.

Survivor benefits are paid to surviving spouses and to the couple's children. There are no similar benefits available to the surviving partner in a same-sex relationship. And their children are denied any benefits unless the state recognized the legal parental status of the decedent. In states where second-parent adoptions are not allowed, this can have a devastating effect on the children involved.

This is true even in Massachusetts, where same-sex marriage is legal. The federal Defense of Marriage Act prohibits treating those marriages the same as heterosexual marriages for Social Security benefits purposes.

Disabled individuals can apply for Social Security disability benefits. If married, the spouse can also receive a spousal disability benefit. Since same-sex relationships are not recognized on the federal level, a lesbian or gay couple would receive less than a similarly situated married couple.

Transgender elders may be in even greater peril. They may not be able to access spousal, survivor, or disability benefits. Heterosexual transgender elders may not marry because their home state does not recognize their gender transition. Transgender elders in same-sex relationships are in the same boat as lesbian and gay couples. Transgender individuals who have married, while technically eligible for Social Security benefits, may be denied them if the marriage is successfully challenged and deemed void *ab initio*.

D. Medicaid

Medicaid (Title XIX of the Social Security Act) is a federally funded, state-run program providing assistance to low-income and low-resource individuals and families. General guidelines are established by the federal government; however, program requirements are set by the individual states.

There are five groups covered by Medicaid:

- Children;
- Pregnant women;
- Adults in families with dependent children;
- Individuals with disabilities; and
- Individuals age 65 and over.

States are responsible for establishing eligibility standards, type, amount, scope and duration of services, rates of payment for services, and the administration of the program. State rules vary; eligibility in one state does not guarantee eligibility in another.

Individual states can also determine, to some extent, which services will be provided. One of the complications about Medicaid is that the rules can, and do, frequently change.

In addition to the federally funded Medicaid program, most states also have "state-only" programs to assist poor persons who do not qualify for Medicaid.

Medicaid is the largest single payor of direct medical services for persons with AIDS (PWAs) and children with AIDS. The Department of Health and Human Services estimates that 50% of PWAs and 90% of children with AIDS receive medical services through Medicaid.

1. Estate Recovery Programs

The 1993 Omnibus Budget Reconciliation Act[14] (OBRA) made changes to the Medicaid Program. Under OBRA, states are required to institute estate recovery programs. These programs are designed to recover money spent by Medicaid from a recipient's estate.

OBRA sets the minimum standards for recovery. These include the population subject to recovery, covered services, and assets subject to recovery. States also have the discretion to make their individual programs more inclusive.

Estate recovery programs apply to persons receiving services paid for by Medicaid. The persons subject to estate recovery include anyone over the age of 55 and those who are permanently institutionalized regardless of age. There is no minimum amount of time to receive services, which can include those provided in both a nursing home and home-based situation.

Of particular importance to lesbian and gay couples, estate recovery includes assets that are conveyed to a survivor, heir, or assignee of the recipient.[15] This means that property is subject to recovery even if held in joint and survivorship tenancy, as tenants-in-common, survivorship, life estate, living trust, or any other arrangement. As a result, lesbian and gay couples must consider their potential liability, and that of their surviving partner, if they decided to seek Medicaid coverage.

If one partner enters a nursing home and applies for Medicaid, he will be required to sell his interest in the home. Unless his partner is able to buy out his interest, the house must be sold in order to qualify for Medicaid. This is another reason to encourage clients to look into long-term care insurance. Some companies offer these policies to same-sex couples at a "couples" rate rather than an individual one.

Congress established a minimum list of possible assets that states must include in their estate recovery programs. That list includes:

- nursing home services;
- community based services;
- drugs;
- inpatient hospital services; and
- Qualified Medicare Beneficiary (QMB) portions of services.

States are not burdened by a statute of limitations in initiating estate recovery procedures. But a recent case out of Illinois gives another opinion.[16] The Illinois Supreme Court ruled that the state could not recover from the estate of the deceased recipient's widow. Mrs. Tutinas died four years after her husband. The Illinois Department of Public Aid filed a claim for $61,000 against Mrs. Tutinas's estate. The court cited the Medicaid Act[17] in support of its decision: "No adjustment or recovery of any medical assistance correctly paid on behalf of an individual under the State plan may be made." One exception permits recovery from the individual's estate but not from the surviving spouse.

This is an interesting decision, but it must be considered in light of the 2005 Deficit Reduction Act, which requires states to initiate estate recovery. If there is no statute of limitations, how long can a state wait before seeking reimbursement? Can a state seek reimbursement from the estate of a surviving domestic partner who dies years after the recipient? Answers to these questions must be litigated.

2. *Look-Back Period*

The "look-back" period comes into play when a Medicaid applicant transfers assets to another party or a trust in order to qualify for coverage. It involves the time that must pass between the transfer and eligibility. The transfers at issue are those made for less than fair market value. Transfers sold at fair market value are not considered, because the money received from the transfer is available to pay for services.

Under the 1993 OBRA law,[18] the look-back period was 36 months. Transfers made to a trust had a look-back period of 60 months. An applicant making a transfer within the look-back period would be ineligible for Medicaid for a specific period. The 2005 Deficit Reduction Act[19] changed the look-back period to 60 months for all transfers.

Transfer of assets before February 8, 2006, are subject to the 36-month look-back period; assets transferred on or after February 8, 2006, are subject to the 60-month look-back period.

3. *Penalty Period*

Under OBRA, the penalty period during which an applicant is ineligible for Medicaid started on the date of the transfer. The start date of the penalty period changed under the 2005 Deficit Reduction Act. The penalty period now starts on the *later* of the first day of the month in which the transfer was made *or* the date on which an individual is eligible for Medicaid benefits and would otherwise be receiving an institutional level of care, based on an approved application for that care, but for the imposition of the penalty period.[20] The regulations for these terms are state-specific.

Determining the period of ineligibility changed with the 2005 Act. Before the change, the states rounded down and partial months were not considered. The new law requires the states to round up and to count partial months. For example, a client who is ineligible for 2.3 months may have the .3 month counted as either one-third of a month or a full month.[21] States may not round down or disregard any fractional period. An applicant's ineligibility is determined under clause (i) or (ii) with respect to the disposal of assets.

4. Hardship Waiver

Before the 2005 Deficit Reduction Act took effect, the penalty period was not applied when "the State determines under procedures established by the State that the denial of eligibility would work an undue hardship as determined on the basis of criteria established by the Secretary."[22]

Section 6011(d) of the Deficit Reduction Act added language to the waiver definition. It defines an "undue hardship" standard and establishes specific elements that states must follow in their mandatory provisions for undue hardship waivers.

5. Annuities

Annuities are treated as assets disposed of for less than fair market value unless the state is the remainder beneficiary. They are treated as a transfer of assets unless (a) the annuity is purchased with retirement funds or with employee pension proceeds or (b) it is irrevocable and non-assignable, actuarially sound, and provides for payments in equal amounts during the annuity's term, and there are no balloon payments.

6. Principal Residence

The 2005 Deficit Reduction Act exempts $500,000 in equity from the applicant's principal residence. States have authority to raise the exemption amount to $750,000. The old law had an unlimited exemption amount on the principal residence.

7. Continuing Care Retirement Communities

The old law did not consider Continuing Care Retirement Communities (CCRC) entrance fees to be an available asset. This changed under the 2005 Act. These entrance fees, which can be considerable, are considered assets available to the applicant. The existence of these fees can interfere with an applicant's Medicaid eligibility.

8. Life Estates

The term "assets" also includes the purchase of a life estate interest in another's home, "unless the purchaser resides in the home for a period of at least 1 year after the date of the purchase."[23]

9. Long-Term Care Partnerships

The 2005 Act permits the states to enter into Long-Term Care Partnership reciprocity agreements. These agreements allow states to make deals with people who buy a specific amount of long-term care insurance to be eligible for Medicaid.

10. Life Insurance

Life insurance may help counter recovery efforts by Medicaid against the estate of a deceased recipient. Proceeds from the insurance policy may be used to pay off Medicaid when the state seeks to recover the cost of care from the decedent's estate. The couple may want to take out life insurance on each other for this contingency.

E. Effect on Lesbian, Gay, Transgender, and Transsexual Elders

Qualified lesbians, gay men, and transgender elders age 65 and over are eligible as individuals for Medicaid assistance. Lesbians and gay men under age 65 are potentially eligible *only* if they fall within one of the categories listed above.

To qualify for Medicaid, the client must spend down assets to a minimal amount. The needs of the applicant's same-sex partner are not considered. Medicaid recipients can have monetary assets of no more than $1,500 or $2,000, depending on the applicant's state of residence.

An individual's Social Security check will be turned over to the nursing home, although the resident will be allowed to keep between $25 and $50 for incidental expenses.

An applicant's primary residence and one automobile are also allowed. That represents the total amount of assets any individual Medicaid recipient can possess to qualify. Unless a qualified individual, such as a spouse or disabled child, lives in the applicant's primary residence, the house must be listed for sale within six months after qualifying for Medicaid.

Same-sex couples who hold joint title in a residence may be required to sell the house to allow the applicant to qualify for Medicaid. There is no consideration given to the "community" partner. The other alternative is for the non-applicant partner to buy out her partner's interest in the house. Unfortunately, this may not be possible, especially if both partners are elderly.

The federal DOMA, mini-DOMAs, and state constitutional amendments make it unlikely that the couple's relationship will be recognized and the non-applicant partner allowed to remain in the residence. An argument can be made, under the estate recovery program, that any money owed to Medicaid can be recovered once the house is sold. Since this is a new field, with new rules, nothing is apparent or certain.

The resident must dispose of all other assets. Any property sold for less than 80% of its fair market value may be viewed as an improper transfer. This determination may result in the applicant being deemed ineligible for Medicaid for a specific period.

LGT elders do not benefit from having a partner. Since same-sex marriages are not currently recognized, each partner will be considered an individual for Medicaid eligibility purposes.

In contrast, married heterosexual couples are generally listed as "resident" and "community" spouses. The "resident" spouse is the Medicaid applicant and the "community" spouse remains in the couple's primary residence. The "community" spouse may qualify for a community spouse payment.

The couple is also allowed to keep their home as long as the community spouse lives in it. It does not matter if the house is titled in the name of one or both spouses. Because spouses are required to support each other, having the house only in the name of the community spouse may not save it from the estate recovery program.

If the applicant does not have a spouse, the residence must be put up for sale within six months of entry into a nursing home. Similar consideration is not given to a same-sex couple, unless the home is titled in the non-applicant partner's name alone.

Medicaid recipients may also be eligible for Medicare. Elderly lesbians, gay men, and transgender elders are eligible to apply for Medicare once they reach 65. Dual eligibility usually comes into play with an elderly person when nursing home care becomes a factor.

Medicare pays for skilled nursing care only. It does not pay for custodial nursing home care. This can be a confusing topic for clients. Briefly, medical conditions that require the services of an RN for medical care such as IVs, post-surgical care, etc., usually qualify as skilled nursing care. Some nursing homes have skilled-care wings on the property.

Custodial care means the resident requires assistance with daily activities such as dressing, eating, and bathing. This type of care does not qualify for Medicare.

As mentioned earlier, an applicant for Medicaid must be impoverished to qualify for benefits. Some people try to create eligibility by transferring their property to others before submitting an application. Mistakes in the transfer of assets to qualify for Medicaid may result in disqualification for a significant period. Knowing what is and is not allowed may make the difference between qualifying for and being denied Medicaid.

Example: The applicant transfers a savings account with $15,000 in it to his partner a month before he applied. This transfer took the applicant's assets to zero dollars. The nursing home costs $5,000 per month. Medicaid would deem the applicant ineligible for three months. This equals the amount of time the applicant would spend down the improperly transferred asset—three months at $5,000 per month.

Under the 2005 Act, only transfers made 60 months before applying will be outside the look-back period. The average nursing home stay is two to three years. If the individual can pay for nursing home care for 60 months, there will be no penalty period. But few people stay in a nursing home for five years.

Example: The resident transfers his only asset, the house, to his partner two years before entering the nursing home. The house fair market value is $100,000. The annual cost of the nursing home is $40,000. The resident will be ineligible for Medicaid for three years and will be required to pay for his care during that time. After three years, he will become eligible for Medicaid because the transfer took place more than 60 months before applying for benefits.

Medicaid also does not cover all expenses. In some cases a Medicaid trust or "special needs trusts" may be appropriate, particularly in situations where one or both partners suffer from a life-threatening disease. A special needs trust may be established to provide for a Medicaid recipient's needs that are not covered by the program. In those situations, it is necessary to research the pertinent state law to determine the type of "special needs trusts" that are available and how to draft them to protect the client.

There are different types of trusts available. States permit these trusts because it will recover its costs upon the death of the recipient. In some cases, the state recovers its expenses up to the amount of services provided. This does not protect the individual's heirs but can provide a more comfortable life for the Medicaid recipient.

Medicaid is a complicated program, and it helps to consult with someone well versed in its intricacies. A state's Long-Term Care Ombudsman office may be very helpful in deciphering the Medicaid rules. Each state is required to establish an Ombudsman office under the requirements of the Older Americans Act.

There may also be gift tax consequences. Lawyers must discuss tax issues with their clients in order for them to be informed about the possible ramifications of their actions.

If the Medicaid recipient has community assets that were not counted when determining eligibility, the state will place a lien on that property. The state then enforces the lien after the resident dies to recover the cost of care. This occurs even if the resident and his partner jointly owned a house and the resident's name remained on the house. The state's lien could continue until the house was sold. Or, the state may force a sale to recover its Medicaid investment in the decedent. The state then recovers an amount equal to the amount of services provided from the sale price.

This is another instance where records of contributions to the purchase of the house and its upkeep are vitally important. If the resident partner cannot prove he contributed to the purchase of the house, the state may argue that the value of the house belongs solely to the Medicaid recipient.

These issues have not been litigated. With the mini-DOMAs many states have in place, the opportunity for litigating these issues is considerable.

F. Counseling of Elders

Medicaid is a tricky subject, and states are cutting back on benefits. It is a welfare program and recipients must be poor. The states and Congress will continue to enact laws and regulations that afford them greater opportunity to recover Medicaid expenditures from a recipient's estate.

In situations involving same-sex couples, documentation concerning joint accounts will become increasingly important. It is likely that states will demand proof of actual joint ownership and contribution when making Medicaid eligibility determinations. These demands will also become *de riguer* when a state moves to recover Medicaid expenses provided to the decedent.

Many clients will not have sufficient documentation to prove who contributed what to where. It may become necessary to re-create the documentation if possible or start from that point forward. Such documentation will also serve the couple well when dealing with the I.R.S and estate tax issues.

G. LGT Elders Who Are Military Veterans

Many elderly LGT persons will be veterans. "Don't ask, don't tell" aside, thousands of lesbians and gay men served honorably in our nation's armed forces. They are entitled to military retirement pay, VA healthcare, and other veterans' benefits. Yet they may be subjected to the anti-gay attitudes of staff and patients at VA hospitals.

Assisting an LGT elder in obtaining veteran benefits, including healthcare, will be a huge benefit to these people. Negotiating the bureaucracy of the Department of Veteran Affairs is a chore for the most astute person. It becomes even more arduous for LGT veterans because of their status as non-heterosexuals. Even if LGT veterans obtain benefits, it is important to maintain contact to ensure they are treated with respect and receive the services to which they are entitled. The VA is not generally known for treating veterans well; its treatment of LGT veterans is apt to be even more hostile.

Lesbian and gay national organizations are in a good position to help attorneys who represent LGT veterans.

H. Retirement Accounts

The unequal treatment does not stop or start with federal benefits. Federal law requires pension plans to protect spouses. There is no similar requirement to protect a same-sex partner, because domestic partners are not synonymous with "spouse."

This discrimination came home to the partner of a Tampa police officer after her partner was killed in the line of duty.

On July 6, 2001, Master Patrol Officer Lois Marrero was shot and killed while on duty with the Tampa Police Department. She died 15 months away from retirement. Officer Marrero left behind her partner of 11 years, Tampa Police Officer Mickie Mashburn.

Unlike the officer's heterosexual counterparts, Officer Mashburn was not entitled to receive any part of Marrero's pension. Florida's pension law provides that only spouses and children are eligible to receive survivor benefits. She also could not receive a refund of the $50,000 paid into the pension fund by Marrero. The eight-member city pension board rejected Mashburn's application and awarded the $50,000 refund to Marrero's mother, who claimed there was no relationship between Marrero and Mashburn. And because Marrero died intestate, her parents inherited her estate.

The National Center for Lesbian Rights is representing Mashburn in a lawsuit challenging the pension board's decision, and the Tampa City Council is reviewing the pension policy. Mashburn has the support of the police and firefighter unions.

Mashburn did receive $25,000 from the Florida crime victims' compensation fund. Florida's Attorney General, Bob Butterworth, approved that payment.

Dramatic changes occurred in 2006 concerning retirement accounts. In July 2006, President Bush signed the Pension Protection Act of 2006.[24] The law became effective on January 1, 2007.

The most significant part of this new law for LGT clients is section 829, titled "Allow Rollovers by Nonspouse Beneficiaries of Certain Retirement Plan Distributions." This section amends section 402(c) of the Internal Revenue Code[25] and permits the owner of specific retirement plans (think I.R.A.) to name a non-spouse beneficiary. Before the change, only spouses could roll over an inherited I.R.A. without being required to begin withdrawals within five years. The new law gives that same right to any named beneficiary. The "spouse only" requirement has been repealed. The complete texts of sections 829 and 402(c) of the Internal Revenue Code are included in Appendix B.

The owner of a retirement plan may name anyone as the beneficiary. The beneficiary has the right to transfer the funds directly into an "inherited I.R.A." This allows the beneficiary to spread out distributions over many years. As with all I.R.A.s, required distributions begin when the owner turns 70.5 years old. These new provisions are effective for distributions made after January 1, 2007.

Under the old law, a decedent could name a non-spouse beneficiary, but the law required that person to begin taking withdrawals within five years. Under the revised provision, a non-spouse beneficiary can transfer the proceeds directly into an inherited I.R.A. and stretch out withdrawals over his life expectancy.

Most company 401(k) plans required withdrawal within five years in a lump sum. The beneficiaries would be responsible for paying federal and state taxes on the full balance. The new law changes that requirement.

The changes also apply to inheritances from 403(b) plans (teachers) and 457 savings accounts (government workers). Tax bills incurred by non-spouse survivors of 9/11 victims prompted the legislation.

When setting up such an account, the financial institution must title it as an "inherited I.R.A," and it must be a separate account; the inherited proceeds cannot be transferred into an existing I.R.A. Arrange for the direct transfer of the proceeds into the inherited I.R.A., as checks sent directly to the beneficiary may trigger a taxable distribution.

Same-sex couples will now be able to leave their retirement funds to their partners with the same benefits as heterosexual married couples. This is a good development for lawyers and their same-sex clients.

I. Public Accommodations

There is no federal legislation banning discrimination based on sexual orientation in employment, housing, or public accommodations. Absent state law restrictions, nursing homes and assisted living facilities are free to discriminate against LGT elders in their admission policies. Even when services and benefits are available, many lesbian and gay seniors are unaware of either their existence or eligibility requirements. This is where good lawyers are essential.

For some lesbians and gay men, an assisted-living facility may seem to be a viable alternative to nursing home care. However, neither the state nor federal governments regulate assisted-living facilities or continuing-care retirement centers (CCRC). These are private-pay facilities, and residents do not qualify for Medicaid. The facilities generally provide limited resources, including a lack of qualified medical personnel to dispense medications. These facilities are often not licensed or equipped to deal with a resident's medical needs. And, on top of everything, these are for-profit operations, and their primary concern is making money to pay shareholders.

Affordable housing is a major concern for all elders, but it is particularly important to LGT elders. LGT persons may have no children or be estranged from their birth family. Some may have no one to call for emergencies.

A growing number of retirement communities are being developed that cater to the LGBT community. Unfortunately, most of them are very expensive. Santa Fe's Rainbow Vision development is a for-profit operation. Condominiums are being sold for $250,000. The cost of housing in these communities perpetuates the stereotype that all lesbians and gay men are wealthy. But because private developers are building these communities, profit is important, and they, by necessity, targeted a high-income market.

Some nonprofit organizations are developing retirement communities that include market price and affordable housing.

Many LGT seniors plan to remain in their homes, but this may not be feasible as they age. The lack of public accommodations law that prohibits discrimination based on sexual orientation will become more apparent over the next 10 to 20 years.

Stories abound of gay and lesbian couples, living in senior communities, who are barred from living together or shunned by the other residents. Unfortunately, the LGBT community has been slow to take up the cause of these seniors. This is changing, albeit slowly. While the LGBT retirement communities are being developed, more needs to be done to address general aging issues. This includes ensuring adequate healthcare for older LGT seniors. There is a dearth of healthcare providers catering to LGT elders. This failure will become worse with time.

J. Nursing Homes and Hospice Care

Statistics from the U.S. Administration on Aging show that at least 40% of people turning 65 will stay in a nursing home at least once in their lifetime. Fifty percent of those entering a nursing home will stay six months or less. One in five will stay a year or more, and one in 10 will stay three years or longer. Most of those over 65 are women. Given these figures, it is likely that an attorney serving this population will have elder clients in need of nursing home care.

According to *Consumer Reports*, 36% of assisted-living residents enter a nursing home because their needs cannot be accommodated elsewhere. Two percent enter a nursing home because they run out of money and can no longer afford to stay at home or in another venue. A percentage of those older persons entering nursing homes will be lesbians and gay men.

Nursing homes or retirement facilities can deny entry to lesbian, gay, or transgender elders because of their sexual orientation or gender identity. And, since there is no legal sanction against sexual orientation discrimination, it is important to determine if the nursing home accepts lesbian and gay residents. Does the facility treat a same-sex couple the same as a married couple? Are same-sex couples allowed to reside in couples' rooms? These are important questions to ask *before* the person enters a nursing home or assisted-living facility. Too often, an openly lesbian or gay couple or individual will be forced back into the closet to be accepted into a nursing home community.

Nursing home litigation has become commonplace. Claims deal with issues such as staff failure to properly care for the resident, assaults, and wrongful death, among others. Nursing homes are beginning to develop strategies to deal with this increase in litigation. Some are converting to limited liability companies, which results in the facility having no money, insurance, or assets to pay any judgments. These are shell corporations established to hide profits from successful litigants. The corporation at the bottom is either a not-for-profit or pass-through entity.

Many nursing homes are in debt, but the owners continue to make money. Large corporations with deep pockets own many individual nursing homes. It is necessary to establish the level of control the corporation exerts over the individual nursing home and its administrators.

A book that may help understand the nuances of piercing the corporate veil is *The Buffalo Creek Disaster*.[26] The book deals with a class-action suit against a coal company. The plaintiffs could only be made whole if the parent company was held responsible. It was and they were.

While the economics involved favor the nursing home industry, individual nursing homes can be worthless. That's why targeting the corporate owner is a better idea.

The Texas 2003 tort reform litigation capped non-economic damages at $250,000. This is just one state where suing a nursing home is not cost-effective.

Discovery is necessary to gather the information required to pierce the corporate veil or show the owner has substantial control over the care given in the institution as well as the policies that contributed to the injury. Seeking disclosure of the ownership statement from the state health department will identify the named insureds on the institution's insurance policy. This allows counsel to argue that the corporation is a shell, as the individuals are the policy beneficiaries and not the corporation.

Discrimination litigation against nursing homes, continuing-care retirement communities, and other entities providing services to the elderly will undoubtedly increase with the rise in LGT residents. One's sexual orientation or gender identity is not grounds for poor treatment or discrimination in providing services. It is important to look at state and local laws and ordinances dealing with discrimination. While laws against same-sex couples are prevalent, local communities, including counties and cities, are providing protection where state law may not. This research allows a lawyer to refute arguments that the LGT client has no cause of action.

A situation arose in Florida when a lesbian couple was denied admission to the Westminster Oaks Retirement Community. The facility denied their application because it violated their policy against allowing unmarried, non-related couples from living together. Florida, however, is one state in which county and local governments have enacted legislation that prohibits housing discrimination based on sexual orientation.

In the Westminster Oaks case, the policy violates a local law protecting lesbians and gay men from housing discrimination. The same law includes prohibitions against discrimination based on gender and marital status. The National Center for Lesbian Rights filed a complaint on behalf of the women involved in the Westminster Oaks case. The Westminster owners settled the case and the couple moved into their new home.

Another Florida case, originating in Boca Raton, involved an apartment complex that refused to rent an apartment to a gay couple. This action violated a county law that protects same-sex couples from housing discrimination. The apartment complex, Colonial Apartments, settled the matter during mediation and agreed to pay $25,000 to each of the men and to Lambda Legal Defense and Education Fund.

Another significant consideration that needs to be addressed is a person's right to privacy in the facility. While many lesbian and gay individuals and couples are open about their relationships, a large number remain closeted. It is important that a facility honors an LGT person's right to privacy. "Outing" an elderly LGT person can be devastating. This is particularly true if the threatened outing is used for nefarious purposes, such as blackmail, or to prevent the senior resident from complaining about her treatment.

Even when a resident is open about her sexuality, she may be subjected to discriminatory conduct by nursing home staff. In one instance, the staff refused to bathe an elderly female nursing home resident because they did not want to touch "the lesbian."

In many nursing home facilities, sexuality is often a problem for the staff. No one wants to think of these "old folks" being sexually active. Many consider gay sex to be deviant behavior.

Each state's Agency on Aging must create a Long-Term Care Ombudsman office. This office provides assistance and information to elderly persons and their families and friends. The office is also charged with visiting nursing homes, receiving and investigating complaints, and providing information on long-term care facilities. The Ombudsman office is also a good source of current information on local nursing homes.

A state's Department of Health is responsible for issuing regulations governing nursing home operations. There is also a federal mandate requiring nursing homes to ensure that each resident is able to maintain, as much as possible, the quality of life he or she enjoyed before entering the facility.

Hospice care allows an individual to remain at home while end-of-life care is provided. For some LGT elders, the hospice concept may be intimidating because they are not open about their gender identity or sexual orientation. Typical LGT patients and families do not exist. Not all LGT persons have partners; some are single, widowed, divorced, and married with opposite-sex spouses. Many have children and grandchildren. Transgender patients may be unwilling to disclose their status during the admission process. Yet it is important for LGT patients to be forthcoming because of the need for proper care. Hospice providers must also be sensitive to the needs of LGT patients and ensure that their employees provide sensitive and proper care.

It is essential that hospice staff determine who has decision-making authority if the patient becomes incompetent. The patient's same-sex partner does not have automatic legal authority. Hospice personnel must, however, honor all advance directives from the patient. When there is no advance directive, state law applies, and the family of origin may be seen as the primary decision-making entity. This often results in the complete exclusion of the patient's partner.

> **Hospices**
>
> Hospice providers can benefit from the following suggestions:
> 1. Include gender-neutral relationships on intake forms.
> 2. Insist on a written advance directive and provide the resource to obtain one.
> 3. Define family of choice and family of origin; identify potential conflicts.
> 4. Encourage the patient to complete advance care and estate planning.
> 5. Identify any psychosocial issues between the family of choice and family of origin.
> 6. Train hospice staff in transgender medical issues.
> 7. Identify any spiritual issues that may arise.
> 8. Provide support for the surviving partner, including grief counseling.
> 9. Collaborate with local LGBT organizations to address patient needs.
> 10. Train hospice staff concerning the needs of LGBT people and end-of-life issues unique to them.
> 11. Identify individual staff misgivings or fears concerning caring for LGBT patients.
> 12. Emphasize respect for the patient and his or her family.

K. Healthcare Issues Affecting Lesbian, Gay, Transgender, and Transsexual Seniors

Throughout the country, healthcare is a concern. This is not just a LGT issue; it affects everyone. LGT persons have additional medical concerns that do not affect the general population.

First, there is doctor bias. Many lesbians do not seek medical assistance because of the bias experienced with homophobic doctors. As with a lawyer, it is essential for a patient to be open and honest with her doctor. If she cannot tell the doctor that she is a lesbian, the quality of care will suffer.

For example, women of childbearing age are always asked about the type of birth control used. Lesbians use the only kind that is 100% effective; they never have sex with men. While the "gayby" boom is in full swing, there are still many more lesbians who, in response to the question "Are you pregnant?" will answer, "Not unless you've seen a star in the East!"

And, as stated earlier, Medicaid treats same-sex couples differently.

Elderly LGT persons are very concerned about the availability of health insurance. Most of these elders do not have supplemental coverage. While an increasing number of corporations and companies of all sizes offer health insurance and other benefits to same-sex couples, these benefits may not be available after retirement. It is something for lawyers representing elderly LGT clients to investigate and consider when advising them.

As a result of these concerns, it is important for lawyers to ensure hat their clients are provided with all the legal documents necessary to protect them in a healthcare facility. This includes hospitals, nursing homes, assisted living facilities, home health-care situations, and the like. It is also important to determine that the client is being treated with respect and that her needs are being met.

L. LGT Elders and Aids

According to the National Association on HIV Over Fifty (NAHOF),[27] between 11% and 15% of U.S. AIDS cases occur in the over-50 age group. NAHOF opines that the number of these cases will increase as the population ages. More people with AIDS are living longer because of improvements in the drug regimen to control the disease. As with other issues affecting the elderly, older persons with HIV are often invisible. This leads to their situation being ignored or overlooked by the organizations dealing with AIDS issues.

Contrary to popular myth, older persons are sexually active, and some may be IV drug users. This places them at greater risk for becoming infected with the HIV virus. Seniors are not routinely tested for HIV infection. This may partially be the result of AIDS organizations not targeting this segment of the population. As a result, older persons are often not diagnosed with HIV until the virus has developed into a more serious health situation that is more difficult and more expensive to treat. Older persons with undiagnosed and untreated HIV infections die sooner than their younger counterparts.

The educational and treatment programs currently in place do not address the needs of elders. While elders continue to be sexually active, they are less likely to consider using preventive measures to avoid sexually transmitted diseases, including HIV. This is most likely because of a generational bias and ignorance of safe-sex preventive methods.

Even when diagnosed with HIV or AIDS, elders face a society that penalizes them because of ageism and prejudice against people with sexually transmitted disease (STD) infections. Elders are also less likely to tell their families for fear of being ostracized.

Some HIV symptoms may be similar to those elders face as a matter of simply aging. Fatigue, dementia, rashes, etc., are often seen in the elderly. This results in misdiagnoses of their condition and that prevents them from being properly treated.

Practitioners counseling this segment of the population should become familiar with the issues surrounding HIV and AIDS and be prepared to address a client's needs in this area. Lawyers serving an elder population are more than mere legal advisers. Elder clients look upon their lawyers as friends and confidants. This places the lawyer in a perfect position to recommend medical treatment if there is any indication that an untreated condition exists.

M. Insurance Concerns of Lesbian, Gay, Transgender, and Transsexual Seniors

It is important for LGT seniors to consider their need for various types of insurance. This includes long-term care insurance, disability insurance, and life insurance.

The long-term care insurance should include coverage for at-home and nursing home care and have an inflation provision. A client may be more comfortable knowing he can remain in his home with proper care and avoid the potential pitfalls of being gay in a heterosexual nursing home.

Life insurance can relieve the couple's concern about the ability of the surviving partner to remain in the home.

Disability insurance can provide a welcome cushion in the event one partner becomes ill and is no longer able to work. The most cost-effective policies come through professional groups or organizations. A policy that waives premiums at a certain point is also beneficial to the couple.

Most lesbians and gay men do not have employers who provide health insurance for domestic partners. Health insurance is an enormous and expensive problem in this country, and lesbians and gay men are not immune. It is important to ascertain whether clients have health insurance.

Medical expenses are often the reason people file bankruptcy. However, under the new bankruptcy law, it is more difficult to discharge debts of any kind. If the couple does not own their home jointly and the titleholder becomes ill, the house may be jeopardized. If the titleholder's health deteriorates to the point where he or she must enter a nursing home, the house is a countable resource for Medicaid eligibility determination. In a same-sex couple, the needs of the resident's partner are not considered.

Likewise, if the titleholder incurs a catastrophic illness, the house is vulnerable to creditors for payment of outstanding medical bills. Unlike married heterosexual couples, there are no spousal rights to the "manor house."

Life insurance can benefit the surviving partner in the tax arena. There is no exemption from having property taxes reassessed at the death of one partner, unlike with a married couple. The I.R.S. presumes that the first person to die owned all the jointly held property. The parties must rebut the I.R.S.'s position through extensive records, including receipts and tax returns.

Transferring property from joint ownership to a sole owner can cause a reassessment of property taxes. The surviving partner may be unable to pay the increased taxes, and that places the house at risk. Life insurance can alleviate this concern and provide sufficient funds to pay the property tax increase.

N. Transgender and Transsexual Elders

Transgender persons and transsexuals, as a class, endure discrimination on many levels. Transgender and transsexual elders are particularly vulnerable to discrimination because of fear and ignorance. They are excluded from homeless shelters, retirement communities, nursing homes, and assisted-living facilities. Transgender elders find it difficult to receive proper medical care. They are also excluded from government-provided social services.

Few laws exist to protect transgender persons. California, Minnesota, and Rhode Island are among those states that prohibit discrimination against transgender persons.

It is also difficult for transgender persons, including elders, to find a lawyer to represent them. They present the same type of legal issues as any other clients. Not all come in with issues relating to their gender identity.

Transgender and transsexual elders may also bring a history of abuse, neglect, and discrimination. Many experienced extreme forms of psychiatric abuse, including electroshock therapy, forced drugging, and aversion therapy. These elders may have suffered permanent physical and psychological damage because of their treatment. The damage may include tardive dyskinesia[28] and other neurological impairments, immune deficiency, and severe depression.

In nursing home or other institutionalized settings, staff may insist on treating and dressing a transgender elder as their biological sex rather than accept them as they are. Some transgender persons die before anyone becomes aware that they are not the gender they present to the world.

Billy Tipton is a case in point. He was a well-known jazz musician who died in 1989 from a bleeding ulcer. He lived his life as a man. It was only at his death that people became aware that he was biologically female. He had not seen a doctor in 50 years.

Many transgender and transsexual elders avoid seeking medical care because they experience multiple forms of discrimination. There are few medical, legal, or social resources available to them. These elders are particularly vulnerable to abuse and neglect.

O. Conclusion

The needs of LGT seniors mirror, in many cases, those of the rest of the senior population. While there are lesbian and gay retirement communities cropping up around the country, most lesbians and gay men have lived in mixed communities all their lives and plan to continue doing so.

Many LGT persons do not have an extended family unit. Often our families are composed of other persons in the gay community.

LGT seniors are entitled to the same benefits as heterosexual seniors. There can be no differentiation based on sexual orientation. This is an untested field of law; however, extensive litigation may be necessary to ensure fair and equitable treatment for all seniors without regard to sexual orientation.

Lawyers representing these clients must familiarize themselves with a plethora of laws that affect their clients. It is a challenging and rewarding field of practice, and lawyers will find themselves benefiting as much as their clients.

Notes

1. *Demographic Profile*, Mature Market Institute, MetLife, www.metlife.com.
2. Alaska, New Hampshire, Vermont, Maine, Maryland, Colorado, Connecticut, Virginia, Wyoming, Washington, New Jersey, Montana, Massachusetts, Minnesota, Oregon, West Virginia, and Wisconsin.
3. *Lesbian, Gay, Bisexual and Transgender (LGBT) Aging: A Fact Sheet for Activists*, Senior Action in a Gay Environment (SAGE), *available at* www.sageusa.org.
4. *Aging*, National Gay and Lesbian Task Force, *available at* www.ngltf.org.
5. M.V.L. Badgett, *Income Inflation: The myth of affluence among gay, lesbian and bisexual Americans* (Dec. 1, 1998), National Gay and Lesbian Task Force Institute, *available at* www.thetaskforce.org/downloads/income.pdf; M.V.L BADGETT, MONEY, MYTHS AND CHANGE: THE ECONOMIC LIVES OF LESBIANS AND GAY MEN, Chicago: Univ. of Chicago Press (2001).
6. *Gender Identity Disorder (GID):* diagnosis given individuals experiencing anxiety over being assigned a sex different from that they feel they are. DIAGNOSTIC AND STATISTICAL MANUAL OF MENTAL DISORDERS, 4th ed. (DSM-IV-TR).
7. Minter & Shannon, *Legal and public policy issues for transgender elders*, *available at* www.nclrights.org/ publications/transelders.htm; *see also* T. Donovan, *Being transgender and older: A first person account*, 13(4) J. GAY & LESBIAN SOCIAL SERVS.: ISSUES IN PRACTICE, POLICY & RESEARCH 19-22.

8. www.jointcommission.org.

9. Find state-specific programs at www.ltcombudsman.org/static_pages/ombudsmen.cfm.

10. Produced by the Met Life Mature Market Institute, American Society on Aging's Lesbian and Gay Aging Issues Network (LGAIN), and Zogby Int'l, November 2006; *available at* www.asaging.org/lgain.

11. Pub. L. 106-501, 114 Stat. 2267 (Nov. 13, 2000); 42 U.S.C. § 3056, et seq.

12. www.eldercare.gov/Eldercare/Public/Home.asp

13. 42 U.S.C. § 401, et seq.

14. 42 U.S.C. § 1396p.

15. 42 U.S.C. § 1396p(a); 42 U.S.C. § 1396r-5.

16. Betty J. Hines, Ex'r of the Estate of Beverly Tutinas v. The Dep't of Public Aid, 221 Ill. 2d 222, May 18, 2006 (No. 10084).

17. 42 U.S.C. § 1396p(b).

18. 42 U.S.C. 1396p(c)(1)(B)(i), (ii), (I), (II)

19. S. 1932, Pub. L. No. 109-171.

20. 42 U.S.C. § 1396p(c)(1)(D).

21. 42 U.S.C. § 1396p(c)(1)(E)(iv).

22. 42 U.S.C. § 1396p(c)(2)(D).

23. 42 U.S.C. § 1396p(c)(1)(J); 26 C.F.R. § 20.2031-7.

24. Pub. L. 109-280.

25. 26 U.S.C. § 402(c).

26. Gerald M. Stern, The Buffalo Creek Disaster, First Vintage Books (1976).

27. http://www.hivoverfifty.org; 816-421-5263.

28. Evidenced by muscular side effects of extended exposure to anti-psychotic drugs. Can occur months or years after taking the drugs. Symptoms include random movements of the tongue, lips and jaw; facial grimacing; movement of the arms, legs, fingers and toes; swaying motion of the trunk. Symptoms may be mild, moderate or severe. There is no definitive, validated or widely accepted treatment. National Alliance on Mental Illness, *available at* www.nami.org.

CHAPTER TEN

Estate Planning

Helping lesbian and gay families prepare their estate-planning documents is an integral part of representing these clients. Most states do not provide coverage for lesbian and gay families in their intestacy statutes. Those that do, including New Jersey, California, Connecticut, Massachusetts, Vermont, Washington, and Oregon, also have domestic partnership or civil union laws or permit same-sex marriage. This fact increases the need for these clients to have the legal documents necessary to protect themselves and their children.

The basic documents that clients need to consider are:

1. Last Will and Testament
2. Trust (testamentary or inter vivos)
3. Advance Directives (Living Will and Healthcare Power of Attorney)
4. Designation of Agent for Healthcare Institutions
5. Durable Power of Attorney for Finances

These documents will allow the client to designate who makes the significant decisions in their lives and after death.

Even attorneys whose practice does not include estate planning must be familiar with the basics. Estate planning is just one facet of a family law practice, and this knowledge will benefit clients.

When starting out, it is important to ask clients what they want to accomplish with their estate plan. With that information, the attorney can determine what documents are best to realize the clients' goals.

Many LGBT clients have not made any effort to develop an estate plan. Many do not believe it is necessary or, as many people do, are procrastinating. Some do not take the necessary steps because they do not want to contemplate their own mortality.

> **Frank and Rob**
>
> Frank and Rob were together for almost four years. As a gift to each other, they were going to celebrate their anniversary by completing an estate plan. One month prior to the anniversary, Rob, a photojournalist, suddenly perished in a helicopter accident while on assignment.
>
> Rob's family, with whom he was not close, swooped in from all over the South. One of Rob's sisters asked Frank to take a walk with her. Upon his return to the home, the locks had been changed and Frank was denied entry. They wouldn't even let him have his dog.
>
> All of the couple's assets were in Rob's name. Frank worked as a manager of a condominium and, for work purposes, kept his driver's license with the address of his condo. The couple were planning to launch a business, so all assets were transferred into Rob's name so the new entity would look highly capitalized.
>
> The cops were called but access was denied, since Frank was not able to show them a driver's license with the address of the home. He couldn't get any of his mail from inside the home to show the police that he, in fact, lived there. We obtained an emergency injunction to allow him entry, but by the time we entered, the home had been stripped bare. All photos were gone; precious possessions were missing. Frank was aghast.
>
> We went to mediation to try to encourage fairness. We asked for the return of the dog. The family asked if Frank had the receipt for the dog's purchase to prove that it was his! With no rights and no written declarations otherwise, the family took absolutely everything. All Frank had were memories and the conviction to tell his story so that this wouldn't happen to other couples in the future.
>
> *Attorney Elizabeth F. Schwartz represented Rob in his attempt to recover his home and the couple's assets. She can be reached at 927 Lincoln Road, Suite 118, Miami Beach, FL 33139; phone: 305.674.9222; fax: 305.674.9002; www.sobelaw.com.*

A. Last Will and Testament

"Testate" means the decedent had a valid will. "Intestate" means the decedent died without a valid will.

When someone dies intestate, the state intestacy statute controls the distribution of the estate. This statute often covers only spouses and blood relatives.

There is usually no provision for same-sex partners.

Many same-sex couples do not understand the difference or significance of "testate" and "intestate" succession. Lawyers can explain to clients what happens if they die without a will. Clients must understand that the surviving partner, and possibly their children, will have no legal right to inherit any part of the probate estate if there is no will and they live in a state without protection for lesbian or gay families.

Some states that recognize gay marriage (Massachusetts), civil unions (Vermont, Connecticut, New Jersey), domestic partnerships (California), or similar relationships (Hawaii) do have provisions for intestate succession between same-sex couples. But the couple must enter into those relationships legally to benefit from the statutory protection.

The Last Will and Testament allows an individual to provide for the distribution of his or her estate after death. Without a will, a person's estate is distributed according to a state's intestate descent and distribution statute.

California, Massachusetts, Washington, and Vermont have led the way by providing that intestate succession statutes include same-sex couples. However, many people do not live in those states. Therefore, it is imperative that clients be encouraged to execute a will containing their decisions concerning the distribution of their estate.

If children are involved, the parties need to discuss whether both of them will be included in their respective testamentary dispositions. This becomes even more crucial if one partner is not a legally recognized parent. The discussion needs to include the disposition of assets and guardianship. The partners may also decide that a co-parent adoption is more appropriate.

Given the myriad complexities of planning an estate for a same-sex couple or LGT individual, drafting client-specific documents is important. "Canned" wills and trusts will not help the client and may, in some cases, create problems after death. As a rule, estate-planning software and form books are geared toward married, heterosexual couples. Few resources are available that were developed for either same-sex or unmarried heterosexual couples.

Lawyers must know their limits and acknowledge them to the client. Bring in help if necessary to avoid committing malpractice and, more important, to ensure that clients' estate plans are prepared to meet their goals.

It is important to know the client well. That engenders a solid relationship in which the clients communicate what they want and the lawyer can provide the services they need. Clients may need help in understanding the documents being prepared.

1. Guardian of Minor Children

Lesbian and gay families are particularly vulnerable regarding their children. Not all states permit second-parent adoptions; few recognize any legal rights between the children and the non-birth parent. This situation can cause major problems for the children if the birth parent dies.

The birth parent must provide a guardian for any minor children. The guardian can be a person or an institution (bank). The birth parent can name her partner as the children's guardian. However, it is important to consider the possibility that a court will refuse to appoint the surviving partner. Given that possibility, the testator can name her partner as guardian of the child's estate, if she is not named guardian of the person. This bifurcates the process and provides for the partner's continued involvement with the child after the birth parent's death.

The legal parents should provide for an interim guardian in addition to anyone named in a testamentary document. The interim guardian will care for the child while the deceased parent's estate is being administered. This provides the child with continuity and security during a difficult and vulnerable time.

The legal parent should also consider which persons, if any, she does *not* want to be named as guardian. Her reasons for excluding those people can be specified. For example, the mother's parents may disapprove of their daughter's same-sex relationship and refuse to permit the surviving partner to continue seeing the child. This hurts both the child and the surviving partner.

Think about and resolve these issues for the benefit of both the child and the decedent's partner.

2. Recognizing the Relationship

Adding a clause dealing with the testator's relationship with his or her partner may help avoid a challenge to the will. In any case, a clause describing the relationship can be used by the executor to rebut a will challenge.

Some lesbian and gay persons are estranged from their families. When they die, the decedent's family may contest the will, arguing that the decedent was not gay or that the relationship was just a friendship. Including a clause in the will in which the testator talks about her relationship will give credibility to the partner's arguments and may cause a judge or jury to look at the family's assertions in a different light. While there is no guarantee, it does allow the testator to talk to those she leaves behind.

There is an emerging school of thought that encourages clients to leave out the adjectives describing their relationship, i.e., "partner," "spouse," "life partner," "domestic partner," and similar terms. And avoid using the word "spouse" in legal documents; that word has a specific legal meaning and does not work with lesbian and gay clients outside of Massachusetts.

The concern is how the mini-DOMAs and state constitutional amendments may be used to interfere with a decedent's estate plan. Will a family member be able to contest a will because the document uses terms that attempt to mimic or imitate marriage? Will a probate court refuse to accept a will because of the language used by the testator to describe her relationship?

On the other hand, no state seems to have a law that specifies what language a testator may use to describe persons named in a will. And lesbian and gay families are doing their best to carve out a place in the heterosexual legal world. When legislatures enacted family and probate codes in the states, they did not consider lesbian and gay individuals or their families. It just was not part of the discussion.

None of these questions have been answered, and it is unknown if they are even being raised. This is virgin territory for everyone, and no one is sure what will happen with some of the draconian language inserted in these amendments. Practitioners may want to discuss the issue with clients and let them make an informed decision.

While it seems unlikely that a court would declare a will void for using terms such as "partner," "domestic partner," "life companion," etc., it is within the realm of possibility.

An ultraconservative judge may be offended by the terminology used and invoke the constitutional language as grounds to invalidate a testamentary bequest. In any event, the cost involved with fighting such a decision may reduce the estate to nothing. The decedent's family may not care because the surviving partner will receive nothing, and that might be their ultimate goal.

Still, the thought of referring to the person sharing your life as "my friend" reduces the commitment the parties shared. Frankly, the words available to lesbian and gay couples are limited. The word "spouse" most clearly describes the relationship but causes the most problems.

These are strange and unnerving times, and lawyers counseling lesbian and gay clients need to be aware of the possible scenarios. This allows the lawyer to discuss potential problems with clients, and informed clients can help the lawyer draft the best documents possible.

3. *Funeral Expenses*

Same-sex couples need to address items that do not necessarily arise with other couples. For example, most states stipulate that family members are authorized to make funeral arrangements. Non-family members will not be able to alter decisions made by the family, even if those decisions are contrary to the decedent's wishes.

Some states, like Ohio, are addressing this issue and amending statutes to permit a person to name whomever he chooses to make funeral arrangements. Ohio's new law became effective in October 2006.

The executor is authorized to pay the funeral expenses. If clients believe there may be a problem with the family, it may be wise to include a clause addressing funeral expenses. The clause may restrict the executor's authority to pay for any funeral expenses that do not correspond with the decedent's wishes. For example, the decedent wanted to be cremated, but the family wants her interred in the family plot.

The executor could notify the funeral director of the will's restrictions on payment. The family would be told they are responsible for paying the funeral expenses, since the contract is between them and the funeral home. Faced with an expensive funeral, the family may reconsider its position. The funeral director may also be reluctant to proceed if there is a possibility the bill will not be paid by the estate. The executor has a duty to protect estate assets from improper expenses.

There is no guarantee this will work, but it is worth trying to ensure that the decedent's wishes are carried out.

An attorney can also recommend prepaying the funeral expenses. Care must be taken, however, to ensure that any subsequent owner of the funeral home will honor the contract. With prepaid funeral contracts, check the fine print to avoid hidden charges.

Another tactic is to research a memorial society that allows members to purchase cremation or burial services in advance. Some of these societies offer low-cost services to their members. If such a contract exists, the family's position would be less tenable and the executor's position enhanced.

4. *"In Terrorum" Clauses*

Discuss using an "in Terrorum" clause in the will. Because many lesbian and gay people are estranged from their families, such a clause may be helpful. It is important to determine if such clauses will be honored in the state where the estate will be probated.

Some states do not permit "in Terrorum" clauses. But these clauses permit the testator or trustor to determine who shall inherit an estate and who shall be excluded.

In 2006, the California Court of Appeals in *Tunstall v. Wells* issued a decision on this issue.[1] The court ruled that a no-contest clause in a testamentary trust does not violate public policy. The court held: "... testator has the right to grant bequests subject to any lawful conditions he or she may select. Beneficiaries of a testamentary instrument have no right to testamentary bequests except subject to the testator's conditions, and it is generally not the role of a court to rearrange those bequests or conditions in keeping with the court's sense of justice."

The testator included a clause that caused the forfeiture of all bequests if one of the beneficiaries contested the will. At least one of the named beneficiaries objected to the terms of the trust. The court, in rejecting those objections, ruled that "[v]alid will and trust may contain terms that might strike outside observers as unfair . . . but a testator may do that, and we would step dangerously outside our proper role were we to rewrite such an instrument to reflect our sense of justice."

The court found that forfeiture clauses often discourage litigation and "thus promote public policy." The court noted similar decisions in Texas, New Jersey, and Pennsylvania. In Ohio, "no contest" clauses are valid and referred to as the "forfeiture rule."[2]

Some lawyers believe the testator or trustor must provide enough of a gift to give a prospective contester pause before proceeding. But, if "no contest," "forfeiture rule," or "in Terrorum" clauses are valid in the state, using them may benefit an LGT client whose family is likely to contest the estate distribution.

5. *Beneficiary Designations*

Include a clause that confirms all beneficiary designations and asset ownership by using a blanket statement indicating that those designations and ownership are intended and stated in the appropriate instrument governing the account or asset. This type of clause can reduce the possibility of a challenge to jointly held property and a claim that it was only for the sake of convenience. The clause will prevent an argument that the decedent never intended the property or asset to pass to the surviving joint owner.

6. *Pet Clauses*

People with pets are concerned about what will happen to them when they die or become incapacitated. Lawyers will serve their clients well if they raise the issue early on in the process.

Providing for pets after the owner's death is important. Some states, like Ohio, permit pet trusts. It is important to ensure that the person named as the caretaker wants the job. It is also preferable to include a specific sum of money for the pet's care. But make sure it is clearly spelled out that the person paying the bills is required to care for the pet.

> **Testamentary Pet Clause**
>
> I leave my pet(s) _____ that I may own at my death to MY FRIEND, with the sum of $3,000 that I ask her to use for their medical care and support. [I believe the amount is sufficient to provide for my pet during life.] [If my pet dies before the funds are exhausted, MY FRIEND may retain the balance.]
>
> If MY FRIEND is unable or unwilling to care for the pet(s), this gift shall lapse. I then direct my Executor to arrange a suitable home for my pet(s) and to prepay their natural lifetime projected medical care and food costs by contractual arrangement with the person or entity taking the pet(s) and their veterinarian. I ask that my Executor act toward my pet(s) as I would act were I to make these arrangements. I authorize the use of up to $10,000 from my funds to make these contractual arrangements for my pet(s).

In addition to a testamentary clause in the will, it is also important to provide for pets during the owner's illness or incapacity. Include a clause in the client's Durable Power of Attorney for Finances. This may require the client to select someone else to actually care for the animal. Some cities have organizations that assist AIDS patients with the care of their pets when they are hospitalized.

It is possible to include pets in the lifetime distribution clauses of a living trust.

> **Pet Clause For Power of Attorney**
>
> To make expenditures for my own care, maintenance, support and general welfare and for the care and support of my domestic pet(s), _____. This includes arranging for regular exercise (daily walks), monthly/weekly/daily grooming, veterinary care and special dietary needs, if any. I authorize payment from my funds for pet care provided by relatives, neighbors, caretakers or professional pet care services.

B. Trusts

Trusts are a valuable tool to use when preparing a client's estate plan. A trust is an empty shell into which assets are transferred by the grantor. The trust then owns the assets and they are no longer part of the grantor's estate. A non-tax reason for trusts is to clarify the lines of inheritance. Trusts can be used to benefit charities or provide for the needs of a disabled child. Trusts can be revocable (changeable during the grantor's lifetime) or irrevocable. Once created, an irrevocable trust cannot be changed.

Testamentary Trusts are included in the body of a will. The trust comes into existence upon the testator's death. The decedent's estate funds the trust.

Inter Vivos Trusts or Living Trusts come into being during the trustor's lifetime. An inter vivos trust can be either revocable or irrevocable. A trustor can change a revocable inter vivos trust during his or her lifetime; an irrevocable inter vivos trust cannot be changed.

A "grantor" or "trustor" establishes trusts for the benefit of beneficiaries. A "trustee" administers the trust. The "trustee" can be the "trustor" or another person or entity. Some trustors elect to name a bank's trust department to administer the trust. This often happens when the trust is very large or the trustor does not have a person capable of administering the trust.

What Is a Trust?

Explaining trusts to a client can be difficult. Here are two possible definitions.

Living Trust: A contract you enter into while you are alive. You can name yourself as the trustee and name someone you trust to manage the trust after you die. You transfer all your assets into the trust while you are alive. The trust tells the trustee how to manage and/or dispose of your assets during your lifetime. After you die, the alternate trustee steps in and continues to carry out your wishes.

Testamentary Trust: Similar to a living trust except it does not become effective until after you die. You set up the trust through your will and designate which assets will go into the trust after your death. You can arrange to have all or some of your assets go into the trust. After your death, your executor pays into the trust the assets you designated in your will. Then the trustee takes over to manage the trust according to your wishes.

A trust becomes effective when it is executed and funded. When this happens, the trust is a distinct legal entity that is separate from any person.

Several triggering events can terminate the trust. These include the death of the last beneficiary, a specific age for the beneficiaries, or death of a partner, at which time the trust is distributed to the remainder beneficiaries. When drafting the trust, a lawyer must determine if the "rule against perpetuities" is followed in the state. This rule provides that a trust can last for "a life in being plus 21 years." The rule prevents a testator from tying up property for multiple generations. Many states have liberalized the rule against perpetuities.

Some clients may ask about joint trusts. These trusts are used almost exclusively in community property states and not at all in common-law states. The trusts fell from favor in common-law states because of concerns about gift and estate tax liabilities. Even in common-law states, joint trusts may be a viable estate-planning tool for clients with no possibility of estate tax liability.

Married couples often use joint trusts when both are grantors. The trusts contain provisions benefiting both parties during their lifetimes. There are also provisions for the surviving spouse and other beneficiaries. The parties' Last Will and Testament contains a pour-over provision to fund the trust upon the individual's death.

All property owned by the couple is transferred to the trust. The trust takes all separate property and makes it joint.

Gay and lesbian couples, even though not married, may be able to use a joint trust but must proceed carefully. Issues that arise with these trusts include:

1. Determining any change in property rights if the parties end their relationship
2. Any gift tax concerns
3. Procedure to remove or replace the trustee
4. Authority to amend or revoke the trust
5. Administration of assets
6. Who is entitled to income and principal during the joint lives

A joint trust may also result in the loss of creditor protection so that the assets of both parties become subject to creditors' claims. In this vein, joint trusts are not helpful for anyone in a profession subject to malpractice claims. These trusts also do not help in qualifying for Medicaid. A joint trust will preclude any sort of Medicaid planning.

Contribution of assets to a joint trust may be construed as gifts resulting in gift tax liability. Since separate property will become "jointly owned," there is a complete divestiture of ownership, and that will probably trigger gift tax consequences.

It is also inadvisable to place a life insurance policy into a joint trust. An irrevocable life insurance trust is a better route to follow.

Joint trusts are not a beginner's tool. If one is considered, it must be done carefully and with a complete understanding of the advantages and disadvantages. Once property is placed into a trust, the parties have less control and may end up with a decent estate plan but a lousy life plan—especially if their relationship ends.

1. Testamentary Trusts

A testamentary trust is funded by the decedent's estate, usually during probate. The trust is included in the body of the Last Will and Testament. The trust does not exist until the testator dies.

The testator can revoke the trust or change its provisions at any time. There is no current interest passed to the beneficiaries in a testamentary trust when the will is signed. The prospective beneficiaries have no standing to challenge any changes before the testator's death. In fact, the beneficiaries have no standing to be told the contents of the testator's will before her death.

Once the testator dies, the beneficiaries do have standing to challenge the will and the testamentary trust. However, the challenge must be based on undue influence, fraud, duress, or incompetence. There is no right to overturn a will simply because a potential beneficiary is unhappy with the contents.

Testamentary trusts are often used to provide for minor children. The trustor can control when the trust terminates, usually when the minor child/children reach a specific age.

Clients must be aware, however, that a trustee can request early termination of the trust if continuing it would no longer be financially responsible. Some states have a minimum threshold for trusts. For example, state law may allow a trustee to request termination through the courts when the trust reaches an amount set by statute.

A client may fund the trust with an amount sufficient to preclude an early termination. It is difficult to predict how long any amount will last. The attorney needs to discuss this issue with the client before the trust is established. Again, the priority is determining what the client wants to accomplish.

Testamentary trusts are also useful if a testator wants to provide for a favorite charity. The charity can be named as the residual beneficiary. Charitable remainder trusts are becoming popular as part of a client's tax plan. The federal estate tax exemption will continue to rise to $3.5 million in 2009. Under current law, the estate tax disappears in 2010, only to reappear in 2011. Congress continues to debate whether to repeal the estate tax permanently.

Attorneys representing clients with substantial estates need to be familiar with the federal exemption amount and the home state estate tax level. Attorneys also need to know and recognize when they are out of their comfort zone and solicit the help of an experienced tax planner. This benefits the client and the attorney. It also precludes possible malpractice.

2. *Inter Vivos Trusts*

Inter vivos trusts are also known as living trusts. This is a contract entered into between the trustor (creator) and the trustee during the latter's lifetime. The trust is either funded with the trustor's current assets or it remains unfunded until a later time. The triggering event for later funding could be the trustor's disability or death. However, the trust must be funded in order to be effective.

Funding is crucial for these trusts. Some attorneys leave the transfer of assets to the client. As a result, many living trusts are not funded or only partially funded. Funding during the trustor's lifetime removes those assets from the probate estate. The probate estate, therefore, is reduced or eliminated. This saves probate costs.

Attorneys can charge the client a fee to transfer the assets into the trust or offer the service as part of an overall estate plan package. Put the offer to transfer assets in writing, mail it to the client, and document any verbal discussions about such a transfer in the file. Many clients refuse and decide to do the work themselves. But transferring assets into a trust is a time-consuming process, and many lay people fail to complete it. That leaves them with an empty trust and a probate estate.

Attorneys whose clients refuse the offer to handle the transfer must be proactive in protecting themselves. One solution is to send the ubiquitous "nag" letter to clients reminding them to transfer the assets. It is crucial for attorneys to send reminder letters and document the advice provided to clients in the file. This helps protect the attorney from allegations of malpractice if the assets are not transferred. In some states, beneficiaries have standing to sue the lawyer for failing to protect their interests. For these reasons, documenting the file is essential to win a malpractice claim.

If the trustor decides to fund the trust after his death, include a "pour-over clause" in the will. This clause results in all estate assets being placed in the trust.

An inter vivos trust is not subject to probate or court supervision, or placed in a public record. This aspect appeals to many clients who want their affairs to remain private. A will, on the other hand, is a public document probated and is available for public view.

The inter vivos trust can be revocable or irrevocable. An irrevocable trust prevents the trustor from making any changes to the trust document after it is executed. An irrevocable trust takes ownership of the assets out of the trustor's hands. Even if the trustor is also the trustee, the trust provisions govern the assets, and the trustee is required to administer the trust according to its provisions. Carefully consider whether to create an irrevocable trust. Most trustors want to retain control over their property while alive.

When a trustor does create an irrevocable trust, he usually names himself as the trustee. That allows the trustor to retain control over his assets, albeit within the confines of the trust.

Another reason to avoid an irrevocable trust involves the possibility that the couple's relationship may end. Transferring property to an irrevocable trust means the parties remain inextricably tied together—and estranged couples tend to avoid that level of contact.

Many people believe a living trust allows them to avoid probate, protects them from their creditors, and avoids all income and estate taxes. It is the lawyer's responsibility to disabuse people of these fanciful notions. Clients are also well-served by consulting with an accountant who is familiar with trusts.

The Internal Revenue Code does not provide for the avoidance of taxes through a trust. If that were the case, everyone would have a trust and no one would pay taxes. A trust will not protect an individual from her legal responsibilities, including child support, alimony, or other judgments.

As long as the trustor retains control over the trust assets, there will be no reduction in income taxes.

Most people use the inter vivos trust to avoid probate and keep their affairs private. Same-sex couples may find it useful in that respect. It is usually more difficult to challenge a trust than a will, but it is possible. Clients also need to know that a probate case may still need to be filed.

Wills, trusts, and probate issues are state-specific. It is important for lawyers with limited experience in these matters to consult with more experienced colleagues.

> **Pet Care Living Trust Provisions**
>
> I intend that my domestic pet(s) remain in my home with me. I want to maintain contact with them for as long as possible. I direct my trustee to arrange for regular exercise (daily walks), veterinary care and companionship when I cannot provide that to my pet(s). I want home care provided that will permit my pet(s) to stay with me. Any home healthcare provider must be comfortable with my pet(s) and treat them kindly. My trustee shall pay for the time spent by my family, friends or neighbors who help care for my pet(s), or to employ a pet care professional to provide that care and companionship. I ask that veterinary care be continued at (name of veterinary clinic) where my pet(s) have always been cared for. If I am forced to leave home because of my health situation, I want my trustee to select a new residence where I may live with my pet(s). If that is not possible, I want my trustee to arrange regular, twice-weekly visits with my pet(s).

3. *Grantor Retained Income Trusts (GRITs)*

Grantor Retained Income Trusts are irrevocable trusts. Chapter 14 of the Internal Revenue Code governs GRITs. This trust permits a transfer of property with little to no gift tax cost. But GRITs are not available for transfers made to a grantor's family. The I.R.C. defines "family" at § 2704(c). The advantage for same-sex couples is that a GRIT is an option, since the definition of "family" does not include "life partner," "domestic partner," or similar designation.

The grantor transfers property during his lifetime but retains the right to income produced by the trust for a designated period. When the specified time expires, the trust ends and the property is distributed to a designated third party. In cases involving lesbian and gay couples, that person can be the grantor's partner.

The grantor can also retain a "reversionary interest." This gives the grantor the power of disposition over the transferred property during his or her lifetime. The transferred interest takes effect only if the grantor dies before the reserved term ends.

Transfers to a GRIT are taxable gifts. The gift amount is determined by the actuarial value of the grantor, any reserved income interest, and the contingent reversionary interest from the property's value. The gift's value is determined by subtracting the actuarial value of the reserved interest from the value of the property transferred into the trust.

Any retained interest must be in either a fixed amount, known as an "annuity interest," or a fixed percentage of the trust's fair market value. The latter is also known as a "unitrust interest."

If the trust's income is less than the reserved amount, the payment is made from the trust principal.

Property transferred into a GRIT can be cash, stocks, bonds, real property, or an interest in a business.

If the grantor survives the designated term, the tax is calculated using the initial value of the property at the time of the transfer. There is no value at the end of the trust. The transferred property is no longer in the grantor's estate and not subject to any estate tax. When the grantor survives the termination of the GRIT, the only taxable event occurred when the trust came into being.

The situation is different if the grantor dies before the designated period expires. In that case, the property reverts to the grantor's estate and is taxed at the existing level. There is no gift tax because no gift was made. This means the entire value of the grantor's gift tax exemption is reinstated. The gift tax lifetime exemption is currently $1 million.

Estate planners may consider using this tool if one partner has a more significant estate than the other. The GRIT protects any increase in the value of the transferred property over the course of the trust. If the grantor survives the trust, the beneficiary receives the current value of the transferred property but is taxed on the value as of the initial transfer.

4. *Total Return Trust*

These trusts allow the grantor to provide for an "income beneficiary" for life. When that person dies, the trust principal is distributed to the "principal beneficiaries." These parties may have differing interests, so it is best to name an independent, objective trustee to administer the trust. The trustee will owe a duty to both the short-term and long-term beneficiaries.

As the beneficiary interests can be at odds, the trustee's duty involves balancing income and growth. One way to resolve the dilemma is to define the "income beneficiary's" income as a percentage of the principal. By doing so, the trustee is able to invest the trust in a way that will satisfy all parties. Setting income as a percentage of the trust means the income grows as the trust grows.

A charitable remainder trust works in a similar manner. This type of trust may allow for the distribution of increased wealth to the beneficiaries—short and long term.

5. *Grantor Retained Annuity Trust (GRAT)*

The grantor receives a fixed annuity from the trust. The balance passes to the named beneficiaries free from any estate tax liability. Once assets are transferred into the GRAT, the grantor no longer owns them. This allows the administration of those assets outside of probate.

C. Charitable Remainder Trusts and Annuities

There are several types of charitable trusts for clients to consider. These trusts are most helpful for clients with large estates who may face federal or state estate taxes. However, the trusts are available to all clients. Since lesbian and gay clients have few other tax-saving estate-planning techniques open to them, these trusts may help clients achieve their estate-planning goals.

There is a Planned Giving Design Center[3] that includes free information about charitable transfers. Individual charitable organizations will also have information on such transfers.

Bequests for foreign charities are also possible, especially when transferred at the donor's death. The U.S. Treasury Department has a Best Practices for International Fund Raising.[4] The American Bar Association also has a free electronic mailing list enabling subscribers to get information about charitable giving.[5]

1. *Charitable Lead Trust (CLT)*[6]

A CLT establishes an annuity of unitrust amount that is paid to a charity for a prescribed number of years. The period involved can be either a specific number of years or the life of an individual. At the end of that time the trust terminates, and any remaining assets are paid to the named beneficiaries, such as the testator's heirs.

CLTs used to earn gift and estate tax deductions are called a "Non-Grantor Lead Trust."

A Charitable Lead Annuity Trust makes a guaranteed fixed payment to a charity. The Charitable Lead Unitrust pays a fixed percentage of the fair market value of the trust assets to the charity. Both trusts must make these payments at least on an annual basis. More frequent payments are also permitted. Under the Charitable Lead Unitrust, the principle's value is determined annually.

These trusts can be used to transfer wealth for generations. Due to the large sums normally involved, the donor usually chooses a professional trustee to manage the trust. When the trust is established, the donor is entitled to a gift or estate tax deduction. The deduction is based on the present value of the trust assets. There is no income tax deduction for Non-Grantor Lead Trusts. Trust management is designed to produce the amount destined for the charity according to the trust terms.

2. Charitable Remainder Unitrust (CRUT)[7]

CRUTs are a variable-income trust used by people who intend to make large gifts to charities and may have complex estates. These trusts offer great flexibility when transferring real estate or other appreciated property to the trust. The trust must pay a fixed percentage, not less than 2% or more than 50% of the net fair market value of the assets, to the income beneficiaries. The value of the assets is determined annually. Trust payments are made at least annually for the life of the income beneficiaries or for a term not to exceed 20 years.

When the trust terminates, the balance of assets is transferred to the named charity, which must be a qualified charitable organization. This usually requires the organization to hold a 501(c)(3) certificate from the Internal Revenue Service. The balance transferred to the charity must be at least 10% of the initial value of assets transferred to the trust.

Donors may make gifts to the trust over time to meet their tax considerations. On funding, the donor may receive a charitable income tax deduction. This depends on the donor's age, trust payment rate, federal discount rate, and the assets' fair market value.

There are four basic types of CRUTs:

a. Net Income Only Unitrust (NICRUT), which distributes the lesser of the required percentage or actual trust income;
b. Net Income Only with Makeup Provision Unitrust (NIMCRUT), which distributes the lesser of the required percentage or the actual trust income. If any distribution is less than required, the trust can make up those shortages in later years;
c. Straight Unitrust, which pays a fixed percentage of the assets without regard to actual trust income; and
d. Flip Unitrust, which results from the conversion of either a NIMCRUT or NICRUT and turns both into a Straight Unitrust when a specific event happens. This is useful for trusts with low- income-producing assets or closely held business assets.

Income beneficiaries that are not charities must report the distributions as income under I.R.C. § 664(b).

3. *Charitable Remainder Annuity Trust (CRAT)*[8]

CRATs are fixed-income trusts designed by donors wishing to make significant charitable gifts and design a charitable life income plan. The payout must be between 5% and 50% of the initial fair market value of the trust assets. The donor retains an income for life, with the remainder going to a qualified charity. This trust allows the donor to defer or eliminate any capital gains taxes on appreciated property.

Under the rules, the ultimate payout to the qualified charity must be at least 10% of the original asset value. The tax treatment for CRATs is the same as for CRUTs.

4. *Charitable Gift Annuity (CGA)*[9]

CGAs involve a contract between a donor and a charity. The donor makes a charitable gift and receives an income of defined payments for life. The payments are made quarterly, semi-annually, or annually and are based on a fixed percentage of the original contribution. The age of the beneficiary determines the payment amount.

Annuities funded with cash gifts allow part of the gift to be free of federal income tax. The other part is taxed at the regular rates. Charities offering this option require a minimum initial donation and a minimum donor age. The usual amount is $10,000 and 60 years old. Charities may also charge an administrative fee to cover risk and expenses.

5. *Remainder Interests in Real Estate/Retained Life Estate*[10]

This gift plan allows a donor to contribute his or her personal residence or farm to a qualified charity. The donor retains a life estate in the property. The term may also be for a lesser number of years.

This involves an irrevocable deed transfer to the charity. The life estate may be for a term of years, the donor's life, or a combination of the two. The donor may also use this tool to transfer a vacation home. The donor remains responsible for all taxes, expenses, maintenance, and upkeep of the property while living in it. When the life estate ends, the charity may keep or sell the property.

An advantage of this gift is to allow a donor to make a charitable contribution, receive current tax benefits, and have a home to live in. These gifts are often used by people who do not plan to leave the property to family members.

6. *Qualified Retirement and IRA Assets*

People may arrange for their retirement or IRA assets to be paid to a qualified charitable organization. IRAs, KEOGH plans, 401(k) accounts, and 403(b) accounts can be used. These accounts, if passed on death to a non-charity beneficiary, may be subject to income and estate taxes. The tax rate may be high, and transferring these assets to a charity will avoid those taxes.

The charity may be named as the beneficiary on the account using the plan's regular beneficiary form. These accounts cannot be transferred to a charity during the donor's lifetime. The donor may donate the money to the charity as it is distributed to him. That gives the donor income but also a charitable deduction during his lifetime.

7. *Life Insurance Gifts*

The owner of a life insurance policy may name a qualified charitable organization as the beneficiary. This allows a person of modest means to make a significant charitable donation.

The donor can either make an irrevocable decision to name the charitable organization as the policy's owner or just as the beneficiary. If the former action is taken, the charity can then name itself as the beneficiary.

Gifts involving an existing policy allow the donor to take a charitable deduction for the policy's value. The charitable deduction is not necessarily the same as the policy's face value. Paid-up policies result in a deduction equal to the policy's replacement value or an amount that does not exceed the donor's tax basis. When premium payments remain, the deduction is usually an amount equal to the terminal reserve value and the proportionate part of the last premium paid before the gift was made.

Charitable gifts can be a valuable estate-planning tool. Lawyers with a limited background in estate tax planning should consider collaborating with a tax lawyer or a legitimate financial planner. Of course, working with a non-lawyer requires the client's informed consent and must not include any fee-sharing. The financial planner and attorney would charge separate fees. Still, such collaboration can be established to serve the client's best interests. The lawyer will be responsible for drafting all legal documents, including wills and trust agreements.

D. Advance Directives

Advance directives are the same as living wills and Health Care Powers of Attorney. These documents allow individuals to advise healthcare providers of their wishes in the event they are unable to voice those intentions.

The 2005 case involving Florida resident Terry Schiavo brought the importance of these documents to the public. The actions by Congress and the Florida

Legislature motivated people to make the decision to sign these directives. No one wants strangers making important decisions for him or her.

These documents are of particular importance to same-sex couples and can prevent interference by family members. They can also be used to prevent hospital or nursing home personnel from banning a patient's partner from the facility. These legal documents are used to identify who is to make the decisions and what those decisions should be.

Even though, unlike a married couple, same-sex couples are not recognized as a legal entity, these documents are helpful in establishing the parties' relationship and are enforceable in court. The applicable state statutes provide a process for contesting decisions made by the patient's healthcare agent.

1. Living Will

A living will is not the same as a Last Will and Testament, but many people do not know the difference.

The generally accepted definition of a living will is that it expresses a person's wishes about artificially prolonging life. Specifically, two doctors must certify that the patient is in a terminal condition from which there will be no recovery. The doctors certify that death is imminent and further medical intervention will not improve the patient's condition. The doctors certify there is no chance of recovery. The patient, through the living will, is stating that he or she wants no heroic measures taken and no artificial means used to prolong life. The living will form may also include a provision allowing the patient to refuse, or have withdrawn, nutrition and hydration but continue comfort medication.

The principal can be very specific concerning the type of medical treatment he or she wants. Some states have adopted standard forms vetted by the state bar association, medical association, and other interested agencies. These forms can be used with the knowledge that the language is approved statewide. Healthcare providers and facilities may also be familiar with and accept the standard forms.

These documents protect the healthcare provider and the facility from liability for carrying out the patient's written instructions.[11]

2. Health Care Power of Attorney

The person named as a patient's attorney in fact for healthcare purposes is authorized to carry out the patient's wishes. Usually, this authority arises when the patient is no longer able to make his or her own decisions or communicate with healthcare personnel.

Without this power of attorney, the default position is to look to the patient's immediate family. This does not include a same-sex partner.

Same-sex couples need this document to establish each partner's legal authority concerning the other for healthcare providers, hospital and nursing home administrators, and, possibly, the patient's family. If there is no legal recognition of the parties' relationship, this document can be used to rebut opposition to the partner making the decision. The document reflects the patient's intentions and is legally recognizable by a court.

There is an unrelenting fear among same-sex couples that they will not be allowed access to each other in a medical situation. These fears are valid. Many same-sex couples worry that the recent spate of state constitutional amendments banning gay marriage will also prevent them from having their legal documents recognized. Imagine the fear anyone would feel if the one person who means the most is not allowed into the hospital room.

Lawyers representing lesbian and gay clients must remember that there is a coordinated attempt in the United States to prevent any legitimization of same-sex relationships. These documents can benefit same-sex couples and their children by smoothing the way in traumatic times. So far, no state has enacted a law that explicitly precludes same-sex couples from naming each other in Advance Directives.

3. Health Insurance Portability and Accountability Act (HIPAA)

Due to the expansion of electronic exchange in healthcare information, the provisions of the Health Insurance Portability and Accessibility Act (HIPAA) guard and protect a person's personal healthcare information.

Including language in the advance directives or in a separate document may prevent confusion in a healthcare setting. The last thing someone needs is to be told by healthcare personnel that they cannot discuss the patient's case with you because of HIPAA; a HIPAA authorization avoids that situation.

Sample language is included in the Appendices. Inserting HIPAA authorization in the Health Care Power of Attorney and the Living Will provides the legal tools for the partner to take an active role in the patient's care. This is a relatively simple process and should become standard in all Advance Directives prepared by any lawyer.

But HIPAA language should also be included in the Designation of Agent and Durable Power of Attorney for Finances. There is concern that including the language only in Advance Directives will prevent the authority from taking place. The Health Care Power of Attorney authorizes the named person to assume responsibility only *after* the grantor becomes incapacitated. HIPAA authority gives the right to discuss the patient's condition with the medical providers. The authority does not occur until after incapacity is determined, and that cannot be determined without the authority. It is a classic Catch-22 situation.

To avoid the possibility, review your General Durable Power of Attorney for Finances to determine if it provides HIPAA authority to the attorney-in-fact. If it does not, you may include HIPAA language in the grantor's Durable Power of Attorney for Finances and Designation of Agent. This may be redundant, but it may also avoid confusion when such a document is needed.

A separate HIPAA authorization is another option. This gives the designee a separate document to present that does not include other, extraneous information. Samples of these documents are included in the Appendix.

E. Designation of Agent

This document is used to designate the person authorized to visit a patient/resident in a healthcare facility (including nursing home, hospice, correctional facility, etc.). Lesbian and gay persons can name their partner as the designated agent. The document can also be used to specify that the designated agent is the one who decides who visits the patient/resident.

Many hospitals limit visits to "immediate family." Same-sex couples do not, in the eyes of many institutions, fall into that category. This document helps refute that position.

This document references the Joint Commission on Accreditation of Healthcare Organizations (JCAHO). JCAHO is responsible for accrediting healthcare organizations. Hospitals need accreditation to operate.

JCAHO defines "family" as "[t]he person(s) who plays a significant role in the individual's (patient's) life. This may include a person(s) not legally related to the individual." (Joint Commission Resources, JCR, 2001 Hospital Accreditation Standards, p. 322)

This can be a powerful argument for a lesbian and gay family to make if they run into difficulty during a partner's hospitalization. A complaint can be made to JCAHO if the healthcare organization refuses to comply with the document.

The Designation of Agent form is also used to authorize the agent to recover the patient/resident's personal property, decide on the disposition of remains, authorize an autopsy, and make funeral arrangements. Most states provide that family members have the authority to make funeral arrangements. Even though there is a designated agent, there is no guarantee that the court will recognize that person. The clause described in the section on Wills may be helpful.

This document is another piece of evidence attesting to your clients' relationship and their intentions.

F. Durable Power of Attorney for Finances

Through this power of attorney (POA), the principal names another person to act in his place. This is a very powerful document, and clients need to understand its significance. The attorney is in a position to caution the client about the document's use and potential misuse.

With a durable power of attorney, the person named as the attorney-in-fact acts in the name of the principal.

There are different forms of powers of attorney. One takes effect immediately and is the most powerful document. The durable nature of the power means it will continue even if the principal becomes disabled. This language is an important part of the power of attorney.

Clients can also execute a "springing power of attorney." This takes effect only when a certain event occurs, usually on the disability of the principal.

A concern with the "springing" power is how to determine the event that triggers the disability. Any dispute about whether the springing POA is in effect may require a court order. A dispute may arise about whether the principal is disabled. The principal's family may contest the designated attorney-in-fact being allowed to exercise the power.

There are limited powers of attorney that restrict the power given to the attorney-in-fact. These are used for a specific purpose or task, such as paying bills, writing checks, or selling real estate.

A general power of attorney gives the attorney-in-fact complete power to operate as the principal would. An extreme example is that the attorney-in-fact sells the principal's house without his actual knowledge.

The client must be sure that the person being given the power will use it wisely and in the principal's interests.

Some financial institutions, brokers, etc., require their own power of attorney form. Either the client or the attorney can contact these institutions and determine if they will accept a POA different from the organization's standard forms. If not, it is in the client's best interests to execute the required form.

1. Nomination of Guardian

Caregiver disputes are growing in number. While there are no national statistics, custody battles over elderly parents, spouses, and grandparents are becoming more common. The same type of dispute may arise in cases involving same-sex couples. Many LGT people are estranged from their families. If the LGT family member becomes ill or incapacitated, the family may show up to take control of the person and his or her estate. That can leave the partner with no legal standing.

The issues that are raised can include where the person is to live, who will be the primary caregiver and, perhaps most important, who controls the person's finances. According to the National Guardianship Association in State College, Pennsylvania, shifting demographics propel many of the disputes. Fractured families and tensions among children and stepfamilies over the relative's care contribute to the situation. Long-standing family rifts can also create a combative situation. Often, the battle begins when large sums of money are at stake.

An increasing number of interstate custody and guardian disputes are made more difficult because of the lack of uniformity among the states. In 2005, 15 states passed 25 guardianship laws; 14 states passed 19 laws in 2004.[12] Some of the new laws limit the guardian's power and provide for more oversight. The Uniform Law Commission is working on a model law that will deal with interstate guardianship feuds. Hopefully, that model will include situations involving LGT persons and provide rights to their partners.

The situation can be difficult even if the couple is in a legally recognized relationship within their domiciliary state. Most states do not recognize same-sex relationships, and removing one person to such a state will invalidate all legal protections available in the home state. Careful planning is crucial.

Include a provision for the nomination of a guardian of the person and the estate in the durable power of attorney. The principal nominates the person he wants appointed as his guardian. This can be used by the Probate Court if there is a move to create a guardianship. That nominee can also be a professionally trained guardian who is sensitive to the needs of a same-sex couple.

Including a mediation clause in advance directives may also be helpful if there is a probability the person's family will object or contest any designation of authority.

Some states refer to this as a conservatorship, so language reflecting both possibilities may be advisable. This is particularly appropriate in situations where the principal lives in one state and his family lives in another.

The clause can provide for an alternative if the court refuses to name the nominee as guardian. This is similar to the guardian clause for minor children in the will. The principal may nominate a specific person or entity to control the estate even if the court appoints someone else as guardian of the person. Some courts have particular people or entities they prefer and may not appoint any family member. The principal's attorney in fact must be prepared to argue in favor of the named nominees.

G. Payable on Death (POD) Bank Accounts

These are different from joint personal accounts. They are similar to naming a beneficiary on a life insurance policy. But they are available only on personal bank accounts. Business accounts must be held in joint tenancy with right of survivorship.

POD accounts provide that the money in the account goes to a specific person when the account holder dies. The beneficiary has no present interest in the account and cannot access the account during your lifetime. There is no gift to the beneficiary because it is not yet complete.

Couples who maintain separate accounts may use this as another part of their estate plan. It allows them to provide for a surviving partner and still avoid probate. The money transfers after death and outside probate. There is no procedure to contest the designation.

It is a simple process, and clients can do this without a lawyer. Each financial institution has the form needed to designate the payee. Usually it is on the signature form completed when accounts are opened.

Clients can ask their financial institution what documentation the payee needs to access the account after the owner dies.

H. Funeral Arrangements

Encourage clients to list their funeral wishes in a letter to the executor. Wills are read *after* the funeral, so it is not practical to put the information in that document.

Clients will ask about prepaid funeral arrangements. It is important to read the contract carefully. Make sure the contract price covers the entire expense of the funeral, burial vault, headstone, casket, lunch, church/memorial service, cremation, etc. The contract terms must specify exactly what is and, just as important, is not covered. Be sure there are no hidden charges, such as opening and closing the grave, placing the headstone, etc.

Negotiate a contract that will be honored by the existing funeral home operator and all successors. International companies are absorbing many family-run funeral homes. The name may be the same, but the owner may have changed.

A new owner may not recognize or accept a prepaid contract entered into with the previous owner. This is an argument against using a prepaid contract. Even if the contract between the client and the operator states it will be honored, there is no contract between the client and a future owner. Even though one may think a future owner is required to honor existing contracts and accept them as part of the sale, there is no guarantee that will happen. Those contracts can be viewed as a liability the new owner is unwilling to accept. Further, it would require litigation to force the issue.

Investing in a life insurance policy to cover the cost of the funeral may be a more prudent way to proceed.

I. Unified Estate and Gift Tax Credit

Every person in the United States has a $1 million lifetime gift tax exemption. Every person also has the right to make a $12,000 annual gift to whomever he chooses. (This annual amount changes, making it necessary to check the Internal Revenue Code regularly.)

The Unified Estate and Gift Tax Credit is important to lesbian and gay couples. Since same-sex couples are not entitled to the marital deduction, they must be careful in their financial dealings with each other.

Holding property in joint and survivorship form can present problems when one partner dies. The I.R.S. assumes that the entire value of the property is in the decedent's estate. That assumption may result in estate tax being levied on the estate. Likewise, when the surviving partner dies, the I.R.S., once again, determines the entire value to be part of the surviving partner's estate. Result: A same-sex couple is taxed twice for the same property. This does not happen with married couples.

Lesbian and gay couples must keep detailed financial records that reflect their individual and joint contributions to the household, particularly all jointly held property.

If the jointly held property increases in value to the point where estate tax is due, the surviving partner, as the sole owner of the house, will be personally liable for the tax. If she cannot pay the tax, a lien will be filed against the property and a forced sale may result.

The parties may use their individual lifetime gift tax exemption to transfer an interest to the other. This allows both to deduct $1 million from the value of the house, and may allow them to avoid all estate tax liability.

Lawyers who are not comfortable or familiar with tax law may want to collaborate with a tax attorney to develop these estate plans.

Same-sex couples may consider holding real estate as tenants in common rather than joint tenants. They would each own a pro-rata share of the property and could leave their share to each other on death. Income and expense sharing can also be divided according to their individual pro-rata share.

Individual states may also allow property titles to transfer on death without giving an interest in the property during life. This is a Transfer on Death deed. It is a valuable tool available to estate planners and their clients.

Each party can also use a revocable living trust to convey an interest in the property to the other. Living trusts are administered outside the probate process.

The transferred interest may be eligible for a reduction of the fair market value that further reduces any potential tax liability. This is the minority interest discount. It can be 10% to 30% of the property's fair market value. With the discount, it may be possible for the surviving partner to take the decedent's interest tax-free.

J. Other Ideas for Estate Distribution

In addition to the ideas presented earlier, clients should be aware of other alternatives.

Designating multiple beneficiaries in retirement plans and IRAs (Roth and traditional) is one way to manage an estate and provide for many people. This may be necessary in situations where one or both partners have children from the relationship or prior relationships.

Irrevocable life insurance trusts are non-probate assets and can provide a means to pay off a house, pay for the funeral, or provide an income for the surviving partner or the parties' children. The trust would also be outside the decedent's estate for tax purposes because it is irrevocable.

For clients with large estates, it may be advisable to begin a regular process of making gifts to family members. One advantage of this is that the giftor is able to note these gifts in his or her will. The testator can then indicate that the gifts were in lieu of any testamentary bequest. It will be necessary to keep records of the gifts given, name, date, and amount in order to rebut any post-death allegation that the giftee received nothing. At present, an individual is able to give $12,000 per year to an unlimited number of people. This annual amount does not count against the $1 million lifetime exemption.

Life estates also present an opportunity to provide for a surviving partner and other beneficiaries. Establishing a surviving partner's right to remain in the couple's home following the death of one may obviate a will challenge.

Couples who have children may also want to study the Section 529 Plans available to pay for college. This is a valid estate-planning option a couple may use to offset the growing cost of college.

Other possibilities are family limited partnerships, charitable remainder trusts, qualified personal residence trusts, and self-canceling installment notes.

Again, the purpose of any estate planning decision is to meet the goals set by the client.

Any estate plan developed for a same-sex couple should build in the possibility that federal law may change and recognize gay marriage, civil unions, and domestic partnerships. Language that addresses this possibility will permit clients to take advantage of changes in the law without rewriting all their documents. The same holds true of changes in the couple's respective state laws.

Some of the benefits governed by federal law and unavailable to same-sex couples include pension benefits (ERISA), self-insured health insurance plans, COBRA benefits that allow a person to continue health insurance after leaving a job, and Family and Medical Leave Act benefits.

Joint financial accounts may create an issue if there is a question about the reason for their creation. Some joint accounts are for the convenience of the account holder. For example, an elderly parent asks his son to sign on to the account to facilitate finance management. This is generally not considered a true survivor account. The son does not deposit any funds. His name is on the account for the convenience of the father.

Specifying, in estate-planning documents, that the parties intend the joint accounts to be treated that way and not as accounts of convenience may alleviate potential future problems. A provision in the will or other documents that reflects the testator's intent that all funds in the joint accounts go to the surviving partner is good planning practice.

Some people create a "deed of convenience" as a supplement to a previous deed. This type of deed must be carefully considered in light of the relevant state law and must be prepared only by a lawyer.

Transferring an interest in real estate may trigger gift tax liability. Real estate can be placed in a trust, but transfer any ownership interest in that real estate outside the trust in an amount equal to the annual exemption. This type of transfer is not taxable. For example, Julius owns the house, and he wants to ensure that his partner, Brutus, gains an interest in the property. For whatever reason, Julius does not want to refinance, and Brutus agrees. Julius transfers the house into a living trust. Outside the trust, he transfers $12,000 in interest to Brutus. The amount equals the annual exemption and does not trigger any gift tax. This most likely will require an annual deed preparation reflecting the new interest as tenants in common.

K. Inherited Individual Retirement Plans

In July 2006, President Bush signed the Pension Protection Act of 2006.[13] The law became effective on January 1, 2007.

Included in this new law is Section 829, titled "Allow Rollovers by Non-spouse Beneficiaries of Certain Retirement Plan Distributions." This language changes Section 402(c) of the Internal Revenue Code.[14] The new law permits the owner of specific retirement plans (think I.R.A.) to name a non-spouse beneficiary. Before the change, only spouses could roll over an inherited I.R.A. without being required to begin withdrawals within five years. The new law gives that same right to any named beneficiary. The "spouse only" requirement has been repealed. The complete texts of Sections 829 and 402(c) of the Internal Revenue Code are included in Appendix B.

The owner of a retirement plan may name a child or other non-spouse as the beneficiary. The beneficiary has the right to transfer the funds directly into an "inherited I.R.A." This allows the beneficiary to spread out distributions over many years. As with all I.R.A.s, required distributions begin when the owner turns 70.5 years old. These new provisions are effective for distributions made after January 1, 2007.

Under the old law, a decedent could name a non-spouse beneficiary. However, the law required that beneficiary to begin taking withdrawals within one year. With the new provision, the non-spouse beneficiary can transfer the proceeds directly into an "inherited I.R.A." and stretch out withdrawals over his life expectancy.

Most company 401(k) plans required withdrawal within five years in a lump sum. The beneficiaries then paid federal and state taxes on the full balance. The changes also apply to inheritances from 403(b) plans (teachers) and 457 savings accounts (government workers). Tax bills incurred by non-spouse survivors of 9/11 victims prompted the legislation.

When setting up these accounts, be sure the financial institution titles it an "inherited I.R.A." This must be a separate account. The inherited proceeds cannot be transferred into an existing I.R.A. It is advisable to arrange for the direct transfer of the proceeds into the "inherited I.R.A." Checks sent directly to the beneficiary may trigger a taxable distribution even if the funds are immediately deposited into the new I.R.A.

Same-sex couples will now be able to leave their retirement funds to their partners with the same benefits as heterosexual married couples. This is a good development for lawyers and their same-sex clients.

L. Conclusion

Lesbian and gay couples do not have the Unified Marital Deduction to use in planning their estates. Most clients want their attorney to maximize their assets and minimize their state and federal tax liability. Each client's situation will be different. This is not a one-size-fits-all situation. That's what makes it so exciting and challenging. These clients present different scenarios concerning their children, real estate, contracts, business interests, investments, and the like. They do not fit into a neat niche that is easily replicated.

Attorneys representing lesbian and gay families are in an excellent position to use their creativity to accomplish their clients' goals. Lawyers can also act to help their clients protect their families when they travel. Estate planning is more than anticipating death. The forms lesbian and gay families need include those used in daily life.

Notes

1. Tunstall v. Wells, 144 Cal. App. 4th 554, 50 Cal. Rptr. 3d 468 (Oct. 31, 2006).
2. Moodie v. Andrews, 2002-Ohio-5765 (9th Dist. Ct. App.); Bradford v. Bradford, 19 Ohio St. 546 (1869); Kirkbride v. Hickok, 155 Ohio St. 293 (1951) ("no good faith exception to 'no contest' clauses").
3. www.pgdc.com
4. www.abanet.org/rppt/cmtes/pt/d2/2003-29Comments.pdf
5. www.abanet.org/rppt/comtes/pt/d2/home.html
6. I.R.C. §§ 170(f)(2)(B), 2055(e)(2)(B), and 2522(c)(2)(B).
7. I.R.C. § 664(d)(2) and Treas. Reg. §§ 1.664-1 and 1.664-3.
8. I.R.C. § 664(d)(1) and Treas. Reg. §§ 1.664-1 and 1.664-2.
9. I.R.C. § 72 and Treas. Reg. §§ 1.170A-1(d) and 1.1011-2.
10. I.R.C. §§ 170(f)(3)(B)(i) and (4), 2522(c)(2), and 2055(e)(2); Treas. Reg. §§ 1.170A-7 and 1.170A-12.
11. The DVD "What You Need to Know About Living Wills" is available from Legal Insight™, www.legalinsight.com; 713-913-0300.
12. American Bar Association Commission on Law & Aging, www.abanet.org/aging.
13. Pub. L. 109-280.
14. 26 U.S.C. 402(c).

CHAPTER ELEVEN

Immigration

Immigration issues may also play a part in representing lesbian and gay clients. This is a highly specialized area of law, and an immigration lawyer experienced in sexual orientation cases will best serve the client's interests.

Under current federal law, lesbian and gay U.S. citizens and permanent legal residents cannot sponsor their same-sex partners for entry into the United States. However, foreign lesbian and gay nationals are no longer excluded from entry into the United States because of their sexual orientation.

Congress is considering legislation, the Uniting American Families Act (UAFA),[1] that will allow U.S. citizens and legal permanent residents to sponsor their same-sex partners.

A. Immigration Law Background

The Immigration Act of 1917 barred lesbians and gay men from immigrating to the United States.[2] In 1952, Congress amended the Act to exclude gay men and lesbians on the basis that they were "... afflicted with psychopathic personality ... or a mental defect."[3]

The 1952 ban continued in full force and effect until 1963, when the Ninth Circuit held it void for vagueness. "[T]he statutory term, 'psychopathic personality' where measured by common understanding and practices does not convey sufficiently definite warning that homosexuality and sexual perversion are embraced therein."[4]

Under the 1952 immigration law, the Immigration and Naturalization Service (INS) referred anyone suspected of being "homosexual" to the U.S. Public Health Service, which examined the foreign national, decided if the person was homosexual, and issued a certification to that effect as authorized by the law.[5] This certificate constituted irrefutable proof of the person's sexual orientation.

Immigration judges used these certificates as the sole basis for their decisions.

In 1965, Congress again amended the immigration law to specifically exclude foreign nationals afflicted with a "sexual deviation," meaning homosexuals.[6]

In 1967, the U.S. Supreme Court resolved a challenge to the language by holding that the term "psychopathic personality" was not unconstitutionally vague.[7] The Court held that Congress intended to exclude homosexuals.

The American Psychiatric Association (APA) removed homosexuality from its official list of disorders in 1973. But that did not stop the Department of Justice (DOJ) from releasing guidelines on the subject in 1980. DOJ guidelines determined there was an ongoing "legal obligation to exclude homosexuals from entering the United States."[8] *Hill v. INS*[9] challenged the DOJ guidelines. The Ninth Circuit held that the government could exclude homosexuals from immigrating only if the Public Health Service issued a certification.

In 1979, after the APA made its decision, the PHS decided it would no longer issue certificates declaring that homosexuals have "psychopathic personalities." The *Hill* decision presented an interesting dilemma for the INS. The Ninth Circuit held the government could only exclude homosexuals with a PHS certificate, but PHS no longer issued them.

The Fifth Circuit held an opposite view in the case *In re Longstaff*.[10] The court held that the petitioner was a homosexual who had not been lawfully admitted to the United States and, therefore, was properly denied naturalization.

Finally, with the Immigration Act of 1990,[11] Congress removed the exclusion. Even with the exclusions removed, foreign nationals who are lesbian or gay are still at risk in immigration cases. Federal law still allows for exclusion based on moral turpitude convictions, lack of "good moral character," and sodomy convictions.[12] The Department of Homeland Security (DHS) has no guidelines in place for dealing with sodomy convictions. In light of *Lawrence v. Texas*,[13] DHS may be hard-pressed to enforce an exclusion based on sodomy. Then again, DHS may interpret *Lawrence* to apply only to U.S. state laws and inapplicable to foreign nationals seeking admission into the United States.

Eighteen countries recognize same-sex couples for immigration purposes. They are: Australia, Belgium, Brazil, Canada, Denmark, Finland, France, Germany, Iceland, Israel, the Netherlands, New Zealand, Norway, Portugal, South Africa, Spain, Sweden, and the United Kingdom.

The Defense of Marriage Act (DOMA)[14] controls the definition of "spouse" under federal law. Federal law defines "spouse" as a husband or wife of the opposite sex. The law explicitly excludes same-sex couples. DOMA has never been successfully challenged in court.[15] In 1982, the Ninth Circuit decided that the Immigration and Naturalization Act's "spouse" definition excluded same-sex couples.[16] Unless DOMA is overturned, the federal immigration laws will continue to exclude same-sex couples.

The Uniting American Families Act[17] will not alter the definition of "spouse." The Act also would not give same-sex couples any rights associated with marriage. It would permit foreign-national same-sex couples to immigrate and seek permanent residency. These immigrants would be classified as "permanent partners." The Act defines "permanent partners" as "anyone over 18 years of age who is:

(i) in a committed, intimate relationship with an adult U.S. citizen or legal permanent resident 18 years of age or older in which both parties intend a lifelong commitment;
(ii) financially interdependent with that other person;
(iii) not married to, or in a permanent partnershipwith, anyone other than that other person;
(iv) unable to contract with that person a marriage cognizable under the Immigration and Naturalization Act; and
(v) is not a first-, second- or third-degree blood relation of that other individual."[18]

The issue of the United States' obligations under international treaties is discussed in *Separated and Unequal*.[19] According to the authors, "[I]nternational treaty law renders a duty upon State Parties to uphold the provisions set forth within a given treaty instrument. States become Party to an international treaty upon signature and ratification of the instrument. Upon such ratification, State Parties are obliged to implement national legislation consistent with the duties and obligation to which the treaty alludes."[20] The authors believe the United States has a duty under the International Covenant of Civil and Political Rights (ICCPR) to implement national legislation that is consistent with the duties and obligations in the treaty. These obligations include the right to family and family unity.[21]

In its present state, U.S. law is behind the immigration laws and policies of its allies. "Family values" in the United States carries a different definition from that commonly acknowledged by many other nations.

B. Basic Immigration Law

The law in the United States does not include sexual orientation as a ground for exclusion from entry into the country. Legally, the Citizenship and Immigration Service (CIS) cannot ask a person about his or her sexual orientation. U.S. immigration law *does* prohibit persons who are HIV-positive from entering the country, although waivers are available.

Permanent immigration into the United States requires sponsorship by specific family members or an employer. Another way is through a lottery system for a government-issued green card. This is a random drawing process. Persons seeking permanent status can also apply for admission as asylum seekers or refugees. A limited number of visas are available each year.

The United States government does not recognize same-sex relationships. The government uses the Defense of Marriage Act (DOMA) to justify this position. Lesbian and gay U.S. citizens cannot use their relationship to sponsor their partners for permanent residence status. The United States also will not recognize foreign marriages between same-sex individuals. These marriages are not permitted in the United States under DOMA and do not merit consideration by the CIS.

Family-based immigration is complicated and based on a preference system. The system requires a relative to submit an I-130 petition establishing the relationship. The CIS then sets a priority date, based on the preference category, before the petitioner can take the next step of applying for a green card. The priority date may be years away.

Immediate family members of U.S. citizens (spouses, parents, unmarried minor children) may file for permanent residency simultaneously with the I-130 petition. A list of the preference categories and priority dates is found at the CIS Web site.[22]

The current state of immigration law in the United States is not favorable to lesbian or gay persons. Overstaying a visa is the most common means used by prospective immigrants to stay in the country. However, this practice carries significant penalties. Remaining in the United States without lawful status for more than six months bars the person from reentering for three years. Stay over a year and the penalty period extends to 10 years. These penalties apply even if the person has an I-130 petition approved.

Applicants for permanent residency must establish that they are unlikely to become a "public charge" and prove their sponsor will provide financial support.

C. Visas

Persons seeking visas to enter the United States must apply at the nearest U.S. Consulate. The applicant must also have a valid passport, issued by his or her home country.

A visa is a stamp in the passport that permits the holder to come to the United States. On arrival at a U.S. airport, U.S. immigration officials must decide whether to admit the person. Visas do not guarantee admission into the United States.

Most Western European citizens do not need a visa to enter the United States. This is a reciprocal agreement, since these countries do not require visas from American citizens or legal residents.

There are two categories of visas: immigrant and non-immigrant. The latter allows the recipient to stay in the United States for a specific and limited time (e.g., student visa); an immigrant visa is also known as a "green card" and allows the holder to stay in the United States permanently.

The U.S. State Department is responsible for issuing visas. The Department of Homeland Security is responsible for immigration policy and administration.

D. Asylum

Lesbians and gays have been eligible to apply for asylum as members of a "particular social group" since 1994. Asylum applications are confidential and will not be released to the government of the applicant's home country.

An asylum applicant must be physically present in the United States, at a border crossing or an airport. These cases are very complicated, and an experienced immigration attorney will best serve those clients with sexual orientation immigration issues.

People seeking asylum in the United States base their appeal on the persecution or torture experienced in their native countries.[23] Application is made under Section 208 of the Immigration and Naturalization Act (INA).[24] Applicants must show that there is a well-founded fear of persecution should they be returned to their country of origin. Evidence can include past persecution or the risk of future persecution. The determinative elements are both subjective and objective.

A person must establish that any persecution is based on his or her membership in a social group.[25] While membership in an identifiable social group is required, the statute does not define "membership" or "social group." A "social group" can comprise persons of similar backgrounds, interests, or status. The first case to recognize homosexuality as a "membership in a social group" is *In re Toboso-Alfonso*.[26] Attorney General Janet Reno instructed immigration judges to adopt this case as precedent in 1994.[27]

Asylum can also be based on "race, religion, nationality . . . or political opinion."[28]

A client fearful of persecution in her home country because of her sexual orientation may be eligible for asylum. However, even applicants who establish persecution and abuse by police in their country of origin may be unable to convince an immigration judge. A Russian lesbian who was subjected to psychiatric treatment because of her sexual orientation failed to convince an immigration judge. The Bureau of Immigration Appeals denied her application because the judge believed the government merely tried to "cure" her and there was no intent to "harm."[29]

The woman successfully appealed her case to the Ninth District Court of Appeals. The court's opinion included the following language: "The fact that a persecutor believes the harm he is inflicting is 'good for' his victim does not make it any less painful to the victim, or indeed, remove the conduct from the statutory definition of persecution."[30] The definition of "persecution" is objective.

Applicants who request asylum while at a border crossing or airport are kept in detention until a decision is made on the application. Applicants must prove an inability or unwillingness to return to their native country due to past persecution and reasonable fear of future persecution. Lesbian and gay applicants can establish persecution, past, present or future, based on sexual orientation or HIV status. More than one ground is acceptable.

An applicant carries the burden of establishing the existence of persecution of gay men and lesbians in his or her home country. Persecution is not discrimination. Losing a job because one is gay is discrimination. Being arrested and tortured because of one's sexual orientation is persecution. An experienced immigration lawyer will be able to help an applicant establish whether persecution existed.

Applications for asylum must be filed within one year of entering the United States. Late filers may be able to show extraordinary reasons for the delay. The date the application is received by the CIS is the filing date. Persons granted asylum may apply for permanent legal residency one year after asylum is approved.

Undocumented persons may also file for asylum. However, the information provided in the application will be used to deport the applicant if asylum is denied.

Requesting asylum, alone, will not guarantee success. A Lebanese man's asylum request came to naught in 2004.[31]

Mohamad Abdul-Karim is a gay man who immigrated from Lebanon. He requested asylum based on his belief he would be persecuted were he to return to Lebanon. Unfortunately, in 1998 the U.S. State Department issued an advisory opinion that Lebanese officials were not enforcing prohibitions against homosexual behavior.

Abdul-Karim based his argument on undated, old newspaper clippings. The immigration judge ruled the evidence was unverifiable and insufficient to overcome the State Department's opinion. The Board of Immigration Appeals and the Ninth Circuit Court of Appeals agreed with that determination. The Ninth Circuit found the State Department's advisories constituted "substantial evidence," and there was no contradictory evidence.

Perhaps if Mr. Abdul-Karim had had well-informed or prepared counsel, the outcome may have been different.

Of special significance, the Ninth Circuit cited a federal regulation[32] that concerns foreign-language translations. Under the regulation, any translated material must consist of a "full English translation which the translator has certified as complete and accurate, and by the translator's certification that he or she is competent to translate from the foreign language into English." Mr. Abdul-Karim submitted unsworn and unsigned translations, an indication that either he had translated them himself and was proceeding *pro se* or his attorney did not know the rules.

On April 16, 2006, the First Circuit denied an asylum request because the petitioner did not present enough evidence showing that he was gay.[33] The petitioner, Robert Kibuuka, denied being in a romantic relationship with a man during the Bureau of Immigration Appeals hearing. This was not true. He presented evidence of a major depressive disorder because of his sexuality. The immigration judge denied the petition because Kibuuka did not convince him he was "a member of the gay community."

This case exposes the dilemma for those seeking asylum based on sexual orientation. Kibuuka feared for his safety if forced to return to Uganda. But the appellate court refused to allow him to introduce evidence about his gay relationship.

Petitioners who fear retribution in their home country may also fear admitting being gay before an American immigration judge. The case also raises the issue of what is considered sufficient evidence to prove one's sexual orientation.

Asylum applicants may fail because what happens in their country of origin could also happen in the United States. If laws in the United States that affect homosexuals are comparable to laws in a foreign country, asylum will be denied. Unfortunately, the United States continues to violate the human rights of some of its own citizens.

E. Immigration for Employment Purposes

Individuals seeking entry into the United States to work must have an employer sponsor them. The exceptions are people of "extraordinary ability," a "special immigrant," or an "investor."

Employers that wish to bring in a foreign worker must first establish that there are no American citizens available to fill the job. Employment visas are based on a preference system, similar to family-based immigration.

The employer must file an application for a "labor certification" with the Department of Labor. This application must establish that there are no United States citizens able, willing, and qualified to fill the open position. The employer must also establish that it has the financial ability to pay the offered wage. Further, the prospective employee must meet the position's minimum requirements.

When the labor certification is approved, the employer submits it to the CIS. After the CIS approves the application, the prospective employee either adjusts his status if he is in the United States or applies for a visa if outside the country. Once the application is approved, the individual becomes a permanent resident of the United States.

F. Green Card Lottery

The prize for winning this random drawing lottery is being allowed to live permanently in the United States. Unlike many lotteries, you need not be present to win.

Participants must be citizens of a low-admission country to enter the lottery. Low-admission countries send less than 50,000 immigrants annually to the United States. Eligible participants include those with a high school diploma (or its equivalent) and work experience within five years of the application that required at least two years of training or experience. Applicants must be in the United States legally to participate in the lottery.

G. Transgender and Transsexual Persons

On May 18, 2005, transgender persons received a welcomed decision from the Bureau of Immigration Appeals (BIA). The case, *Matter of Lovo-Lara*,[34] dealt with a petition filed by Ms. Lovo to bring her Salvadoran husband into the United States.

In September 2001, Ms. Lovo underwent sex reassignment surgery. She married her husband in September 2002. The state of North Carolina issued an amended female birth certificate and driver's license. North Carolina also issued a marriage license.

Ms. Lovo submitted the I-130 petition with an affidavit from her medical doctor concerning the surgery. The Nebraska Service Center responsible for processing these applications denied her application, citing a 2004 memo that prohibits recognition of marriages when one or both of the participants are transsexuals.

The BIA used a two-prong test in arriving at their decision. They first considered whether the marriage was valid under state law. The BIA concluded Ms. Lovo's marriage is valid because North Carolina issued a marriage record. Second, the appellate panel considered whether the marriage was valid under the Immigration and Nationality Act (INA). Again, the BIA found in favor of Ms. Lovo. The INA did not address transsexuals. Further, contrary to the arguments made by the Department of Homeland Security, the federal Defense of Marriage Act does not address the issue either. DOMA is intended to prohibit "homosexual marriages." Congress made no reference to transsexuals.

The BIA found, for immigration purposes, that Ms. Lovo entered into a heterosexual marriage. The BIA also held that marriage has always been a matter of state law. This decision further confirms that the law of the state where the marriage is performed determines the validity of any marriage.

H. Sham Marriages

Some immigrants enter into sham marriages to gain admission to the United States. Immigration officials are aware of these attempts and take precautions to ensure that any marriage between a U.S. citizen and a foreign national is legitimate. The penalties can be severe. The foreign national is deported, and the U.S. citizen may face felony charges that carry fines and a prison sentence.

In 2005 the U.S. Sixth Circuit Court of Appeals[35] denied an asylum request because the petitioner engaged in a sham marriage that destroyed his credibility. Saleh Safadi came to the United States in 1988 on a student visa. He originally planned to attend Wichita State University. In 1989 he moved to Detroit.

He married a U.S. citizen in 1992 and applied for an immigrant visa. He unsuccessfully requested an adjustment in his status from student to immigrant. After immigration officials denied his request, he divorced his wife.

Safadi claimed to be involved in a committed, same-sex relationship at the same time he was married. After the divorce, Safadi sought asylum because of being homosexual. He claimed deportation would subject him to prosecution if he returned to Jordan. The immigration judge denied the application and found that Safadi had not proven he was gay. The judge did not question whether homosexuality can be the basis for an asylum request.[36] The judge found that Safadi lacked credibility, since he had claimed to be in a legitimate marriage. The Board of Immigration Appeals upheld the decision.

The Sixth Circuit held that the discrepancies in Safadi's claims and the fraudulent marriage were sufficient to support the BIA's ruling.

Foreign nationals who want to enter the United States must be wary of engaging in questionable activities that will haunt them in the future. Given the current overall political climate, any conduct that shows an attempt to circumvent U.S. law will not bode well for the prospective immigrant.

I. Persons Living with HIV/AIDS

U.S. immigration policy has historically been unfavorable to applicants who are HIV-positive or have AIDS. Existing federal law prevents foreigners who are HIV-positive or are living with AIDS to enter or permanently remain in the United States without a waiver.[37] There is evidence that this situation is changing. A Togolese immigrant received asylum because he belonged to the social group of persons afflicted with HIV.[38]

People seeking asylum in the United States who are also HIV-positive or living with AIDS often do so because medical care is unavailable in their home countries. They may also see the United States as a country that is less judgmental toward those with these illnesses. Lesbian, gay, and transgender foreigners may also find that their sexual orientation is less a hindrance if they are also infected with HIV/AIDS.

J. Pending Congressional Action

The Uniting American Families Act[39] was introduced in the U.S. House of Representatives and Senate in May 2007. Under current immigration law, U.S. citizens and permanent residents may sponsor their spouses and other family members to immigrate into the United States..

The existing laws do not apply to same-sex partners of U.S. citizens or those with permanent residency. Same-sex partners are not considered "spouses" under U.S. immigration law and do not qualify as "family." The Uniting American Families Act (UAFA), if passed, will remedy the situation. The UAFA was previously called the Permanent Partners Immigration Act.

According to the Human Rights Campaign, 19 countries recognize same-sex couples under their immigration laws. They are: Australia, Belgium, Brazil, Canada, Denmark, Finland, France, Germany, Iceland, Israel, the Netherlands, New Zealand, Norway, Portugal, South Africa, Spain, Sweden, Switzerland, and the United Kingdom.

If enacted, the UAFA will allow same-sex couples to sponsor their foreign national partners if they meet the same requirements as married couples. Couples must provide proof of their relationship, which can include affidavits from persons attesting to its existence.

The UAFA will define a "permanent partner" as a person who is 18 or older, in a committed, intimate relationship with another adult (18 or older). The parties will have established their intent to establish a lifelong commitment. Both parties must be financially interdependent and not married to or in a permanent relationship with another person. Further, the parties must show they are unable to marry under the Immigration and Nationality Act.

K. Who Can Help

There are several organizations that can assist lesbian and gay clients with immigration issues. Some of these organizations provide direct legal assistance to clients in need of immigration advice. Others can provide referrals to immigration lawyers sympathetic to the unique needs of lesbian and gay clients seeking immigration assistance.

Organizations Providing Assistance in LGBT Immigration Cases

1. Lesbian & Gay Immigration Rights Task Force, New York, 350 W. 31st St., Ste. 505, New York, NY; 212-714-2904; www.lgirtf.org (also in South Florida, Texas, New Orleans, and San Diego.
2. Greater Boston Legal Services, 197 Friend St., Boston, MA 02114; 617-371-1270; www.gbls.org.
3. HIV Law Project, 161 William St., New York, NY 10038; 212-577-3001; www.hivlawproject.org.
4. Safe Horizon Immigrant Legal Services Project, 74-09 37th Ave., Rm. 308, Jackson Heights, NY; 718-899-1233, ext. 129; www.safehorizon.org.

> 5. Illinois Coalition for Immigrant and Refugee Rights, 36 S. Wabash, Ste. 1425, Chicago, IL; 312-332-7360; www.icirr.org.
> 6. Heartland Alliances Midwest Immigrant & Human Rights Center, 208 S. LaSalle St., Ste. 1818, Chicago, IL 60604; 312-660-1370; www.heartlandalliance.org.
> 7. Human Rights Initiative of North Texas, 2501 Oak Lawn Ave., Ste 850, Dallas, TX 75219; 214-855-0520; www.hrionline.org.
> 8. Immigration/Asylum Project, National Center for Lesbian Rights, 870 Market St., Ste. 570, San Francisco, CA; 415-392-6257, ext. 304; www.nclrights.org.
> 9. Immigration Law Project, 1625 N. Schrader Blvd., Los Angeles, CA 94103; 323-993-7670, ext. 3.
> 10. International Gay and Lesbian Human Rights Commission, 1360 Mission St., Ste. 200, San Francisco, CA 94103; 415-255-8680; www.iglhrc.org.
> 11. Northwest Immigrant Rights Project, 909 8th Ave., Seattle, WA 98104; 206-587-4009; Toll Free: 888-201-1014; www.nwjustice.org.

The services provided by the various organizations include legal information, educational seminars in immigration issues, assistance to LGBT and HIV-positive immigrants and their attorneys, direct representation for low-income LGBT clients, and pro bono referrals for income eligible clients.

L. Conclusion

Even though lesbian, gay, and transgender immigrants have made progress, there is no growing body of case law. Identity and conduct remain issues for homosexuals seeking to immigrate to the United States. There is also ongoing evidence that an applicant's success may depend on the personal biases and prejudices of the immigration officer and the B.I.A. judge.

Stereotypes continue to plague immigration seekers. Applicants who do not meet the stereotypical view of what a lesbian or gay man should look, act or sound like may be denied. Applicants must present evidence to support their claims. A bias remains against admitting lesbian, gay, and transgender persons into this country. Some people may not be gay enough and others may be too gay when it comes to convincing the Bureau of Immigration Affairs to grant asylum.

Immigration is highly visible now. Illegal immigration is a major political topic. We may be a nation of immigrants, but many Americans, including too many politicians, prefer their immigrants to look, sound, and live like they do.

Immigration will continue to be an important legal arena for lesbian, gay, and transgender persons seeking the shelter of the Lady in New York's harbor.

Notes

1. H.R. 3006, 109th Cong. (2005).
2. 8 U.S.C. § 136, repealed by Immigration and Naturalization Act, § 403(a)(13),(16),(18); 66 Stat. 279, 280 (1952).
3. 8 U.S.C. § 1182 (1)-(3), (5)-(7), amended 1990.
4. Fleuti v. Rosenberg, 302 F.2d 652 (9th Cir. 1962), *vacated on other grounds*, 374 U.S. 449 (1963).
5. 8 U.S.C. §§ 1222, 1226(d).
6. Act of Oct. 3, 1965, Pub. L. No. 89-236, § 15(b), 79 Stat. 911, 919, *amending* 8 U.S.C. § 1182(a)(4).
7. Boutilier v. INS, 387 U.S. 118 (1967).
8. Press Release, Dept. of Justice Guidelines and Procedures for the Inspection of Aliens Who are Suspected of Being Homosexual, Sept. 9, 1980.
9. 714 F.2d 1470 (9th Cir. 1983).
10. 716 F.2d 1439 (5th Cir. 1983).
11. Pub. L. No. 101-649, § 601, 104 Stat. 4978, 5067-78 (1990); 8 U.S.C. § 1182 (1990).
12. 8 U.S.C. § 1182(a)(2)(A)(i)(I) (2000).
13. 539 U.S. 558 (2003).
14. 1 U.S.C. § 7 (2000).
15. Smelt v. County of Orange, 374 F. Supp. 2d 861 (C.D. Cal. 2005); Wilson v. Ake, 354 F. Supp. 2d 1298 (M.D. Fla. 2005); *In re* Kanda, 315 B.R. 123 (Bankr. W.D. Wash. 2004).
16. Adams v. Howerton, 673 F.2d 1036, 1039 (9th Cir. 1982).
17. H.R. 3006, 109th Congress (2005).
18. LENA AYOUB & SHIN-MING WONG, SEPARATED AND UNEQUAL 572-73, National Center for Lesbian Rights, 2004.
19. *Id.* at 581-91.
20. *Id.* at 582.
21. ICCPR, art. 17, Dec. 19, 1966, 999 U.N.T.S. 171, effective March 23, 1973; SEPARATED AND UNEQUAL, *supra* note 18, at 582.
22. http://uscis.gov/graphics/services/imm_visas.htm
23. For an excellent evaluation of asylum law, see Hollis V. Pfitsch, *Homosexuality in Asylum and Constitutional Law: Rhetoric of Acts and Identity*, 15 LAW & SEXUALITY 59 (2006), published by Tulane Univ. School of Law.
24. I.N.A. § 208(a), 8 U.S.C.A. § 1158(a) (2005).
25. This is the most common basis for LGBT asylum seekers; 8 U.S.C.A. § 1158(b)(1)(B).
26. 20 I.&N. Dec. 819, 822 (B.I.A. 1990).
27. Att'y Gen. Order No. 1895-94 (June 19, 1994).
28. 8 U.S.C.A. § 1101(a)(42)(A).

29. Alan G. Bennett, Note, *The "Cure" that Harms: Sexual Orientation-Based Asylum and the Changing Definition of Persecution*, 29 GOLDEN GATE U.L. REV. 279, 299 (1999).

30. Pitcherskaia v. INS, 118 F.3d 641, 648 (9th Cir. 1997).

31. Abdul-Karim v. Ashcroft, 2004 WL 1435149 (June 24, 2004) (not selected for publication).

32. 8 C.F.R. § 103.2(b)(3).

33. Kibuuka v. Gonzalez, 2006 WL 964746 (April 14, 2006).

34. 23 I&N 746 (BIA 2005) (Interim Decision No. 3512).

35. Safadi v. Gonzales, 2005 WL 2175937, 2005 Fed. App. 0682N (6th Cir. Aug. 9, 2005).

36. 8 U.S.C. § 1101(a)(42)(A).

37. 8 U.S.C.A. § 1182(a)(1)(A)(i) (2000).

38. Zachary Bromer, Case Notes, *Boer-Sedano v. Gonzalez: The Increasing Influence of HIV/AIDS Status on Asylum Claims Based on Homosexual Identity*, 15 LAW & SEXUALITY 163, 172 (2006), Tulane Univ. School of Law, 73 No. 6 Interpreter Releases 901 (July 8, 1996).

39. H.R. 2221, sponsored by Rep. Jarrold Nadler (D-NY); S. 1328, sponsored by Sen. Patrick Leahy (D-VT).

APPENDIX A

Case Law

A. United States Supreme Court Cases

Lawrence v. State of Texas, 539 US 558 (2003)
Boy Scouts of America v. Dale, 530 U.S. 640 (2000)
Romer v. Evans, 517 U.S. 620 (1996)
Bowers v. Hardwich, 478 U.S. 186 (1986), overruled by *Lawrence v. Texas*
Davis v. Monroe County Board of Education, 526 U.S. 629 (1999)
Franklin v. Gwinnett County Public Schools, 503 U.S. 60 (1992)
Tinker v. Des Moines Indep. Comm. Sch. Dist., 393 U.S. 503 (1969)
Hazelwood Sch. Dist. v. Kuhlmeier, 484 U.S. 260 (1988)
Good News Club v. Milford Central Sch., 533 U.S. 98 (2001)
Gebser v. Lago Vista Indep. Sch. Dist., 524 U.S. 274 (1998)
Board of Educ. of Westside Community Sch. v. Mergens, 496 U.S. 226 (1990)
Hurley v. Irish-American Gay, Lesbian & Bisexual Group, 515 U.S. 557 (1995)
Smith v. Organization of Foster Families, 431 U.S. 816 (1977)
Zablocki v. Redhail, 434 U.S. 374 (1978)
Quilloin v. Walcott, 434 U.S. 246 (1978)
Michael H. v. Gerald D., 491 U.S. 110 (1989)
Palmore v. Sidoti, 466 U.S. 429 (1984)
Loving v. Virginia, 388 U.S. 1 (1967)
Santosky v. Kramer, 455 U.S. (1982)

B. Federal Cases

Chandler v. McInnville Sch. Dist., 978 F. 2d 524 (9th Cir. 1992)
Chambers v. Babbitt, 2001 WL 533664 (D. Minn. May 17, 2001)
Saxe v. State College Area Sch. Dist., 240 F.3d 200 (3rd Cir. 2001)

Downs v. Los Angeles Unified Sch. Dist., 228 F.3d 1003 (9th Cir. 2000)
DiLoreto v. Downey Unified Sch. Dist. Bd. of Ed., 196 F.3d 958 (9th Cir. 1999)
Boy Scouts of America v. Till, 136 F. Supp. 1295 (S.D. Fl. 2001)
Boyd County High School Gay Straight Alliance v. Board of Educ. of Boyd County, 258 F. Supp. 2d 667, 690 (E.D. Ky. 2003)
Latino Officers Ass'n v. City of New York, 196 F.3d 458 (2d Cir. 1999)
Colin v. Orange Unified Sch. Dist., 83 F. Supp. 2d 1135, 1148 (C.D. Cal. 2000)
Theno v. Tonganoxie Unified School District, 377 F. Supp. 2d 952 (D. Kan. 2005)
DiRuggerio v. Rodgers, 743 F.2d 1009 (3rd Cir. 1984)
Flood v. Braaten, 727 F.2d 303 (3rd Cir. 1984)

C. Equal Access Act

Caudillo v. Lubbock Indep. Sch. Dist., 311 F. Supp. 2d 550 (N.D. Tex. 2004)

D. Dress Code

Boroff v. Van Wert City Bd. of Educ., 220 F.3d 465 (6th Cir. 2000)
Scott v. Sch. Bd. of Alachua City, 324 F.3d 1246 (11th Cir. 2003)
Jeglin v. San Jacinto Unified Sch. Dist., 827 F. Supp. 1459 (C.D.Cal. 1993)
Syphiewski v. Warren Hills Regional Bd. of Educ., 307 F.3d 243 (3d Cir. 2002)

E. Curriculum

Fleischfresser v. Directors of Sch. Dist. 200, 15 F.3d 680 (7th Cir. 1994)
Leebaert v. Harrington, 332 F.3d 134 (2d Cir. 2000)

F. School Board/Districts Liability Harassment Discrimination

Davis v. Monroe Cty. Bd. of Educ., 526 U.S. 629 (1999)
Ray v. Antioch Unified Sch. Dist., 107 F. Supp.2d 1165 (N.D. Cal. 2000) (Undisclosed financial settlement)
McLaughlin v. Board of Educ. of Pulaski County Special Sch. Dist., 296 F. Supp.2d 960 (E.D. Ark. 2000); student harassed by teacher; district liable; administration knew and condoned the teacher's behavior; took no action.
Fricke v. Lynch, 491 F. Supp. 381 (D. R.I. 1980)
Nabozny v. Podlesny, 92 F. 3d 446 (7th Cir. 1996) ($962,000)

Ray v. Antioch Unified School District, 107 F. Supp. 2d 1165 (N.D. Cal. 2000)

Henkle v. Gregory, 150 F. Supp. 2d 1067 (D. Nev. 2001), U.S. Dist. Court Settlement Agreement, August 2002 ($451,000)

Massey v. Banning Unified Sch. Dist. 256 F. Supp. 1090 (C.D. Cal. 2003) ($45,000)

Montgomery v. Indep. School Dist. No. 709, 109 F. Supp. 2d 1081 (D. Minn. 2000) (Undisclosed financial settlement)

O.H. V. Oakland, 2000 WL 33376299 (N.D. Cal. 2000) (Confidential settlement)

Flores, et.al. v. Morgan Hill Unified School Dist., 324 F.3d 1130 (9th Cir. 2003) ($1,100,000)

George Loomis v. Visalia Unified School Dist. U.S. Dist. Ct. Consent Decree & Order (August 2002) ($130,000)

Snelling v. Fall Mountain Regional Sch. Dist., 2001 WL 276975 (D.N.H. 2001)

Vance v. Spencer, 2000 WL 1651376 (6th Cir. 2000) ($220,000)

G. School Activities/Restrictions on Speech/Viewpoints

Downs v. Los Angeles Unified Sch. Dist., 228 F.3d 1003 (9th Cir. 2000)
Hansen v. Ann Arbor Public Schools, 293 F. Supp.2d 780 (E.D. Mich. 2003)
Widmar v. Vincent, 454 U.S. 263 (1981)

H. Bankruptcy

In re Russell L. Goodale, 298 BR 886 (Bankr. W.D. Wash. 2003) judgment granted one same-sex partner against another; one issue whether creditor partner could meet definition of "spouse" under federal bankruptcy law.

I. State Cases

Doe v. Yunits, 2000 WL 33162199 (Mass. Super. 2000)
Gay Activists Alliance v. Lomenzo, 31 N.Y. 2d 965 (1973)
Wadlington v. Holmdel Township Board of Education, Superior Court of Monmouth County, New Jersey
Ramelli v. Poway Unified School District, June 8, 2005, Superior Court, San Diego County, Calif., Judge Steven R. Denton
In re Parentage of L.B., 155 Wn.2d 679, 122 P.3d 161 (2005), appealed U.S. Supreme Court, No. 05-974, Feb. 1, 2006, *cert. denied*, May 15, 2006

J. Second Parent Adoptions

Russell v. Bridgens, 264 Neb. 217, 647 NW2d 56 (Neb. 2002); Nebraska must recognize second-parent adoption granted in Pennsylvania even though such adoptions are not permitted in Nebraska.

K. Custody Cases

Alabama, Mississippi, Missouri and Virginia consider sexual orientation in custody decision. States involved below require showing of adverse impact (nexus test) of parent's actions and harm to child before sexual orientation becomes relevant.

S.N.E. v. R.L.B., 699 P. 2D 875 (Alaska, 1985)

In re: Marriage of Birdsall, 197 Cal.App.3d 1024, 243, Cal.Rptr. 287 (Cal.App. 4 Dist., 1988)

Maradie v. Maradi, 1996 Fla. App. LEXIS 7574 (July 16, 1996)

Buck v. Buck, 233 S.E.2d 792 (Ga. 1977)

Teegarden v. Teegarden, 642 N.E.2d 1007 (Ind. Ct. App. 1994)

In re the Marriage of Wiard, 505 N.W.2d 506 (Iowa App. 1993)

Stone v. Stone, No. 79-141, Me. Sup. Ct., Knox Cty, July 15, 1980, *rev'g* No. 71-2-D111, Me. Dist. Ct. Knox Cty, July 26, 1979

Whitehead v. Black, 2 Fam.L.Rep. (BNA) 2593 (ME Super Ct., Cumberland Cty. 1976)

Doe v. Doe, 16 Mass.App.Ct. 499, 452 N.E.2d 293 (Mass.App.Ct. 1983)

Bezio v. Patenaude, 381 Mass. 563, 410 N.E.2d 1207 (Mass., 1980)

M.P. v. S.P., 169 N.J.Super. 425, 404 A.2d 1256 (N.J.Super.A.D. 1979)

A.C. v. C.B., 113 N.M. 581, 829 P.2d 660 (N.M.App. 1992)

State ex rel. Human Serv. Dept. in the Matter of Jacinta M., 107 N.M. 769, 764 P.2d 1327 (N.M.App. 1988)

Anonymous v. Anonymous, 120 A.D.2d 983, 503 N.Y.S.2d 466 (N.Y.A.D. 4 Dept. 1986)

Guinan v. Guinan, 120 A.D.2d 963, 477 N.Y.S.2d 830 (N.Y.A.D. 3 Dept. 1984)

Large v. Large, 1993 WL 498127 (Ohio App. 10 Dist.)

Conkel v. Conkel, 31 Ohio App. 3d 169, 509 N.E.2d 983 (Ohio App. 1987)

Fox v. Fox, 1995 WL 422057 (Okla. July 18, 1995)

Stroman v. Williams, 291 S.C. 376, 353 S.E.2d 704 (S.C. App. 1987)

Blew v. Verta, 420 Pa. Super. 528, 617 A.2d 31 (Pa. Super. 1992)

Tucker v. Tucker, 247 Utah Adv. Rep. 26 (Ut. Ct. App. Sept. 6, 1994)

Nickerson v. Nickerson, 158 Vt. 85, 605 A.2d 1331 (Vt. 1992)

Medeiros v. Medeiros, 8 Fam.L.Rep. (BNA) 2372 (Vt. Super. 1982)
Matter of Marriage of Cabalquinto, 43 Wash.App. 518, 718 P.2d 7 (Wash. App. 1986)
Schuster v. Schuster, 90 Wash.2d 626, 585 P.2d 130 (Wash. 1978)
M.S.P. v. P.E.P., 178 W.Va. 183, 358 S.E.2d 442 (W.Va. 1987)
Rowsey v. Rowsey, 174 W.Va. 692, 329 S.E.2d 57 (W.Va. 1985)
Dinges v. Montgomery, 514 N.W.2d 723 (Wis.App. 1993)

L. Awarding Property Rights to Unmarried Cohabitants

Wilbur v. DeLapp, 119 Or. App. 348, 850 P.2d 1151
Vasquez v. Hawthorne, 145 Wash. 2d 103, 33 P.3d 735 (Wash. 2001)

M. Statutes

District of Columbia: custody determined without reference to race, color, national origin, political affiliation, sex or sexual orientation;
D.C. Code Sext. 16-911(a)(5) (1999)
Equal Access Act (EAA), 20 U.S.C. ß4071(a), (b) Arizona, California, Nevada and Utah require written parental consent before students can participate in classes discussing sex, sexuality and AIDS. Consent not required when discussing harassment/discrimination because of sexual orientation or gender identity.
Ariz. Rev. Stat. ß15-716 (2003)
Cal. Educ. Code ß51550 (West 2003)
Nev. Rev. Stat. ß389.065 (2003)
Utah Code Ann. ß53A-13-101 (2003)
Protection of Pupil Rights Amendment (PPRA); parents can limit child's participating in surveys or questionnaires on controversial or sexual subjects; 20 U.S.C. ß1232h (2004)

N. State Law Decisions re: Same-Sex Marriage & Related Issues

Alabama:

In re: H.H., 830 So. 2d 21, 26 (Ala. 2002) ("homosexual conduct of a parent—conduct involving a sexual relationship between two persons of the same gender—creates a strong presumption of unfitness that alone is sufficient justification for denying that parent custody of his or her own children or prohibiting the adoption of the children of others") (Moore, J. concurring);

Alaska:
Brause v. Bureau of Vital Statistics, 1998 WL 88743 (Alaska Sup. Ct. 1998) (Court ruled that state needs a compelling interest to refuse to recognize same-sex marriage, but this case was overruled by constitutional amendment);

Arizona:
Standhardt v. Superior Court ex rel. County of Maricopa, 77 P.3d 451 (Ariz. App. 2003), review denied (2004) (no fundamental right to same-sex marriage);

Colorado:
Adams v. Howerton, 673 F.2d 1036 (9th Cir.), cert. denied, 458 U.S. 1111 (1982) (male America citizen and male Australian alien who had been ceremonially "married" by a minister in Colorado does not qualify alien as citizen's spouse);

Connecticut:
Rosengarten v. Downes, 802 A.2d 170 (Conn. App. Ct.), cert. granted in part but dismissing case as moot upon death of the party, 806 A.2d 1066 (Conn. 2002) (a Vermont civil union is not "marriage" recognized under this state because the union was not entered into between one man and one woman);

District of Columbia:
Dean v. District of Columbia, 653 A.2d 307 (D.C. 1995) (marriage statute prohibited clerk from issuing license to same-sex couple and same-sex marriage is not a fundamental right protected by the Due Process Clause);

Florida:
Frandsen v. County of Brevard, 800 So. 2d 757, 759, 760 (Fla. 5th DCA 2001), rev. denied, 828 So. 2d 386 (Fla. 2002) (classifications based on sex are not subject to strict scrutiny, noting that the Constitution Revision Commission refused to add the term "sex" to the Florida constitution so as to avoid any possibility that Florida courts might conclude the provision required recognition of same-sex marriages);

Georgia:
Burns v. Burns, 560 S.E.2d 47 (Ga. App.), reconsideration denied, cert. denied (2002) (a Vermont civil union is not marriage, and even if it were, Georgia would not recognize it as such, because the state authorizes only the union of one man and one woman and prohibits same-sex marriage);

Hawaii:
Baehr v. Lewin, 852 P.2d 44 (Haw. 1993), aff'd, 950 P.2d 1234 (Haw. 1997) (authorizing strict scrutiny for marriage classifications but decision was overruled by constitutional referendum);

Illinois:
In re Estate of Hall, 707 N.E.2d 201, 206 (Ill. App. 1998) (challenge to statute proscribing same-sex marriage was moot and petitioner was never legally married—"We cannot retroactively redefine petitioner and Hall's relationship as a lawful marriage or even confer the benefits of a legal marriage upon the relationship. If we did, we would essentially be resurrecting common law marriage . . .";

Indiana:
Morrison v. Sadler, 2003 WL 23119998 (Ind. Super. Ct.), cert. denied (2003) (dismissing challenge to Indiana's DOMA which limits marriage to one man and one woman);

Kansas:
In re Estate of Gardiner, 42 P.3d 120 (Kan. 2002) (a post-operative male-to-female transsexual is not a woman within the meaning of the statutes recognizing marriage, and thus a marriage of a male-to-female transsexual to another male is void);

Kentucky:
Jones v. Hallahan, 501 S.W.2d 588 (Ky. 1973) (a same-sex union is not recognized as marriage);

Maryland:
Jennings v. Jennings, 315 A.2d 816, 820 n.7 (Md. Ct. App. 1974).

Massachusetts:
Goodrich v. Department of Public Health, 440 Mass. 309, 798 N.E.2d 941 (Mass. 2003) (first court to sanction same-sex marriage);
Albano v. Attorney General, 769 N.E.2d 1242 (Mass. 2002) (initiative for constitutional amendment banning same-sex marriage permissible);

Minnesota:
Baker v. Nelson, 191 N.W.2d 185, 186, 187 (Minn. 1971) (upholding statute that does not authorize marriage between persons of the same sex. "The institution of marriage as a union of man and woman, uniquely involving the procreation and rearing of children within a family, is as old as the

book of Genesis" and recognizing "there is a clear distinction between a marital restriction based merely upon race and one based upon the fundamental difference in sex.");

New Jersey:

M.T. v. J.T. 355 A.2d 204 (N.J. App. 1976) (male transsexual who underwent sex reassignment surgery may be considered female for marital purposes); *In re Bacharach*, 780 A.2d 579 (N.J. App. 2001) (change of name to include last name of same-sex partner was not for an inappropriate purpose);

Lewis v. Harris, 2003 WL 23191114 (N.J. Sup. Ct. 2003) (unpublished) (New Jersey is not required to allow same-sex marriage).

New York:

Anonymous v. Anonymous, 325 N.Y.S.2d 499 (N.Y App. Div. 1971) (a marriage between two males was a nullity notwithstanding that "husband" believed "wife" was a female at the time of the ceremony, and notwithstanding that "she" had subsequent sex surgery);

Storrs v. Holcomb, 645 N.Y.S.2d 286 (N.Y. App. Div. 1996) ("same-sex marriage . . . is not presently recognized under the laws of any state of the Union." The "long tradition of marriage, understood as the union of male and female, testifies to a contrary political, cultural, religious and legal consensus [opposed to same-sex marriage] concluding that New York does not recognize or authorize same-sex marriage and that the City Clerk correctly refused to issue the license.");

In re Estate of Cooper, 564 N.Y.S.2d 684, 688 (N.Y. Fam. Ct. 1990) ("the state has a compelling interest in fostering the traditional institution of marriage whether based on self-preservation, procreation, or nurturing and keeping alive the concept of marriage and family as a basic fabric of our society";

Ohio:

In re Bonfield, 780 N.E.2d 241 (Ohio 2002) (cohabiting same-sex partner of biological mother was not a "parent");

In re Ladrach, 513 N.E.2d 828 (Probate Court 1987) ("There is no authority in Ohio for the issuance of a marriage license to consummate a marriage between a post-operative male-to-female transsexual person and a male person");

In re Nash, 2003WL23097095 (Ohio App. 11 Dist., Dec 31, 2003) (public policy in Ohio prohibited post-operative female-to-male transsexual from marrying female);

Pennsylvania:

De Santo v. Barnsly, 476 A.2d 952 (Pa. Super. Ct. 1984) (two persons of the same sex cannot contract a common-law marriage);

Texas:

Littleton v. Prange, 9 S.W.3d 223 (Tex. App. 1999), cert. denied, 531 U.S. 870 (2000) (ceremonial "marriage" between a man and a transsexual born as a man, who was surgically and chemically altered to have the physical characteristics of a woman, is not valid);

Vermont:

Baker v. State, 744 A.2d 864 (Vt. 1999) (holding that while the Vermont constitution requires that same-sex couples be afforded the same benefits of traditional marriage, the constitution does not require the state to issue a same-sex marriage license);

Washington:

Singer v. Hara, 522 P.2d 1187, 1192 (Wash. App. 1974) (statutory prohibition of same-sex marriage does not violate state constitution).

APPENDIX B

Legal Resources

Part I:
Law Review/Articles/Books

Harris Interactive and GLSEN (2005), *From Teasing to Torment: School Climate in America, A Survey of Students and Teachers.* New York: GLSEN

Beyond the Binary: A Toolkit for Gender Identity Activism in Schools (2004), by Stephanie Cho, Carolyn Laub & Sean Saifa M. Wall of GSA Network; Chris Daley of the Transgender Law Center and Courtney Joslin of NCLR

U.S. Dept. of Education, Office of Civil Rights, Revised Title IX Guidance (Jan. 2001); OCR Revised Guidance, § III

Fifteen Expensive Reasons Why Safe Schools Legislation is in Your State's Best Interest, January 2004; Gay, Lesbian and Straight Education Network and National Center for Lesbian Rights; www.nclrights.org; www.glsen.org

Law Review & Journal Articles

Lesbian (M)Otherhood: Creating an Alternative Model for Settling Child Custody Disputes, Nadine A. Gartner, 16 Tul. J.L. & Sexuality 45 (2007)

Privatizing Same-Sex "Marriage" Through Alternative Dispute Resolution: Community-Enhancing Versus Community Enabling Mediation, Clark Freshman, 44 UCLA L. Rev. 1687 (1997)

Protecting Families: Standards for Child Custody in Same-Sex Relationships, Gay & Lesbian Defenders and Advocates, 10 UCLA Women's L.J. 151 (1999)

A Same-Sex Marriage and Divorce: A Proposal for Child Custody Mediation, Jeffrey A. Dodge, 44 Family Court Rev. 87 (Jan. 2006)

The Right to Define One's Own Concept of Existence: What Lawrence Can Mean for Intersex and Transgender People, Chai Feldblum, 7 Georgetown J. Gender & L. 115 (2006)

Recognition of Same-Sex Legal Relationships in the United States, Peter Hay, 54 Am. J. Comp. L. 257 (Fall 2006)

Etsitty v. Utah Transit Authority: Transposing Transsexual Rights Under Title VII, Tracey Hoskinson, 15 L. & Sexuality 175 (2006)

"Because of... Sex": Rethinking the Protections Afforded Under Title VII in the Post-Oncale World, Andrea Meryl Kirshenbaum, 69 Albany L. Rev. 139 (2005)

Where Is My Other Mommy?: Applying the Presumed Father Provision of the Uniform Parentage Act to Recognize the Rights of Lesbian Mothers and Their Children, Maggie Manternach, 9 J. Gender, Race & Justice 385 (Winter 2005)

Not Gay Enough for the Government: Racial and Sexual Stereotypes in Sexual Orientation Asylum Cases, 15 L. & Sexuality 135 (2006) (NLGLA Michael Greenberg Writing Competition Winner)

Advance Planning by Same-Sex Couples, Ellen D.B. Riggle, Sharon S. Rostosky and Robert A. Prather, 27 J. Fam. Issues 758, 2006; WLNR 928762 (June 1, 2006)

Children of Same-Sex Parents Deserve the Security Blanket of the Parentage Presumption, Jennifer L. Rosato, 44 Family Court Rev. No. 1, 74 (Jan. 2006)

Are You My Mother? Defending the Rights of Intended Parents in Gestational Surrogacy Arrangements in Pennsylvania, Krista Sirola, 14 Am. Univ. J. Gender, Social Pol'y & L. 131 (2006)

The Unheard Victims of the Refusal to Legalize Same-Sex Marriage: The Reluctance to Recognize Same-Sex Partners as Parents Instead of Strangers, Laura L. Williams, 9 J. Gender, Race & Justice 419 (Winter 2005)

Parenthood by Pure Intention: Assisted Reproduction as the Functional Approach to Parentage, Richard F. Storrow, 53 Hastings L.J. 597 (2002)

What Does It Mean to Be a Parent? The Claims of Biology as the Basis of Parental Rights, John Lawrence Hill, 66 N.Y.U. L. Rev. 353 (1991)

Marital Agreements, 849 T.M. (BNA 2003), Linda J. Ravdin

When Harry Met Larry and Larry Got Sick: Why Same-Sex Couples Should Be Entitled to Benefits Under the Family and Medical Leave Act, Bell, Alana, 22 Hofstra Lab. & Emp. L.J. 276 (Fall 2004)

Making Gay Straight Alliance Student Groups Curriculum-Related: A New Tactic for Schools Trying to Avoid the Equal Access Act, Berkley, Brian, 61 Wash. & Lee L. Rev. 1847 (Fall 2004)

Same-Sex Unions: The New Civil Rights Struggle or an Assault on Traditional Marriage, Bossin, Phyllis, 40 Tulsa L. Rev. 381 (Spring 2005)

Inscribing Lesbian and Gay Identities: How Judicial Imaginations Intertwine With the Best Interests of Children, Carnahan, Christopher, 11 Cardozo Women's L. J. 1 (Fall 2004)

Status or Contract? A Comparative Analysis of Inheritance Rights Under Equitable Adoption and Domestic Partnership Doctrines, Drake, R. Brent, 39 Georgia L. Rev. 675 (Winter 2005)

Equitable Considerations for Families with Same-Sex Parents: Russell v. Bridgens, Fougeron, Katie A., 83 Neb. L. Rev. 915 (2005)

Homosexual or Female? Applying Gender-Based Asylum Jurisprudence to Lesbian Asylum Claims, Neilson, Victoria, 16 Stanford L. & Pol'y Rev. 417 (2005)

Uncharted Territory: Choosing an Effective Approach in Transgender-Based Asylum Claims, Neilson, Victoria, 32 Fordham Urban L.J. 265 (March 2005)

When Harry Met Lawrence: Allowing Gays and Lesbians to Adopt, Shkedi, Nicole M., 35 Seton Hall L. Rev. 873 (2005)

Unconstitutionality of Oklahoma's Statute Denying Recognition to Adoptions by Same-Sex Couples from Other States, Spector, Robert G., 40 Tulsa L. Rev. 467 (Spring 2005)

The Right to Marry, Sunstein, Cass R., 26 Cardozo L. Rev. 2081 (April 2005)

Homosexuality in Asylum and Constitutional Law: Rhetoric of Acts and Identity, Pfitsch, Hollis V., 15 L. & Sexuality 59 (2006)

The End of Marriage, Wardle, Lynn D., 44 Family Court Rev. No. 1, 45 (Jan. 2006)

The Expanding Rights of Transsexuals in the Workplace, Dishman, Neil, 21 The Labor Lawyer 121 (Fall 2005)

A Historical Guide to the Future of Marriage for Same-Sex Couples, Goldberg, Suzanne B., 15 Colum. J. Gender & L. 249 (2006)

Clothes Don't Make the Man (or Woman), But Gender Identity Might, Levi, Jennifer L., 15 Colum. J. Gender & L. 90 (2006)

Letting Go of a National Religion: Why the State Should Relinquish All Control Over Marriage, Miller, Amelia A., 38 Loy. L.A. L. Rev. 2185 (Dec. 2005)

Parental Responsibilities: New Definitions in Same-Sex Families, 36 Fam. L. (UK) 120, (Feb. 2006)

The Religious Liberty Argument for Same-Sex Marriage and Its Effect Upon Legal Recognition, Russell, Jeremiah H., 7 Rutgers J. L. & Religion 4 (Dec. 2005)

Do Mom and Mom and Baby Make A Family?, Friedlander, William S. ATLA Publications, Vol. 40, Issue 13 (Dec. 2004), www.atla.org/publications/trial/0412/contents

Lesbian and Gay Families: Gender Nonconformity and the Implications of Difference, Ball, Carlos, 31 Capital U. L. Rev. 691 (2003)

Adoptions by Lesbian and Gay Parents Must Be Recognized by Sister States Under the Full Faith and Credit Clause Despite Anti-Marriage Statutes That Discriminate Against Same-Sex Couples, Cox, Barbara J., 31 Capital U. L. Rev. 751 (2003)

Living Together: Estate Planning Basics, Donahue, Scott M., 38 New Eng. L. Rev. 547 (2003-4)

Gay Divorce As New Practice Area: Lawyers Prepare for Uncharted Waters, Jones, Leigh, Natl. L.J., June 28, 2004, p. 1

Rewriting the Legal Family: Beyond Exclusivity to a Care-Based Standard, Kavanagh, Matthew M., 16 Yale J.L. & Feminism 83 (2004)

The Children of Art (Assisted Reproductive Technology): Should the Law Protect Them From Harm?, Rosato, Jennifer L., 2004 Utah L. Rev. 57

Adoption and the Best Interests of the Child: On the Use and Abuse of Studies, Strasser, Mark, 38 New Eng. L. Rev. 629 (2003-4)

The Fight to Be A Parent: How Courts Have Restricted the Constitutionally-Based Challenges Available to Homosexuals, Gesing, Erica, 38 New. Eng. L. Rev. 841 (2003-4)

Caregiving Among Older LGBT New Yorkers, study by Marjorie H. Cantor and coauthors published by the NGLTF Policy Institute in 2004, www.thetaskforce.org/downloads/Caregiving.pdf

Caregiving and Postcaregiving Experiences of Midlife and Older Gay Men and Lesbians, a 2001 doctoral dissertation by Kristina Hash; offering a qualified analysis of a sample of older lesbian and gay caregivers experiences; www.kmhash.tripod.com/disspage.htm

Legal Recognition of Same-Sex Relationships in the United States: A Social Science Perspective, Gregory M. Herek, University of California, Davis, *American Psychologist*, p. 607, September 2006

Who May Adopt, Be Adopted, or Place a Child for Adoption? Summary of State Laws, Child Welfare Information Gateway, Children's Bureau/ACYF; www.childwelfare.org

Books

Living Together, Legal Guide for Unmarried Couples, Warner, Ihara & Hertz, 13th Ed. Nolo Press, 2006; www.nolo.com

Legal Guide for Gay and Lesbian Couples, *Curry, Clifford & Hertz, 13th Ed., Nolo Press 2005; www.nolo.com*

Sexual Orientation and the Law (Two Volumes), Achtenberg & Moulding, Thomson-West, 2nd Ed. 2006

Part II:
Information on Benefits for Same-Sex Couples

California

To register for a domestic partnership: www.ss.ca.gov (look under "Special Programs Information").

Colorado

Refer to www.hrc.org. in "What's Happening in My State" to learn about the new additions to Colorado's anti-discrimination law. The law that now includes sexual orientation and gender identity took effect on August 3, 2007.

Connecticut

See www.state.ct.us.

Hawaii

To obtain information about registering a Reciprocal Relationship, check the Hawaii Vital Records office at www.state.hi.us/dob/records/rbrfaq.htm.

Hawaii

To obtain information about registering a Reciprocal Beneficiary Relationship, check the Hawaii Vital Records office at www.state.hi.us/doh/records/rbrfaq.htm.

Iowa

Refer to www.hrc.org. under "What's Happening in My State" to learn more. Iowa enacted a law that prohibits discrimination in employment, housing, public accommodations, credit, and education because of sexual orientation or gender identity. The law became effective July 1, 2007.

Maine

Domestic Partnership information at www.state.me.us.

New Hampshire

Effective January 1, 2008, New Hampshire's Civil Union law becomes effective. For more information, go to www.glad.org (serving all of New England) or the Freedom to Marry Coalition New Hampshire, www.nhftm.org.

Citations N.H. Rev. Stat. Ann. 457:1; N.H. Rev. Stat. Ann. 457:2; N.H. Rev. Stat. Ann. 457:3; N.H. Rev. Stat. Ann. 457:43.

New Jersey

Information on new Civil Union law at www.state.nj.us.

Oregon

For information on Oregon's new Domestic Partnership law and expanded anti-discrimination law, go to www.basicrights.org, the website for Basic Rights Oregon.

Vermont

Information on Civil Unions and Reciprocal Beneficiaries can be found at www.sec.state.vt.us/municipal/civil_mar.htm.

Washington

Information about Washington's new Domestic Partnership law can be found at www.secstate.wa.gov/corps/domestic partnerships.

Part III:
Pension Protection Act of 2006
(Enrolled as Agreed to or Passed by Both House and Senate)

SEC. 829. ALLOW ROLLOVERS BY NONSPOUSE BENEFICIARIES OF CERTAIN RETIREMENT PLAN DISTRIBUTIONS.

(a) In General-

(1) QUALIFIED PLANS- Section 402(c) of the Internal Revenue Code of 1986 (relating to rollovers from exempt trusts) is amended by adding at the end the following new paragraph:

'(11) DISTRIBUTIONS TO INHERITED INDIVIDUAL RETIREMENT PLAN OF NONSPOUSE BENEFICIARY-

'(A) IN GENERAL- If, with respect to any portion of a distribution from an eligible retirement plan of a deceased employee, a direct trustee-to-trustee transfer is made to an individual retirement plan described in clause (i) or (ii) of paragraph (8)(B) established for the purposes of receiving the distribution on behalf of an individual who is a designated beneficiary (as defined by section 401(a)(9)(E)) of the employee and who is not the surviving spouse of the employee—

'(i) the transfer shall be treated as an eligible rollover distribution for purposes of this subsection,

'(ii) the individual retirement plan shall be treated as an inherited individual retirement account or individual retirement annuity (within the meaning of section 408(d)(3)(C)) for purposes of this title, and

'(iii) section 401(a)(9)(B) (other than clause (iv) thereof) shall apply to such plan.

'(B) CERTAIN TRUSTS TREATED AS BENEFICIARIES- For purposes of this paragraph, to the extent provided in rules prescribed by the Secretary, a trust maintained for the benefit of one or more designated beneficiaries shall be treated in the same manner as a trust designated beneficiary.'.

(2) SECTION 403(a) PLANS- Subparagraph (B) of section 403(a)(4) of such Code (relating to rollover amounts) is amended by inserting 'and (11)' after '(7)'.

(3) SECTION 403(b) PLANS- Subparagraph (B) of section 403(b)(8) of such Code (relating to rollover amounts) is amended by striking 'and (9)' and inserting ', (9), and (11)'.

(4) SECTION 457 PLANS- Subparagraph (B) of section 457(e)(16) of such Code (relating to rollover amounts) is amended by striking 'and (9)' and inserting ', (9), and (11)'.

(b) Effective Date- The amendments made by this section shall apply to distributions after December 31, 2006.

Part IV:
Sec. 402. Taxability of Beneficiary of Employees' Trust

TITLE 26, Subtitle A, CHAPTER 1, Subchapter D, PART I, Subpart A, Sec. 402

STATUTE

(a) Taxability of beneficiary of exempt trust

Except as otherwise provided in this section, any amount actually distributed to any distributee by any employees' trust described in section 401 (a) which is exempt from tax under section 501 (a) shall be taxable to the distributee, in the taxable year of the distributee in which distributed, under section 72 (relating to annuities).

(b) Taxability of beneficiary of nonexempt trust

(1) Contributions

Contributions to an employees' trust made by an employer during a taxable year of the employer which ends with or within a taxable year of the trust for which the trust is not exempt from tax under section 501 (a) shall be included in the gross income of the employee in accordance with section 83 (relating to property transferred in connection with performance of services), except that the value of the employee's interest in the trust shall be substituted for the fair market value of the property for purposes of applying such section.

(2) Distributions

The amount actually distributed or made available to any distributee by any trust described in paragraph (1) shall be taxable to the distributee, in the taxable year in which so distributed or made available, under section 72 (relating to annuities), except that distributions of income of such trust before the annuity starting date (as defined in section 72 (c)(4)) shall be included in the gross income of the employee without regard to section 72 (e)(5) (relating to amounts not received as annuities).

(3) Grantor trusts

A beneficiary of any trust described in paragraph (1) shall not be considered the owner of any portion of such trust under subpart E of part I of subchapter J (relating to grantors and others treated as substantial owners).

(4) Failure to meet requirements of section 410 (b)

(A) Highly compensated employees

If 1 of the reasons a trust is not exempt from tax under section 501 (a) is the failure of the plan of which it is a part to meet the requirements of section 401 (a)(26) or 410 (b), then a highly compensated employee shall, in lieu of the amount determined under paragraph (1) or (2) include in gross income for the taxable year with or within which the taxable year of the trust ends an amount equal to the vested accrued benefit of such employee (other than the employee's investment in the contract) as of the close of such taxable year of the trust.

(B) Failure to meet coverage tests

If a trust is not exempt from tax under section 501 (a) for any taxable year solely because such trust is part of a plan which fails to meet the requirements of section 401 (a)(26) or 410 (b), paragraphs (1) and (2) shall not apply by reason of such failure to any employee who was not a highly compensated employee during—

(i) such taxable year, or

(ii) any preceding period for which service was creditable to such employee under the plan.

(C) Highly compensated employee

For purposes of this paragraph, the term "highly compensated employee" has the meaning given such term by section 414 (q).

(c) Rules applicable to rollovers from exempt trusts

(1) Exclusion from income

If—

(A) any portion of the balance to the credit of an employee in a qualified trust is paid to the employee in an eligible rollover distribution,

(B) the distributee transfers any portion of the property received in such distribution to an eligible retirement plan, and

(C) in the case of a distribution of property other than money, the amount so transferred consists of the property distributed,

then such distribution (to the extent so transferred) shall not be includible in gross income for the taxable year in which paid.

(2) Maximum amount which may be rolled over

In the case of any eligible rollover distribution, the maximum amount transferred to which paragraph (1) applies shall not exceed the portion of such distribution which is includible in gross income (determined without regard to paragraph (1)). The preceding sentence shall not apply to such distribution to the extent—

(A) such portion is transferred in a direct trustee-to-trustee transfer to a qualified trust which is part of a plan which is a defined contribution plan and which agrees to separately account for amounts so transferred, including separately accounting for the portion of such distribution which is includible in gross income and the portion of such distribution which is not so includible, or

(B) such portion is transferred to an eligible retirement plan described in clause (i) or (ii) of paragraph (8)(B).

In the case of a transfer described in subparagraph (A) or (B), the amount transferred shall be treated as consisting first of the portion of such distribution that is includible in gross income (determined without regard to paragraph (1)).

(3) Transfer must be made within 60 days of receipt

(A) In general

Except as provided in subparagraph (B), paragraph (1) shall not apply to any transfer of a distribution made after the 60th day following the day on which the distributee received the property distributed.

(B) Hardship exception

The Secretary may waive the 60-day requirement under subparagraph (A) where the failure to waive such requirement would be against equity or good conscience, including casualty, disaster, or other events beyond the reasonable control of the individual subject to such requirement.

(4) Eligible rollover distribution

For purposes of this subsection, the term "eligible rollover distribution" means any distribution to an employee of all or any portion of the balance to the credit of the employee in a qualified trust; except that such term shall not include—

(A) any distribution which is one of a series of substantially equal periodic payments (not less frequently than annually) made—

(i) for the life (or life expectancy) of the employee or the joint lives (or joint life expectancies) of the employee and the employee's designated beneficiary, or

(ii) for a specified period of 10 years or more,

(B) any distribution to the extent such distribution is required under section 401 (a)(9), and

(C) any distribution which is made upon hardship of the employee.

(5) Transfer treated as rollover contribution under section 408

For purposes of this title, a transfer to an eligible retirement plan described in clause (i) or (ii) of paragraph (8)(B) resulting in any portion of a distribution being excluded from gross income under paragraph (1) shall be treated as a rollover contribution described in section 408 (d)(3).

(6) Sales of distributed property

For purposes of this subsection—

(A) Transfer of proceeds from sale of distributed property treated as transfer of distributed property

The transfer of an amount equal to any portion of the proceeds from the sale of property received in the distribution shall be treated as the transfer of property received in the distribution.

(B) Proceeds attributable to increase in value

The excess of fair market value of property on sale over its fair market value on distribution shall be treated as property received in the distribution.

(C) Designation where amount of distribution exceeds rollover contribution

In any case where part or all of the distribution consists of property other than money—

(i) the portion of the money or other property which is to be treated as attributable to amounts not included in gross income, and

(ii) the portion of the money or other property which is to be treated as included in the rollover contribution, shall be determined on a ratable basis unless the taxpayer designates otherwise. Any designation under this subparagraph for a taxable year shall be made not later than the time prescribed by law for filing the return for such taxable year (including extensions thereof). Any such designation, once made, shall be irrevocable.

(D) Nonrecognition of gain or loss

No gain or loss shall be recognized on any sale described in subparagraph (A) to the extent that an amount equal to the proceeds is transferred pursuant to paragraph (1).

(7) Special rule for frozen deposits

(A) In general

The 60-day period described in paragraph (3) shall not—

(i) include any period during which the amount transferred to the employee is a frozen deposit, or

(ii) end earlier than 10 days after such amount ceases to be a frozen deposit.

(B) Frozen deposits

For purposes of this subparagraph, the term "frozen deposit" means any deposit which may not be withdrawn because of—

(i) the bankruptcy or insolvency of any financial institution, or

(ii) any requirement imposed by the State in which such institution is located by reason of the bankruptcy or insolvency (or threat thereof) of 1 or more financial institutions in such State.

A deposit shall not be treated as a frozen deposit unless on at least 1 day during the 60-day period described in paragraph (3) (without regard to this paragraph) such deposit is described in the preceding sentence.

(8) Definitions

For purposes of this subsection—

(A) Qualified trust

The term "qualified trust" means an employees' trust described in section 401 (a) which is exempt from tax under section 501 (a).

(B) Eligible retirement plan

The term "eligible retirement plan" means—

(i) an individual retirement account described in section 408 (a),

(ii) an individual retirement annuity described in section 408 (b) (other than an endowment contract),

(iii) a qualified trust,

(iv) an annuity plan described in section 403 (a),

(v) an eligible deferred compensation plan described in section 457 (b) which is maintained by an eligible employer described in section 457 (e)(1)(A), and

(vi) an annuity contract described in section 403 (b).

If any portion of an eligible rollover distribution is attributable to payments or distributions from a designated Roth account (as defined in section 402A), an eligible retirement plan with respect to such portion shall include only another designated Roth account and a Roth IRA.

(9) Rollover where spouse receives distribution after death of employee

If any distribution attributable to an employee is paid to the spouse of the employee after the employee's death, the preceding provisions of this subsection shall apply to such distribution in the same manner as if the spouse were the employee.

(10) Separate accounting

Unless a plan described in clause (v) of paragraph (8)(B) agrees to separately account for amounts rolled into such plan from eligible retirement plans not described in such clause, the plan described in such clause may not accept transfers or rollovers from such retirement plans.

(d) Taxability of beneficiary of certain foreign situs trusts

For purposes of subsections (a), (b), and (c), a stock bonus, pension, or profit-sharing trust which would qualify for exemption from tax under section 501 (a) except for the fact that it is a trust created or organized outside the United States shall be treated as if it were a trust exempt from tax under section 501 (a).

(e) Other rules applicable to exempt trusts

(1) Alternate payees

(A) Alternate payee treated as distributee

For purposes of subsection (a) and section 72, an alternate payee who is the spouse or former spouse of the participant shall be treated as the distributee of any distribution or payment made to the alternate payee under a qualified domestic relations order (as defined in section 414 (p)).

(B) Rollovers

If any amount is paid or distributed to an alternate payee who is the spouse or former spouse of the participant by reason of any qualified domestic relations order (within the meaning of section 414 (p)), subsection (c) shall apply to such distribution in the same manner as if such alternate payee were the employee.

(2) Distributions by United States to nonresident aliens

The amount includible under subsection (a) in the gross income of a nonresident alien with respect to a distribution made by the United States in respect of services performed by an employee of the United States shall not exceed an amount which bears the same ratio to the amount includible in gross income without regard to this paragraph as—

(A) the aggregate basic pay paid by the United States to such employee for such services, reduced by the amount of such basic pay which was not includible in gross income by reason of being from sources without the United States, bears to

(B) the aggregate basic pay paid by the United States to such employee for such services.

In the case of distributions under the civil service retirement laws, the term "basic pay" shall have the meaning provided in section 8331 (3) of title 5, United States Code.

(3) Cash or deferred arrangements

For purposes of this title, contributions made by an employer on behalf of an employee to a trust which is a part of a qualified cash or deferred arrangement (as defined in section 401 (k)(2)) or which is part of a salary reduction agreement under section 403 (b) shall not be treated as distributed or made available to the employee nor as contributions made to the trust by the employee merely because the arrangement includes provisions under which the employee has an election whether the contribution will be made to the trust or received by the employee in cash.

(4) Net unrealized appreciation

(A) Amounts attributable to employee contributions

For purposes of subsection (a) and section 72, in the case of a distribution other than a lump sum distribution, the amount actually distributed to any distributee from a trust described in subsection (a) shall not include any net unrealized appreciation in securities of the employer corporation attributable to amounts contributed by the employee (other than deductible employee contributions within the meaning of section 72 (o)(5)). This subparagraph shall not apply to a distribution to which subsection (c) applies.

(B) Amounts attributable to employer contributions

For purposes of subsection (a) and section 72, in the case of any lump sum distribution which includes securities of the employer corporation, there shall be excluded from gross income the net unrealized appreciation attributable to that part of the distribution which consists of securities of the employer corporation. In accordance with rules prescribed by the Secretary, a taxpayer may elect, on the return of tax on which a lump sum distribution is required to be included, not to have this subparagraph apply to such distribution.

(C) Determination of amounts and adjustments

For purposes of subparagraphs (A) and (B), net unrealized appreciation and the resulting adjustments to basis shall be determined in accordance with regulations prescribed by the Secretary.

(D) Lump-sum distribution

For purposes of this paragraph—

(i) In general The term "lump-sum distribution" means the distribution or payment within one taxable year of the recipient of the balance to the credit of an employee which becomes payable to the recipient—

(I) on account of the employee's death,

(II) after the employee attains age 591/2,

(III) on account of the employee's separation from service, or

(IV) after the employee has become disabled (within the meaning of section 72 (m)(7)),

from a trust which forms a part of a plan described in section 401 (a) and which is exempt from tax under section 501 or from a plan described in section 403 (a). Subclause (III) of this clause shall be applied only with respect to an individual who is an employee without regard to section 401 (c)(1), and subclause (IV) shall be applied only with respect to an employee within the meaning of section 401 (c)(1). For purposes of this clause, a distribution to two or more trusts shall be treated as a distribution to one recipient. For purposes of this paragraph, the balance to the credit of the employee does not include the accumulated deductible employee contributions under the plan (within the meaning of section 72 (o)(5)).

(ii) Aggregation of certain trusts and plans For purposes of determining the balance to the credit of an employee under clause (i)—

(I) all trusts which are part of a plan shall be treated as a single trust, all pension plans maintained by the employer shall be treated as a single plan, all profit-sharing plans maintained by the employer shall be treated as a single plan, and all stock bonus plans maintained by the employer shall be treated as a single plan, and

(II) trusts which are not qualified trusts under section 401 (a) and annuity contracts which do not satisfy the requirements of section 404 (a)(2) shall not be taken into account.

(iii) Community property laws. The provisions of this paragraph shall be applied without regard to community property laws.

(iv) Amounts subject to penalty. This paragraph shall not apply to amounts described in subparagraph (A) of section 72 (m)(5) to the extent that section 72 (m)(5) applies to such amounts.

(v) Balance to credit of employee not to include amounts payable under qualified domestic relations order. For purposes of this paragraph, the balance to the credit of an employee shall not include any amount payable to an alternate payee under a qualified domestic relations order (within the meaning of section 414 (p)).

(vi) Transfers to cost-of-living arrangement not treated as distribution. For purposes of this paragraph, the balance to the credit of an employee under a defined contribution plan shall not include any amount transferred from such defined contribution plan to a qualified cost-of-living arrangement (within the meaning of section 415 (k)(2)) under a defined benefit plan.

(vii) Lump-sum distributions of alternate payees. If any distribution or payment of the balance to the credit of an employee would be treated as a lump-sum distribution, then, for purposes of this paragraph, the payment under a qualified domestic relations order (within the meaning of section 414(p)) of the balance to the credit of an alternate payee who is the spouse or former spouse of the employee shall be treated as a lump-sum distribution. For purposes of this clause, the balance to the credit of the alternate payee shall not include any amount payable to the employee.

(E) Definitions relating to securities

For purposes of this paragraph—

(i) Securities. The term "securities" means only shares of stock and bonds or debentures issued by a corporation with interest coupons or in registered form.

(ii) Securities of the employer. The term "securities of the employer corporation" includes securities of a parent or subsidiary corporation (as defined in subsections (e) and (f) of section 424) of the employer corporation.

[**(5)** Repealed. Pub. L. 104–188, title I, §?1401(b)(13), Aug. 20, 1996, 110 Stat. 1789]

(6) Direct trustee-to-trustee transfers

Any amount transferred in a direct trustee-to-trustee transfer in accordance with section 401 (a)(31) shall not be includible in gross income for the taxable year of such transfer.

(f) Written explanation to recipients of distributions eligible for rollover treatment

(1) In general

The plan administrator of any plan shall, within a reasonable period of time before making an eligible rollover distribution, provide a written explanation to the recipient—

(A) of the provisions under which the recipient may have the distribution directly transferred to an eligible retirement plan and that the automatic distribution by direct transfer applies to certain distributions in accordance with section 401 (a)(31)(B),

(B) of the provision which requires the withholding of tax on the distribution if it is not directly transferred to an eligible retirement plan,

(C) of the provisions under which the distribution will not be subject to tax if transferred to an eligible retirement plan within 60 days after the date on which the recipient received the distribution,

(D) if applicable, of the provisions of subsections (d) and (e) of this section, and

(E) of the provisions under which distributions from the eligible retirement plan receiving the distribution may be subject to restrictions and tax consequences which are different from those applicable to distributions from the plan making such distribution.

(2) Definitions

For purposes of this subsection—

(A) Eligible rollover distribution

The term "eligible rollover distribution" has the same meaning as when used in subsection (c) of this section, paragraph (4) of section 403 (a), subparagraph (A) of section 403 (b)(8), or subparagraph (A) of section 457 (e)(16).

(B) Eligible retirement plan

The term "eligible retirement plan" has the meaning given such term by subsection (c)(8)(B).

(g) Limitation on exclusion for elective deferrals

(1) In general

(A) Limitation

Notwithstanding subsections (e)(3) and (h)(1)(B), the elective deferrals of any individual for any taxable year shall be included in such individual's gross income to the extent the amount of such deferrals for the taxable year exceeds the applicable dollar amount. The preceding sentence shall not apply to the portion of such excess as does not exceed the designated Roth contributions of the individual for the taxable year.

(B) Applicable dollar amount

For purposes of subparagraph (A), the applicable dollar amount shall be the amount determined in accordance with the following table:

For taxable years The applicable beginning in dollar amount: calendar year: 2002 $11,000; 2003 $12,000; 2004 $13,000; 2005 $14,000; 2006 or thereafter $15,000.

(C) Catch-up contributions

In addition to subparagraph (A), in the case of an eligible participant (as defined in section 414 (v)), gross income shall not include elective deferrals in excess of the applicable dollar amount under subparagraph (B) to the extent that the amount of such elective deferrals does not exceed the applicable dollar amount under section 414 (v)(2)(B)(i) for the taxable year (without regard to the treatment of the elective deferrals by an applicable employer plan under section 414 (v)).

(2) Distribution of excess deferrals

(A) In general

If any amount (hereinafter in this paragraph referred to as "excess deferrals") is included in the gross income of an individual under paragraph (1) (or would be included but for the last sentence thereof) for any taxable year—

(i) not later than the 1st March 1 following the close of the taxable year, the individual may allocate the amount of such excess deferrals among the plans under which the deferrals were made and may notify each such plan of the portion allocated to it, and

(ii) not later than the 1st April 15 following the close of the taxable year, each such plan may distribute to the individual the amount allocated to it under clause (i) (and any income allocable to such amount).

The distribution described in clause (ii) may be made notwithstanding any other provision of law.

(B) Treatment of distribution under section 401 (k)

Except to the extent provided under rules prescribed by the Secretary, notwithstanding the distribution of any portion of an excess deferral from a plan under subparagraph (A)(ii), such portion shall, for purposes of applying section 401 (k)(3)(A)(ii), be treated as an employer contribution.

(C) Taxation of distribution

In the case of a distribution to which subparagraph (A) applies—

(i) except as provided in clause (ii), such distribution shall not be included in gross income, and

(ii) any income on the excess deferral shall, for purposes of this chapter, be treated as earned and received in the taxable year in which such income is distributed.

No tax shall be imposed under section 72 (t) on any distribution described in the preceding sentence.

(D) Partial distributions

If a plan distributes only a portion of any excess deferral and income allocable thereto, such portion shall be treated as having been distributed ratably from the excess deferral and the income.

(3) Elective deferrals

For purposes of this subsection, the term "elective deferrals" means, with respect to any taxable year, the sum of—

(A) any employer contribution under a qualified cash or deferred arrangement (as defined in section 401 (k)) to the extent not includible in gross income for the taxable year under subsection (e)(3) (determined without regard to this subsection),

(B) any employer contribution to the extent not includible in gross income for the taxable year under subsection (h)(1)(B) (determined without regard to this subsection),

(C) any employer contribution to purchase an annuity contract under section 403 (b) under a salary reduction agreement (within the meaning of section 3121 (a)(5)(D)), and

(D) any elective employer contribution under section 408 (p)(2)(A)(i).

An employer contribution shall not be treated as an elective deferral described in subparagraph (C) if under the salary reduction agreement such contribution is made pursuant to a one-time irrevocable election made by the employee at the time of initial eligibility to participate in the agreement or is made pursuant to a similar arrangement involving a one-time irrevocable election specified in regulations.

(4) Cost-of-living adjustment

In the case of taxable years beginning after December 31, 2006, the Secretary shall adjust the $15,000 amount under paragraph (1)(B) at the same time and in the same manner as under section 415 (d), except that the base period shall be the calendar quarter beginning July 1, 2005, and any increase under this paragraph which is not a multiple of $500 shall be rounded to the next lowest multiple of $500.

(5) Disregard of community property laws

This subsection shall be applied without regard to community property laws.

(6) Coordination with section 72

For purposes of applying section 72, any amount includible in gross income for any taxable year under this subsection but which is not distributed from the plan during such taxable year shall not be treated as investment in the contract.

(7) Special rule for certain organizations

(A) In general

In the case of a qualified employee of a qualified organization, with respect to employer contributions described in paragraph (3)(C) made by such organization, the limitation of paragraph (1) for any taxable year shall be increased by whichever of the following is the least:

(i) $3,000,

(ii) $15,000 reduced by the sum of—

(I) the amounts not included in gross income for prior taxable years by reason of this paragraph, plus

(II) the aggregate amount of designated Roth contributions (as defined in section 402A (c)) for prior taxable years, or

(iii) the excess of $5,000 multiplied by the number of years of service of the employee with the qualified organization over the employer contributions described in paragraph (3) made by the organization on behalf of such employee for prior taxable years (determined in the manner prescribed by the Secretary).

(B) Qualified organization

For purposes of this paragraph, the term "qualified organization" means any educational organization, hospital, home health service agency, health and welfare service agency, church, or convention or association of churches. Such term includes any organization described in section 414 (e)(3)(B)(ii). Terms used in this subparagraph shall have the same meaning as when used in section 415 (c)(4) (as in effect before the enactment of the Economic Growth and Tax Relief Reconciliation Act of 2001).

(C) Qualified employee

For purposes of this paragraph, the term "qualified employee" means any employee who has completed 15 years of service with the qualified organization.

(D) Years of service

For purposes of this paragraph, the term "years of service" has the meaning given such term by section 403 (b).

(8) Matching contributions on behalf of self-employed individuals not treated as elective employer contributions

Except as provided in section 401 (k)(3)(D)(ii), any matching contribution described in section 401 (m)(4)(A) which is made on behalf of a self-employed individual (as defined in section 401 (c)) shall not be treated as an elective employer contribution under a qualified cash or deferred arrangement (as defined in section 401 (k)) for purposes of this title.

(h) Special rules for simplified employee pensions

For purposes of this chapter—

(1) In general

Except as provided in paragraph (2), contributions made by an employer on behalf of an employee to an individual retirement plan pursuant to a simplified employee pension (as defined in section 408 (k))—

(A) shall not be treated as distributed or made available to the employee or as contributions made by the employee, and

(B) if such contributions are made pursuant to an arrangement under section 408 (k)(6) under which an employee may elect to have the employer make contributions to the simplified employee pension on behalf of the employee, shall not be treated as distributed or made available or as contributions made by the employee merely because the simplified employee pension includes provisions for such election.

(2) Limitations on employer contributions

Contributions made by an employer to a simplified employee pension with respect to an employee for any year shall be treated as distributed or made available to such employee and as contributions made by the employee to the extent such contributions exceed the lesser of—

(A) 25 percent of the compensation (within the meaning of section 414 (s)) from such employer includible in the employee's gross income for the year (determined without regard to the employer contributions to the simplified employee pension), or

(B) the limitation in effect under section 415 (c)(1)(A), reduced in the case of any highly compensated employee (within the meaning of section 414 (q)) by the amount taken into account with respect to such employee under section 408 (k)(3)(D).

(3) Distributions

Any amount paid or distributed out of an individual retirement plan pursuant to a simplified employee pension shall be included in gross income by the payee or distributee, as the case may be, in accordance with the provisions of section 408 (d).

(i) Treatment of self-employed individuals

For purposes of this section, except as otherwise provided in subparagraph (A) of subsection (d)(4),[1] the term "employee" includes a self-employed individual (as defined in section 401 (c)(1)(B)) and the employer of such individual shall be the person treated as his employer under section 401 (c)(4).

(j) Effect of disposition of stock by plan on net unrealized appreciation

(1) In general

For purposes of subsection (e)(4), in the case of any transaction to which this subsection applies, the determination of net unrealized appreciation shall be made without regard to such transaction.

(2) Transaction to which subsection applies

This subsection shall apply to any transaction in which—

(A) the plan trustee exchanges the plan's securities of the employer corporation for other such securities, or

(B) the plan trustee disposes of securities of the employer corporation and uses the proceeds of such disposition to acquire securities of the employer corporation within 90 days (or such longer period as the Secretary may prescribe), except that this subparagraph shall not apply to any employee with respect to whom a distribution of money was made during the period after such disposition and before such acquisition.

(k) Treatment of simple retirement accounts

Rules similar to the rules of paragraphs (1) and (3) of subsection (h) shall apply to contributions and distributions with respect to a simple retirement account under section 408 (p).

APPENDIX C

Forms

Form # 1   Will Questionnaire
Form #2   Will Format
Form #3   Client Estate-Planning Checklist
Form #4   Designation of Agent
Form #5   Durable Financial Power of Attorney
Form #6   Springing Power of Attorney Language
Form #7   Notice of Revocation of Power of Attorney
Form #8   HIPAA Release
Form #9   Nomination of Guardian for a Minor
Form #10   Parental Consent for Medical Treatment of a Minor
Form #11   Consent for Medical Treatment of a Minor (Alternative Form)
Form #12   Domestic Partnership Agreement (Complex Form)
Form #13   Domestic Partnership Agreement, Maintaining Separate Property
Form #14   Domestic Partnership Agreement (Simple Form)
Form #15   Termination of Domestic Partnership Agreement
Form #16   Shared Parenting Agreement, with UCCJEA/PKPA Language
Form #17   Memorandum of Understanding; Transsexual/Transgender Spouse
Form #18   Confirmation of Designation of Beneficiary
Form #19   Definition of Relationship
Form #20   Sperm/Ova Donor Agreement

Form #1
Confidential Will Questionnaire

Your answers to this questionnaire serves as the basis for your estate plan. The questionnaire also serves as a tool for you to identify issues you want to consider and information you may have forgotten. Please answer all applicable questions as completely as possible. The information you provide is strictly confidential and included in the Attorney-Client Confidential Relationship. We will discuss any questions you have when we meet.

Please have any previous Wills, Divorce Decrees, Domestic Partnership or similar agreements, Custody/Visitation orders or agreements, Parenting Agreements and similar documents available at the interview.

1. Your legal name: _____

2. Partner's legal name: _____

3. Do you currently have a will? [ ] Yes   [ ] No

4. Do you have a Domestic Partnership or similar agreement? [ ] Yes   [ ] No

5. Home address: _____

    Telephone Number: _____

6. Date of birth: _____
    Place of Birth: _____
    Citizenship: _____

7. Have you been married [ ] Yes   [ ] No
    If "Yes" did marriage end in [ ] death or [ ] divorce.
    Year marriage ended: _____
    If there was a divorce, please have a copy of the divorce decree available.

8. Do you have a domestic partnership agreement in effect? [ ] Yes   [ ] No
        (If "Yes" please have a copy available for review)

9. Do you have any children?   [ ] Yes [ ] No
    (Skip to Question 9 if you have no children)

(a) Do any of your children have special needs or are any handicapped?
[ ] Yes [ ] No

(b) Who has physical custody of the children: _____

(c) PLEASE LIST ALL OF YOUR CHILDREN, INCLUDING ADOPTED CHILDREN. Include names, city, state and ages.

Name	City, State	DOB
_____	___ _____	_____
_____	___ _____	_____
_____	___ _____	_____

(d) Please identify any children who may have predeceased you: _____
_____

10. What is your legal relationship to the child(ren)? _____
_____

SPECIFIC BEQUESTS OF PROPERTY TO SPECIFIC PERSONS

You decide how to divide your personal property and to whom it will go. You can either include specific gifts of specific items in your Will or through a separate listing that can be referenced in the Will. Listing the items separate from the Will leaves you free to change list without needing to rewrite your Will. You may use the Will to make a specific bequest if you are concerned your wishes will not be honored. A specific bequest may also be appropriate if you intend to leave an item to a non-family member.

11. Please indicate the specific item(s) you want distributed and the name of the person(s) to whom you are leaving the item(s). _____
_____
_____

12. PETS. Consider what happens to your pets after your death. You may want to designate a specific individual to care for them. You may also consider providing a specific monetary bequest to that person for the care of the pet. _____

_____

_____

BENEFICIARIES OF YOUR ESTATE

Think about who you want to inherit your estate after the Executor distributes any specific bequests. Example: Do you want everything to go to your partner? How do you want to provide for children? Grandchildren? Other family members? Do you want everyone to receive equal shares?

13. Name the person(s) to whom you want to leave your estate:

    Name: _____
    Relationship: _____
    City/State: _____

    Name: _____
    Relationship: _____
    City/State: _____

14. Name the person(s) you wish to be the alternate beneficiary of your estate:

    Name: _____
    Relationship: _____
    City/State: _____

    Name: _____
    Relationship: _____
    City/State: _____

    Name: _____
    Relationship: _____
    City/State: _____

15. GUARDIANSHIP OF MINOR CHILDREN.

Consider naming a guardian for any minor children you have. Natural parents have priority in these maters. You can name someone to be the guardian of the person and of the estate. If you do not name a guardian, and there is no other natural parent, the probate court will appoint one for any minor child(ren).

(a) FIRST CHOICE for Guardian:

Name: _____
Relationship: _____
City/State: _____

(b) ALTERNATE CHOICE for Guardian:

Name: _____
Relationship: _____
City/State: _____

16. EXECUTOR.

The Executor is responsible for collecting all estate property, paying all legal debts, taxes and expenses of the estate and dividing the estate according to your directions. The Executor must be over the age of 18; it can also be an institution (e.g. a bank). Name an alternate executor in case your first choice is unable or unwilling to accept the appointment. Your Executor mayl be compensated from the estate assets according to Ohio law. The Executor may also choose to waive the fee.

(a) FIRST CHOICE for Guardian:

Name: _____
Relationship: _____
City/State: _____

(b) ALTERNATE CHOICE for Guardian:

Name: _____
Relationship: _____
City/State: _____

17. WILL CONTEST.

Consider whether any family member is apt to file a Will contest. If you think that may happen, you may want to include a provision to deter people from contesting your Will. You may provide that anyone contesting the Will receives nothing from the estate. Generally, you will need to leave a specific bequest sufficient to make an heir think twice before contesting your will.

18. TAX ISSUES.

In order to determine if tax planning is required for your estate it is important to estimate the overall value of your accumulated property. This includes life insurance and all property listed in your name. The current exemption for federal estate tax for the year _____ is $_____. If your total estate is over $_____ more extensive estate planning may be required. We will discuss this at the interview.

(a) Estimated value of your total assets at present: (Check one)

A. [ ] Under $_____

B. [ ] Over $_____

19. Do you want to sign a Durable Power of Attorney for Finances [ ] Yes [ ] No

(a) Who do you want to name as your attorney-in-fact (the person to whom you are giving the authority to act on your behalf)?

Name: _____

Address: _____

Telephone No.: _____

Relationship: _____

(b) Alternate Attorney-in-fact:

Name: _____

Address: _____

Telephone No.: _____

Relationship: _____

20. Do you want to sign a Health Care Power of Attorney and Living Will?
[ ] Yes   [ ] No

(a) First Choice (the person designated to make health care decisions for you):

Name: _____

Address: _____

Telephone No.: _____

Relationship: _____

(b) Second Choice (the alternate person designated to make health care decisions):

Name: _____

Address: _____

Telephone No.: _____

Relationship: _____

21. Do you want to execute a Designation of Agent? This document allows you to name someone to make decisions concerning who will visit you in a health care facility (including nursing home, hospice, etc.), disposition of personal effects, disposition of remains and funeral arrangements. While these documents have not been tested in court, it does give you the opportunity to make your intentions known.   ___ Yes   ___ No

ASSETS

Generally, a will does not list each and every item of property that you want to convey following your death. However, it is important to list the **FORM OF OWNERSHIP AND THE APPROXIMATE VALUE OF YOUR PROPERTY**. If you are unsure as to the form of ownership you can ask your insurance agent or your mortgage holder. If you are still uncertain please have the documents available and we will review them together. It is important that you complete the answers concerning the following assets as best you can.

22. (a) REAL PROPERTY (i.e. residence, vacant land, rental property, vacation home). Please have your deeds available for review.

(1) Location: _____

Market value and mortgage balance: _____

Exact way owner(s) are named on deed: _____

_____

(1) Location: _____

Market value and mortgage balance: _____

Exact way owner(s) are named on deed: _____

_____

(b) BANK ACCOUNTS (Indicate whether checking, savings, brokerage account or CDs)

Name/location of financial institution: _____

Account Balance: _____

Name of Account Holder (specify joint or POD): _____

Name/location of financial institution: _____

Account Balance: _____

Name of Account Holder (specify joint or POD): _____

Name/location of financial institution: _____

Account Balance: _____

Name of Account Holder (specify joint or POD): _____

(c) LIST IRAs, RETIREMENT PLANS (including 401k accounts)

Name/location of financial institution:_____

Account Balance: _____

Name of Account Holder (specify joint or POD): _____

Name of beneficiary: _____

Name/location of financial institution:_____

Account Balance: _____

Name of Account Holder (specify joint or POD): _____

Name of beneficiary: _____

Name/location of financial institution:_____

Account Balance: _____

Name of Account Holder (specify joint or POD): _____

Name of beneficiary: _____

(d) STOCKS, BONDS, MUTUAL FUNDS, INCLUDING U.S. SAVINGS BONDS

Name(s) of stocks/bonds/funds:_____

How are holdings held: _____

Approx value: _____

Name(s) of stocks/bonds/funds:_____

How are holdings held: _____

Approx value: _____

Name(s) of stocks/bonds/funds:_____

How are holdings held: _____

Approx value: _____

(e) TITLED VEHICLES; list all cars, trucks, boats and motorcycles:

Year/Make/Model: _____
Titled Owner: _____
Approx Value: _____

Year/Make/Model: _____
Titled Owner: _____
Approx Value: _____

(f) OTHER IMPORTANT ASSETS (i.e. stamp/coin/other collections, business interests, partnerships, lottery winnings) _____
_____
_____

(g) LIFE INSURANCE POLICIES:

Name on Policy: _____

Face Value: _____

Beneficiary: _____

Name on Policy: _____

Face Value: _____

Beneficiary: _____

Please note any additional questions you want to discuss during the interview.

Form #2
Last Will and Testament

Of _____

I, _____, of _____, _____, hereby make, publish and declare this to be my Last Will and Testament and revoke any previous wills and codicils made by me.

Section 1. Identification of Family

1.01 My [partner's] name is _____. All references in this will to my partner, whether or not specifically named, shall mean only my partner, _____.

1.02 I have [no] living children or issue. [**Specify names of children and whether they are minors or adults. If minors, the Will must also include a Guardian of Person and Estate clause in conformance with state law. Include the partner's children in the definition of children whether biological or adopted; include any children where the partner's adoption petition has not been finalized.**]

Section 2. Nomination of Executor

2.01 I hereby nominate _____ to serve as my Executor. Should this person be unable or unwilling at any time to serve in that capacity, I nominate _____ of _____, _____ as my Alternate Executor.

2.02 I direct that my Executor, and any successor, be permitted to serve without bond in any jurisdiction.

Section 3. Disposition of Tangible Personal Property

3.01 I give, devise and bequeath my tangible personal property to [my partner], _____. [The tangible personal property is: _____.]

or [A list and description of my tangible personal property to which _____ is entitled to receive is incorporated by reference to my Will. It is marked, "List of Tangible Personal Property."]

My Executor has sole discretion to sell any of the property that is not suitable for distribution. The proceeds of any sale shall become part of my residuary estate. If the devisee named in this section predeceases or does not survive me, I direct that the said property be sold and the proceeds distributed with the residue of my estate.

Section 4. Residuary Devise

4.01   My residuary estate shall consist of all property or money owned by me at the time of my death and not otherwise effectively disposed of in this Will. It includes all insurance proceeds or other death benefits that are payable to my estate. My residuary estate does not include any property over which I may have a power of appointment.

All valid claims asserted against my estate and all expenses incurred in administering my estate, including expenses of administering nonprobate assets, are excluded from my residuary estate.

4.02   I give, devise and bequeath my residuary estate to [my partner], _____. My devisee must survive me by 30 days to receive any part of my estate.

4.03   If [my partner] or _____ predeceases or fails to survive me I give, devise and bequeath my residuary estate to _____.

[4.04   I am leaving my estate to my partner, _____, because he/she is my life partner. I am not making these provisions out of any disrespect or lack of affection or love for my family. It is my intention that my partner, _____, inherits my estate.]

Section 5. Specific Provision Regarding My Pet(s)

5.01   If [my partner], _____, predeceases or fails to survive me, I bequeath any pets I own at the time of my death to _____. _____ is willing and able to care for my pets in a comfortable setting with a standard of care similar to what I have provided for them.

I bequeath to _____, the sum of $500.00 per pet, for accepting this responsibility. I intend that this bequest be used to defray the costs of providing care to my pets. Any amount left over after the death of my pets shall become the property of _____.

5.02   If _____ is unable to accept and care for my pets, I authorize and request my Executor to select an appropriate person who is willing assume this responsibility and agrees to maintain my pets in a comfortable setting with a standard of care similar to what I have provided for them.

I bequeath to the person agreeing to be responsible for the care of my pets the sum of $500.00 per pet. I intend that this bequest be used to defray the costs of providing care to my pets. Any amount left over after the death of my pets shall become the property of _____.

Section 6. Powers of Executor

6.01   My Executor, and any successor thereto, shall have all powers granted to Executors and fiduciaries under the probate code and other applicable laws of the State of _____, including the power to execute any joint or individual tax return on my behalf or on behalf of my estate.

6.02   My Executor shall be entitled to reasonable compensation for services actually performed and to reimbursement of expenses properly incurred.

> (A) My Executor shall have, in addition to any other powers, the power to invest, reinvest, sell, mortgage, lease or otherwise transfer or dispose of any part or all of my estate, without the necessity of obtaining prior or subsequent court approval;
>
> (B) To make repairs or improvements to my property as may be deemed necessary to preserve or enhance the value of my estate.
>
> (C) To borrow funds for use in estate administration if there are insufficient liquid assets in my estate;
>
> (D) To employ persons, including attorneys, investment advisors or other agents for assistance or advice, or not to employ such persons, as my Executor deems appropriate.

(E) To compromise and settle any claims against or in favor of my estate on such terms and conditions as my Executor deems best.

(F) To make determinations as to the allocation of receipts and the apportionment of expenditures between income and principal. My Executor shall not be required to follow any provision of law regarding such determinations, including Chapter 1340 of the Ohio Revised Code.

6.03   My Executor may make distributions either in cash or in kind. Distributions in kind may be made at the discretion of my Executor. My Executor may make any distributions under this will either (1) directly to the beneficiary, (2) in any form allowed by applicable state law for gifts or transfers to minors or persons under disability, (3) to the beneficiary's guardian, conservator, or caregiver for the benefit of the beneficiary, or (4) by direct payment of the beneficiary's expenses.

Section 7. Construction and Definitions

The following rules and definitions shall apply in the construction of this instrument and in the administration of my estate:

7.01   Any reference to my "Executor" in whatever form refers to the person, persons, or
institution then acting as the personal representative of my estate.

7.02   If any devisee or other beneficiary under this will dies within 30 days after my death or under such circumstances where there is insufficient evidence in the judgment of my Executor to determine whether such person has died within 30 days after my death, the devisee or beneficiary shall be deemed to have failed to survive me.

7.03   The laws of the State of _____ shall govern all questions as to the validity and construction of this.

7.04   The term "estate and death taxes" shall mean all estate, inheritance, transfer, succession, or other taxes or duties payable by reason of my death, including interest and penalties thereon.

Section 8. Payment of Taxes and Expenses

8.01   I direct my Executor to pay the expenses of administering my estate, the expenses created by reason of my death, and all estate and death taxes payable with respect to property includable in my gross estate or taxable by reason of my death, whether or not such property is part of my probate estate and whether or not such taxes are payable by my estate or by the recipient of any such property. Such taxes and expenses should be paid out of my residuary estate without apportionment.

[OPTIONAL CLAUSE]

8.02   I direct my Executor to pay only those expenses dealing with my funeral and interment that conform to my expressed wishes. I have written down what I want for my funeral and interment. It is in an envelope marked, "Funeral" and is located _____.

If anyone interferes with my expressed wishes concerning my funeral, memorial service or interment or fails to abide by my expressed wishes, that person or persons shall be wholly responsible for any and all expenses. My estate shall be held harmless for any expenses incurred that do not conform to my wishes.

I ask that the Court and everyone else involved honor my expressed wishes, even if those wishes run counter to those of my immediate family. It is my intention that _____ make all funeral and interment decisions in accord with my expressed wishes.

IN WITNESS WHEREOF, I hereby subscribe my name to this instrument this _____ day of _____, _____ at _____, _____ .

_____
Testator

STATEMENT OF WITNESSES

Each witness declares, under penalty of perjury and the laws of the State of _____, that the following is true and correct. I am over the age of eighteen years and competent to be a witness to the will of _____. The Testator signed this Last Will and Testament on the _____ day of _____, _____ declaring it to be the Testator's Last Will and Testament. The Testator signed this Last Will and Testament in the presence of each of us. We, at the Testator's request and in the Testator's presence, and in the presence of each other now subscribe our names as witnesses.

We do hereby declare that the Testator signed and executed the instrument, as _____ last will, that the Testator signed willingly and freely and voluntarily executed it for the purposes expressed. We also declare that each of the witnesses, in the presence and hearing of the Testator, signed the Will as witness and that to the best of our individual knowledge the Testator was at the time 18 or more years of age, of sound mind and under no constraint or undue influence.

_____
Witness Signature

_____
Witness Name

_____
Witness Address

_____
Witness Signature

_____
Witness Name

_____
Witness Address

Form #3
Client Estate-Planning Checklist

This list is designed to assist you or your heirs in locating important documents and information needed to settle your estate. You should review this document on a regular basis and update as needed.

1. Will
    a. Date signed:_____
    b. Where located: _____
    c. Who is named Executor? _____

2. Trust
    a. Date signed:_____
    b. Where located: _____
    c. Who is named Executor? _____

3. Durable Power of Attorney for Finances
    a. Date signed:_____
    b. Where located: _____
    c. Who is named Executor? _____

4. Living Will
    a. Date signed:_____
    b. Where located: _____

5. Health Care Power of Attorney
    a. Date signed:_____
    b. Where located: _____
    c. Who is named to make health care decisions: _____

6. Health Insurance

    a. Name of Carrier: _____

    b. Carrier's address/phone number: _____

    c. Policy number: _____

7. Disability Insurance

    a. Name of Carrier: _____

    b. Carrier's address/phone number: _____

    c. Policy number: _____

8. Long-term Care Insurance

    a. Name of Carrier: _____

    b. Carrier's address/phone number: _____

    c. Policy number: _____

9. Life Insurance

    a. Name of Carrier: _____

    b. Carrier's address/phone number: _____

    c. Policy number: _____

    d. Named Beneficiary: _____

10. Retirement/Employee Benefits

    a. Company name, address & phone number: _____
    _____

    c. Named beneficiary: _____

11. Letter of instructions (funeral and burial; insurance papers; location of will and trust; location of safe deposit box; names/addresses/phone numbers of: lawyer, accountant, broker and clergy member; instructions for distribution of tangible personal property; expression of wishes for family/friends; business instructions.)

12. Personal financial information including credit cards, loans, checking and saving accounts, brokerage accounts, stocks, bonds and U.S. Savings bonds, mutual funds, outstanding loans both owing and owed.

13. List of doctors.

14. Statement of wishes concerning personal matters.

15. Current and complete references to all personal property currently owned.

16. Location of business buy/sell agreements, partnership papers, corporate filings and other business related paperwork.

17. Irrevocable insurance trust.

18. Specification of all property, individual, joint, community and mixed.

19. Any gift tax returns filed? When/Where. Type of gift.

20. Deeds to all real property.

Form #4
Designation of Agent with Authority Re: Health Care Visitation, Receipt of Personal Property, Disposition of Remains, and Making Funeral Arrangements

I, _____, designate [my partner], _____, as my agent empowered with the following authority.

A. VISITATION AUTHORITY: If I am admitted to a medical facility of any type, a nursing home, hospice or similar health care, skilled nursing or custodial facility, my agent, _____, shall be designated as "family" as that term is defined by the Joint Commission on Accreditation of Healthcare Organizations. JCAHO defines "family" as, "The person(s) who plays a significant role in the individual's [patient's] life. This may include a person(s) not legally related to the individual." (Joint Commission Resources, JCR, 2001 Hospital Accreditation Standards, p. 322).

My agent shall have priority in being admitted to visit me in such facility. This authority supersedes any policy existing in any health care, medical, nursing home, hospice or similar facility. [My partner,] as my agent, is designated as the person to be consulted by medical or health care personnel concerning my care and treatment. This is in keeping with the Health Care Power of Attorney I executed. My agent shall also have the authority to determine who will be permitted to visit me while in the facility and during any recovery at home.

This authorization supersedes any preference given to parties related to me by blood or by law or other parties desiring to visit me. These instructions shall remain in full force and effect unless and until I freely give contrary written instructions to competent medical personnel on the premises involved. My subsequent disability or incapacity shall not affect these instructions.

B. RECEIPT OF PERSONAL PROPERTY: My agent shall have the right to receive any and all items of personal property and effects that may be recovered from or about my person by any health care, medical, nursing home, hospice or similar facility, police agency or any other person or public/private entity at the time of my illness, disability or death. This specifically includes cash or other liquid asset(s).

C. DISPOSITION OF REMAINS/AUTOPSY and AUTHORIZATION for FUNERAL ARRANGEMENTS: My agent shall have the authority to authorize an autopsy if it is deemed necessary or is required by law.

In matters concerning the disposition of my remains and funeral arrangements, I provide that my agent, or any other person directed by my agent to dispose my remains, shall follow my instructions for any funeral services. Any limitations on this authority are specified in this document.

My agent is to direct the disposition of my remains by the following method:
burial _____ cremation _____. The specific instructions are found in:
_____

In this regard, my agent has the authority to make all decisions necessary for my obituary notice, funeral arrangements, including any mortician's role, burial services, interment or cremation of my body, including, but not limited to the selection of a casket or urn, selection, care and tending of a grave site and selection of a gravestone including any inscription.

D. ADDITIONAL AUTHORITY:

My agent shall have access to all medical records and information pertaining to me and concerning treatments, procedures, treatment plans, etc. This includes the right to disclose this information to other people. I explicitly authorize any medical or health care provider to release information requested by my agent to him/her and consider my agent an authorized person to receive such information under the Health Information Portability and Accessibility Act (HIPAA)

This Authorization applies to any health information protected by the federal Health Insurance Portability and Accountability Act of 1996 (HIPAA), and the regulations implementing it (45 C.F.R. ßß160-164). It is intended to comply with all specific requirements of those regulations (45 C.F.R. ß164.508(c)), and with the relevant privacy provisions of _____ law.

My agent has the authority to admit or discharge me from any hospital, nursing home, residential care, assisted living or similar facility or service entity. My agent also has the authority to hire and fire medical, social service and other support personnel. My agent is primarily responsible for my medical and health care.

_____   _____
        Date   Principal

State of _____

County of _____

    Before me, a Notary Public in and for said County and State, personally appeared the above named, _____, who acknowledged that he did sign the foregoing two-page instrument, and that the same is his free act and deed.

    In Testimony Whereof, I have hereunto set my hand and official seal at _____, _____, this _____ day of _____, 20____.

_____
           Notary Public

<u>A COPY OF THIS DOCUMENT SHALL HAVE THE SAME EFFECT AS THE ORIGINAL</u>

Form #5
General Durable Power of Attorney

This document provides your designated attorney in fact with broad powers to act on your behalf concerning all your property, persona and business affairs. The powers you grant continue until you revoke them or die. These powers continue even if you become disabled, incapacitated or incompetent.

You have the right to revoke or terminate this Durable Power of Attorney at any time. But, you must revoke the power in writing.

I, _____ , the Principal, create this General Power of Attorney to enable the person named below to act as my agent and attorney-in-fact on all matters at all times, either before or after the my disability.

1. **Designation of Agent.** I hereby designate and appoint _____ , to be my agent and attorney-in-fact and to act in my name and stead for all purposes.

2. **Effective Date.** This General Power of Attorney and the powers conferred shall be effective as of the date I execute this document.

3. **Disability or Disappearance of Principal.** This General Power of Attorney shall not be affected by my disability. The powers and authority conferred on my agent in this instrument shall be fully exercisable by my agent even after my subsequent disability or incapacity or the later uncertainty as to whether I am alive or dead.

All acts performed by my agent under this General Power of Attorney, during any period of my disability or incompetence or during any period of uncertainty as to whether I am alive or dead, shall have the same effect, and inure to the benefit of and bind me, my heirs, devisees, and personal representative, to the same extent as if the I were alive, competent and not disabled.

4. **Nomination of Guardian of Person and Estate.** In the event I become disabled and am unable to manage my own affairs, I hereby nominate _____ , as the Guardian of my person and estate.

I nominate her as my Guardian because he is best suited to carry out my wishes, desires and intentions concerning my estate. He is also the person who has my best interests at heart. I trust her completely and ask the Probate Court to honor my selection of my Guardian. I also ask that my nominee serve without bond.

In the event the Probate Court does not name my nominee as the Guardian of my person and estate, I demand that the person selected by the Court be required to post a bond to serve in the capacity of Guardian.

5. **Powers of Agent.** The Agent acting under this General Power of Attorney shall have the full power and authority to do and perform every act and thing to the same extent as the Principal could do if personally present and under no disability. The Agent shall have all of the powers, rights, discretions, elections, and authority conferred by statute, the common law, or rule of court or governmental agency that are reasonably necessary for the Agent to act on the Principal's behalf for any purpose. In addition to these general powers, the Agent shall have the following specific powers:

A. The power to request, ask, demand, sue for, recover, sell, collect, forgive, receive, and hold money, debts, dues, commercial paper, checks, drafts, accounts, deposits, legacies, bequests, devises, notes, interests, stocks, bonds, certificates of deposit, annuities, pension and retirement benefits, insurance proceeds, any and all documents of title, choses in action, personal and real property, intangible and tangible property and property rights, and demands whatsoever, liquidated or unliquidated, as now are, or may become, owned by, or due, owing, payable, or belonging to the Principal, or in which the Principal has or may hereafter acquire an interest; to have, use, and take all lawful means and equitable and legal remedies, procedures, and writs in the Principal's name for the collection and recovery thereof, and to adjust, sell, compromise, and agree for the same; and to make, execute and deliver for the Principal, on the Principal's behalf and in the Principal's name, all endorsements, acceptances, releases, receipts, or other sufficient discharges for the same.

B. The power to prepare, sign, and file joint or separate income tax returns or declarations or estimated tax returns for any year or years; to prepare, sign, and file gift tax returns with respect to gifts made by the Principal, or by the Agent on the Principal's behalf, for any year or years; to consent to any gift and to utilize any gift-splitting provision or other tax election; and to prepare, sign, and file any claim for refund of any tax. This power is in addition to and not in limitation of the tax powers granted in the next paragraph.

C. The power and authority to do, take, and perform each and every act and thing that is required, proper, or necessary to be done, in connection with executing and filing any tax return, receiving and cashing any refund checks with respect to any tax filing, and dealing with the Internal Revenue Service and any state and local tax authority concerning any gift, estate, inheritance, income, or other tax, and any audit or investigation of same. This power shall include the power to do all acts that could be authorized by a properly executed Form 2848, entitled "Power of Attorney and Declaration of Representative," granting the broadest powers provided therein to the Agent.

D. The power to conduct, engage in and transact any lawful matter of any nature, on behalf of or in the name of the Principal, and to maintain, improve, invest, manage, insure, lease, or encumber, and in any manner deal with any real, personal, tangible, or intangible property, or any interest in them, that the Principal now owns or may later acquire, in the name of and for the benefit of the Principal, upon such terms and conditions as the Agent shall deem proper. This includes renewing my license plates and/or license stickers with the Ohio Bureau of Motor Vehicles.

E. The power to exercise or perform any act, power, duty, right, or obligation that the Principal now has, or may later acquire, including, without limiting the foregoing, the right to enter into a contract of sale and to sell any real, personal, tangible, or intangible property on the Principal's behalf and the right to renounce or disclaim any testamentary or nontestamentary transfer intended for the Principal.

F. The power to: make, receive, sign, endorse, acknowledge, deliver, and possess insurance policies, documents of title, bonds, debentures, checks, drafts, stocks, proxies, and warrants, relating to accounts or deposits in, or certificates of deposit, other debts and obligations, and such other instruments in writing of any kind or nature as may be necessary or proper in the exercise of the rights and powers herein granted.

G. The power to sell any and all shares of stocks, bonds, or other securities now belonging to or later acquired by the Principal that may be issued by any association, trust, or corporation, whether private or public, and to make, execute, and deliver any assignment, or assignments, of any such shares of stocks, bonds, or other securities.

H. The power to conduct or participate in any business of any nature for and in the name of the Principal; execute partnership agreements and amendments thereto; incorporate, reorganize, merge, consolidate, recapitalize, sell, liquidate, or dissolve any business; elect or employ officers, directors, and agents; carry out the provisions of any agreement for the sale of any business interest or the stock therein; and exercise voting rights with respect to stock, either in person or by proxy, and exercise stock options.

I. The power to enter any safe deposit box rented by the Principal, and to remove all or any part of the contents thereof, and to surrender or relinquish said safe-deposit box. Any institution in which any such safe-deposit box may be located shall not incur any liability to the Principal or the Principal's estate as a result of permitting the Agent to exercise the powers herein granted.

J. The power to make outright gifts of cash or property to adults or to minors in custodial form under an applicable Gifts to Minors Act, in amounts not to exceed the amount established by the Internal Revenue Service for individual annual gifts to each adult or minor donee in any calendar year. Permissible donees hereunder shall include my partner, any of my children or stepchildren and their descendants, or any descendant of a brother or sister of mine or of any person to whom I shall have been married, as well as any person who shall be married to any of the foregoing.

K. The power to convey or assign any cash or other property of which the Principal shall be possessed to the trustee or trustees of any trust that the Principal may have created, provided that such trust is subject to revocation by the Principal, which power shall be exercisable hereunder by the Agent.

L. The power to purchase United States Government Bonds known as "Flower Bonds," which may be used in payment of death taxes from the Principal's estate.

M. Subject to the provisions of section 1 above, the power to appoint a substitute or alternate agent and attorney-in-fact, who shall have all powers and authority of the Agent.

N. INSERT APPROPRIATE HIPAA LANGUAGE

O. INSERT LANGUAGE CONCERNING THE PRINCIPAL'S DOMESTIC PETS, IF NECESSARY.

6. **Limitation of Power of Agent.** Regardless of any other provision of this General Power of Attorney, the Agent shall have no rights or powers hereunder

with respect to any act, power, duty, right or obligation relating to any person, matter, transaction or property held or possessed by me as a trustee, custodian, personal representative or other fiduciary capacity. In addition, the Agent shall have no power or right to perform any of the following functions:

---

7. **Ratification.** I hereby ratify, acknowledge and declare valid all acts performed by the Agent on my behalf before the effective date of this General Power of Attorney.

8. **Revocation and Termination.** This General Power of Attorney is revocable by me, provided that insofar as any governmental agency, bank, depository, trust company, insurance company, other corporation, transfer agent, investment banking company or other person who shall rely upon this power, this power may be revoked only by a notice in writing executed by me and delivered to such person or institution.

This General Power of Attorney shall not be revoked or otherwise become ineffective in any way by the mere passage of time, but rather shall remain in full force and effect until revoked by me in writing.

I hereby revoke all general powers of attorney previously executed by me, if any, and the same shall be of no further force or effect. However, I do not intend in this General Power of Attorney to affect, modify or terminate any special, restricted or limited power or powers of attorney previously granted by me in connection with any banking, borrowing or commercial transaction.

9. **Construction.** This General Power of Attorney is executed and delivered in the State of _____, and the laws of the State of _____ shall govern all questions as to its validity and as to the construction of its provisions. This instrument is to be construed and interpreted as a general durable power of attorney. The enumeration of specific powers is not intended to limit or restrict the general powers granted to the Agent in this instrument.

10. **Reliance.** Third parties may rely upon the representations of the Agent as to all matters related to any power granted to the Agent in this instrument, and no person who acts in reliance upon the representation of the Agent shall incur any liability to my estate or me by permitting the Agent to exercise any power. Third parties may rely upon a photocopy of this executed General Power of Attorney to the same extent as if the copy were an original of this instrument. This document consists of _____ pages.

IN WITNESS WHEREOF, I have executed this Durable General Power of Attorney on the _____ day of _____ 20___.

_____,
_____PRINCIPAL

State of _____
County of _____

_____, the Principal, executed and acknowledged this Durable Power of Attorney for Finances before me this _____ day of _____, 20___.

_____
Notary Public

Form #6
Springing General Durable Power of Attorney

This document provides your designated attorney in fact with broad powers to act on your behalf concerning all your property, persona and business affairs. The powers you grant become effective when you become disabled as specified. The powers continue until you are no longer disabled, incapacitated, incompetent or die.

You have the right to revoke or terminate this Springing Durable Power of Attorney at any time before you become incompetent or incapacitated. But, you must revoke the power in writing.

I, _____, of _____, the Principal, create this General Power of Attorney to enable the person named below to act as my agent and attorney-in-fact on all matters at all times, either before or after the my disability.

1. **Designation of Agent.** I hereby designate and appoint _____, to be my agent and attorney-in-fact and to act in my name and stead for all purposes.

2. **Designation of Personal Representative.** The designation of my agent, _____, as my Personal Representative, with the legal authority to make health care decisions for me shall become effective immediately upon the signing of this document. I intend this authorization and designation to comply with the federal regulations, 45 C.F.R. ß164.508(c). My physicians are authorized to release protected health information, including information about my capacity to make informed decisions. I intend this authorization to be construed broadly.

3. **Effective Date.** This Springing Durable Power of Attorney and the powers conferred under paragraph 6 shall become effective when I become incapacitated or incompetent. My incapacity or incompetence shall be determined either by an affidavit signed by the physician treating me or by my Personal Representative based on the Personal Health Information provided to him by my health care providers.

Incapacity or incompetence is defined as: being physically, mentally and/or legally unable to manage my personal and/or business affairs. This definition shall include my inability to speak with, write to, or otherwise communicate my

intentions and wishes to my agent, _____,
or my treating physician.

It shall also include my inability to communicate my wishes concerning my finances or health care with my agent or my physician. Any physician who certifies in good faith, by affidavit, that I am incompetent or incapacitated shall be held harmless from all liability for that certification.

Any actions taken by my agent, _____, on my behalf and based on the certification that I am disabled, incapacitated or incompetent shall be recognized and honored by all persons. No person or entity that complies with requests from my agent, under the terms of this Power of Attorney, shall incur any liability to anyone for acting in good faith reliance on this instrument.

4. **Health Insurance Portability and Accountability Act of 1996 (HIPAA).** My Personal Representative and agent, _____, shall have the authority, under the Health Insurance Portability and Accountability Act of 1996 (HIPAA) to receive any and all Protected Health Information (PHI) from any health care provider is treating me or has treated me. I intend this authority to meet all requirements of the federal regulations implementing HIPAA and found at 45 C.F.R. §§ 160-64.

5. **Disability or Disappearance of Principal.** This General Power of Attorney shall not be affected by my disability. The powers and authority conferred on my agent in this instrument shall be fully exercisable by my agent even after my subsequent disability or incapacity or the later uncertainty as to whether I am alive or dead.

All acts performed by my agent under this General Power of Attorney, during any period of my disability or incompetence or during any period of uncertainty as to whether I am alive or dead, shall have the same effect, and inure to the benefit of and bind me, my heirs, devisees, and personal representative, to the same extent as if the I were alive, competent and not disabled.

6. **Nomination of Guardian of Person and Estate.** In the event I become disabled and am unable to manage my own affairs, I hereby nominate _____, as the Guardian of my person and estate.

I nominate him as my Guardian because he is best suited to carry out my wishes, desires and intentions concerning my estate. He is also the person who has my best interests at heart. I trust him completely and ask the Probate Court to honor my selection of my Guardian. I also ask that my nominee serve without bond.

In the event the Probate Court does not name _____, as the Guardian of my person and estate, I demand that the person selected by the Court be required to post a bond to serve in the capacity of Guardian.

7. **Powers of Agent.** The Agent acting under this General Power of Attorney shall have the full power and authority to do and perform every act and thing to the same extent as the Principal could do if personally present and under no disability. The Agent shall have all of the powers, rights, discretions, elections, and authority conferred by statute, the common law, or rule of court or governmental agency that are reasonably necessary for the Agent to act on the Principal's behalf for any purpose. In addition to these general powers, the Agent shall have the following specific powers:

A. The power to request, ask, demand, sue for, recover, sell, collect, forgive, receive, and hold money, debts, dues, commercial paper, checks, drafts, accounts, deposits, legacies, bequests, devises, notes, interests, stocks, bonds, certificates of deposit, annuities, pension and retirement benefits, insurance proceeds, any and all documents of title, choses in action, personal and real property, intangible and tangible property and property rights, and demands whatsoever, liquidated or unliquidated, as now are, or may become, owned by, or due, owing, payable, or belonging to the Principal, or in which the Principal has or may hereafter acquire an interest; to have, use, and take all lawful means and equitable and legal remedies, procedures, and writs in the Principal's name for the collection and recovery thereof, and to adjust, sell, compromise, and agree for the same; and to make, execute and deliver for the Principal, on the Principal's behalf and in the Principal's name, all endorsements, acceptances, releases, receipts, or other sufficient discharges for the same.

B. The power to prepare, sign, and file joint or separate income tax returns or declarations or estimated tax returns for any year or years; to prepare, sign, and file gift tax returns with respect to gifts made by the Principal, or by the Agent on the Principal's behalf, for any year or years; to consent to any gift and to utilize any gift-splitting provision or other tax election; and to prepare, sign, and file any claim for refund of any tax. This power is in addition to and not in limitation of the tax powers granted in the next paragraph.

C. The power and authority to do, take, and perform each and every act and thing that is required, proper, or necessary to be done, in connection with executing and filing any tax return, receiving and cashing any refund checks with respect to any tax filing, and dealing with the Internal Revenue Service and any state and local tax authority concerning any gift, estate, inheritance, income, or other tax, and any audit or investigation of same. This power shall include the power to do all acts that could be authorized by a properly executed Form 2848, entitled "Power of Attorney and Declaration of Representative," granting the broadest powers provided therein to the Agent.

D. The power to conduct, engage in and transact any lawful matter of any nature, on behalf of or in the name of the Principal, and to maintain, improve, invest, manage, insure, lease, or encumber, and in any manner deal with any real, personal, tangible, or intangible property, or any interest in them, that the Principal now owns or may later acquire, in the name of and for the benefit of the Principal, upon such terms and conditions as the Agent shall deem proper. This includes renewing my license plates and/or license stickers with the Ohio Bureau of Motor Vehicles.

E. The power to exercise or perform any act, power, duty, right, or obligation that the Principal now has, or may later acquire, including, without limiting the foregoing, the right to enter into a contract of sale and to sell any real, personal, tangible, or intangible property on the Principal's behalf and the right to renounce or disclaim any testamentary or nontestamentary transfer intended for the Principal.

F. The power to: make, receive, sign, endorse, acknowledge, deliver, and possess insurance policies, documents of title, bonds, debentures, checks, drafts, stocks, proxies, and warrants, relating to accounts or deposits in, or certificates of deposit, other debts and obligations, and such other instruments in writing of any kind or nature as may be necessary or proper in the exercise of the rights and powers herein granted.

G. The power to sell any and all shares of stocks, bonds, or other securities now belonging to or later acquired by the Principal that may be issued by any association, trust, or corporation, whether private or public, and to make, execute, and deliver any assignment, or assignments, of any such shares of stocks, bonds, or other securities.

H. The power to conduct or participate in any business of any nature for and in the name of the Principal; execute partnership agreements and amendments thereto; incorporate, reorganize, merge, consolidate, recapitalize, sell, liquidate, or dissolve any business; elect or employ officers, directors, and agents; carry out the provisions of any agreement for the sale of any business interest or the stock therein; and exercise voting rights with respect to stock, either in person or by proxy, and exercise stock options.

I. The power to enter any safe deposit box rented by the Principal, and to remove all or any part of the contents thereof, and to surrender or relinquish said safe-deposit box. Any institution in which any such safe-deposit box may be located shall not incur any liability to the Principal or the Principal's estate as a result of permitting the Agent to exercise the powers herein granted.

J. The power to make outright gifts of cash or property to adults or to minors in custodial form under an applicable Gifts to Minors Act, in amounts not to exceed the amount established by the Internal Revenue Service for individual annual gifts to each adult or minor donee in any calendar year. Permissible donees hereunder shall include my partner, any of my children or stepchildren and their descendants, or any descendant of a brother or sister of mine or of any person to whom I shall have been married, as well as any person who shall be married to any of the foregoing.

K. The power to convey or assign any cash or other property of which the Principal shall be possessed to the trustee or trustees of any trust that the Principal may have created, provided that such trust is subject to revocation by the Principal, which power shall be exercisable hereunder by the Agent.

L. The power to purchase United States Government Bonds known as "Flower Bonds," which may be used in payment of death taxes from the Principal's estate.

M. Subject to the provisions of section 1 above, the power to appoint a substitute or alternate agent and attorney-in-fact, who shall have all powers and authority of the Agent.

N. **INSERT LANGUAGE CONCERNING THE PRINCIPAL'S DOMESTIC PETS, IF NECESSARY.**

8. **Limitation of Power of Agent.** Regardless of any other provision of this General Power of Attorney, the Agent shall have no rights or powers hereunder with respect to any act, power, duty, right or obligation relating to any person, matter, transaction or property held or possessed by me as a trustee, custodian, personal representative or other fiduciary capacity. In addition, the Agent shall have no power or right to perform any of the following functions:

_____

_____

9. **Ratification.** I hereby ratify, acknowledge and declare valid all acts performed by the Agent on my behalf before the effective date of this General Power of Attorney.

10. **Revocation and Termination.** This General Power of Attorney is revocable by me, provided that insofar as any governmental agency, bank, depository, trust company, insurance company, other corporation, transfer agent, investment banking company or other person who shall rely upon this power, this power may be revoked only by a notice in writing executed by me and delivered to such person or institution.

This General Power of Attorney shall not be revoked or otherwise become ineffective in any way by the mere passage of time, but rather shall remain in full force and effect until revoked by me in writing.

I hereby revoke all general powers of attorney previously executed by me, if any, and the same shall be of no further force or effect. However, I do not intend in this General Power of Attorney to affect, modify or terminate any special, restricted or limited power or powers of attorney previously granted by me in connection with any banking, borrowing or commercial transaction.

11. **Construction.** This General Power of Attorney is executed and delivered in the State of _____, and the laws of the State of _____ shall govern all questions as to its validity and as to the construction of its provisions. This instrument is to be construed and interpreted as a general durable power of attorney. The enumeration of specific powers is not intended to limit or restrict the general powers granted to the Agent in this instrument.

12. **Reliance.** Third parties may rely upon the representations of the Agent as to all matters related to any power granted to the Agent in this instrument, and no person who acts in reliance upon the representation of the Agent shall incur any liability to me or my estate by permitting the Agent to exercise any power. Third parties may rely upon a photocopy of this executed General Power of Attorney to the same extent as if the copy were an original of this instrument.

IN WITNESS WHEREOF, I have executed this Durable General Power of Attorney on the _____ day of _____ 20___.

_____, ,
PRINCIPAL

State of _____
County of _____

_____, the Principal, executed and acknowledged this Springing Durable Power of Attorney for Finances before me this _____ day of _____, 20___.

_____
Notary Public

Form #7
Notice of Revocation of Power of Attorney

I, _____, of _____,

City of _____, County of _____,

State of _____, hereby give notice that I have

revoked, and do hereby revoke, the power of attorney dated _____,

given to _____ (name of attorney in fact),

empowering said _____, to act as my true and

lawful attorney in fact, and I declare that all power and authority granted under

said power of attorney is hereby revoked and withdrawn.

DATED: _____   _____
                                         Signature of Principal

WITNESSES:

_____ Residing at _____

_____ Residing at _____

State of _____
County of _____

On this _____ day of _____, 20__, _____ personally appeared before me and executed this document in my presence.

_____
Notary Public

Form #8
Authorization to Release Health Insurance and/or Medical Records Protected Under the Health Information Portability and Accountability Act (HIPAA)

I, _____, am the patient and I authorize the disclosure and use of the designated health information as listed on this form. I authorize the custodian of this health information to permit the person or persons named in this form to review or inspect the health information. I also authorize the custodian of the HIPAA protected health information to provide copies of the information to the named person or persons if requested to do so.

DOB: _____
Patient's Social Security No. _____

Provide as specific and explicit description of the information to be released, including the date and place of service if applicable:
_____
_____
_____
_____

I authorize the following healthcare provider or custodian of records to release and disclose the described health information: _____
_____

I authorize the healthcare provider or records custodian to release and disclose the health information to my designee: _____.

This request is for the following purpose(s):
___ Personal injury litigation   ___ Other pending litigation
___ Medical malpractice litigation   ___ Other (describe):
_____
_____

My designee ___ is ___ is not authorized to disclose the described health information to others.

I have the right to revoke this Authorization, in writing, at any time by notifying the person named as my designee to request the information. I shall also notify any healthcare provider or records custodian named on this form. Any revocation shall be prospective in nature and shall not affect any actions taken by the designee or healthcare provider or records custodian prior to the date those persons or entities received the written revocation.

My healthcare provider cannot require me to sign this Authorization as a condition of providing medical treatment or continuing to provide medical treatment.

This Authorization expires on: _____, or when the following event occurs: _____

_____ _____
Signature of Patient/Authorized Representative   Date

Authority of Representative:
___ Patient is a minor and I am the patient's parent and natural guardian.

___ Patient is a minor and I am the patient's guardian appointed by:
_____

___ Patient is a ward; I am the patient's guardian, appointed by:
_____

___ Patient is deceased. I am the patient's domestic partner, surviving spouse, executor or administrator of the patient's estate appointed by:
_____

___ I am the patient's agent, designated in the patient's Health Care Power of Attorney

___ I am the patient's attorney in fact, with the power to make the foregoing request under the terms of the patient's Durable General Power of Attorney and/or Durable Power of Attorney for Finances   ___ Other:
_____

IN WITNESS WHEREOF, personally executed this HIPAA Release on the _____ day of _____, 20___.

_____,
Principal

State of _____
County of _____

_____, the Principal, personally appeared before me and executed and acknowledged this Durable Power of Attorney for Finances before me this _____ day of _____, 20_____.

_____
Notary Public

This Authorization to Release Health Information and/or Medical Records is meant to conform to the requirements of a valid authorization as set forth in the Standards for Privacy of Individually Identifiable Health Information (the HIPAA Privacy Rule), 45 C.F.R. PARTS 160 and 164. Section 164.508 describes these requirements.

A PHOTOCOPY OR FACSIMILE OF THIS AUTHORIZATION SHALL HAVE THE SAME EFFECT AS THE ORIGINAL DOCUMENT.

Form #9
Nomination of Guardian for Estate and Person of a Minor Child

Contributed by:

Susan M. Murray
Attorney at Law
Langrock Sperry & Wool, LLP
111 S. Pleasant Street
P. O. Box 351
Middlebury, VT 05753-0351
802.388.6356 (v)
802/388.6149 (f)
smurray@langrock.com

I, _____, am the natural mother/father of the minor child, _____, who was born on _____, hereby make the following nomination of a legal guardian of the person and property of my minor child, in the event I am unable, physically or mentally, to care for my child.

I

In the event I become unable to care for my minor child, it is my desire, and I hereby nominate, my friend, companion and life partner, _____, currently residing in _____, _____, to be the legal guardian of the person and property of my minor child, _____. He/She is to serve without having to post a bond.

This nomination is based on the fact that a loving and parental relationship exits between _____ and _____. Furthermore, my minor child, _____, has lived with this adult and looks to her for guidance, support and affection. It would be detrimental to my child, _____, to deprive him/her of this established relationship at a time when I am unable to provide the security and care necessary to my child's health development. It is in the child's best interest that _____ be named the guardian of my minor child. It is my strong belief that it would be in _____'s best interests to be placed in the care and custody of _____ notwithstanding the interest or availability of each and every one of my family members so to act as guardian.

    I have chosen _____ as _____'s guardian because he/she is the person most suitable and capable of helping and guiding _____. I believe that _____ can and will provide a warm, stable and loving home for my child, and care for him/her and teach him/her with understanding and love.

    I have given this matter long and careful contemplation before choosing any guardian for my child. I have considered each of my family members as well as close friends as possible guardians. After long and thoughtful reflection, for all of the above reasons, I firmly believe that it will be in _____'s best interests that _____ be named guardian of the person and estate (property) of my minor child in the event of my disability.

II

    In the event that _____ is unable to serve as guardian or is disqualified by a Court of law from serving, I nominate _____ to serve as the guardian of the person and property of my child, _____.

III

    [Both the identity and whereabouts of the minor child's natural father are unknown to me.]

OR

    [The minor child was conceived through alternative insemination by an anonymous donor and has no natural father.]

OR

[The minor child was conceived through alternative insemination by donor. Said donor waived, in writing, any and all rights he may have to object to my nomination of a guardian.]

I have purposefully not nominated my parents or siblings to be the guardians of my child in the even of my disability. It is my belief that they lack an established, close and warm relationship with my child. I believe it would be detrimental to _____ to remove him/her from _____ and place him/her with adults who are, for all practical purposes, stranger.

IN WITNESS WHEREOF, I have hereunto signed my name this _____ day of _____, 20___.

_____
Client's Name

WITNESSES

_____ executed this document, consisting of _____ pages in our presence. At his/her request, and in his/her presence, we have hereunto subscribed our names as attesting witness thereto. Each of us declares that _____ appears to be of sound mind and free from duress or undue influence at the time he/she signed this document. He/She affirmed that he/she is aware of the nature of the document and signed it freely and voluntarily.

_____ Residing at _____

_____ Residing at _____

State of _____

County of _____

At _____, _____ on the ___ day of 20__, _____ personally appeared before me. He/She acknowledged this instrument, by him/her sealed and subscribed, to be his/her free act and deed.

_____
Notary Public

Form #10
Parental Consent to Authorize Medical Treatment of Minor

I/We, _____ is/are the parent(s) of: _____, born (state DOB for each minor child)_____.
I/We am/are placing my/our child(ren) into the care of _____ during our absence. I/We authorize _____, to consent to any medically necessary X-ray, examination, anesthetic, medical or surgical diagnosis or treatment and hospital care recommended for the benefit of my/our child(ren). Such medical care is to be rendered to said child under the care, supervision and advice of a physician or other medical care provider licensed to practice medicine in any sate in the United States. I/We further authorize _____, to consent to any X-ray, examination, dental or surgical diagnosis or treatment and hospital care to be rendered to my/our minor child(ren) by a dentist licensed to practice dentistry in any state in the United States.

This authority shall be valid from _____ to _____, 20__. Executed this _____ day of _____, 20__ at _____, _____.

_____
Parent's Signature

_____
Parent's Signature

State of _____
County of _____

On _____, 20__, _____

_____, personally appeared before me and executed this document. WITNESS my hand and official seal.

_____
Notary Public

Form #11

Authorization to Consent to Medical, Surgical or Dental Examination or Treatment of a Minor and Authorization to Deal With Minor's School

Contributed by:

Susan M. Murray
Attorney at Law
Langrock Sperry & Wool, LLP
111 S. Pleasant Street
P. O. Box 351
Middlebury, VT 05753-0351
802.388.6356 (v)
802/388.6149 (f)
smurray@langrock.com

  I, _____, being the mother of _____, a minor child, do hereby authorize, _____ of _____, _____, to consent to any x-ray examination, anesthetic, medical or surgical diagnosis or treatment and hospital care to be rendered to said minor child under the general and/or special supervision and up on the advice of a physician and/or surgeon licensed to practice medicine in any state of the United States, or to consent to any x-ray, examination, anesthetic, dental or surgical diagnosis or treatment and hospital care to be rendered to said minor child by a dentist licensed to practice dentistry in any state of the United States.

  I direct any hospital, medical staff or physician treating said minor child to give to _____ the same priority in visitations that would be extended to me as said minor child's mother in the event that said minor child is a patient in any hospital or other health care facility.

I authorize any school, day care or similar institution providing services to me for my minor child, _____, to release any and all records, information or documentation relating to said minor child to

_____.

I further direct such school, day care or institution to accept _____'s signature or consent in lieu of mine with regard to parental authorization to enable said minor child to take part in outside or in-school activities or day care activities, to sign for report cards or similar notices, to provide notice of said minor child's absence from school and the like. I further authorize these acts as the sole physical and legal custodian of said minor child under the laws of the State of _____.
In the event of emergency, I direct that the school, day care or institution make a reasonable effort to contact _____ and me immediately.

I further direct that in a medical emergency the school, day care or other institution has my permission to send said minor child immediately to a hospital with a trauma center which is reasonable close to the place where such medical emergency took place.

I declare that any act lawfully done or authorized hereunder by _____ shall be binding on myself, my heirs, legal and personal representatives, and assigns. I agree for myself, my heirs and assigns to same harmless and indemnify all persons, hospitals, agencies and/or institutions acting in reasonable reliance on the authority herein conferred.

IN WITNESS WHEREOF, I have hereunto signed my name this ____ day of _____, 20__ at _____, _____.

_____
CLIENT'S NAME

State of _____

County of _____

At _____, _____ on the ___ day of 20__, _____ personally appeared before me. He/She acknowledged this instrument, by him/her sealed and subscribed, to be his/her free act and deed.

_____
Notary Public

Form #12
Domestic Partnership Agreement (Complex)

AGREEMENT, made this _____ day of _____, 20__, between _____, residing at _____ (hereinafter referred to as "_____") and _____, residing at _____, hereinafter referred to as "_____").

WHEREAS, the parties intend to establish a domestic partnership and raise children together, and desire to set forth their agreements and expectations regarding their financial, property and other rights and obligations arising out of the contemplated domestic partnership; and,

WHEREAS, by execution of this Agreement, the parties hereby revoke and nullify any and all written agreements previously executed by either or both parties; this Domestic Partnership Agreement superceded any and all previously executed or unexecuted Domestic Partnership Agreements between the parties;

NOW, THEREFORE, in consideration of the mutual promises and agreements herein contained, the parties hereto agree as follows:

1. <u>Separate Property of Each Party</u>

The parties wish to identify what will remain the separate property of each party during the domestic partnership, and to determine their rights in the event of a separation or dissolution of their domestic partnership, as hereinafter discussed.

The following shall constitute and remain the "separate property" of the respective parties: (a) property, whether real or personal, and whether vested, contingent or inchoate, belonging to or acquired by a party prior to the contemplated domestic partnership of the parties, including without limitation the property listed on Schedules A-1 and A-2; (b) all property acquired by a party at any time by bequest, devise, inheritance, distribution from a trust, or by gift; (c) salary, wages and other compensation for personal services; (d) retirement and pension benefits; (e) compensation for personal injuries; (f) proceeds of insurance policies received from any sources; (g) the increase in value of such property, whether or not such increase in value is due in whole or in part to the contributions or efforts of the other party; (h) rents, issues, profits, dividends, interest or other income derived from other distributions upon such property; (i) the proceeds of the sale of such property; (j) property acquired in exchange for such property or acquired with the proceeds of the sale of such property; (k) any other property identified or defined as separate property elsewhere in this Agreement; and (l) any assets or property acquired at any time by either party in their singular name, or jointly with another person. It is the agreement of the parties that unless property is denoted in this Agreement as joint property, it shall be considered separate property. Except as otherwise expressly provided in this Agreement, or by way of an addendum to this Agreement, each party shall be responsible for his/her own debts, unless a debt was undertaken in a joint manner, as evidenced by the documents creating such debt. Each party hereby indemnifies and holds harmless the other for any debt incurred by the party that is not a joint debt.

Except as otherwise expressly provided in this Agreement, each party shall keep and retain sole ownership, enjoyment, control and power of disposal of his/her separate property of every kind and nature, now owned or hereafter acquired by such party, free and clear of any interest, rights or claims of the other party by reason of the domestic partnership or otherwise. These rights include the right to dispose of his/her separate property by gift, sale, testamentary transfer or in any other manner, and to encumber, pledge or hypothecate such property.

Each party covenants and agrees not to make any claim or demand on the separate property of the other party or on the heirs, legal representatives, executors or administrators of the other party with respect to the separate property of the other party, except as otherwise may be expressly provided in this Agreement.

If the parties commingled their separate property to acquire new property, the interests of the parties in this new property shall be separate property interests in proportion to their original contributions to the acquisition of such property.

Except as otherwise expressly provided in this Agreement, the separate property now or hereafter owned by one party can become joint or the property of the other party only by a written instrument reclassifying the property for purposes of this Agreement executed by the party whose separate property is thereby reclassified. No acts, conduct or statements by either party shall change the status of separate property, other than an instrument executed by the party whose separate property is thereby reclassified.

No contribution by either party to the care, maintenance, improvement, custody or repair of the separate property of the other party, whether such contributions are in the form of money, property or personal services rendered, shall in any way after or convert any of such separate property, or any increase in the value thereof, to the status of joint property. Any contributions by either party to the care, maintenance, improvement, custody or repair of the separate property of the other party shall become part of the separate property of the other party and the contributing party shall not have any claim for reimbursement. No use by either party of earnings or other separate property for joint or household expenses shall be construed to imply joint ownership of such assets.

Each party agrees, upon request, to cooperate with the other in connection with procuring loans secured by the other party's separate property, including the execution of instruments waiving all rights with respect to the other's separate property. The party owning the separate property shall indemnify and hold the party requested to execute such instruments harmless from and against any liability with respect thereto. Any proceeds derived from loans secured by a party's separate property shall be said party's separate property.

2. <u>Joint Property</u>

The parties recognize that they may from time to time acquire property in their joint names. This may include, for example, sums deposited into bank accounts in their joint names and stock and bond portfolios, certificates of deposit and money market funds in their joint names.

Title to any and all savings accounts, certificates of deposit, money market certificates, cash reserve accounts, money management accounts, stocks, bonds, savings plans, securities or any other funds or assets of the same or a similar nature (other than joint checking accounts) acquired jointly by both of the parties during the domestic partnership shall be placed in the names of both parties hereto in such manner that such assets may not be withdrawn or disposed of without the signatures of both parties thereto.

3. <u>Gifts</u>

All gifts given to the parties jointly shall be the joint property of the parties. Any gifts given from one party to the other prior to or during the domestic partnership shall be considered the separate property of the recipient of the gift, unless the party making the gift specifies that the property is to be the joint property of the parties. Such specification shall be in writing and attached to this Domestic Partnership Agreement as an Attachment.

4. <u>General Living Expenses</u>

The day-to-day living expenses of the parties, such as normal expenses for food, clothing and entertainment shall be paid by the parties in such proportions as they from time to time may agree upon in light of the then available resources of each party.

5. <u>Joint Checking Account</u>

The parties shall establish a joint checking account from which either party may withdraw funds for the payment of household and other joint living expenses, including living expenses of the child(ren). The parties shall contribute funds to this checking account as they from time to time may agree in light of the available resources and income of each party.

The funds in this checking account, and property purchased using these funds, shall be the joint property of the parties. This checking account is for the convenience of the parties, and the amounts deposited in the account are not intended to reflect the actual cost of living of either or both of the parties.

6. <u>The Parties' Residence</u>

_____ and _____ are the owners of a house known as _____ (primary residence). Said primary residence is encumbered by a mortgage and the principal balance presently outstanding is approximately $_____.

It is the intention of the parties to reside in said primary residence with their children.

The expenses of ownership of the primary residence, including without limitation utilities, homeowners' insurance, real estate taxes, maintenance and ordinary repairs, shall be paid by the parties in such proportions as they from time to time may agree upon in light of the then available resources of each party.

If, during the domestic partnership, the primary residence is sold and another residence is purchased in its place, the substitute residence shall be treated in the same manner under this Agreement as the primary residence for which it was substituted, unless the parties otherwise agree in a written instrument amending this Agreement.

The furniture, furnishings and other household effects in the primary residence shall be the joint property of the parties, with the exception of items which were the pre-domestic partnership separate property of either party and art, antiques or collectibles acquired as separate property of either party.

7. <u>Other Real Estate</u>

The parties from time to time may own real property other than the primary residence. If a party acquires such property in his/her sole name, it shall be said party's separate property for purposes of this Agreement. If the parties acquire such property as tenants in common, the interests of each party shall be separate property interests in the proportions set forth in the deed. If the parties acquire such property as joint tenants with rights of survivorship, it shall be joint property. The rights of the parties with respect to such property shall be governed by this Agreement unless they agree to some other treatment of such property in a written instrument amending this Agreement.

8. <u>Pensions</u>

Any pension plans of either party, heretofore or hereafter created, shall be and shall remain separate property of such party, free from any claim of the other party, notwithstanding the domestic partnership of the parties. Any pension plans that are the separate property of a party shall not be subject to equitable distribution and shall not be considered assets to which the other party would be entitled to share in, unless, in the event of death, the other party is designated on the pension plan documents as a beneficiary.

As used herein, "pension plan" shall mean any kind of pension plan, 401(k) plan, retirement plan, profit sharing plan, employee benefit plan or any other form of deferred compensation to which a party may be entitled because of his/her employment or work. References to a party's pension plan shall be deemed to include all monies held in such party's pension plan or thereafter added to or accumulated in that pension plan, and any increments, accretions or increases in the value of such pension plan, and any other rights such party has to the pension plan or such monies.

9. <u>Children</u>

It is the intention of the parties to have or adopt one or more children during the domestic partnership. It is the intention of the parties that during their domestic partnership, when one partner has a child, that partner will consent to the other partner's undertaking of any and all steps to adopt that child.

It is the intention of each party to create an irrevocable life insurance trust that will be funded by their separate funds, and that will provide for the maintenance of the surviving partner, if the domestic partnership is still in effect at the time the other partner dies. Regardless of the status of the domestic partnership, the irrevocable life insurance trust will provide for the maintenance, health, education and welfare of the parties' child(ren). The parties agree that each will continue to fund their own irrevocable life insurance trust until such time the life insurance policy has been paid in full or the youngest child reaches the age of twenty-five. The parties hereby agree that all indicia of life insurance shall be set forth in Schedule C, attached hereto.

10. Termination of the Domestic Partnership

The parties recognize that it is in their best interests to set forth their agreement as to their respective rights in the event of a termination of their domestic partnership by separation or dissolution of their domestic partnership.

The parties agree that the value of the primary residence and/or any other property that is owned jointly or by another entity whereby both are beneficiaries or own an equitable interest, shall be determined by obtaining a current appraisal from the lending institution that possesses a mortgage on the property. If either party feels the lending institution's appraisal is inaccurate, then a second appraisal will be obtained at the cost of the party seeking another appraisal. Both appraisals will be averaged and that average shall be the price the parties will use to determine the fair market value of the property.

The parties intend to agree upon which party will be able to remain in the primary residence, depending upon a variety of factors, the most important factor being the best interest of their child(ren). To exercise the option to purchase the primary residence one party (the Proposed Buyer) must give the other party (the Proposed Seller) written notice of her election to purchase the Proposed Seller's interest within 90 days after termination of the domestic partnership. Termination of the domestic partnership shall be considered as written notice defined herein. If the parties cannot agree upon which party will remain in the primary residence, the primary residence will be placed with a real estate broker at listing price of the fair market value as determined by the method set forth above.

If practicable, the closing of title shall take place on a date not more than 60 days after the fair market value of the primary residence is determined. At the closing of title, the Proposed Buyer shall pay the amount due to the Proposed Seller and the Proposed Seller shall deliver good and clear title, free from encumbrances and any documents that may be necessary or appropriate to transfer all of his/her right, title and interest in the primary residence to the Proposed Buyer.

If either party elects to purchase the interest of the other party in the primary residence, the party who so elects shall also simultaneously purchase the interest of the other party in the jointly owned furniture, furnishings and other household effects of the residence for the fair market value of such interest.

If neither party exercises the aforesaid options, the primary residence shall be promptly listed for sale with a broker mutually agreeable to the parties. The parties shall jointly agree to the listing price. If the parties cannot agree, then the average of the appraisals discussed earlier in this section shall be used to determine the listing price.

If the primary residence does not sell at the listing price within a reasonable period of time, said price shall be reduced until the residence is sold. A reasonable period of time is agreed upon to be six to eight months. The parties agree that the reduction in price will begin at five percent of the listing price. The reduction will continue in increments of five percent until the primary residence is sold.

The net proceeds from the sale of the primary residence, after deducting for all related expenses in connection with the sale, shall be divided equally between the parties. Any liens and encumbrances levied against the primary residence as the result of a debt owed by either party shall be paid by that party with his/her own separate assets prior to the passing of title to the Proposed Buyer.

In the event of the termination of the domestic partnership, the parties shall have joint legal custody of any minor children of the parties. It is the expectation of the parties, however, that the children will reside predominantly with their respective birth or legal parent, [however, the other party shall have frequent and meaningful contact/parenting time with the child(ren).]
Each party agrees to pay reasonable amounts, in light of his/her available income and resources, for the support of any minor children of the parties, at a minimum, in an amount that is set forth in the current child support guidelines of the state in which the parties reside. The parties agree to consult and negotiate in good faith regarding the children's education, visitation, payment of medical expenses and other issues that may arise regarding the children in the event of the termination of the domestic partnership.

In the event of the termination of the domestic partnership any joint property acquired by the parties during the domestic partnership shall be divided equally between the parties, notwithstanding the percentage contribution each party may have made to acquire of create such property.

The parties recognize that some items of joint property, such as tangible personal property, cannot be readily divided into shares. If the parties cannot agree on the division of any such items or the fair compensation that one party should pay to the other for his/her share of such items, such items shall be sold so that the proceeds of sale may be divided equally.

Each party hereby irrevocably waives, releases and relinquishes any and all claims or rights that he/she now or hereafter might otherwise have to or against the separate property now owned or hereafter acquired by the other party. This includes, without limitation, laws relating to equitable distribution, marital property, community property, curtesy, dower or any other interest or right of distribution of property by reason of domestic partnership, cohabitation, union or marriage. Each party recognizes that this waiver includes rights he/she might otherwise have or acquire in the future under the laws of the state in which the parties resided at the time the domestic partnership terminated.

As used herein, the term "termination of the domestic partnership" shall mean either party sending the other party written notice of their intent to terminate the domestic partnership.

Notice shall be sent by first class mail, certified mail or any other form of mailing by which confirmation of delivery can be ascertained. Notice shall be sent to the party's current residence where that person normally receives mail or to the party's last known address.

11. Death of the Parties

The parties recognize that it is in their best interests to set forth their Agreement as to their respective rights upon the death of either party during the domestic partnership.

All jointly owned property shall pass in accordance with the laws of the state in which the property is located. Title to property held jointly with rights of survivorship will pass to the survivor in accordance with state law.

Each party retains sole control over his/her separate property. Each party shall have the right to dispose of that separate property either by will or inter vivos or in accordance with the rules of intestate succession of the state in which the decedent was domiciled.

Nothing in this Agreement shall restrict the right of either party to bequeath or give property to the other party. If either party should provide that the other party shall receive property, as a bequest or gift under his/her last will and testament or otherwise, including without limitation life insurance proceeds, pension or profit sharing plan benefits and assets held as joint tenants with rights of survivorship, such other party shall have the right to receive such property. The parties agree, however, that no promises of any kind have been made by either of them to the other with respect to any such bequest or gift.

The obligations set forth in this Article 11 shall terminate and cease to be binding in the event of the termination of the domestic partnership by separation or dissolution of their domestic partnership or annulment, except separate property shall always remain separate property.

If, upon the death of either party, an action for separation or dissolution of their domestic partnership or annulment has been commenced but a judgment has not been entered, any rights of the surviving party to share in the estate of the deceased party shall be extinguished and the surviving party shall be entitled to receive from the decedent's estate only what the surviving party would have been entitled to pursuant to the Agreement had a judgment of separation or dissolution of their domestic partnership been entered.

12. Full Disclosure

A copy of the parties' current net worth statement is attached hereto as Schedule B. The parties affirm that the contents of the net worth statement are accurate and true.

Each party has made independent inquiry, to his/her own satisfaction, into the complete financial circumstances of the other, and acknowledges that he/she is fully informed of the income, assets and financial prospects of the other.

[Neither of the parties has been previously married. Neither of the parties has living children.]

13. Legal Representation

The parties acknowledge that they have retained and have been represented by separate and independent legal counsel of their own choosing in connection with the negotiation of this Agreement. _____ consulted with Attorney _____. _____ consulted with Attorney _____. Each has been separately and independently advised regarding this Agreement including the rights waived or otherwise released herein.

14. <u>Notices</u>

Any notice, demand or other communication required or permitted under this Agreement shall be in writing and shall be delivered by hand or by Federal Express courier or by certified or registered mail, return receipt requested, to a party at his/her address stipulated above or at such other address as the party may designate.

15. <u>General Provisions</u>

This Agreement is entire and complete and embodies all understandings and agreements between the parties. All prior understandings, agreements, conversations, communications, representations, correspondence and other writings are merged into this instrument, which alone sets forth the understanding and agreement of the parties.

Each party acknowledges that all of the matters embodied in this Agreement, including all terms, covenants, conditions, waivers, releases and other provisions contained herein, are fully understood by each; that this Agreement is fair, just and reasonable; that each party is entering into this Agreement freely, voluntarily and after due consideration of the consequences of doing so; and that this Agreement is valid and binding upon each party.

This Agreement and each provision thereof shall not be amended, modified, discharge, waived or terminated except by a writing executed by the party sought to be bound. Failure of a party to insist upon strict performance of any provision of this Agreement shall not be construed as a waiver of any subsequent default of the same or similar nature, nor shall it affect the parties' rights to require strict performance of any other portion of this Agreement. Any waiver by either party of any provision of this Agreement, or of any right or option hereunder shall not be deemed a continuing waiver and shall not prevent such party from thereafter insisting upon the strict performance or enforcement of such provision, right or option.

The parties agree that each of them, upon request of the other party or the legal representatives of the other party, shall execute and deliver such other and further instruments as may be necessary or appropriate to effectuate the purposes and intent of this Agreement. Each party, upon request of the other, shall execute and deliver a confirmation that this Agreement remains in full force and effect.

This Agreement and all rights and obligations of the parties hereunder shall be governed by and construed in accordance with the laws of the State of _____. The laws of the State in which the parties reside with their child(ren) shall govern irrespective of whether either or both of the parties heretofore or hereafter reside or are domiciled in any other jurisdiction and irrespective of whether any property is located in any other jurisdiction. If any provision of this Agreement should be held to be invalid or unenforceable under the laws of any State, county or other jurisdiction in which enforcement is sought, the remainder of this Agreement shall continue in full force and effect.

This Agreement shall be binding upon and shall inure to the benefit of the parties hereto and their respective heirs, executors, administrators, successors and assigns.

IN WITNESS WHEREOF, the parties hereto have executed this Agreement on the date first written above, of his/her own free will and attests that neither is under the influence of any alcohol, drug or other substance that would affect the party's decision-making capability. Each party attests that he/she is competent to enter into this Agreement.

_____
Signature

_____
Signature

State of _____

County of _____

_____, the Principal, personally appeared before me and executed and acknowledged this Domestic Partnership Agreement before me this _____ day of _____, 20___.

_____
Notary Public

State of _____

County of _____

_____, the Principal, personally appeared before me and executed and acknowledged this Domestic Partnership Agreement before me this _____ day of _____, 20___.

_____
Notary Public

Form #13
Simple Domestic Partner Agreement Maintaining Separate Property

We, _____ and _____ make the following agreement:

1. We enter into this contract to set forth our rights and responsibilities to each other. [Recite the consideration for the contract.]

2. We intend to abide by the provisions of this agreement in the spirit of love, joy, cooperation and good faith.

3. We agree that all property owned by either of us, as of the date of this agreement, shall be considered to be and shall remain, the separate property of each. Neither of us will have any claim to the separate property of the other absent a written agreement transferring ownership. A list of our major items of separate property are attached and incorporated into this agreement.

4. Our individual income and any property accumulated from that income shall remain the separate property of the person earning the income. Neither of us shall have any claim to this separate property.

5. Each of us shall maintain separate bank accounts. This includes, checking, savings and credit card accounts.

6. Neither of us shall be liable or responsible for the individual debts incurred by the other in her/his own name.

7. We agree to be jointly responsible for all debts we enter into together.

8. We agree to equally divide all household and living expenses. This includes, but is not limited to: groceries, utilities, rent and daily household expenses.

9. We agree that there may be a need to maintain a joint bank account (checking or savings) for a specific purpose. In that event, we agree to contribute an equal amount to the bank account. Neither party will have the right to withdraw funds from that account without the permission and consent of the other.

10. We also agree that we may, at some time, agree to own property jointly. Any jointly held property ownership shall be reflected either in writing or on the title to said property. In the event we dissolve our domestic partnership, we provide that any jointly held property will be divided into equal shares, unless we provide otherwise in a written document.

11. Any property received by one of us through gift or inheritance remains the separate property of the recipient. The other party has no claim on that separate property unless provided for in a written instrument.

12. Neither of us has any rights to, nor any financial interest in, any real estate owned entirely or partially by the other person. This includes any real property accumulated before or during our relationship.

13. We agree that either party can terminate this contract by giving the other party a one-week written notice of that intent. If either of us seriously considers leaving the relationship we both agree to, at least, three counseling sessions with a professional counselor or therapist.

14. In the event that this relationship is terminated we agree to divide all jointly held property equally. Neither of us shall have any claim against the other for support, property or financial assistance.

15. We agree to resolve any dispute arising from this agreement through mediation. The mediator shall be an objective third party who is mutually agreed upon. The mediator's role shall be to help us dissolve our relationship and resolve any differences concerning a division of jointly held property or other issues in a mature and unemotional manner. We agree to enter into mediation in good faith.

16. In the event that our attempt at good-faith mediation is unsuccessful to resolve all issues in dispute, either party may seek to resolve the issues through arbitration through the use of the following protocol:

    (a) Deliver a written demand for arbitration to the other person and name one arbitrator;

    (b) The other party shall respond with the name of a second arbitrator within five days from receipt of the notice;

(c) The two named arbitrators shall select and name a third arbitrator;

(d) The arbitration meeting will take place within seven days following the selection of the third arbitrator;

(e) Each party is entitled to retain legal counsel at his/her own expense;

(f) Each party may present witnesses and evidence at the arbitration hearing;

(g) The arbitrators shall issue their decision within five days after the hearing. Their decision shall set forth their findings and conclusion and shall be in writing. The decision shall be binding upon each of us. We agree that neither party shall seek relief from the arbitration decision in court.

(h) If the person to whom an arbitration demand is made fails to respond within five days, the other party may give an additional five days written notice of his/her intent to proceed. If there is still no response, the person initiating the arbitration may proceed with the arbitration before an arbitrator he/she has designated. Any award shall have the same force and effect as if all three arbitrators had settled it.

17. This agreement represents our complete understanding concerning our domestic partnership. It replaces any and all prior agreements, written or oral. We agree that this document can only be amended in writing and must be signed by both of us.

18. We agree that, in the event a court finds any portion of this contract to be illegal or otherwise unenforceable, the remainder of the contract shall remain in full force and effect.

Signed this _____ day of _____, 20__ at _____,

_____.

_____	_____
Signature	Signature

State of _____

County of_____

_____ and _____, personally appeared before me and executed and acknowledged this Domestic Partnership Agreement before me this day of _____, 2003.

_____
Notary Public

Exhibit A:
  Separate Property of _____

Exhibit B.
  Separate Property of _____

Form #14
Simple Domestic Partner Agreement Sharing Most Property

We, _____ and _____ make the following agreement:

1. We enter into this contract to set forth our rights and responsibilities to each other.

2. We intend to abide by the provisions of this agreement in the spirit of love, joy, cooperation and good faith. [Specify the consideration for the contract].

3. We agree that all property owned by either of us, as of the date of this agreement, shall be considered to be and shall remain, the separate property of each. Neither of us will have any claim to the separate property of the other absent a written agreement transferring ownership. A list of our major items of separate property are attached and incorporated into this agreement.

4. Our individual income, earned while we are living together and during this relationship shall belong to both of us in equal shares. Likewise, all property accumulated from that income shall belong to both of us in equal shares. In the event we separate and/or terminate this domestic partnership we agree to divide all such accumulated property, in whatever form, equally between us.

5. We agree to maintain joint bank accounts. This includes checking and savings accounts. In the event we decide to obtain a joint credit card account we agree to be jointly liable for the credit card balance.

6. Neither party shall be responsible or liable for any credit card debt incurred by the other on his/her individual credit card accounts.

6. Neither of us shall be liable or responsible for the debts incurred by the other as an individual.

7. We agree to be jointly responsible for all joint debts and expenses.

8. We agree to equally divide all household and living expenses. This includes, but is not limited to: groceries, utilities, rent and daily household expenses.

9. We also agree that we may, at some time, agree to own real property jointly. Any jointly held real property ownership shall be reflected either in writing or on the title to said property. In the event we dissolve our domestic partnership, we provide that any jointly held property will be divided into equal shares, unless we provide otherwise in a written document.

10. Any property received by one of us through gift or inheritance remains the separate property of the recipient. The other party has no claim on that separate property unless provided for in a written instrument.

11. Neither of us has any rights to, nor any financial interest in, any separate real estate owned entirely or partially by the other person. This includes any real property accumulated before or during our relationship.

12. We agree that either party can terminate this contract by giving the other party a one-week written notice of that intent. If either of us seriously considers leaving the relationship we both agree to, at least, three counseling sessions with a professional counselor or therapist.

13. In the event that this relationship is terminated we agree to divide all jointly held property equally. Neither of us shall have any claim against the other for support, property or financial assistance.

14. We agree to resolve any dispute arising from this agreement through mediation. The mediator shall be an objective third party who is mutually agreed upon. The mediator's role shall be to help us dissolve our relationship and resolve any differences concerning a division of jointly held property or other issues in a mature and unemotional manner. We agree to enter into mediation in good faith.

15. In the event that our attempt at good-faith mediation is unsuccessful to resolve all issues in dispute, either party may seek to resolve the issues through arbitration through the use of the following protocol:

   (a) Deliver a written demand for arbitration to the other person and name one arbitrator;
   (b) The other party shall respond with the name of a second arbitrator within five days from receipt of the notice;

(c) The two named arbitrators shall select and name a third arbitrator;

(d) The arbitration meeting will take place within seven days following the selection of the third arbitrator;

(e) Each party is entitled to retain legal counsel at his/her own expense;

(f) Each party may present witnesses and evidence at the arbitration hearing;

(g) The arbitrators shall issue their decision within five days after the hearing. Their decision shall set forth their findings and conclusion and shall be in writing. The decision shall be binding upon each of us. We agree that neither party shall seek relief from the arbitration decision in court.

(h) If the person to whom an arbitration demand is made fails to respond within five days, the other party may give an additional five days written notice of his/her intent to proceed. If there is still no response, the person initiating the arbitration may proceed with the arbitration before an arbitrator he/she has designated. Any award shall have the same force and effect as if all three arbitrators had settled it.

16. This agreement represents our complete understanding concerning our domestic partnership. It replaces any and all prior agreements, written or oral. We agree that this document can only be amended in writing and must be signed by both of us.

18. We acknowledge that both of us have had the opportunity to consult with an attorney of our choice to review this document. We also acknowledge that each of us, as individuals, is responsible for consulting with an attorney. The failure or refusal of either or both of us to do so shall not be construed to mean this Domestic Partnership Agreement was not entered into willingly, freely and voluntarily by both of us.

17. We agree that, in the event a court finds any portion of this contract to be illegal or otherwise unenforceable, the remainder of the contract shall remain in full force and effect.

Signed this _____ day of _____, 20__ at _____, _____.

_____   _____
          Signature   Signature
State of _____

County of _____

_____ and _____, personally appeared before me and executed and acknowledged this Domestic Partnership Agreement before me this day of _____, 2003.

                              _____
                                       Notary Public

Exhibit A:
    Separate Property of _____

Exhibit B.
    Separate Property of _____

Exhibit C.
    Jointly Held Property of _____ **and** _____.

Form #15
Termination of Domestic Partnership

1. It is hereby agreed that _____ and _____, who have been domestic partners living together at (specify address, type of premises, apartment or house), shall separate and go their own way. At this time neither party has the intention of resuming their former domestic partnership arrangement.

2. It is also agreed that the each party shall retain complete and total control over his/her separate property, including any furnishings or furniture, the each brought into the relationship. A list of each party's separate property is attached hereto as Exhibit A.

3. It is further agreed that the items listed in Exhibit B were purchased and are owned jointly by the parties. The parties divided these items in a fair and equitable manner. Each party is entitled to complete and total control over the items listed under their respective names in Exhibit B.

4. The parties agree to dispose of any and all joint debts and other joint obligations in the following manner: [specify each creditor, amount owed, who will pay obligation, indemnification clause].

5. The parties also agree that [both of them are leaving the shared premises] or [that _____ is leaving the shared premises and _____ will remain in the shared premises. The one staying shall assume all responsibility for said premises from this date forward, except for any common debts incurred by the parties during their relationship. _____ will take whatever action is required to [remove _____'s name from the lease] or [refinance the mortgage].

6. The party who is leaving agrees not to reenter the premises without the remaining party's permission, nor will he/she remove any items from the premises without the other party's knowledge.

7. [Specify how jointly owned real estate is to be valued, listed and sold].

8. Neither party shall have any claim against the other party's business interests, pension or retirement funds, insurance proceeds, rights of inheritance or any other property not specifically described in this Agreement.

9. Neither party shall have a claim to compensation from the other for services rendered during the time they lived together, for financial support of any kind or for any other property, assets or money not described in this Agreement.

10. The parties agree to resolve any dispute arising from this agreement through mediation. The mediator shall be an objective third party who is mutually agreed upon. The mediator's role shall be to help the parties dissolve their relationship and resolve any differences concerning a division of jointly held property or other issues in a mature and unemotional manner. The parties agree to enter into mediation in good faith. [Parties agree to engage attorneys practicing collaborative law in order to resolve the issues involved in the termination of their relationship. Both parties understand that the collaborative process is engaged in with the specific intent to avoid litigation.]

11. In the event that the parties' attempt at good-faith mediation is unsuccessful to resolve all issues in dispute, either party may seek to resolve the issues through arbitration through the use of the following protocol:

- (a) Deliver a written demand for arbitration to the other person and name one arbitrator;
- (b) The other party shall respond with the name of a second arbitrator within five days from receipt of the notice;
- (c) The two named arbitrators shall select and name a third arbitrator;
- (d) The arbitration meeting will take place within seven days following the selection of the third arbitrator;
- (e) Each party is entitled to retain legal counsel at his/her own expense;
- (f) Each party may present witnesses and evidence at the arbitration hearing;

(g) The arbitrators shall issue their decision within five days after the hearing. Their decision shall set forth their findings and conclusion and shall be in writing. The decision shall be binding upon each party. The parties agree that neither one shall seek relief from the arbitration decision in court.

(h) If the person to whom an arbitration demand is made fails to respond within five days, the other party may give an additional five days written notice of his/her intent to proceed. If there is still no response, the person initiating the arbitration may proceed with the arbitration before an arbitrator he/she has designated. Any award shall have the same force and effect as if all three arbitrators had settled it.

12. Each party states that he/she entered into this Agreement freely, voluntarily, without fraud, duress, threats or coercion.

The parties, by signing below, indicate their intention to participate in this Agreement and the provisions set forth herein. Signed this ___ day of _____, 20__.

_____   _____
            Signature   Signature

State of _____

County of _____

_____ and _____, the Principals, personally appeared before me and executed and acknowledged this Termination of Domestic Partnership/Living Together Arrangement before me this _____ day of _____, 20__.

_____
        Notary Public

Form #16
Sample Shared Parenting Agreement

This agreement is made this ____ day of _____, 20__, by and between _____ and _____.

In consideration of the promises made to each other, and in consideration of our mutual contributions toward the [creation by in vitro fertilization; artificial insemination] or [adoption] of a child [born] or [adopted] on the ____ day of _____, 20__, and in acknowledgment that state law is unsettled in this area of parental rights, and in acknowledgment of the parties' mutual belief that the best interests of our child, _____, require stable sources of financial, academic, medical and emotional support, the parties enter into this Agreement to guarantee that their child will receive the full benefit of having each and both of the parties as parents, including current and future financial and emotional support, rights to inheritance and to guarantee that both _____ and _____ shall be considered natural and legal parents of _____.

Therefore, we agree as follows:

1. Each party acknowledges and agrees that they live together in a primary family relationship and have since _____. The parties further acknowledge that during the course of their relationship [_____ gave birth to _____ (child or children) on _____] or [they adopted _____ (child or children) on _____.]

2. The decision to have a child was a joint decision of the parties and was based on the commitment of each party to parent the child(ren) jointly. The parties acknowledge that both partners

have been primary parents and caregivers to the child(ren) since birth. It is our intent to raise this child [these children] together as a family unit.

3. Each party acknowledges and agrees that, while they now live together as a family, there may come a time when the parties no longer do so. In that event, the parties agree that they will continue to provide for their child(ren) as follows:

   a. Both parties will have joint custody of the child(ren).
   b. Both parties will take whatever action is necessary to obtain a shared parenting agreement from the court having jurisdiction over these matters.
   c. The child will spend approximately one-half of his/her time with each parent. Each parent shall share equally in the responsibility for the care of the child(ren) during school vacations or illness either by personally caring for the child(ren) or making arrangements for proper care.
   d. Each parent will pay one-half of the normal daily living expenses and costs of the child(ren) while they live together; or the entire cost of daily living expenses when the child(ren) is/are with each one, should they stop living together.
   e. Each parent shall claim the child(ren) as a dependent for tax purposes in alternate years. _____ shall claim the child(ren) during even numbered tax years and _____ during odd numbered tax years.
   f. Each parent shall maintain the child(ren) as a beneficiary(ies) of a life insurance policy in the minimum amount of _____ until the child(ren) shall attain the age of [majority] or [specify age].

4. Both parents acknowledge and agree that all major decisions regarding the physical location, support, education, medical care

and religious training of the child(ren) shall be made by them jointly.

5. Both parents agree that each will make a good faith effort to remain in _____ (name community) until the child(ren) complete high school. Neither parent may move out of the designated community without the prior written consent of the other parent. The other parent shall not unreasonably withhold such consent.

6. The parties agree that should a significant discrepancy occur in their respective net monthly income, following a separation, they will negotiate child support payments consistent with the child support schedule then in effect in their State of domicile.

7. Each parent agrees that, in the event either of them is no longer able to care and provide for the child(ren) because of death or legal disability, it will be in the best interests of the child(ren) to remain with the other parent. Neither parent will allow the child(ren) to be adopted by any other person so long as both parents are living.

8. Each parent agrees that any dispute pertaining to this Agreement will be resolved through mediation. The mediator shall be an objective third party who is mutually agreed upon. The mediator's role shall be to help us resolve any disputes, dissolve our relationship and/or resolve any differences concerning the child(ren). The parties agree to enter mediation in good faith. [Can include clause/provision concerning collaborative law efforts to resolve disputes in addition to, in lieu of, or as an alternative to mediation.]

9. In the event that the parties' attempt at good-faith mediation is unsuccessful to resolve all issues in dispute, either party may seek to resolve the issues through arbitration through the use of the following protocol:

(a) Deliver a written demand for arbitration to the other person and name one arbitrator;

(b) The other party shall respond with the name of a second arbitrator within five days from receipt of the notice;

(c) The two named arbitrators shall select and name a third arbitrator;

(d) The arbitration meeting will take place within seven days following the selection of the third arbitrator;

(e) Each party is entitled to retain legal counsel at his/her own expense;

(f) Each party may present witnesses and evidence at the arbitration hearing;

(g) The arbitrators shall issue their decision within five days after the hearing. Their decision shall set forth their findings and conclusion and shall be in writing. The decision shall be binding upon each of us. We agree that neither party shall seek relief from the arbitration decision in court.

(h) If the person to whom an arbitration demand is made fails to respond within five days, the other party may give an additional five days written notice of his/her intent to proceed. If there is still no response, the person initiating the arbitration may proceed with the arbitration before an arbitrator he/she has designated. Any award shall have the same force and effect as if all three arbitrators had settled it.

10. Each party understands that there are legal questions raised by the issues involved in this Agreement that are not yet settled by statute or prior court decisions. Notwithstanding the knowledge that certain clauses stated in this Agreement may be unenforceable in a court of law, the parties choose to enter into this Agreement to clarify their intent to jointly provide and nurture

their child(ren), even when they are no longer living together in a single family residence.

11. Specifically, the parties recognize that the current state of law regarding financial support of children may not obligate the non-legally recognized parent to provide support to the child(ren).

12. The parties also recognize that current law gives the natural/legal parent no enforceable right to collect support on behalf of the child(ren) from the other parent.

13. Notwithstanding the current state of the law regarding support each party agrees to support the minor child(ren) and to be bound by current and future support obligations for the child(ren) pursuant to the laws of the State in which the child is domiciled.

14. The parties intend that this Agreement create an enforceable right for either party to collect child support on behalf of the child(ren), including the right to request that support be extended beyond minority consistent with the child support laws of the State of domicile.

15. The parties agree to do everything legally possible to create a legal relationship between the child(ren) and the non-legally recognized parent, _____. This will be done for purposes of custody, visitation, support, inheritance, health care insurance and guardianship of the minor child(ren).

16. Each party agrees to leave at least one-half of his/her estate to the child(ren). If a trust is created for the child(ren), the trustor shall name the other parent as the trustee. Likewise, both parties agree to name the other as the child(ren)'s guardian in their respective wills. The parties agree to jointly decide on an alternate guardian of the child(ren).

17. The parties intend this Agreement to guide the Court should one become involved in determining the best interests of the child(ren). The parties agree that the Court shall have jurisdiction over any disputes arising during the child(ren)'s minority regarding custody, support or visitation.

18. The parties agree to participate in Court-ordered mediation concerning issues of custody or visitation and to be bound by court orders regarding the child(ren). Specifically, _____ agrees to be bound by a court order compelling him/her to pay support for the child(ren) or to have contact with the child(ren) on a set schedule. Likewise, _____, the natural parent, agrees to be bound by any court order granting visitation and/or joint custody to _____. Both parties agree that they will not raise legal arguments intended to interfere with the ongoing relationship between the other parent and the child(ren).

19. The parties agree to put aside any personal differences they may have with each other, in the event of their separation or termination of the relationship, in order to do what is in the best interests of the child(ren).

20. If either party contests the Court's jurisdiction over any dispute involving the child(ren), including custody, support, care or visitation, then that party may be stopped from defeating the Court's jurisdiction by reason of having accepted the benefits of the mutual promises contained in this Agreement. It either party contests the Court's jurisdiction over any issue involving the custody, care, support or visitation of the child(ren), and is successful in defeating the Court's jurisdiction, then that party shall be liable for liquidated damages in the amount of $_____ for each year that this Agreement was in

effect. The contesting party shall also be responsible for paying all costs and attorney fees incurred by the defending party.

21. Both parties agree that the Uniform Child Custody Jurisdiction Enforcement Act (UCCJEA) and the Parental Kidnapping Protection Act (PKPA) shall apply to any children we parent together and to any court order and to this agreement.

22. This Agreement contains the entire understanding of the parties. There are no promises, understandings, agreements or representations between them that are not reflected in this Agreement.

23. Each party agrees that he/she signed this Agreement voluntarily and freely, of his/her own volition, without any duress of any kind whatsoever.

24. Both parties acknowledge that legal counsel represented them in the discussions and negotiations that led to the creation of this Agreement. _____, Attorney at Law represented _____. And, _____, Attorney at Law represented _____. Each party acknowledges that he/she had legal advice prior to signing this Agreement and that each fully understands the terms of this Agreement.

IN WITNESS WHEREOF, the parties hereunto have executed this Agreement, on the ____ day of _____, 20__ in _____, _____.

Dated: _____ _____
                                             Signature

Dated: _____ _____
                                             Signature

State of _____

County of _____

_____ and _____, personally appeared before me and executed and acknowledged this Shared Parenting Agreement before me this day of _____, 20_____.

_____

Notary Public

Form #17
Memorandum of Understanding

This Memorandum is entered into on the date shown below between
_____("Husband") and
_____ ("Wife").

This Memorandum of Understanding sets forth the position of the Husband and Wife concerning the fact that _____ is transsexual/transgender. Both parties enter into this marriage with the full knowledge and understanding of that fact. Both parties enter into this marriage voluntarily and with full acceptance that _____ is transsexual/transgender.

I. Recitals

A. _____ and _____, upon their marriage, acknowledge that they have knowledge that _____ is transsexual/transgender.

B. Through this Memorandum, _____ and _____ intend to make clear that they both understand that _____ was identified as [male/female] at birth.

C. By entering into their marriage and through this Memorandum of Understanding, _____ and _____ intend to acknowledge their mutual understanding that _____ is legally [female/male].

D. Both parties acknowledge and accept the rights and responsibilities typically associated with marriage in _____, despite the fact that _____ is transsexual/transgender.

E. Both parties agree that if this marriage is dissolved, through divorce or dissolution, that neither party will make arguments, in or out of any litigation that are based on _____ being transsexual/transgender.

F. Neither party will deny the other's rights or their own responsibilities typically associated with marriage in _____ or challenge the validity of the marriage because _____ is transsexual/transgender.

G. Both parties having full knowledge that _____ is transsexual/transgender and they will be unable to conceive a child together.

H. Both parties agree that any child born during the marriage, by whatever means, will be considered the natural and legal child of both.

II. Representations and Waivers

A. Each party has in good faith fully disclosed all relevant information concerning _____ status as transsexual/transgender.

B. Both Husband and Wife have in good faith fully answered all questions presented by the other about _____ being transsexual/transgender and the possible effects of said status on their marriage in _____.

C. Neither party has any remaining questions about _____ being transsexual/transgender and the possible effects of said status on their marriage in _____.

D. Both parties recognizes that this Memorandum may alter legal rights each might otherwise have under _____ law.

E. Both parties, by signing this Memorandum of Understanding expressly waives all such rights whether known or unknown at the time of signing.

F. This memorandum takes effect at the time when a marriage license is issued.

G. The later invalidation of the marriage license or the ensuing marriage does not invalidate this agreement.

H. In the event that any provision of this Memorandum is deemed invalid or unenforceable, the remaining provisions are severable and remain effective.

I. Both parties agree that this is a binding legal contract between them, their heirs and assigns and acknowledge receipt of valid consideration for the rights waived and the rights, responsibilities and obligations that are inherent in the marital contract.

In witness thereof, the parties have entered into this agreement on:

_____   _____
         Date   Husband

_____   _____
         Date   Wife

State of _____

County of _____

_____ and _____, the Husband and Wife, personally appeared before me and executed and acknowledged this Memorandum of Understanding before me this _____ day of _____, 20___.

_____
Notary Public

Form #18
Confirmation of Ownership and Beneficiary Designations

[Insert into the Last Will and Testament.]

I may have certain accounts in specific financial institutions and/or other assets, including real estate, titled jointly with _____.

Title to these accounts and assets, wherever located, have been established in such form that they are transferable to _____ upon my death, if _____ survives me, and without the need for probate administration.

Through this clause, I intend to confirm _____'s absolute right to ownership in those accounts and assets at my death. _____'s entitlement to these accounts and assets is dependent upon _____ surviving me.

If any of those accounts or assets are in a form that presents any doubt as to whether _____ is the owner of the balance remaining in any account or assets at my death, I give the balances in such accounts and assets to _____, if he/she survives me.

I also confirm that all accounts, including any retirement or pension accounts and insurance policies owned or held by me at my death that name one or more beneficiaries are intended to pass to the named beneficiary or beneficiaries.

I specifically, and without limiting any of the previous language, confirm that any accounts or insurance policies in which I have named _____ as the beneficiary are his/her sole property.

Form #19
Definition

[Include in any Domestic Partnership Agreement]

"My partner" refers to _____, even if our relationship is not legally recognized by any applicable state law under which my estate or any portion of my estate is probated and/or administrated.

_____ shall not be deemed my heir under this Last Will and Testament if our relationship ends or is dissolved, whether through a court or by agreement of the parties.

If a legal dissolution of our relationship is not possible, the relationship shall be deemed dissolved upon receipt of written notice by either _____ or myself to the other of an intention to dissolve the relationship.

Form #20
Donor Insemination Agreement

This Agreement is made between _____, _____ and _____. The following agreement is entered willingly and voluntarily.

1. _____ agrees to donate [his sperm]/[her eggs] to _____ for the purpose of donor insemination. _____ will donate [his sperm]/[her eggs] once per month for the _____ months following the signing of this Agreement. If _____ does not conceive during this time the parties agree to discuss extending this agreement.

2. [Sperm donor] _____ agrees to coordinate his donation of sperm to coincide with _____'s monthly cycle [or as her doctor indicates]. He also agrees to permit his sperm donation to be frozen for later use at _____'s discretion.

2. [Egg donor] _____ agrees to coordinate her donation of ova with _____ and her doctor.

3. [_____ will pay _____ $1.00 each time he donates sperm. This shall constitute full and complete consideration for this contract.]

3. [_____ will pay _____ $1.00 each time she donates ova for _____'s benefit. This shall constitute full and complete consideration for this contract.]

4. _____ will pay for any medical expenses not covered by _____'s health insurance. This includes expenses incurred for a physical examination, blood screening, semen analysis, HIV screening and any other medically required examinations that occur before the first

donation of sperm. She will also reimburse _____ for any costs directly associated with office visits he makes to accomplish the sperm donation.

_____ also agrees to pay _____ transportation expenses that are limited to gas, toll charges, parking fees or public transportation fares. _____ agrees to submit receipts and a list of expenses within 14 days of incurring them.

5. _____ acknowledges he/she has been tested for HIV and other sexually transmitted diseases and received negative results. He/She acknowledges that he/she has used "safe sex" practices during the ____ months before signing this contract. He/She also agrees, as a requirement under this contract, to continue practicing "safe sex" during the term of this contract. He/She also agrees to notify _____ immediately if there is any possibility that he/she engaged in any unsafe sex practices. Such activity will be cause of _____ to immediately terminate this contract with no further liability on the part of any party.

6. All parties to this contract are single. None of them are presently involved in a legal marriage recognized by the State of _____. _____ and _____ are in a [committed relationship], [registered Domestic Partnership], [Civil Union] and intend to be the legal parents of any child or children born as a result of artificial insemination. Both _____ and _____ intend to seek legal recognition of their parental rights as soon as possible after the birth. This includes, but is not limited to _____ seeking to adopt the child.

_____ agrees to cooperate with any adoption petition or other legal action needed to confer legal parental recognition on _____.

7. _____ agrees to waive all rights to the child or children that may be bon as a result of this insemination. He makes this decision freely, voluntarily and with full knowledge that he will have no involvement in the child's life as a parent.

8. _____ agrees that he will not attempt, in any way, to establish a parent-child relationship with the child, that he will not seek legal recognition of his parental rights, that he will not seek custody or visitation with the child. He accepts and recognizes that he will have no parental rights concerning any child resulting from the insemination.

9. _____ will make all sperm donations to [a licensed medical doctor] or [a sperm bank]. [This shall be done to comply with any state law concerning anonymous sperm donations.]

10. _____ and _____ will have sole authority and responsibility to name any child born as a result of the inseminations.

_____'s name, as the sperm donor, will not be listed as "father" on the child's birth certificate.

11. Once their parental rights are established, _____ and _____ will have sole and complete authority to determine the child's upbringing, education, naming a guardian and providing all care.

_____ will have no claim on being named the child's guardian.

12. _____ relationship will be determined by the child's mothers. He will be considered a "family friend." _____ and _____ reserve the right to end all contact between _____ and the child if they, in their sole discretion, determine such action to be in the child's best interests.

13. If the child becomes curious its father, the mothers reserve the right, in their sole discretion, to tell the child about _____ and the method used to give birth. They will tell the child that _____ is the biological father and the sperm donor.

14. Any information given by the mothers to the child about its paternal history is solely for the benefit of the child and does not waive any provisions of this contract, nor grant _____ and parental rights or rights to custody or visitation.

15. _____ may/may not disclose his biological connection to any child that results from the insemination with his sperm. But, if he does disclose the information to his family or anyone else, he agrees not to assist any family member in any effort to establish contact with the child or to achieve any legal rights concerning the child. Any visitation between the child and _____'s family will be in the sole and complete discretion of _____ and _____.

16. _____ and _____ agree that they will be solely responsible for the financial needs of the child. They agree to hold _____ harmless for any support at any time. They also agree not to seek, either individually or jointly, any court-ordered child support. They, individually and jointly, agree to assist _____ should any person attempt to hold him responsible for child support.

17. The parties acknowledge that the law in the area of Artificial Reproductive Technology is not settled. They understand that this contract may not be enforceable in court. They enter into this contract in good faith and without hesitation or remorse.

18. Any dispute arising out of this contract shall be resolved through mediation. All parties agree to participate in mediation in good faith with the intent to resolve all differences. [If, after _____ sessions with the mediator, the parties have not resolved their dispute, they agree to submit the dispute to binding arbitration.] The parties will be jointly responsible for any mediation [or arbitration] expenses.

19. If mediation is unsuccessful, the parties agree to submit it to their friend, _____ to resolve the dispute. All parties agree to accept the decision reached by _____.

20. All parties are aware of their individual right to seek legal advice and counsel before signing this contract.

21. Any changes to this contract must be made in writing and signed by all parties.

22. If any provision in this contract is determined to be unenforceable, the remaining provisions will continue in full force and effect.

_____   _____
Date   (Sperm/Egg Donor)

_____   _____
Date   Birth Mother

_____   _____
Date   Other Mother

Form #21
For Transgender Individuals Entering into Heterosexual Marriage/Relationship

MEMORANDUM OF UNDERSTANDING

This Memorandum of Understanding is entered into on the date shown below between _____, Husband and _____, Wife.

Both parties acknowledge, by their signatures, the receipt of adequate consideration to bind them to the provisions of this Memorandum of Understanding.

RECITALS

A. The parties, upon entering into marriage, desire to establish that both have knowledge that _____ is transgender.

B. By entering into this Memorandum of Understanding, both parties wish to make clear that they understand that _____ was identified as [male/female] at birth.

C. By entering into this Memorandum of Understanding, both parties make clear that they both understand that _____ is [male/female].

D. By entering into this Memorandum of Understanding, both parties make clear that they each fully accept the rights and responsibilities typically associated with marriage in the State of _____, despite the fact that _____ is transgender.

E. Both parties agree that if this marriage is dissolved, neither party will make arguments based on _____ being transgender. And, neither party will deny the other's rights or their own responsibilities typically associated with marriage in the State of _____.

F. By entering into Memorandum of Understanding, both parties have full knowledge that because _____ is transgender they will be unable to conceive a child together. They also agree that any child or children born during this marriage will be considered the legal child of both parents. The parties further agree that they will assume all parental responsibilities, rights and obligations concerning the children. Neither party will take any action that will interfere with the parent-child relationship. Both parties agree that the child's or children's best interests are served by continuing the parent-child relationship even if the marriage is dissolved.

REPRESENTATIONS AND WAIVERS

A. Each party has, in good faith, fully disclosed all relevant information concerning _____'s status as transgender.

B. Each party has, in good faith, fully answered all questions presented by the other about _____'s status as transgender and the possible legal or emotional effect that status may have on their marriage.

C. Neither party has any remaining questions about _____'s transgender status and the possible legal or emotional effect it may have on their marriage.

D. The parties recognize that this Memorandum of Understanding may give them legal rights, responsibilities and obligations that might not exist under existing state and federal law.

E. By entering into this Memorandum of Understanding, each party expressly waives such rights. Each party also expressly waives any constitutional rights they may have to be the sole determinant of the best interests of any child or children born during this marriage.

F. This Memorandum of Understanding takes effect when the marriage license is issued.

G. Any later invalidation or dissolution of this marriage does not invalidate or dissolve this Memorandum of Understanding.

H. If any provision of this Memorandum of Understanding is determined to be invalid or unenforceable, the remaining provisions are severable and remain effective. But, both parties agree that they intended to enter into this Memorandum of Understanding even though there may be an argument that it is contrary to a State's professed public policy.

I. Both parties acknowledge that they have the opportunity to retain (or: have retained) independent counsel to explain their legal rights, responsibilities and obligations and the effect of this Memorandum of Understanding on them.

In Witness thereof: The parties have entered into this Memorandum of Understanding on the _____ day of _____, _____.

_____ _____
WIFE   HUSBAND

_____ _____
Counsel for Wife   Counsel for Husband

OR

On the ____ day of _____, _____, the parties appeared before me and signed this document as a voluntary act.

_____
NOTARY

Form #22
HIPAA Authorization

FROM: _____
Current Address: _____
Date of Birth: _____
Social Security No. (last 4 digits): _____

This Authorization applies to any health information protected by the federal Health Insurance Portability and Accountability Act of 1996 (HIPAA), and the regulations implementing it (45 C.F.R. §§160-164). It is intended to comply with all specific requirements of those regulations (45 C.F.R. §164.508(c)), and with the relevant privacy provisions of _____ law.

I hereby authorize and direct all "covered entities" under HIPAA, and those entities' "business associates" as follows:

(1) **Information to be disclosed:** All of my protected health information and medical records regarding any past, present or future medical or mental health condition, and including all information relating the diagnosis and treatment of sexually transmitted disease, mental illness and drug or alcohol abuse;

(2) **Person(s) who can request disclosure:** (initial authorized person(s))

_____ (a) _____;

_____ (b) Any individual named as my agent or alternate agent in my Durable General Power of Attorney;

_____ (c) Any individual named as my agent or alternate agent in my Springing Durable General Power of Attorney to determine my incapacity or incompetency;

_____ (d) To the Trustee or Successor Trustee of any trust of which I am a beneficiary, for the purpose of determining my capacity as defined in the trust agreement.

(3) **Person(s) to whom information may be disclosed:**

Those persons identified in Paragraph (2).

(4) **Purpose of release:**

   The purpose of disclosure to persons named or identified in Paragraphs (2)(a) - (d) is to enable those individuals to monitor and evaluate my health and my health care, to evaluate my financial circumstances and obligations and to take such actions as are necessary to ensure my general well being. The purposes of disclosure to persons identified in Paragraph (2)(d) is as stated in that Paragraph.

(5) **Expiration.** This Authorization shall continue until my death, unless I revoke it in writing.

(6) **Revocation.** I may revoke or amend this Authorization in a subsequently dated written instrument, but no standard form generally used by a "covered entity" shall be effective to do so.

(7) **Information subject to re-disclosure.** I understand that the information disclosed pursuant to this Authorization may be subject to re-disclosure and may no longer be protected by HIPAA or other privacy laws.

(8) **No liability for disclosure.** No "covered entity" or "business associate," who acts in good faith under the terms of this Authorization, shall be subject to any liability of any kind to my family, heirs, successors, assigns or others acting in my name.

_____   _____
   Date   Name of Grantor

State of _____

County of _____

   On _____, 20__, _____, the Grantor, appeared before me and willingly signed this instrument as a free and voluntary act and deed. In testimony, I subscribe my name and affix my Notary Seal on _____, 20___.

Form #23
Sample Living Together Agreement

_____, and _____, who live or will live together in the future at [Address]_____, _____, _____, enter into the following agreement.

1. Both parties wish to establish their respective rights and responsibilities regarding their individual income and property and any income and property that may be acquired, either separately or jointly, during their relationship.

2. The parties have made a full and complete disclosure to each other of all of their financial assets and liabilities.

3. Except as provided below, the parties waive the following rights (A sample of waived rights is given):

    a   To share in each other's estates upon their death.

    b   To "palimony" or other forms of support or maintenance, both temporary and permanent.

    c   To share in any increase in value during the period of their relationship of their separate property.

    d   To share in the pension, profit sharing, or other retirement accounts of the other.

    e   To the division of the separate property of the parties, whether currently held or later acquired.

    f   To any other claims based on their relationship.

    g   To claim the existence of a legal relationship (Domestic Partnership, Civil Union, Marriage).

4. [SET FORTH RELEVANT EXCEPTIONS HERE. For instance, if both parties are contributing to the mortgage on the home owned by one party, they may agree that any increase in equity during their relationship will be fairly divided between them. This is important in order to avoid any pay-

ments being perceived as a gift to the title owner.] If the parties intend to become parents, a separate Child Co-Parent Agreement is recommended. Children may also be mentioned in this agreement.

5. The parties agree to divide the household expenses as follows:

Monthly Expenses

Rent or Mortgage	$_____	$_____

Utilities:

Telephone	$_____	$_____
Gas	$_____	$_____
Electricity	$_____	$_____
Water & Sewer	$_____	$_____
Garbage Collection	$_____	$_____
Cable Television	$_____	$_____
Cellular Phone	$_____	$_____
Internet Service	$_____	$_____
Property Taxes	$_____	$_____

Insurance:

Homeowners/Renters	$_____	$_____
Auto(s)	$_____	$_____
Recreational Vehicle	$_____	$_____

Debt Payments:

Vehicle #1	$_____	$_____
Vehicle #2	$_____	$_____
Home Equity Loan	$_____	$_____
Other Loans	$_____	$_____
Credit Card #1	$_____	$_____
Credit Card #2	$_____	$_____
Credit Card #3	$_____	$_____
Day Care	$_____	$_____

Transportation Expenses:

Gasoline	$_____	$_____
Parking/Commuting	$_____	$_____
Vehicle Maintenance	$_____	$_____
Licenses	$_____	$_____

Food:

Groceries	$_____	$_____
Take-out Food	$_____	$_____
Restaurants	$_____	$_____
School Lunches	$_____	$_____

Household Expenses:

Cleaning Supplies	$_____	$_____

Cleaning Service	$_____	$_____
Yard Maintenance	$_____	$_____
Home Maintenance	$_____	$_____
Home Security	$_____	$_____
Home Improvements	$_____	$_____
Home Furnishings	$_____	$_____
Appliances	$_____	$_____

Personal Expenses:

Entertainment	$_____	$_____
Travel	$_____	$_____
Gifts	$_____	$_____
Hobbies	$_____	$_____
Babysitting	$_____	$_____
Pet-care Costs	$_____	$_____
Donations	$_____	$_____
Other Expenses	$_____	$_____
	$_____	$_____
	$_____	$_____

TOTAL EXPENSES:

$_____ $_____

6. [ADDITIONAL PROVISIONS HERE. Example: custody of pets, allocating household chores. While the legal obligation to pay child support to any children of the parties cannot be modified by agreement of the parties, the non-legal parent may agree to support the child even though there is no legal obligation to do so.]
7. Each party is represented by separate and independent legal counsel of his or her own choosing.
8. The parties have separate income and assets to independently provide for their own respective financial needs.
9. This agreement constitutes the entire agreement of the parties and may be modified only in writing signed by both of them.
10. In the event it is determined that a provision of this agreement is invalid because it is contrary to applicable law, that provision is deemed separable from the rest of the agreement, such that the remainder of the agreement remains valid and enforceable.
11. This agreement is made in accordance with the laws of the State of _____, and any dispute regarding its enforcement will be resolved by reference to the laws of that state.
12. Nothing in the agreement shall be construed to reflect a marriage-like relationship if such is prohibited by State law.

I HAVE READ THE ABOVE AGREEMENT, I HAVE TAKEN TIME TO CONSIDER ITS IMPLICATIONS, I FULLY UNDERSTAND ITS CONTENTS, I AGREE TO ITS TERMS, AND I VOLUNTARILY SUBMIT TO ITS EXECUTION. I HAVE RECEIVED ADEQUATE CONSIDERATION FOR THIS AGREEMENT.

_____   _____
Witnessed by:
_____   _____
(Witness or counsel signature)   (Witness or counsel signature)

State of _____

County of _____

Before me, a Notary Public in and for said County and State, personally appeared the above named individuals who acknowledged that they signed the foregoing instrument, and did so freely.

In Testimony Whereof, I have hereunto set my hand and official seal at _____, _____, this _____ day of _____, 20__.

_____
Notary Public

Form #24
Possible Definitions for Legal Documents

A. **<u>My spouse/partner</u>** refers to _____, whether or not my marriage/relationship to him/her is recognized, or she/he is recognized as my spouse/partner, under the applicable state law in which my estate or any portion of my estate is probated and/or administered. This includes any ancillary administration/probate of my estate.

_____ shall not be deemed my spouse/partner under this document if we divorce or if our relationship has been dissolved by any other legal manner. If a legal dissolution of my marriage/relationship with my spouse shall be unavailable, our marriage/relationship shall be deemed dissolved upon written notice from either of us to the other of the intention to dissolve such marriage/relationship.

(Clarifying that the joint accounts are intended to be held jointly with right of survivorship is the purpose of the following language. Some joint accounts are for convenience only. Ex. mother puts daughter's name on her checking account for help with finances; daughter contributes nothing to the account.)

B. I may have established certain accounts in financial institutions and/or own other assets, including real estate, jointly with my spouse/partner. These accounts and assets are held jointly. Any jointly held account or asset is not to be construed as having that form as a matter of convenience to me. Title to these accounts and assets have been established in such form that they are payable or transferable to him/her at my death, if he/she survives me.

I intend by this article to confirm my spouse's/partner's absolute ownership of these accounts and assets at my death, if he/she survives me. If any of those accounts or assets are in such form that there is any doubt as to whether my spouse/partner is the owner of the remaining account balances, I intend this paragraph to correct any such deficiencies. It is my intention that those accounts belong to my spouse/partner.

I hereby also confirm that any and all accounts, including retirement accounts and insurance policies held by me that name one or more beneficiaries are intended to pass to the named beneficiary or beneficiaries. Specifically, without limiting the generality of the foregoing, I confirm any accounts or insurance policies in which I designate my spouse/partner as the beneficiary.

Form #25
Dissolution Agreement

Format Provided by:

Tamara E. Kolz, Partner
Private Wealth Services
Holland & Knight, LLP
Ten St. James Avenue
Boston, MA 02116
617.573.5887
tamara.kolz@hklaw.com

THIS AGREEMENT is made and entered into this 15th day of March, 2007 by and between G. Julius Caesar (Julius) and Marcus J. Brutus (Marc), both of Rome, New York, and hereinafter referred to as the "Party" or "Parties."

WITNESSETH:

WHEREAS Julius and Brutus have been involved in a long-term relationship involving cohabitation and shared expenses;

WHEREAS the Parties purchased property located at 100 Ancienthera Avenue, Rome, New York (the "Property"), the current value of which is $600,000, and hold title to that Property in their joint names with right of survivorship;

WHEREAS the Parties are joint signatories on a promissory note to Cossutia Bank (Bank), loan number 102.100 BCE, which secures the mortgage deed of the Property from both Parties to the Bank. The outstanding balance on the mortgage loan is approximately, $250,450.00;

WHEREAS the Parties are jointly and severally liable for the outstanding balance due on the mortgage loan;

WHEREAS the Parties have each contributed equal amounts toward the purchase, mortgage loan payments and maintenance of the Property;

WHEREAS the Parties wish to dissolve their relationship and cohabitation;

WHEREAS the Parties wish to memorialize their intentions with respect to the disposition, rights and obligations concerning the Property as well as other assets and expenses that the Parties have shared during their cohabitation;

WHEREAS both Parties are educated persons in good health and each has independent economic potential; and

WHEREAS both Parties agree that no change in their respective health or economic potential shall effect, modify or abrogate any portion of this Agreement.

NOW, THEREFORE, in consideration of the mutual understandings contained in and of the mutual promises exchanged between the Parties in this Agreement, and for good and valuable consideration, each to the other given, the Parties mutually covenant and agree to the following:

ARTICLE 1 - PERSONAL PROPERTY

1. The Parties acknowledge and agree that all property of a personal nature, such as clothing, jewelry and personal effects, shall be retained by the person for whose use such items are intended, regardless of how such items were actually acquired or who actually provided payment for such items.

2. The Parties acknowledge that both the title and note for the 2007 Legionnaire vehicle are currently in Caesar's sole name and the Parties agree that it shall remain his sole property.

3. The Parties acknowledge that the household items and furnishing located at the Property belong to Caesar and shall remain his sole property.

4. The Parties acknowledge that the Rubicon River Bank checking account, number 10448, which was previously a joint account, has been transferred into Marcus' individual name. All sums in the account as of the date of transfer and any sums deposited after that date are Marcus' sole property.

5. The Parties acknowledge that there is an account located at the Rubicon River Bank that is in Marcus' sole name. Caesar has deposited 10,475.00 into that account. The Parties agree that any contributions by Caesar currently held in that account may be used toward the property located at 5554 Tiber River Lane,

Falmouth, Massachusetts. Brutus leased that property through December 2008. Caesar waives all rights to any amounts remaining in that account or in any other account currently or subsequently established in Brutus' name, and such accounts shall remain Brutus' sole and exclusive property.

ARTICLE 2 - REAL PROPERTY

6. The Parties acknowledge that the Property is now listed for sale and they agree to cooperate and use their best efforts, in good faith, to bring about a final sale of the Property.

7. Notwithstanding the fact that the Property is listed for sale, the Parties agree that they shall execute a new deed under which they shall hold title to the Property as "tenants in common." This new deed shall be executed contemporaneously with the execution of this Agreement and then recorded with the County Registry of Deeds within 10 days of the signing.

8. That Parties acknowledge and agree that each of them owns an undivided one-half interest in the Property ("ownership interest").

9. Each of the Parties shall have such rights and duties of tenants in common between themselves and with respect to third persons, as determined by the laws of the State of New York, except as otherwise provided in this document. To the extent permitted by law, the provisions of this Agreement shall take precedence over those provisions of New York law that describe the incidents of tenancy in common and shall be binding on the Parties.

10. The Parties agree that if one or both die, each Party's ownership interest shall pass according to the provisions of such individual's Last Will and Testament, or if one should die intestate, according to applicable law.

11. The Parties acknowledge that Cossutia Bank is escrowing real estate taxes and homeowner's property insurance. Each Party shall provide contents insurance for their respective property. Such expenses are paid as a portion of the monthly mortgage loan payment.

12. The Parties agree that Caesar shall be responsible for 100% of the monthly mortgage loan payment through the date the Property is sold. Any tax deductions

attributable to such payments shall be available solely to Caesar. The Parties acknowledge it is their intention to sell the property before September 1, 2007.

13. The Parties agree that Caesar shall be responsible for the payment of 100% of all utility bills, including, but not limited to water, sewer, electricity, telephone, cable and heat until the Property is sold and title transfers.

14. Caesar shall make all mortgage loan and utility payments on or before the due date. This applies even if Caesar is not occupying the Property.

15. The Parties agree that each shall be responsible for 50% of all major repairs and improvements, including but not limited to roof repairs. The Parties shall agree, in writing and in advance, to any improvements or repairs, unless otherwise provided in this Agreement. Neither Party may unreasonable withhold his consent to any repairs or improvements. Major repairs or improvements are defined as costing $500 or more per item. Emergency repairs shall not require the prior written approval of both Parties. Emergency repairs may be made by either Party without the prior approval of the other, but only to the extent necessary to prevent or avoid serious and/or permanent damage. While both Parties acknowledge being responsible for 50% of all major improvements or repairs, they further agree that Caesar shall be responsible for making all payments for any major repairs or improvements until the Property is sold. Marcus shall reimburse Caesar for his share of any payments made for repairs or improvements as specified in Paragraph 17 and Paragraph 25, Subparagraph (C).

16. The Parties agree that Caesar shall be responsible for 100% of all ordinary repairs and maintenance, including but not limited to painting and heating equipment. Ordinary repairs or maintenance is defined as those costing less than $500 per item.

17. If it is necessary for Caesar to pay for repairs or maintenance under Paragraph 15, he shall be entitled to reimbursement from Marcus as provided in that Paragraph. If prior written approval is required and Caesar fails to obtain it, he shall not be entitled to reimbursement and shall be the expense alone, without receiving any credit for having done so, either at the time the Property sells or at

any other time. The Parties may mutually agree to other reimbursement provisions in writing or forego any reimbursement requirements. Unless otherwise agreed to in writing by the Parties, when the Property sells under Article III, 50% of the amount of any expenditure made or indebtedness incurred by Caesar under Paragraph 15 shall be reimbursed to him. There shall be a priority in the distribution of the sale proceeds as specified in Article III, Paragraph 25, Subparagraph (C), before any distribution of the remaining proceeds to Caesar and Marcus under Subparagraph (D) of Paragraph 25. If Caesar buys Marcus' ownership interest under Article III, Paragraph 24, 50% of such amount shall be charged against Marcus according to Paragraph 25, Subparagraph (C) before any distribution of the remaining proceeds to the Parties under Paragraph 25, Subparagraph (D).

18. If Caesar fails to make the payments, specified in Paragraphs 12, 13, 15 or 16 of this Agreement, within 30 days of the due date, Brutus may make the payments on Caesar's behalf in order to prevent a default on any obligation concerning the Property. If Brutus makes such payments, he shall have a lien against Caesar's interest in the Property in an amount equal to two times the aggregate of all such payments by on Caesar's behalf. The Parties may agree to other reimbursement provisions in writing or forego any reimbursement. Any payments owed to Brutus under this Paragraph shall be paid when the Property is sold and before any distribution of the remaining proceeds to the Parties under Paragraph 25, Subparagraph (D).

19. Neither Party shall directly or indirectly, voluntarily or involuntarily, suffer or permit any lien or encumbrance to attach to their respective interests in the Property without the prior written consent of the other.

20. Any sale of the Property shall be made in accordance with Article III.

ARTICLE III - SALE OF REAL ESTATE

21. In marketing the Property, the Parties shall engage a mutually agreed upon and qualified real estate agent or broker selected by them to list the Property. The Property shall be listed at its fair market value and the listing shall be

included in any multiple listing service (MLS), electronic property listing (if available), unless otherwise agreed upon by the Parties. If the parties cannot agree on a qualified real estate agent or broker, each shall select an agent or broker and those two individuals shall agree on a third agent or broker.

22. The Property's fair market value shall be mutually agreed upon by the Parties or determined by an appraisal under Article III, Paragraph 26.

23. If the Property does not sell to a third party by September 1, 2007, Caesar shall have the right to purchase Brutus' ownership interest in the Property at the fair market value determined by Paragraph 25. If Caesar intends to exercise this right, he shall follow the terms established in Paragraph 25.

24. If Caesar desires to purchase Brutus' ownership interest under Paragraph 23, he shall notify Brutus of his intention. An offer and a $1,000 refundable deposit shall accompany the notice. The offer may not be rejected unless the offer amount does not reflect the Property's fair market value, in which event a new offer may be submitted at the agreed upon fair market value. The Parties shall enter into a Purchase and Sales Agreement within 10 days from the date of the accepted offer. This may be contingent for 45 days to secure financing, unless the Parties agree otherwise. Payment shall be by cash, certified or bank cashier's check and the closing shall be within one month after signing the Purchase and Sales Agreement. Caesar shall arrange refinancing or a novation so that Brutus shall have no further liability on the mortgage loan, or other arrangements mutually agreed upon by the Parties. When the sale closes any amounts due a Party under Paragraph 25 shall be credited to or charged against, as the case may be, the payments made to Brutus for an interest in the property.

Form #26
Client Intake Checklist

_____ Review Will Questionnaire

    _____ Executor and Alternate

    _____ Living Will/HCPON Designees
    _____ Including HIPPA language

    _____ Durable POA for Finances/Attorney in Fact
    _____ Include HIPPA language
    _____ Designation of adult guardianship arrangement

_____ Trust
    _____ Revocable Living Trust
    _____ Irrevocable Living Trust
    _____ Special Needs Trust
    _____ Trust for minor child(ren)
    _____ Pour-over Trust provisions
    _____ Testamentary Trust

_____ Real Estate
    _____ J &S Deed
    _____ TOD Deed
    _____ Home equity line of credit

_____ Distribution of Estate

_____ Federal/State Estate Taxes (exemption ceilings)
    _____ Federal
    _____ State

_____ Designation of Agent

_____ Insurance:
    _____ Health
    _____ Life
    _____ Long Term Care
    _____ Homeowner insurance (flood, earthquake, water, tornado/wind, identity theft)

_____ Renter's insurance (renting or if partner not on title to house)
_____ Umbrella policy
_____ Any antiques? Properly insured?
_____ Home business insurance
_____ Professional liability insurance

_____ Children/Grandchildren (per stirpes/per capita)
(Explain difference between PS & PC)
    _____ name guardian; estate & person
    _____ Health care authorization for minor for non-parent

_____ Develop/Maintain home recordkeeping system
    _____ if both parties don't own home, records of contributions essential
    _____ both parties own home; individual contributions to purchase or maintenance
    _____ records needed for tax purposes; pre/post death

_____ Safe-deposit box or home fire/waterproof safe

_____ Comprehensive current inventory of household furnishings/possessions

_____ Listing of credit cards/bank accts/important papers/numbers

_____ Financial planning: does client have financial planner?

_____ Bank accounts (joint/separate; payable on death)

_____ Retirement plans (401-k, TSP, IRAs, KEOGHs)
    _____ automatic payroll deductions

_____ Emergency fund

_____ Letters of instruction
    _____ funeral wishes
    _____ specific items not included in will
    _____ final comments to family/friends
    _____ location of papers/records/stuff

_____ Business ownership considerations
    _____ business succession

_____ buying/selling business
_____ business insurance

_____ Intellectual property
    _____ copyright
    _____ trademark
    _____ patents
    _____ inventions

APPENDIX D

State Laws

Birth Certificate Statutes

I. States with specific statutory authorization to amend after sex reassignment surgery

ALABAMA	Ala. Code §22-9A-19(d)
ARIZONA	Ariz. Rev. Stat. § 36-326 (A)(4)
ARKANSAS	Ark. Code Ann. § 20-18-307
CALIFORNIA	Cal. Health & Safety Code § 103425
COLORADO	Colo. Rev. Stat. 25-2-115
CONNECTICUT	Conn. Gen. Stat. §19a042
DISTRICT OF COLUMBIA	D.C. Code Ann. §7-217(d)
GEORGIA	Ga. Code Ann. §31-10-23(e)
HAWAII	Haw. Rev. Stat. 338-17.7(4)
ILLINOIS	410 Ill. Comp. Stat. 535/17(d)
KENTUCKY	Ky. Rev. Stat. Ann. §213.121 (5)
LOUISIANA	La. Rev. Stat. Ann. 40:62
MARYLAND	Md. Code Ann. Health-General §4-214
MASSACHUSETTS	Mass. Gen Laws ch. 46. §13(e)
MICHIGAN	Mich. Comp. Law S. §333.2831(c)
MISSOURI	Mo. Rev. Stat. §193.215
NEBRASKA	Neb. Rev. Stat. §71-606.01
NEW JERSEY	N.J. Stat. Ann. 26:8-40.12
NEW MEXICO	N.M. Stat. Ann. §24-14-25(D)
NORTH CAROLINA	N.C. Gen. Stat. §130A-118
OREGON	Or. Rev. Stat. §432.235

UTAH	Utah Code Ann. §26-2-11
VIRGINIA	Va. Code Ann. §32.1-269
WISCONSIN	Wis. Stat. §69.15

2. States with general statutes that authorize changes to "sex" designation.

ALASKA	Alaska Stat. §18.50.320
DELAWARE	Del Code Ann. tit. 16 § 3131
FLORIDA	Fla. Stat. Ch. 29, § 382.016
INDIANA	Ind. Code §16-37-2-10
IOWA	Iowa Code IV §144.38
MINNESOTA	Minn. Stat. §144.218(4)
MISSISSIPPI	Miss. Code Ann. §41-57-21
MONTANA	Mont. Code Ann. §50-15-204
NEW HAMPSHIRE	N.H. Rev. Stat. Ann. 126.23-a
NORTH DAKOTA	N.D. Cent. Code §23-02.1-25
OKLAHOMA	Okla. Stat. tit. 63, §1-321
PENNSYLVANIA	35 Pa. Cons. Stat. §450.603
RHODE ISLAND	R. I. Gen. Laws §23-3-21
SOUTH CAROLINA	S.C. Code Ann. §44-63-150
SOUTH DAKOTA	S.D. Codified Laws §35-25-51
TEXAS	Tex. Stat. Ann. §§191.028, 192.011
VERMONT	Vt. Stat. Ann. tit. 18 §5075
WEST VIRGINIA	W. Va. Code §16-5-24
WYOMING	Wyo. Stat. Ann. §35-1-424

3. The rest of the story.

KANSAS — Kansas does not have a controlling statute on the subject; Kan. Admin. Regs. 28-17-20(b)(1)(A)(i) permits the amendment of a birth certificate after sex reassignment.

OHIO — *In re Ladrach*, 513 N.E.2d 828 (Ohio Prob. Ct. 1987); Ohio's birth certificate statute does not permit correction of sex designation for transsexuals.

TENNESSEE — Tenn Code Ann. §68-3-203(d); "the sex of an individual will not be changed on the original certificate of birth as a result of sex change surgery."

States with Pro-LGBT Non-discrimination Laws

Twelve states and the District of Columbia ban discrimination based on sexual orientation and gender identity.

California (1992, 2003)
Colorado (2007)
District of Columbia (1977, 2006)
Illinois (2006)
Iowa (2007)
Maine (2005)
Minnesota (1993)
New Jersey (1992, 2007)
New Mexico (2003)
Oregon (Jan. 2008)
Rhode Island (1995, 2001)
Vermont (1991, 2007)
Washington (2006)

Eight states prohibit discrimination based on sexual orientation.

Connecticut (1991)
Hawaii (1991)
Maryland (2001)
Massachusetts (1989)
Nevada (1999)
New Hampshire (1998)
New York (2003)
Wisconsin (1982)

A complete listing of state adoption laws is available at: www.hrc.org.

State Adoption Laws
(accurate as of 7/1/2007)

Second parent adoptions allow a same-sex parent to adopt the child of his/her partner without the partner terminating parental rights. Since these are court-ordered actions, other states must recognize the adoptions even if they would not be allowed in that state. The U.S. Constitution's Full Faith and Credit Clause applies to court decisions from other states.

Russell v. Bridgens, 647 N.W.2d 56 (Neb. 2002), Nebraska must recognize Pennsylvania decision granting a second-parent adoption even though Nebraska law does not permit them.

Starr v. Erez, COA99-1534 (N.C. Ct. App., Nov. 27, 2000), North Carolina must honor second parent adoption granted by Washington State court.

Finstuen v. Edmonson, 2006 U.S. Dist., LEXIS 32122 (W.D. Okla., May 19, 2006), Oklahoma's Adoption Invalidation Law, prohibiting recognition of adoptions from other states involving same-sex couples violates the Constitution's Full Faith and Credit Clause. The 10th Circuit Court of Appeals upheld this ruling in August 2007, Case No. 06-6213, issued August 3, 2007.

A. Second parent adoptions permitted by statute and appellate court decisions (1):

    California: CAL. FAM. CODE §9000(f) (2004) (registered domestic partners only); *Sharon S. v. Superior Court of San Diego County*, 73 P.3d 554 (CA 2003).

B. Second parent adoptions permitted by Statute (3):

    Colorado: COLO REV. STAT. §§19-5-203(1), 19-5-210(1.5), 19-5-211(1.5) (2007)

    Connecticut: CONN. GEN. STAT. §45a-724(3) (2004), superseding *Adoption of Baby Z.*, 724 A.2d 1035 (1999)

Vermont: VT. STAT. ANN. tit. 15A, §1-102(b) (2004), codifying *In re Adoption of B.L.V.B. & E.L.V.B.*, 628 A.2d 1271 (Vt. 1993)

C. Second parent adoptions permitted by appellate court decision (7):

District of Columbia: *In re M.M.D. v. B.H.M.*, 662 A.2d 837 (D.C. 1995)

Illinois: *In re Petition of K.M. & D.M.*, 653 N.E.2d 888 (Ill. App. Ct. 1995)

Indiana: *In re Adoption of K.S.P.*, 804 N.E.2d 1253 (Ind. Ct. App. 2004); *In re Adoption of M.M.G.C.*, 785 N.E.2d 267 (Ind. Ct. App. 2003)

Massachusetts: *In re Adoption of Tammy*, 619 N.E.2d 315 (Mass. 1993)

New Jersey: *In re Adoption of Two Children by H.N.R.*, 666 A.2d 535 (N.J. Super. 1995)

New York: *In re Jacob, In re Dana*, 660 N.E.2d 397 (N.Y. 1995)

Pennsylvania: *In re Adoption of R.B.F. & R.C.F.*, 803 A.2d 1195 (Pa. 2002)

D. Second parent adoptions permitted by trial courts (15):

Alabama
Alaska
Delaware
Hawaii
Iowa
Louisiana
Maryland
Minnesota
Nevada
New Hampshire
New Mexico
Oregon
Rhode Island
Texas
Washington

E. Appellate court decisions against second parent adoptions (3):

Ohio: *In re Adoption of Doe*, 719 N.E.2d 1071 (Ohio Ct. App. 1998)

Nebraska: *In re Adoption of Luke*, 640 N.W.2d 372 (Neb. 2002)

Wisconsin: *Interest of Angel Lace M.*, 516 N.W.2d 678 (Wis. 1994)

F. Unclear whether second parent adoptions are permitted (22):

>Arizona
Arkansas
Florida (state prohibits all adoptions by homosexuals)
Georgia
Idaho
Kansas
Kentucky
Maine
Mississippi
Missouri
Montana
New Hampshire
North Carolina
North Dakota
Oklahoma
South Carolina
South Dakota
Tennessee
Utah
Virginia
West Virginia
Wyoming

Anti-LGBT Adoption Laws
(accurate as of 7/1/2007)

1. North Dakota's 2003 law permits agencies placing children to discriminate because of religious or moral objections.

2. Oklahoma's law prohibiting recognition of adoptions finalized in other states where the parents are of the same sex. The trial court struck down the law in 2006. The 10th Circuit Court of Appeals upheld that decision August 3, 2007; *Finstuen v. Edmondson*, No. 06-6213.

3. In 2000, Utah amended its adoption law to prohibit adoptions by a person "cohabitating in a relationship that is not a legally valid and binding marriage." This law also applies to foster home placements.

    In 2007, Utah further amended its adoption law to give preference to married couples over single adults. Utah's constitution bans same-sex marriage.

4. Nebraska's adoption policy prohibits allowing individuals who are "known to the agency to be homosexual" to adopt. Nebraska policy also prohibits unmarried and cohabiting adults from adopting. No one is sure if Nebraska enforces this policy. Nebraska also prohibits placing foster children in homes with a person known to be "homosexual."

5. Florida's 1977 law expressly prohibits "homosexual" individuals from adopting. Ironically, Florida has no similar prohibition for foster home placements.

6. In 2000, Mississippi joined Florida in expressly prohibiting adoption by persons of the same gender.

The websites for the Human Rights Campaign, Lambda Legal and Education Defense Fund and the Lesbian and Gay Task Force were used to help compile this information.

States with Civil Unions, Marriage, and Domestic Partnerships
(accurate as of 8/1/2007)

Marriage

Massachusetts remains the only state that permits same-sex marriage.

Civil Unions/Domestic Partnerships with Full Spousal Rights

Vermont, Civil Unions, 2001
Connecticut, Civil Unions, 2005
California, Domestic Partnerships, 2006
New Hampshire, Civil Unions, eff. Jan. 2008
New Jersey, Civil Unions, 2007
Oregon, Domestic Partnerships, eff. Jan. 2008

Civil Unions/Domestic Partnerships with Partial/Comparable Spousal Rights

Hawaii, Reciprocal Beneficiaries, 1997
Maine, Domestic Partnerships, 2004
Washington, Domestic Partnerships,* 2007
District of Columbia, Domestic Partnerships, 2002**

---

*   Washington's Domestic Partnership law is virtually identical to Vermont, New Hampshire and New Jersey. The use of "Domestic Partnership" was a political compromise.

** The District of Columbia enacted its Domestic Partnership law in 1992 but did not implement it until 2002. Congress opposed implementation until then.

APPENDIX E

LGBT Community Resources

Legal Resources

1. **Lambda Legal Defense and Education Fund**

   A. National Office
   120 Wall Street, Ste. 1500
   New York, New York 10005-3904
   212-809-8585 (voice)
   212-809-0055 (fax)
   www.lambdalegal.org

   B. Midwestern Regional Office
   11 East Adams Street, Ste. 1008
   Chicago, Illinois 60603-6303
   312-663-4413 (voice)
   312-663-4307 (fax)

   C. Southern Regional Office
   1447 Peachtree Street, NE, Ste. 1004
   Atlanta, Georgia 30309-3027
   404-897-1880 (voice)
   404-897-1884 (fax)

   D. Western Regional Office
   3325 Wilshire Blvd., Ste. 1300
   Los Angeles, California 90010-1729
   213-382-7600 (voice)
   213-351-6050 (fax)

E. South Central Regional Office
3500 Oak Lawn Avenue, Ste. 500
Dallas, TX 75219-6722
214-219-8585 (voice)
214-219-4455 (fax)

2. **National Center for Lesbian Rights**
870 Market Street, Ste. 570
San Francisco, CA 94102
415-392-6257 (voice)
415-392-8442 (fax)
www.nclrights.org

3. **National Lesbian and Gay Lawyers Association**
601 Thirteenth Street, N.W., Suite 1170 South
Washington, D.C. 20005-3823
(202) 637-6384
www.nlgla.org
Email: info@nlgla.org

4. **Lesbian and Gay Immigration Rights Task Force**
Sponsored by the NCLR and seeking equal application of U.S. immigration laws toward lesbian and gay couples; advocates for persons facing HIV/AIDS discrimination and those seeking asylum due to sexual orientation.

870 Market Street, Ste. 570
San Francisco, California 94102
415-392-6257 (voice)
415-392-8442 (fax)
www.lgirtf.org/SF
Email: lgirtf@hotmail.com

5. **Transgender Law and Policy**
Comprehensive transgender legal resource site.
www.transgenderlaw.org
Email: info@transgenderlaw.org

6. **Gay and Lesbian Advocates and Defenders (GLAD)**
   30 Winter Street, Ste. 800
   Boston, Massachusetts 02108
   617-426-1350 (v)
   www.glad.org
   Email: gladlaw@glad.org

Social Service Resources

7. **National Association of Professional Geriatric Care Managers**
   1604 N. Country Club Blvd.
   Tucson, Arizona 85716-3102
   520-881-8008 (voice)
   520-325-7975 (fax)
   www.caremanager.org

8. **Healthcare, Elder Law Programs (HELP)**
   1404 Cravens Avenue
   Torrance, California 90501-2701
   310-533-1996 (voice)
   310-533-1949 (fax)
   www.help4srs.org
   Email: questions@help4srs.org

9. **Human Rights Campaign**
   1640 Rhode Island Avenue, NW
   Washington, D.C. 20036-3278
   202-628-4160 (voice)
   202-347-5323 (fax)
   202-216-1572 (TTY)
   www.hrc.org

Family Net website deals with issues concerning lesbian, gay, bisexual and transgendered families.

   www.hrc.org/familynet

10. **Love Sees No Borders**
Dealing with issues affecting same-sex immigration in the United States

    P. O. Box 60486
    Sunnyvale, California 94088
    413-502-4758 (fax)
    www.loveseesnoborders.org
    Email: info@loveseesnoborders.org

11. **ACLU National Lesbian and Gay Rights Project**
    132 West 43rd Street
    New York, New York 10036
    212-549-2500 (voice)
    www.aclu.org/issues/gay/hmgl/html

12. **Gay and Lesbian Alliance Against Discrimination (GLAAD)**
Promotes and ensures fair, accurate and inclusive representation in the media.

    West Coast Office:
    5455 Wilshire Blvd., Ste. 1500
    Los Angeles, California 90036
    323-933-2240 (voice)
    323-933-2241 (fax)

    East Coast Office:
    248 W. 35th Street, 8th Floor
    New York, New York 10001
    212-629-3322 (voice)
    212-629-3325 (fax)
    www.glaad.org

13. **National Gay and Lesbian Task Force (NGLTF)**
Civil Rights organization for the LGBT Community

    1700 Kalorama Rd., NW
    Washington, D.C. 20009
    202-332-6483 (voice)
    202-332-0207 (fax)
    202-332-6219 (TTY)
    www.ngltf.org

14. **Gay, Lesbian and Straight Education Network (GLSEN)**
Provides information on establishing a safe school environment for LGBT students.

>   212-727-0135 (voice)
>   www.glsen.org
>   Email: glsen@glsen.org

15. **Parents and Friends of Lesbians and Gays (PFLAG)**
National organization providing group support services for parents and friends.

>   1726 M Street, NW, Ste. 400
>   Washington, D.C. 20036
>   202-467-8180 (voice)
>   202-467-8194 (fax)
>   www.pflag.org
>   Email: info@pflag.org

16. **ABA AIDS Coordination Project**
>   750 15th Street, NW
>   Washington, D.C. 20005-1009
>   202-662-1025 (voice)
>   www.abanet.org/AIDS/home.html

17. **Benefits Checkup**
A free, comprehensive web-based screening tool designed to match seniors to federal, state and local benefits and services. The survey takes about 15 minutes and is anonymous. The output generated highlights programs the user may be eligible for and explains the application process.

>   www.BenefitsCheckUp.org

18. **Gay and Lesbian Medical Association (GMLA)**
>   415-255-4547
>   Email: info@glma.org
>   www.lccp.org

19. Kaiser Permanente
Provides a handbook on care that address LGBT issues.

A Provider's Handbook on Culturally Competent Care: Lesbian, Gay, Bisexual and Transgendered Population.
Kaiser Permanente National Diversity Hotline: 510-271-6663

20. Joint Commission on Accreditation of Healthcare Organizations (JCAHO)
This organization evaluates and accredits hospitals nationwide. It provides the essential seal of approval that reflects the hospitals high performance standards. JCAHO has a system for reviewing complaints against an accredited health care facility. They will investigate the situation and recommend changes to prevent future repetition. Complaints can be mailed, emailed or faxed. Submit a 1-2 page summary describing the situation encountered and state your concerns. Identify the healthcare organization by name, address and try to identify the personnel with whom you dealt.

Hotline: 800-994-6610
E-mail: complaint@jcaho.org
Office of Quality Monitoring, Fax: 630-790-5636

21. Insurance for same-sex couples

Automobile:
  AETNA
  Commerce
  Hartford (888-466-9675; 35 states & Washington, D.C.)
  Metropolitan
  Travelers

Homeowner:
  Hartford (888-466-9675; 35 states & Washington, D.C.)
  Allstate
  IDS/AMEX

Renter's:
  GEICO

22. **Family Caregiver Alliance**
Seeks to improve caregiver's quality of life through education, services, research and advocacy.

    690 Market St., Ste. 600
    San Francisco, Cal 94104
    800-445-8106
    415-434-3388
    www.caregiver.org
    Email: info@caregiver.org

23. **Association of Gay & Lesbian Psychiatric Referral Services**
Source for referrals to gay or lesbian providers of psychotherapy services.

    215-222-2800
    www.aglp.org

24. **Mary-Helen Mautner Project for Lesbians with Cancer**
Provides assistance for lesbians diagnosed with cancer.

    202-332-5536
    www.mautnerproject.org

25. **National Association on HIV over 50**
Resource site for persons diagnosed as HIV+ and over age 50.

    816-421-5263
    www.hivoverfifty.org

26. **Assistance in paying for cost of medications**
    www.body.com

27. **Source for gay-friendly senior housing**
    www.hrc.org/familynet
    www.retirementliving.com
    www.arbours.org
    www.gayretirement.org
    www.glinn.com
    www.pridesenior.org
    www.resortoncb.com

28. List of health insurance plans for domestic partners

www.gogay.net/insurlist.htm

29. National Hospice & Palliative Care Organization

1700 Diagonal Road, Ste. 625
Alexandria, VA 22314
703-837-1500
www.nhpco.org

30. Euthanasia World Directory

www.finalexit.org

31. Organ Donations

United National Organ Sharing (UNOS) is the agency coordinating organ donations. This group will NOT accept donations from gay donors due to a fear of HIV and AIDS. Some medical centers also prohibit gay donors for HIV and AIDS patients.

www.organdonor.gov

32. Source for life insurance for those who are HIV+

www.HIVpositive.com

33. Current information on individual state adoption laws

www.hrc.org/familynet/adoptions_laws.asp

34. Lesbian and gay parenting resources

www.proudparenting.org
www.lesbian.org
www.familypride.org
www.queerparents.org
www.familieslikeours.org
www.ourfamily.org
www.gayfamilyoptions.org
www.colage.org
www.pflag.org

35. Association of Conflict Resolution

Mediation and arbitration.

202-667-9700
www.acresolution.com

36. **Colage**
International support organization for children with lesbian or gay parents.

> 3543 18th Street, Ste. #1
> San Francisco, CA 94110
> 415-861-5437
> www.colage.org

37. **Lesbian- and gay-friendly therapists**

> www.glitse.com

38. **Senior Action in a Gay Environment (SAGE)**
Activist lesbian and gay senior organization.

> 212-741-2247
> www.sage.org

39. **Gay and Lesbian Victory Fund**

> www.victoryfund.org

40. **Freedom to Marry Collaborative**

> www.freedomtomarry.org

41. **American Society on Aging Lesbian and Gay Aging Issues Network**

> www.asaging.org/lgain.html

42. **Pride Senior Network**

> www.pridesenior.org

43. **The Gay and Lesbian Association of Retired Persons (GLARP)**

> P. O. Box 30808
> Los Angeles, CA 90024
> www.gaylesbianretiring.org

44. **The Institute for Gay and Lesbian Strategic Studies**

   P.O. Box 2603
   Amherst, MA 01004
   413-577-0145
   www.lglss.org

45. **LGBT Caregiver Discussion Group**
Sponsored by the Family Caregiving Alliance (FCA); a free online support group for LGBT people caring for elders and loved ones with chronic conditions.

   www.caregiver.org/caregiver/jsp/content_node.jsp?nodeid=490

46. **Gay, Lesbian & Bisexual Veterans Association**

   PO Box 29317
   Chicago, IL 60629
   www.glbva.org

47. **Gay and Lesbian Outreach to Elders**
A program of New Leaf: Services to Our Community

   1853 Market Street
   San Francisco, CA 94103
   415-626-7000
   http://bayarea.citysearch.com/E/G/SFOCA/1000/08/86

48. **Golden Threads**
A worldwide network for older lesbians

   www.goldenthredsptown.org

49. **International Longitudinal Transgender and Transsexual Aging Research Institute**

   PO Box 28089
   Richmond, VA 23228-28089
   804-421-2428
   www.int-trans.org

50. **National Senior Citizens Law Center (NSCLC)**

   www.nsclc.org

APPENDIX F

Uniform Child Custody Jurisdiction Enforcement Act Adoptions (UCCJEA)

Jurisdiction	Citation
Alabama	Code 1975, §§ 30-3B-101 to 30-3B-405
Alaska	AS 25.30.300 to 25.30.910
Arizona	A.R.S. §§ 25-1001 to 25-1067
Arkansas	A.C.A. §§ 9-19-101 to 9-19-401
California	West's Ann.Cal. Family Code §§ 3400 to 3465
Colorado	West's C.R.S.A. §§ 14-13-101 to 14-13-403
Connecticut	C.G.S.A. §§ 46b-115 to 46b-115jj
Delaware	13 Del.C. §§ 1901 to 1943
District of Columbia	D.C. Official Code, 2001 Ed. §§ 16-4601.01 to 16-4604.02
Florida	West's F.S.A. §§ 61.501 to 61.542
Georgia	O.C.G.A. §§ 19-9-40 to 19-9-104
Hawaii	HRS §§ 583A-101 to 583A-317
Idaho	I.C. §§ 32-11-101 to 32-11-405
Illinois	S.H.A. 750 ILCS 36/101 to 36/403
Iowa	I.C.A. §§ 598B.101 to 598B.402
Kansas	K.S.A. §§ 38-1336 to 38-1377

Kentucky	KRS §§ 403.800 to 403.880
Maine	19-A M.R.S.A. §§ 1731 to 1783
Maryland	MD FAMILY §§ 9.5-101 to 318
Michigan	M.C.L.A. §§ 722.1101 to 722.1406
Minnesota	M.S.A. §§ 518D.101 to 518D.317
Mississippi	MS ST §93-24-1 to 93-24-75
Montana	MCA §§ 40-7-101 to 40-7-317
Nebraska	R.R.S. 1943, §§ 43-1226 to 43-1266
Nevada	N.R.S. 125A.005 to 125A.605
New Jersey	N.J.S 2A:34-53 to 95
New Mexico	NMSA 1978, §§ 40-10A-101 to 40-10A-403
New York	McKinney's Domestic Relations Law, §§ 75 to 78-a
North Carolina	G.S. §§ 50A-101 to 50A-317
North Dakota	NDCC §§ 14-14.1-01 to 14-14.1-37
Ohio	R.C. 3109.21, et seq.
Oklahoma	43 Okla. St. Ann. §§ 551-101 to 551-402
Oregon	ORS 109.701 to 109.834
Pennsylvania	PA ST Prec. 23 PaC.S.A § 5401 to 5482
Rhode Island	Gen. Laws 1956, §§ 15-14.1-1 to 15-14.1-42
Tennessee	T.C.A. §§ 36-6-201 to 36-6-243
Texas	V.T.C.A. Family Code §§ 152.001 to 152.317
Utah	U.C.A. 1953, §§ 78-45c-101 to 78-45c-318
Virginia	Code 1950, §§ 20-146.1 to 20-146.38
Washington	West's RCWA 26.27.011 to 26.27.931
West Virginia	Code §§ 48-20-101 to 48-20-404

INDEX

A

A.H. v. M.P 117
Abdul-Karim v. Ashcroft 260
Adams v. Howerton 259
adoption 85–97
   advantages for children 90
   common statutory requirements 85
      cutoff provision 85–86
   costs 92
   developing law 94–96
      Full Faith and Credit Clause 95
      Lambda Legal Defense and Education Fund 95
   foster care 87
   international 87
      China 89–90
      U.S. Department of State 89
   legal relationship between children and parents 90
   lesbian and gay individuals and couples 92–94
   placement agencies 88
   practice points 92
   private 87, 89
   second-parent 90–92
      procedures 90
   transracial 87
Affirmation of Marriage Act 14
Alison D. v. Virginia M. 112
American Academy of Pediatricians 78, 81
American Bar Association
   Model Rule of Professional Conduct 1.7(b) 7
American Civil Liberties Union of Southern California 150
American Law Institute 117
Americans with Disabilities Act 159, 172
Anderson v. King County 18
annuities 232–35
   charitable gift annuity 234
   charitable lead trust 232–33
   charitable remainder annuity trust 234
   charitable remainder unitrust 233
National Center for Lesbian Rights 155

B

Baker v. Vermont 14, 25
Beyond Marriage coalition 33
   goals 33
Black's Law Dictionary 52
Boutilier v. INS 259
Bowers v. Hardwick 2, 19
Bradford v. Bradford 246
Britain v. Carver 75
Bureau of Immigration Appeals 255
Burns v. Burns 122

C

California Domestic Partner Rights and Responsibilities 25
Carvin v. Britain 115
children 61–83
   benefits of families 77–81
      American Academy of Pediatrics 78
      custody and visitation rights 78
      health, safety, and well-being of the children 78
   best interests of the child 62
   Canadian legislation 81–82
      three legal parents 81
   health care 62
   Human Rights Campaign 61
   inheritance rights 62
   legal documents 62

no difference between straight and gay
    parents 63–64
parental rights 75–77
    adopted children 76–84
    illegitimacy 76
    one partner as legal parent 75
    Uniform Parentage Act 75
putting intentions in writing 74
same-sex couples raising 61
second-parent adoption 61
Social Security benefits 62
starting a family 64–70
Civil Rights Act of 1964 157, 159, 169
civil unions 25–26
    defined 16
    difficulties in terminating 25
    history of 25
Colin v. Orange Unified School District 148
Congressional Budget Office 81
Cote-Whitacre v. Department of Public Health 12

D

Dale v. Boy Scouts 2
Daly v. Daly 166
Davenport v. Little-Bowser 97
Defense of Marriage Act 2, 11–17, 20, 31, 43, 195, 200, 248–50, 255
    effects of 11
    Full Faith and Credit Clause 16
    mini-DOMAs passed by states 12
    state response to 16–17
Deficit Reduction Act 198–99
Dept. of Human Services, et al. v. Howard et al. 97
DeSylva v. Ballentine 55
divorce 40–43
    children 41
        Parent Coordinator statutes 41
    property, division of 43
Doe v. Yunits 146
domestic partnerships 25–26
    California law 25
    defined 16
Domestic Partner Act, California 29
domestic partnership agreements 57
issues to consider 37
Oregon legislation 46
state employee benefits 26–29
D.R. v. Ontario (Deputy Registrar General) 82

E

Education Amendment Act of 1972
    Title IX 145
Eisenstadt v. Baird 56
elders 189–214
    AIDS 211–12
        National Association on HIV Over Fifty 211
    counseling of 203
    discrimination against 213–14
    healthcare issues 210
        Medicaid 210
    insurance concerns 212–13
        disability insurance 212
        life insurance 212
    Medicaid 196, 200–03
        annuities 199
        continuing care retirement communities 199
        estate recovery programs 196–98
        hardship waiver 199
        life estates 199
        life insurance 200
        long-term care partnerships 199
        look-back period 198
        Omnibus Budget Reconciliation Act 196
        penalty period 198
        principal residence 199
        qualifying for 200
    Metlife Study of Lesbian and Gay Baby Boomers 191–92
    military veterans 203–04
        U.S. Department of Veteran Affairs 203
    misunderstandings about healthcare financing 192

National Council on Aging 193
National Family Caregiver Support
    Program 193
    support services 193
nursing homes and hospice care 206–10
    denial of entry to 207
    discrimination litigation 208
    nursing home litigation 207
    right to privacy 208
    suggestions for hospice providers
        210
    U.S. Administration on Aging 206
Older Americans Act 192–93
public accommodations 205–06
    assisted-living facilities 205
    continuing-care retirement centers
        205
retirement accounts 204–05
    401(k) plans 205
    I.R.A.s 205
    Pension Protection Act of 2006 204
Social Security 193
    Defense of Marriage Act 195
    family status, determination of 194
    Old Age, Survivors and Disability
        Insurance program 193
    Supplemental Security Income 193
    survivor benefits 195
    U.S. Administration on Aging 193
Elisa B. v. Superior Court 129
Employee Retirement Income Security Act
    15, 20, 39, 175
Equal Access Act 148
Equal Protection Clause 145–46, 170, 178
Establishment Clause of the First Amend-
    ment 31
estate planning 217–46
    advance directives 235–38
        health care power of attorney 236
        Health Insurance Portability and
            Accountability Act 237
        living will 236
    agent designation 238
        Joint Commission on Accreditation
            of Healthcare Organizations 238

durable power of attorney for finances
    239–40
    attorney-in-fact 239
    nomination of guardian 239–46
    springing power of attorney 239
estate distribution possibilities 243–44
funeral arrangements 241–42
    contract negotiation 241
    put arrangements in writing 241
inherited individual retirement plans
    244–45
    Pension Protection Act of 2006 246
last will and testament 218–24
    beneficiary designations 223
    funeral expenses 221
    guardian of minor children 220
    in terrorum clauses 222–23
    intestate 218
    pet clauses 223
    recognizing the relationship 220
    testate 218
payable on death bank accounts 241
trusts. *See also.*
unified estate and gift tax 242–43
Etsitty v. Utah Transit Authority 173

F

families 51–59
    attacks on nontraditional 52
    benefits of 77–81
    defined 51
    evolving traditions 51
    family law 55–57
        existence of a marriage, presump-
            tion of 56
        senior citizens 55
        Social Security benefits 55
        state experimentation with 55
    issues facing lesbian and gay 53–54
        funerals 53
        important legal areas 53
        sources of U.S. family law 54
    legal documents 57–58
        advance directives 57
        designation of agent 57
        domestic partnership agreements 57

durable power of attorney for finances 57
marital contracts, categories of 57
parenting agreements 57
pre-pregnancy donor agreements 57
moving to another state 58
steps to consider 58
starting 64–70
artificial reproductive technology 65–66
family-related laws 64
Parental Kidnapping Prevention Act 64
parenting documents 64
surrogacy. *See also.*
Uniform Child Custody Jurisdiction Enforcement Act 64
Family Medical Leave Act 20
Finstuen v. Crutcher 97
Finstuen v. Edmondson 1, 97
First Amendment and the Due Process Clause 147
Fleuti v. Rosenberg 259
Flores, et al. v. Morgan Hill Unified School Dist. 144
Full Faith and Credit Clause 16, 19, 95

G

Gay, Lesbian, Straight Education Network 138, 153
Gay-Straight Alliance Network 138–42, 147–49
"gayby" boom 61
Gender Identity Disorder 155–56
defined 155
Gonzales v. O Centro Espirita Beneficente Uniao Do Vegetal, et al. 31
Goodridge v. Dept. of Public Health, et al. 12
Government Accounting Office
study on marriage rights 20
Griswold v. Connecticut 3, 55
GSA Network & Loomis v. Visalia Unified School Dist. 144
GSA/Transgender Law Center/NCLR report 140–42

H

Harris Interactive and GLSEN Study 139–40
Health Insurance Portability and Accountability Act 237
Hernandez v. Robles 24
Hill v. INS 248
Human Rights Campaign 61

I

immigration 247–58
asylum 251–54
basis for 252
Immigration and Naturalization Act 251
request at border crossing 252
basic law
Citizenship and Immigration Service 250
Defense of Marriage Act 250
sponsorship 250
for employment purposes 254
U.S. Department of Labor 254
green card lottery 254
Immigration and Naturalization Service 247
law background 247–49
Defense of Marriage Act 248
Immigration Act of 1990 248
Immigration and Naturalization Act 249
International Covenant of Civil and Political Rights 249
U.S. Department of Homeland Security 248
Uniting American Families Act 249
organizations providing assistance 257
pending congressional action 256–57
Permanent Partners Immigration Act 257
persons living with HIV/AIDS 256
sham marriages 255–56
transgender and transsexual persons 255

Bureau of Immigration Appeals 255
Defense of Marriage Act 255
Immigration and Nationality Act 255
Uniting American Families Act 257
visas 251
Immigration and Naturalization Act 251, 255
Immigration and Naturalization Service 247
In re Adoption Petition of N 97
In re Custody of H.S.H.-K. 112
In re Estate of Gardiner 161
In re Jacob 86
In re Kanda 259
In re Marriage of Simmons 163
In re Visitation With C.B.L. 164
Internal Revenue Code 20, 205, 229–30, 246
Internal Revenue Service 38–40
   dependent claims 40
   gift tax liability 38
International Covenant of Civil and Political Rights 249

J

Joint Commission on Accreditation of Healthcare Organizations 191, 238

K

K.M. v. E.G 68, 132
Kantaras v. Kantaras 163
Kastl v. Maricopa County Community College 170
Koebke v. Bernardo Hts. Country Club 29
Kristine J. v. Lisa R. 132

L

Lambda Legal Defense and Education Fund 94–95, 151, 155
Langan v. St. Vincent's Hospital of New York 29
language

potentially offensive terms 3–4
Lawrence v. Texas 2, 30, 54, 93, 248
Lehr v. Robertson 76
Linda Kaufman v. Va. Dep't of Social Servs. 97
Littleton v. Prange 162
Lofton v. Secretary of Dept. of Children and Family Services 93
Loving v. Virginia 2, 24
Lozoya v. Sanchez 29

M

M.L.B. v. S.L.J. 75
M.T. v. J.T. 162
Manago v. Barnhart 159
Mark Lewis and Dennis Winslow, et al. v. Gwendolyn 19
marriage 17–20
   acceptance of relationships other than marriage 33
   alternatives to traditional 32–34
   Beyond Marriage coalition 33
      goals 33
   civil, defined 16
   civil unions in New Jersey 20
   cohabitation 17
   common-law 23
      elements of 23
   domestic partnership law, Washington 19
   Full Faith and Credit Clause 19
   federal rights 20–21
   foreign recognition of same-sex 24–25
   mixed-race 17
   New York's domestic relations law 18
   religion 31–32
   religious, defined 16
   rights of 18
   survey of state laws 20
   traditional 22–24
   transsexual spouses 167–68
Marriage of D.F.D. 165
Massey v. Banning Unified School Dist. 144
Medicaid 196, 200–03

annuities 199
continuing care retirement communities 199
estate recovery programs 196–98
hardship waiver 199
life estates 199
life insurance 200
long-term care partnerships 199
look-back period 198
Omnibus Budget Reconciliation Act 196
penalty period 198
principal residence 199
qualifying for 200
Miles v. New York University 174
Miller-Jenkins v. Miller-Jenkins 101–07
Montgomery v. Independent School District No. 709 145
Moodie v. Andrews 246

N

Nabozny v. Podlesny 145
National Association on HIV Over Fifty 211
National Center for Lesbian Rights 91, 140–42, 153, 204
National Center for State Courts 87
National Conference of Commissioners on Uniform Laws 105
National Conference of Commissioners on Uniform Statutes 65, 102
National Council on Aging 193
National Family Caregiver Support Program 193
National Gay and Lesbian Task Force 160
Nemcek v. Paskey 69
nursing homes and hospice care 206–10
  denial of entry to 207
  discrimination litigation 208
  nursing home litigation 207
  right to privacy 208
  suggestions for hospice providers 210
  U.S. Administration on Aging 206

O

Occupational Safety and Health Administration 171
Oiler v. Winn-Dixie 173
Old Age, Survivors and Disability Insurance program 193
Older Americans Act 192–93
Omnibus Budget Reconciliation Act 196
Oncale v. Sundowner Offshore 170

P

parent coordinators 41–42
Parental Kidnapping Prevention Act 38, 64, 100
parenting rights 99–132
  applicable laws 100–07
    Parental Kidnapping Prevention Act 100–01
    Uniform Child-Custody Jurisdiction and Enforcement 102–05
    Uniform Parentage Act 105
  changing ways to become a parent 109–10
  co-parenting agreements 119–23
    child's best interest 120
    divorce 122
    financial support of the child 123
    intent 123
    provisions of 120
    state laws 123
  Miller-Jenkins v. Miller-Jenkins 107–09
  parent, defined 110–19
    adoptions, finalizing 119
    child's best interests 112
    de facto parent 116
    in loco parentis 115
    in loco parentis relationship 113
    legal protections for same-sex couples 110
    non-parents seeking custody and visitation 111
    parent-like relationship, demonstrating 113
    parents by estoppel 117

psychological parent 113–15
   rights of the non-legal parent 112
   same-sex parenting case law 123–31
      California 129
      Canada 131
      Colorado 124
      New Jersey 126–27
      Pennsylvania 128
      Tennessee 127–28
      West Virginia 125
Pension Protection Act of 2006 204, 246
Permanent Partners Immigration Act 257
Pitcherskaia v. INS 260
Planned Giving Design Center 232
potentially offensive terms
   attitude 4–5
Price Waterhouse v. Hopkins 152, 170, 173

R

Ramelli v. Poway Unified School District 151
Reciprocal Beneficiary Act, Hawaii 30
Rehabilitation Act of 1973 159, 172
relationships 11–47
   alternatives to traditional 32–34
      acceptance of relationships other than marriage 33
      Beyond Marriage coalition 33
      definition of family, new 33
   benefits denied 21–22
      health insurance 21
   civil unions 25–26
      difficulties in terminating 25
      history of 25
   common-law marriage 23
      elements of 23
   Defense of Marriage Act 11, 16–17
      effects of 11
      Full Faith and Credit Clause 16
      mini-DOMAs passed by states 12
      state response to 17
   denial of equal protection 13
   dependent claims 40

divorce 40–43
   children 41
   Parent Coordinator statutes 41
   property, division of 43
domestic partnerships 25–26
   California law 25
   children of same-sex couples, California 26
   issues to consider 38
   state laws, cost of 26
   state employee benefits 26–29
Employee Retirement Income and Security Act 39
federal marriage rights 20–21
   Defense of Marriage Act 20
   Employee Retirement Income Security Act 20
   Family Medical Leave Act 20
   Government Accounting Office study 20
   Internal Revenue Code 20
foreign recognition of same-sex marriage 24–25
history of 14–16
   California 15
   Connecticut 15
   Hawaii 14
   New Jersey 15
   Vermont 14
Internal Revenue Service 38
life insurance 39
marriage 17–20
   civil unions in New Jersey 20
   cohabitation 17
   domestic partnership law, Washington 19
   Full Faith and Credit Clause 19
   mixed-race 17
   New York's domestic relations law 18
   rights of 18
   survey of state laws 20
marriage, traditional 22–24
Massachusetts 12
   residency requirements 12

Medicaid
   Partnership Program 39
post-separation agreement issues 43
reciprocal beneficiaries law 30
   Reciprocal Beneficiary Act, Hawaii 30
religion and marriage 31–32
   Defense of Marriage Act 31
   Establishment Clause of the First Amendment 31
starting 34–40
   financial considerations 35
   living trusts 36
   parenting agreements 38
   putting intentions to writing 34–40
   real estate considerations 34
state constitution bans on same-sex marriages 13
tax consequences 21–22
termination protocol 43–45
   child custody 45
   domestic violence 44
   financial considerations 44
   taking specific actions 44
terminology 16
   civil marriage 16
   civil union 16
   domestic partnership 16
   religious marriage 16
unmarried cohabitants 29–30
   Unruh Civil Rights Act 29
Virginia 14
   Affirmation of Marriage Act 14
representation 1–9
   civil same-sex marriages 4
   civil unions 4
   domestic partnerships 4
   ethical considerations 7–8
      ABA Model Rule of Professional Conduct 1.7(b) 7
      estate planners 7
      joint representation 7
   language 3
      potentially offensive terms 3
   potential conflicts
      limits of the representation 6
      potential conflicts 6–7
      separate acknowledgment 6
      transitory nature of the law 6
   reciprocal beneficiary relationships 4
   significant case law 2–3
   transgender clients 8
Romer v. Evans 2, 54
Rosa v. Park West Bank & Trust Co. 173
Rose v. Rose 55

S

Safadi v. Gonzales 260
schools 137–53
   gender nonconforming, defined 139
   drag queens/kings, defined 139
   female/male cross-dressers, defined 139
   Fifteen Expensive Reasons Why Safe Schools Legislation Is In Your State's Best Interest 153
   gay-straight alliances 147–49
      curriculum-related groups 149
      efforts to prevent 147
      Equal Access Act 148
      First Amendment right to 148
      non-curriculum-related clubs 149
   gender expression, defined 138
   gender identity, defined 138
   gender queer, defined 139
   gender-nonconforming students 137
   GSA/Transgender Law Center/NCLR Report 140–42
      gender-nonconforming students 140–41
      harassment, forms of 141
   handling discrimination and harassment 142–45
      Equal Protection Clause 145
      Flores, et al. v. Morgan Hill Unified School Dist. 144
      GSA Network & Loomis v. Visalia Unified School Dist. 144
      inadequate response 144
      Massey v. Banning Unified School Dist. 144
      meeting with school officials 143

Nabozny v. Podlesny 145
    parent/guardian involvement 142
    police report, filing 143
    timeliness of action 144
    written complaint with principal 142
    written documentation 142
harassed students, reactions of 150–53
Harris Interactive and GLSEN Study 139
LGBTQ, defined 139
pertinent laws
    Equal Protection Clause 146
    First Amendment and the Due Process Clause 147
    state laws 147
    Title IX 145–46
sexual orientation, defined 139
Student Safety and Violence Prevention Act of 2000 142
transgender 138
transgender youth, defined 141
transsexual 138
Smelt v. County of Orange 259
Smith v. Smith 97
Social Security 193–96
    Defense of Marriage Act 195
    family status, determination of 194
    Old Age, Survivors and Disability Insurance program 193
    Supplemental Security Income 193
    survivor benefits 195
Social Security Act 159
Stanley v. Illinois 76
Student Safety and Violence Prevention Act of 2000 142
surrogacy 66–70
  considerations 69–72
  contracts 67–73
    clauses 71
    egg donation from one lesbian partner to the other 73
    egg/sperm donor 72
    restrictions on 70
    specification of legal rights 70
    with egg donors 69
  requirements for establishing parentage 68

T

Tanner v. Oregon Health Sciences University 46
Title VII 157
total return
    grantor retained annuity 232
transgender clients 8
Transgender Law Center 140–42, 155, 160
transgender/transsexual clients, representing
  areas of law affecting 157
  attitude toward clients 158
  Civil Rights Act of 1964 157
  correct name, importance of 158
  employment 169–74
    Americans with Disabilities Act 172
    Civil Rights Act of 1964 169
    disability laws 172
    Equal Protection Clause 170
    federal laws 173–80
    Occupational Safety and Health Administration 171
    Rehabilitation Act of 1973 172
  family law issues 160–69
    estate planning 168
    marriage 167
    psychological effect on the children 164
    terminating parental rights 166
  gender dysphoria 156
    treatment for 156
  Gender Identity Disorder 155
    defined 155
    diagnosing 156
    therapeutic response to 156
    triadic therapy 156
  identification 180–83
    birth certificates 181
    determining a person's legal sex 180
    name changes 182

Lambda Legal Education and Defense
    Fund 155
National Center for Lesbian Rights 155
networking 158
sex reassignment surgery 174–76
    Employee Retirement Income
        Security Act 175
    Medicaid reimbursement 174
    private insurer exclusion of 175
statutory projections
    Rehabilitation Act of 1973, 1997
        159
statutory protections 158–60
    Americans with Disabilities Act
        159
    overview of transgender legislation
        160
    Social Security Act 159
    Social Security disability benefits
        159
Title VII 157
transsexuals in prison 176–80
    deliberate indifference 176
    Eighth Amendment 176, 179
    Equal Protection Clause 178
    hormone treatment 178
    job condition of probation 177
    placement decisions 179
    plea-bargaining 177
    segregation 177
Transgender Law Center 155
transitioning during trial 157
transgender/transsexual clients, represent-
    ing 155
Troxel v. Granville 52, 62, 75, 111, 118,
    124
trusts 225–32
  annuities 232–35
  charitable gift annuity 234
  charitable lead annuity trust 232
  charitable lead trust 232
  charitable lead unitrust 232
  charitable remainder 232–35
  charitable remainder annuity trust 234
  charitable remainder trust 231

charitable remainder unitrust 233
    types of 233
grantor 225
grantor retained income 230–31
    Internal Revenue Code governing of
        230
    irrevocable 230
    tax calculation 231
    taxable gifts 230
inter vivos (living) 228–30
joint 226
    key issues 226
    loss of creditor protection 226
life insurance gifts 235
living (inter vivos) 228–30
    funding of 228
    Internal Revenue Code 229
    irrevocable 229
    not subject to probate or court
        supervision 228
    pet care provisions 230
    pour-over clause 228
living trust, defined 225
non-grantor lead trusts 233
Planned Giving Design Center 232
qualified retirement and IRA assets 234
remainder interests in real estate 234
retained life estate 234
testamentary 227–28
    donations to charity 227
    early termination of 227
    funding of 227
    providing for minor children 227
    revocation 227
testamentary trust, defined 225
total return 231
    income beneficiary for life provision
        231
triggering events for termination 226
trustee 225
trustor 225
Tunstall v. Wells 222

U

U.S. Administration on Aging 193, 206
U.S. Department of Health and Human Services
  Adoption and Foster Care Analysis Reporting System 87
U.S. Department of Homeland Security 248
U.S. Department of Labor 254
U.S. Department of State 89
U.S. Department of Veteran Affairs 203
Ulane v. Eastern Airlines, Inc. 173
Uniform Child-Custody Jurisdiction and Enforcement Act 38, 64, 102–07
  bases for initial jurisdiction 103
  custody orders, making/modifying 103
  home state, defined 102
  interstate custody battles, elimination of 102
  original jurisdiction, continuance of 103
  prosecutors, authority of 104
  protracted custody litigation, avoidance of 102
  registration
    defenses available to an order seeking 104
  registration procedure for out-of-state orders 103
  registration process 104
  requirements tailored to PKPA 102
Uniform Interstate Family Support Act 107
Uniform Law Commission 240
Uniform Parentage Act 75
  1973 version 105
  2002 amendment 106
  articles of 106
  legal father, defined 106
  National Conference of Commissioners on Uniform Laws 105
  Uniform Child Custody Jurisdiction and Enforcement 107
  Uniform Interstate Family Support Act 107

Uniform Putative and Unknown Fathers Act 105
Uniform Status of Children of Assisted Conception 105
Uniform Putative and Unknown Fathers Act 105
Uniform Status of Children of Assisted Conception 105
Uniting American Families Act 249, 257
Unruh Civil Rights Act 29

W

Wakeman v. Dixon 120
Williams Institute at the University of Los Angeles 81
Wilson v. Ake 259

Z

Zablocki v. Redhall 18